S0-BJF-880

HISTORY OF ANCIENT ART

Johann Joachim
WINCKELMANN

HISTORY
OF ANCIENT ART

VOLUMES I and II

With Johann Gottfried Herder's essay
Winckelmann
Translated from the German by Alexander Gode

FREDERICK UNGAR PUBLISHING CO.
NEW YORK

N
5330
W743
vol. 1-2

11-19-72 Nicholas 885

Translated from the original German
Geschichte der Kunst des Altertums
by G. Henry Lodge

61440

Copyright © 1968 by Frederick Ungar Publishing Co.

Printed in the United States of America

Library of Congress Catalog Card Number 68-8114

O.K.L.T. 11/17/72

A Biographical Note on
Johann Joachim Winckelmann

Johann Joachim Winckelmann is often called the father of
scientific archeology. He was the first towering representative
and—possibly—the precipitating agent of that German-Greek
"elective affinity" that was the principal determinant—ideolog-
ically, aesthetically, and linguistically—in the genesis, course,
and creative output of German classicism. The marriage of
Faust and Helen (in Goethe's Faust drama) is both symbol
and symptom and an unforgettably glorious monument of it.
Lessing's *Laokoon* (1766) could not have been written without
Winckelmann. The title of Goethe's work, *Winckelmann und
sein Jahrhundert* (1805) [Winckelmann and His Century],
speaks for itself.

Winckelmann was born on December 9, 1717, the son of a
poor shoemaker in Stendal in Prussian Saxony. The rector of
the local school took the boy into his home in which he made
himself useful as a guide and reader to his benefactor who was
about to lose his eyesight. In 1735 the rector sent young
Winckelmann to school in Berlin and Salzwedel, where he acquired a sound grounding in Latin and Greek. On one occasion,
between terms, he traveled on foot to Hamburg to buy a number of classical works, begging on the way the needed money
from clergymen and country gentlemen. From 1738 to 1740 he
was matriculated at the University of Halle as a student of
theology, but he spent the better part of his time studying art
and archeology and earning his living as a private tutor. For
the next seven years Winckelmann held various posts as a teacher and teacher's assistant but still found time to learn Italian
and English and to pursue his classical studies. In 1748 the Sax-
on minister, Count von Bünau, appointed Winckelmann secre-

tary and librarian at his country seat near Dresden, and thus afforded him the opportunity to broaden his concepts in direct contact with artists and scholars.

In 1754 Winckelmann became a convert to the Roman Catholic Church and obtained the position of librarian to Cardinal Passionei. The following year he published his *Gedanken über die Nachahmung der griechischen Werke in Malerei und Bildhauerkunst* [Reflections on the Imitation of Greek Works in Painting and Sculpture], after which he was sent to Rome on a two-year pension that had been granted him through the good offices of the papal nuncio by Augustus III, elector of Saxony and king of Poland.

Winckelmann established himself in Rome permanently. He had good contacts at the Vatican, was received by Pope Benedict XIV, had charge of all antiquities in and near Rome (from 1763), and held the titles of papal antiquary and scriptor. He visited Florence, Pompeii, Naples, and Herculaneum, and published *Description des pierres gravées du feu Baron de Stosch* (1760) [Description of the Gems in the Collection of the late Baron Stosch], *Anmerkungen über die Baukunst der Alten* (1762) [Observations on the Architecture of the Ancients], *Sendschreiben von den herculanischen Entdeckungen* (1764) [A Letter on the Discoveries at Herculaneum], and *Nachricht von den neuesten herculanischen Entdeckungen* (1764) [A Report on the Newest Discoveries at Herculaneum]. The work that made Winckelmann immortal was his *Geschichte der Kunst des Altertums* [History of Ancient Art], which appeared in 1764 in Dresden. This was followed (in 1767) by a volume of *Monumenti Antichi Inediti* [Unpublished Monuments of Antiquity].

In 1768 Winckelmann planned a trip to Greece but postponed it in favor of one to Berlin, where his magnum opus was to appear in a French translation. He reached Vienna, where he was received with great honors by Empress Maria Theresa. The thought of having to move still farther away from Italy depressed him to such an extent that he decided to go back. He retreated as far as Trieste, where he arrived in the company of an Italian, one Francesco Arcangeli, who had been condemned to death in Vienna and was leaving Austria in compliance with the condition on which he had been pardoned. At an inn in Trieste Winckelmann showed his companion some coins he had been given by the Austrian empress. Arcangeli murdered him. The date was June 8, 1768.

Winckelmann's body was interred in the churchyard of the cathedral of St. Giusto at Trieste. His collected works were published from 1808 to 1820.

A.G.

WINCKELMANN

A Commemorative Essay by
Johann Gottfried Herder

Had no line of printed text been left behind by Winckelmann, still his life, his letters, his fate would show that he was a man out of the ordinary, that he felt a purpose in being born. His youth was lost in poverty and hardship. Beyond his thirtieth year he breathed the dusty air of a small-town school at which he drilled the boys in conjugation. Yet, his was not a life to be stunted. He did not lose the vision of a better existence. His love of history, his love of Greece and of the higher nobility of human thought, his hatred of German metaphysics, of the barbarism of the theology of the schools, and of the trivial and quadrivial arts, his thirst for freedom, friendship, and the nobility of mind of the ancients, which he gladly paid for with poverty, simplicity, and untitled modesty—all that distinguished him by the standards of our morals to such a degree that I would eagerly, if I but could, set up for him, with no justification other than these attitudes of his, a hermaic pillar among those honoring the wise of antiquity. No one can read those first wretched and oppressed letters addressed by him to Bünau without hearing that the voice of this man, stricken and abandoned by fortune, is also the voice of a noble man who has remained firm, who has remained unbending to the fawning follies of his age, who feels that he is what he is, who respects himself, and who, from his dungeon, will not cry out but at most sigh.

O you, who read those letters, if you are young, if possibly your fate is akin to Winckelmann's fate, find in them a source of new courage. Germany has long been a dense forest, but even where it is at its densest, you will not lose your sense of the cardinal points if you have but kept this virtue, this posture of the ancients: the awareness that it is for a reason that you are here on earth, that you depend on no one in your true honor, your perfect usufruct of life, that you have power to renounce false goals, to refuse to run after the gold tinsel of title and rank, of comfort and pleasure, that it is easy to be poor and to forfeit honors if you but come to be what you are to be and live on in your work. This feeling of integral oneness and truth, of proud nobility and of the readiness to sacrifice oneself for the sake of the calling for which nature made him, in short, this restrained greatness of centuries reveals itself as Winckelmann's distinction in all his writings, in all his letters. We need but read, for example, the letter in which he took leave of Bünau asking understanding—simply, shyly, feelingly—for the change of religion to which he had had to submit. Let us read once more of the joy that filled him as he left Germany to hasten his steps toward the site that was his destiny, that is, Rome and the world of antiquity for which it stood, of how, in this beautiful dream—in this beautiful delusion—he erred, often and, as it were, voluntarily, willfully, in his conception of men, of circumstances, and even of works of art, and of how he was rich in his poverty, proud in his lowliness, proud and great and blessed. There was to him but one way of feeling alive, the way of living in these thoughts, in these endeavors, in this enjoyment.

Yet, as I now turn my thoughts away from him and from his motives and emotions to view the external circumstances that surrounded him, the assistance that was accorded him on his way through life, the fated way he had to follow—forgive me, Germany, if once again I intone the old song and accuse you of being callous, of being heedless. Had he been born among the Cimmerians, could life have been harder on him than it was? Poor and unrecognized, he made the rounds of German universities, and what their chairs were willing to mete out to him under the guise of food for spirit and mind was of a kind unfit and lacking nourishment for him. Find me elsewhere in civilized lands examples similar to that set by Winckelmann's life. To his fortieth year he was assistant to the master of the school at Seehausen or obliged to excerpt barbarous chronicles of monks just to keep body and soul together. Nowhere was there an opportunity open to him—despite his abundance of knowledge, of awareness, of acuity—to find but one man ready and able to redeem him from his plight. Even after he had published a work of such excellence as his *Reflections on the Imitation of Greek Works in Painting and Sculpture,* there was no possibility of proceeding along the path of his unique destiny other than that provided by the intercession and annuity of a proselytizer. And later on, after he had produced in Rome—under conditions of pressing indigence yet in a spirit of enthusiasm for his homeland, for the German nation and its language—a work of the rank of his *History of Ancient Art,* a work that will keep its rank as long as the German language lives, his only reward for all he had done exhausted itself in sordid criticism mitigated at best by a few words of vacuous praise. Then, finally, he had to die as he had lived, a wretched beast of sacrifice at the border of two nations, from which and to which he fled like an exiled stranger. If elsewhere in civilized lands you can find for me many examples similar to this, I shall be sorely distressed. In Germany there is in this nothing out of the ordinary. By its very constitution, this country, as the British lord put it, is a *drôle de corps,* a strange body that has been provided with so many heads for no other reason but that none may know its limbs; that has been provided with so many universities, offiicial agencies, and institutions for no other reason but that there may be, for a free and noble spirit that has proved itself to be free and noble, no place and no condition other than that of the burdensome yoke of breadwinning toil. What are the channels through which our Medicis and d'Estes can be made aware of the useful and the good that is there in plain daylight before their very noses? Possibly by way of Paris, through translations which—though they be mere parodies—our maecenases will read more readily than the originals, letting things go as they will and allowing to happen what can happen through itself. Perhaps, after a man is dead . . . But must I continue?

> —Quis talia fando
> Temperet a lacrimis?—
>
> [Who, on hearing such tales,
> Would restrain his tears?]

I shall, I hope, be forgiven that I have spoken as I did for the sake of the place where I stood. A man's grave is sacred, and if the one bitter truth that his entire life points out to us may not be uttered there, where else and when else shall it be uttered? Through what, I ask, did Germany deserve that

Winckelmann wrote just one line of what he has left us? Is the answer through subjecting him to eight years of toil as a master's assistant in Seehausen, through letting him excerpt chronicles, or through allowing him an annuity paid out by a Catholic father confessor? To which we may add that his life was embittered by thoughtless, petty German pedantries, that it was held against him that now and again he did fail to quote correctly, that he did not at all times make proper use of the sources (because in his state he surely could not have used them), in short, that he was not omniscient or able to produce in lieu of his writings by the work of his hands new Apollos and new Laocoöns to fill the museums in German lands.

Forgive me, noble departed, that I give vent to my anger at your grave, while you yourself showed yourself able to bear your nation's cold ingratitude—if on occasion not without murmurs—always, after you had regained your strength, in perfect steadfastness preferring to forget and not to complain. Precisely for this reason, because you did not raise your voice in accusation, it is for me to do so, not on your behalf or on mine but on behalf of one who at some future time may prove to be your equal. Enough, and not another word!

Winckelmann's first work was written at Oeser's home; and the suggestions received from Oeser's refined mind—even his profound love of allegory—can be discerned in it. It was thus a friend and artist to whose credit it accrued—unthought of by any of the great, the well-off, the sated—that he helped to call forth and to unfold the germ that lay in Winckelmann and that no one had to plant in him. In this slender work—and in the next two following—lies, I believe, the full bud of his soul. Rome, later on, could not do more than make it sprout in learned laurel or have it bear the fruit of riper, more decided judgement. What Winckelmann was to see in Rome, what he wanted to see there, he already bore within him.

May no one misunderstand this or take it to be belittling. I point therefore to the fairly general experience that in most instances, as the whole tree in the bud, the full stature of the human mind and all the future manifestations of it lie in its very first products, provided someone is on hand who is able to see what is there and to help it emerge. I speak here of fruits of the mind and not of premature monstrosities, for Winckelmann was almost forty years old when he wrote his first book, and even then he wrote with all the hesitant shyness of youth. He had had time to evolve the ideas that he bore within himself, which seemed to be innate in him, and which for so long, throughout all the vicissitudes of life, had been his most reliable friends and companions. What was to follow could never be more than application, fuller corroboration and clearer definition, a more concise delineation in detail. At that age man's soul is no longer subject to change, and no one is born a second time. It is for this reason that all the writings by Winckelmann are one in feeling, thought, and expression to an extent that a writer whose productivity extends from his fifteenth year to his ninety-fifth cannot maintain and which—if he is well advised—he does not try to maintain. The most personal letters of Winckelmann were written, too, in this selfsame spirit as though he expected them—which he most certainly did not—to be read by all the world, then and in times to come. That German baron who notes with displeasure that Winckelmann arrived late in Italy, with all the forces of his mind and his soul fully developed, and hence, to be sure, brought with him not only his knowledge but also his enthusiasm—let him, if he will, get himself born in Rome so that he may then determine what his unprejudiced eyes are able to see in antiquity and what not.

What is divine in us is born with us: Learning, books, and marble cannot plant it where it is not from nature. Countless are the cicerones who have viewed and shown antiquities. Countless, too, perhaps the ones who did so with incomparably greater learning and minutious knowledge than Winckelmann ever had —than he could have or would. But how many among them were or could have been, after what Winckelmann was, his equals? This is the way it goes in all the arts, in all the sciences. What else in the world could be called upon to explain that those dedicated to excellence, that those who know and are able to manage the highest perfection in every science and in every art are so few in number? Legion is the name of painters who ground colors as Raphael did, who saw what he saw, but not with his eyes, not with his response. So then, for better or worse, they had to abandon the thought of becoming Raphaels, no matter how strictly, how meticulously they trained themselves in the mechanical craft of the art, succeeding—perhaps— in surpassing him in this or that technical skill. In regard to the *Idea* which Raphael—as he said—bore within himself (implying

that the world around him merely provided him with the opportunity to gather the concepts which the innate idea was in
need of) in regard to his only a second Raphael could, and can
surpass him. This precisely is Winckelmann's case, both in his
philosophy and in his doctrine. "From Plato on," he wrote,
"up to the present time, writings of this kind purporting to be
treatises of the beautiful as a general concept have been hollow,
providing no instruction and carrying little content. As for the
beautiful in art, some recent writers have undertaken to touch
it—without having known it." This and numerous passages of
similar import have been interpreted as evidence of his arrogance.
Instead they were clearly statements of what he felt, and—apart
from any reference to Winckelmann—they are true. The ideal
share in art, the beholder's sublime awareness of the beautiful
and of beauty, these he found treated nowhere as he felt them
in his soul, as he wished them to be treated. For that reason he
spoke as he did. His personal letters likewise bear witness to his
living, at all times of heightened emotions, in the empyreal
sphere of abstracted feelings and to his approaching even the
Highest Being on the wings of enthusiasm derived quite often
from very minor objects. Not everybody, said d'Alembert, has
the gift of being able to rise to the rings of Saturn, but he who
was born on that planet lives there as in his native country.

It is not right, therefore, if one neglects to view Winckelmann's writings under this aspect—the only one that is true—
and sees them instead incompletely and in a false light. I should
think that he himself has been explicit enough in pointing out
to us the proper point of view. Before he went to Rome, he
wrote his *Reflections on the Imitation of Greek Works,* in which
the experience of the beautiful animates every line. In Rome
he began his descriptions of individual works of art, of their
ideas, the idea of Apollo, of Laocoön, and of others; and the
projected essay on the restoration of ancient hermae and the like
(which Cavaceppi no doubt was better qualified to write than
he was), he wisely set aside. But in the *Treatise on the Experience of the Beautiful in Art,* his soul rose up. It did so in his
History of Art and wherever else he reached out into the realm
of these sublime conceptions and awarenesses. What then do
they mean who say that his *History* of Art is defective and in-
complete? Could it be otherwise? Was it Winckelmann's intent
to write it otherwise? Is it meaningful to ask for a complete his-

tory of the art of antiquity when the greater part of that art has perished, when so few and miserly reports of it have been preserved, and when the handful of letters that did speak of it stand there like broken cliffs of a once continuous shoreline? The entire forest of fifty thousand statues in Rome and throughout the rest of the world, and the gems, coins, vessels, and buildings thrown in for good measure—are they more than a haphazard pile of ruins compared to what once (when Pausanias lived and Pliny let alone in earlier times) was called the living history of art? Let him step forward who still feels he has a right to demand that poor old Winckelmann should have burrowed his way through this forest of temples and statues and museums all over the world in order to provide him (without charge) with a *catologus realis* that fitted Winckelmann's design as little as it does mine. His objective was to present in his *History* of Art a system, and he said so himself clearly enough. It was to become the history of the genesis of the beautiful in the art of antiquity, and that it has become. That it still would be, even if it lacked ten times more than in fact it does. The edifice of his historical doctrine has been completed and is complete. The simple Greek temple with its supreme sanctuaries and vast perspectives stands there before us. Should we, could we wish to induce the genius of art to restore for us what fell at the hands of Arabs, Turks, and barbarians, to inform us of what has been lost with lost writings and may lie hidden in sundry places, and to show us to what period each individual work of art might belong, to what artist it should be ascribed, from whom the Etrurians learned and from whom the Greeks, and what little fact exerted an influence hither and which one thither? Come, let us pray, each and all, that this genius of light, this good fairy of eons and nations may appear and provide us with all the answers. Still more, let us be eager to help him, to correct and to compile what there is in the world that can be corrected and that can be compiled. This history of art of antiquity will thereby be greatly enlarged. I doubt, however, that it will enlarge— necessarily and in essentials—the history of art of Winckelmann. In this, such storerooms of learning are but outbuildings or a wing and not the main structure. This is built on a few ideas— great and, I think, eternally unchanging ideas—both of the nature of the beautiful itself and of the genetic origins of it. The arguments leading to them may, if such be the case, undergo changes in this detail or that. The work itself, including the epochs of its art, whatever the number of defects that these may have in matters of detail, the work itself as an ideal whole—and that is what Winckelmann worked for—is right, for it is founded in the order of the ages, in the nature of the thing itself.

A different matter is Winckelmann's *Essay on Allegory,* and I readily admit that this is not his principal work. He was in it rather out of his element. His concept of allegory is indefinite, and he confused it frequently with historical attributes and pursued it, in fact, into the realm of language. Still more indefinite is the manner in which he applied it to the several arts, peoples, and eras. Allegorization in one art cannot ever be entirely what it is in another. It cannot be in one people what it is in another, or in this era what it is in the next. So much depends here on numerous delicately shaded concepts of known and unknown objects and of familiar or foreign ideas, and also on the distinctive coloring of the prevailing taste, the local customs, the particular language, that without them the book of allegory—particularly since it was hewn from solid rock—will forever remain to the public at large a book with seven seals. The history of allegory in literature and art requires, I believe, as much its special man as Winckelmann proved to be the special man for the history of the art of the beautiful. A work on allegory requires a kind of minutial acuity that perhaps Winckelmann with his sense of undivided sublimity and grandeur, could not have. Still, his essay on allegory is the beginning of a most useful collection of allegorical concepts and images in which his special genius, after all, did not abandon him. The author himself announced it as a modest initial effort in a field in which nothing had been done, and it would hence have been wiser to adopt this same viewpoint than to chide him crudely and on the surface, particularly since chiding him required but little art. The frigid reception that this work was given—a work by Winckelmann in spite of everything—hurt the good man deeply, and he decided to write nothing further in German. He did—O sorrow!—keep his word, for after the second volume of his *Monumenti Inediti* his hard and bitter fate overtook him.

A hard, a bitter fate, indeed. As we read of the eager longing in which he thought for years of his friends, of Germany, of his homeland; as we read his announcements of the journey northward reflecting the childlike joy that filled his heart in anticipation, and then observe in our reading how sudden fear of death, a sense of horror, overcame him when he had reached German lands again, when he saw the mountains, the houses and huts that at the time of his journey southward into Italy he had described with so much warmth and feeling: no friend, no argument can hold him, he must go back, he does go back and—at the border of the two countries—he finds death, a death devoid of dignity, replete with repulsive horror; as we are told, and if it be true, that he had just sat down to write a note to the future publisher of his *History* of Art when the hand of the murderer reached out to slay him; as, finally, we reflect that it was again two endearing flaws in his character—his innocent joy of renown and his guilelessness in hastily offering friendship even to those who did not deserve it—that it was again these two idols, dear to him throughout his life, called upon by him so often for solace and encouragement, though followed time and again by rude disappointments, that it was these that were now pressed into service to guide to him the terrible goddess with rope and dagger— who among us will not shudder? Who among us can hold back his tears over Winckelmann's awesome death-seeking premonition? O noble man, you were felled by the hand of the inexorable moira at the border of the country to which you had come to be a stranger, from which you were hurrying away to reach that other country that had bestowed honor upon you and joy, in which now once again you sought peace and strength. You did find that peace, you found it in your grave; you found the strength for which your soul was yearning; you found the friendship that you had looked for here below in a quest beset with deceit; you found the beauty, the wisdom, and the simplicity to which you had dedicated your life and to whose abode in the arms of the godhead your enthusiasm so often helped you rise— you found them where alone you could, in the purer world beyond.

> Auch in Welschlands Tale
> War's nicht gelebt; nun lebest du
> Die zweite schönre Himmelsjugend —

> [Nor were southern valleys
> Homeland of life; but now you live
> A second gladder springtime beyond —]

As I gather these thoughts here at this site of sadness, at

Winckelmann's grave, I cannot but recall that it was Winckelmann's hand that guided me on my pilgrimage of dreams
through antiquity; and I feel not unlike the wanderer who has
searched, in scorching thirst, with tired burning feet, the ruins
of Persepolis and Egypt, of Greece and Rome, who has seen
with every step the wreckage of a fallen city of kings, of a
broken world fated never to return, who has felt the meaning of vanity, the vanity of all things human, but who now—
looking once more, for the last time, at these regions, at these
works, which he is about to leave behind and which he will
never see again, not in ruins and certainly not in the flower
and glory of their ancient life—steps onto the planks of his ship,
with sadness in his heart but also in joyful expectation, in order
to return to his own world, which is a new world and hence
a different world, but in which he will see again his wife, his
children, his friends, whom he will embrace in real life and not
merely in the realm of ideas. Where are you now, O childhood
of the world of the ancients, sweet beloved age of simplicity
in imagery, plastic works, and character? You are gone, gone
is your dream replete with pleasing truth; and the call of those
who long for you, the ardent desire of those who love you, will
never arouse you from the dust. Tied to the wheel of Chronos,
we roll on without surcease—to where? whereto?—and shall
never return to where we once were. Your dream, too, Winckelmann, whom I love and revere, your dream of beautiful figures
of men, of noble friendship of youth, of the wisdom of the ages,
has lived out its term in this world. You lost the springtime
of your life and were granted a few short days of beautiful
harvest. You were spared the winter, which might well have
robbed you of all sweet delusions that are the best flower of
life. From the realm of specular beauty, from the realm of ideas,
you passed on to a truer world in which you no longer yearn
for Greece and the figures of its gods. Farewell! Your murdered
body rests in peace though no monument helps the pilgrim
find your grave. Your body rests beyond the borders of your
fatherland, and these poor pages have not the power to go back
and turn into a monument within your country.—Would, then,
that they give thanks to all friends of Winckelmann, to each
one of his friends who came to the assistance, in whatever small
way it may have been, of the poor pilgrim while he was ours,
and provided for him a good day. The names of his friends

have attained life sempiternal in his writings and letters, and as long as these are read, the shades of the memory of his friends will be loved and revered in the spirit in which the noble man praised their goodness in the effusion of his heartfelt gratitude.

—JOHANN GOTTFRIED HERDER

1781

CONTENTS.

HISTORY OF ANCIENT ART.

Volume I

BOOK I.

THE ORIGIN OF ART, AND THE CAUSES OF ITS DIF-FERENCE AMONG DIFFERENT NATIONS.

CHAPTER I.

THE SHAPES WITH WHICH ART COMMENCED.

CHAPTER II.

MATERIALS USED IN STATUARY.

CHAPTER III.

INFLUENCE OF CLIMATE ON CONFORMATION.

BOOK II.

ART AMONG THE EGYPTIANS, PHŒNICIANS, AND PERSIANS.

CHAPTER I.

CAUSES OF THE PECULIAR CHARACTER OF EGYPTIAN ART.

CHAPTER II.

PRIMITIVE STYLE OF EGYPTIAN ART.

CHAPTER III.

LATER EGYPTIAN STYLE.

CHAPTER IV.

MECHANICAL PART OF EGYPTIAN ART.

CHAPTER V.

ART AMONG THE PHŒNICIANS AND PERSIANS.

BOOK III.

ART OF THE ETRUSCANS AND THEIR NEIGHBORS.

CHAPTER I.

PRELIMINARY REMARKS.

CHAPTER II.

CONFORMATION OF GODS AND HEROES PECULIAR TO THE ETRUSCANS.

CHAPTER III.

STYLE OF ETRUSCAN ARTISTS.

CHAPTER IV.

ART OF THE NATIONS BORDERING ON THE ETRUSCANS.

Volume II

BOOK IV.

ART AMONG THE GREEKS.

CHAPTER I.

GROUNDS AND CAUSES OF THE PROGRESS AND SUPERIORITY OF GREEK
ART BEYOND THAT OF OTHER NATIONS.

CHAPTER II.

THE ESSENTIAL OF ART.

BOOK V.

ART AMONG THE GREEKS (*continued*).

CHAPTER I.

THE CONFORMATION AND BEAUTY OF THE MALE DEITIES AND HEROES.

CHAPTER II.

THE CONFORMATION AND BEAUTY OF THE FEMALE DEITIES AND HEROINES.

CHAPTER III.

THE EXPRESSION OF BEAUTY IN FEATURES AND ACTION.

CHAPTER IV.

PROPORTION. — COMPOSITION.

CHAPTER V.

BEAUTY OF INDIVIDUAL PARTS OF THE BODY.

CHAPTER VI.

BEAUTY OF THE EXTREMITIES, BREAST, AND ABDOMEN. — DRAWING OF THE FIGURES OF ANIMALS BY GREEK MASTERS.

Volume I

PREFACE.

1. THE History of Ancient Art which I have undertaken to write is not a mere chronicle of epochs, and of the changes which occurred within them. I use the term History in the more extended signification which it has in the Greek language; and it is my intention to attempt to present a system. In the first part, — the treatise on the Art of Ancient Nations, — I have sought to execute this design in regard to the art of each nation individually, but specially in reference to that of the Greek. The second part contains the History of Art in a more limited sense, that is to say, as far as external circumstances were concerned, but only in reference to the Greeks and Romans. In both parts, however, the principal object is the essential of art, on which the history of the individual artists has little bearing; the reader, therefore, need not expect to find here those details which have been gathered together on this point by others. On the other hand, those monuments of art which can in any way elucidate the subject are carefully noticed even in the second part.

2. *The History of Art* is intended to show the origin, progress, change, and downfall of art, together with the different styles of nations, periods, and artists, and to prove the whole, as far as it is possible, from the ancient monuments now in existence.

3. A few works have been published under the title of a *History of Art*. Art, however, had but a small share in them, for their authors were not sufficiently familiar with it, and therefore could communicate nothing more than what they had learned from books or hearsay. There is scarcely one who guides us to the essential of art, and into its interior; and those

who treat of antiquities either touch only on those points in which they can exhibit their learning, or, if they speak of art, they do so either in general terms of commendation, or their opinion is based on strange and false grounds. Of this kind is Monier's *History of Art*, amd Durand's translation and explanation of the last Books of Pliny, under the title of *History of Ancient Painting*. Turnbull's *Treatise on Ancient Painting* also belongs to this class. Aratus, who, as Cicero says, did not understand astronomy, was able to write a celebrated poem on it; but I doubt whether even a Greek with no knowledge of art would have been able to say anything worthy of it.

4. In the large and valuable works descriptive of ancient statues which have hitherto been published, we seek in vain for research and knowledge in regard to art. The description of a statue ought to show the cause of its beauty, and the peculiarity in its style. It is necessary, therefore, to touch upon particulars in art before it is possible to arrive at a judgment on works of art. But where are we taught the points in which the beauty of a statue consists? What writer has looked at beauty with an artist's eyes? What has been written of this kind in modern days is not better than the *Statues of Callistratus*. This meagre sophist might have described even ten times as many as he did, without ever having seen a single one. Our ideas contract over most descriptions of this sort, and what was great shrinks to the compass of an inch.

5. A figure is usually determined to be of Greek or Roman origin by its dress or its excellence. A mantle, clasped on the left shoulder, will show that the work was executed by Greeks, — in Greece, in fact. It has even been suggested to seek the native land of the artist who made the statue of Marcus Aurelius in the beautiful hair on the head of the horse. Some resemblance to an owl has been found in it; and by this resemblance the artist intended to signify Athens.

A good figure, merely because not dressed as a senator, is immediately pronounced to be Greek; yet, notwithstanding, there are senatorial statues by Greek artists whose names are known. A group in the Borghese villa is presumed to be Marcius Coriolanus with his mother; and it is so called. From this presumption the inference is drawn that the work was executed at the time of the republic; and, on this account, it is considered worse than it actually is. The name of Egizzia, the

Gypsy, has been bestowed upon a marble statue in the same villa; hence, the real Egyptian style has been discovered in the head, which shows anything else, and which, together with the hands and feet, likewise of bronze, was the work of Bernini. This, in architecture, is accommodating the style to the edifice. Not less unfounded is the appellation — universally adopted without attentive observation — which has been given to the presumed group of Papirius with his mother, in the Ludovisi villa; and Du Bos finds in the countenance of the young man a crafty smile, though there is, in reality, not the slightest indication of such an expression (1). It rather represents Phædra and Hippolytus, for his face shows consternation at a declaration of love from a mother. The incidents represented by Greek artists — and Menelaus, the artist of this work, was a Greek — were drawn from their own mythological and heroic history.

6. In regard to the superiority of a statue, it is not enough to consider the statue of Pasquin, the most beautiful of all the ancient statues, — as Bernini did (2), probably from thoughtless boldness; but a writer must also assign his reasons for claiming such superiority. In precisely the same manner he might have adduced the Meta Sudans, in front of the Coliseum, as an example of ancient architecture.

7. A few writers have, from a single letter, boldly designated the artist; and the author who omits to mention the names of a few artists found on statues, — as, for example, of Papirius, or rather Hippolytus, to which I have just referred, and Germanicus, — pronounces the Mars of John of Bologna, in the Medici villa, to be an antique statue : others have been misled by the assertion. Another, in order to describe a bad antique statue, — the supposed Narcissus (3) in the Barberini palace, — instead of a good figure, relates the fable concerning him ; and the author of a treatise on three statues in the Campidoglio — Roma, and the two Barberini captive kings — gives the reader, quite unexpectedly, a history of Numidia ; in other words, as the Greeks say, " Leucon bears one thing, and his ass another."

8. Descriptions of extant antiquities, of the galleries and villas at Rome, afford quite as little instruction : they rather mislead than instruct. In the catalogues of the statues of the Earl of Pembroke, and of the Cardinal Polignac, two statues of Hersilia, the wife of Romulus, and a Venus by Phidias in Pina-

roli, have the heads of Lucretia and Cæsar, copied from life.
Among the statues at Wilton, the seat of the Earl of Pembroke,
in England, which have been etched badly enough by Cary Creed
on forty plates, large quarto, there are said to be four by a Greek
artist, named Cleomenes. It is impossible not to feel astonishment at the confidence in the credulity of mankind, when it is
asserted in the same work that an equestrian statue of Marcus
Curtius was executed by a sculptor whom Polybius — the general, I presume, of the Achæan league, and the historian —
brought with him from Corinth to Rome. It would not have
been more impudent to have pretended that he sent the artist
to Wilton.

9. Richardson has described the palaces and villas in Rome,
and the statues in them, like one who had seen them only in a
dream. Many palaces he did not see at all, on account of his
brief stay in the city, and some, according to his own statement, he visited but once ; and yet his work, in despite of its
many deficiencies and errors, is the best we have. We must not
be too severe if he has regarded a modern painting, in fresco,
from the hand of Guido, as an antique. Keissler's *Travels* are
not even to be taken into account in regard to what he alleges
of works of art in Rome and other places ; for he has copied,
for this purpose, the most trashy books. Manilli, with great
industry, has made a book especially about the Borghese villa,
and yet he has not noticed three very remarkable pieces in it.
One of them is the arrival of Penthesilea, Queen of the Amazons, near Priam, in Troy, to whom she offers her assistance ;
the second is Hebe, who, having been deprived of her office of
serving the deities with ambrosia, is on her knees, entreating
the forgiveness of the goddesses, as Jupiter had already installed
Ganymedes in her place ; the third is a beautiful altar, on which
Jupiter is represented as riding a Centaur, — which has not been
noticed either by him or any other person, because it stands in
the cellar of the palace.

10. Montfaucon, having compiled his work at a distance from
the treasuries of ancient art, saw with the eyes of others, and
formed his opinions from engravings and drawings, by which he
has been led into great errors. Hercules, with Antæus, in the
Pitti palace, at Florence, — a statue of inferior rank, and of
which more than one half is of modern restoration, — is, according to him and Maffei, nothing less than a work of Polycletus.

The statue of Sleep, of black marble, by Algardi, in the Borghese villa, he pronounces an antique ; and one of the large
modern vases, of the same sort of marble, executed by Silvio of
Veletri, which are ranged near the statue, and which he found,
in an engraving, placed near it, is intended to denote a vase
containing a soporific juice. How many remarkable things he
has neglected ! He acknowledges that he never saw a marble
Hercules with a horn of plenty ; yet in the Ludovisi villa the
hero is so represented, of life-size, in the shape of a Hermes ;
and the horn is really antique. On a broken burial-urn among
the fragments of antiquities belonging to the Barberini family,
which were sold a short time since, is a Hercules with the same
symbol. It occurs to me that another Frenchman, Martin by
name, — who presumes so far as to declare that Grotius did not
understand the Septuagint, — decisively and boldly declares that
the two Genii on ancient urns cannot denote Sleep and Death ;
and yet the altar on which they are seen in this significance,
with the ancient superscription of Sleep and Death, is publicly
exposed in the court of the Albani palace. Another of his
countrymen charges the younger Pliny with falsehood in his
description of his villa ; but the ruins convince us of its truth.

11. The approval of certain mistakes, committed by writers
on antiquities, and the lapse of time, have, as it were, secured
them against refutation. An engraving of a round marble
work, in the Giustiniani villa, to which certain additions have
given the form of a vase, with a Bacchanal scene in relievo, has,
since it was first made known by Spon, been introduced into
many books, and has served the purpose of illustration. Indeed, a lizard creeping up a tree has led to a conjecture that the
work on which it is found may be from the hand of Sauros,
who, in connection with Batrachus, built the portico of Marcellus ; nevertheless, it is of modern workmanship. The reader
may find in the *Notes upon Architecture* my remarks in reference
to these two architects. So too the vase on which Spon has
written a special treatise must be modern, as its appearance
denotes to the eyes of connoisseurs of antiquity and of good
taste.

12. The mistakes of learned men in regard to things of antiquity proceed mostly from inattention to restoration, as many
of them have been unable to distinguish the repairs by which
mutilated and lost portions have been replaced from those really

antique. A large volume might be written about mistakes of
this kind, for the most learned antiquarians have failed in this
particular. From a relievo in the Mattei palace, which represents a hunt by the Emperor Gallienus, Fabretti wished to
prove that horseshoes, nailed upon the foot in the mode of the
present day, had already come into use at that time : he did
not know that the leg of the horse had been repaired by a
sculptor not versed in such matters. Restorations have given
occasion to laughable explanations. For example, Montfaucon
sees in the roll or baton in the hand of Castor or Pollux, in the
Borghese villa, which is modern, an emblem of the laws of
horse-racing at the games ; and in a similar roll of modern addition, which is held by a Mercury in the Ludovisi villa, he finds
an allegory of difficult elucidation ; just as Tristan, in respect
to a strap on a shield, held by a figure presumed to be Germanicus, on the celebrated agate at St. Denis, has regarded it as a
peaceful appendage. In other words, St. Michael baptized a
Ceres. Wright looks upon a modern violin, which has been
placed in the hand of an Apollo, in the Negroni villa, as a genuine antique ; and refers to another modern violin, belonging to
a small bronze figure, at Florence, which Addison also mentions.
The former believes himself to be vindicating the honor of
Raphael, since there is a probability, as he thinks, that this
great artist borrowed the shape of the violin which he placed
in the hand of Apollo on Parnassus, in the Vatican, from the
statue mentioned above, which was repaired for the first time by
Bernini more than one hundred and fifty years after the painter's time. An Orpheus with a violin, on an engraved gem,
might be cited with just as much propriety. In the same way
persons imagined that they saw among the paintings that formerly covered the ceiling of the ancient temple of Bacchus, outside of Rome, a small figure with a modern violin ; but Santes
Bartoli, who made a drawing of the figure, allowed himself to
be better informed, and erased the instrument from his copperplate, — as I see by the impression which he has added to his
colored drawings of ancient paintings in the museum of the
Cardinal Alexander Albani. The ball in the hand of the statue
of Cæsar in the Campidoglio was intended by the ancient artist
— according to the commentary of a later Roman poet — to
signify his desire for absolute sovereignty : he did not see that
the hands and arms are modern. Mr. Spence would not have

found fault with the sceptre of a Jupiter, if he had noticed that the arm is modern, and consequently the staff also.

13. Restorations ought to be pointed out, either in the engravings, or in the explanations of them ; for the head of the Ganymedes in the gallery at Florence, as seen in the engraving, must produce an unfavorable impression ; and it is still worse in the original. How many other heads of ancient statues in that place are modern, which have never been considered as such ! as, for example, the head of an Apollo, whose laurel crown is cited by Gori as something singular. The statues of Narcissus, of the so-called Phrygian priest, of a seated Matron, of the Venus Genetrix, have modern heads ; the heads of a Diana, of a Bacchus with a Satyr at his feet, and of another Bacchus holding a bunch of grapes on high, are frightfully ugly. Most of the statues that belonged to Christina, queen of Sweden, and which now stand at St. Ildefonso, in Spain, likewise have modern heads ; and of the eight Muses there, the arms also are modern.

14. Many mistakes of authors originate from incorrect drawings ; as, for example, in Cuper's explanation of the *Apotheosis of Homer*. The draughtsman considered Tragedy to be a male figure, and the buskin, which is very visible in the marble, was not observed. Moreover, a scroll, instead of a plectrum, is placed in the hand of the Muse which stands on high. The commentator wishes to make an Egyptian Tau out of a sacred tripod, and he asserts that he sees three lappets on the mantle of the figure in front of the tripod : they are, however, not to be found.

15. Hence it is difficult, indeed almost impossible, to write in a thorough manner of ancient art, and of unknown antiquities, anywhere but in Rome. Even a residence there of two years is insufficient for the purpose, as I learn by the laborious preparation required in my own case. We must not, therefore, be astonished, if some one says that he has been unable to discover in Italy any unknown inscriptions. This is true ; and none of those which are above ground, especially in public places, have escaped the attention of the learned. Yet he who has time and opportunity is still always finding obscure inscriptions, which were discovered a long time ago ; and those which I have cited in this work, as well as in the *Description of the Engraved Gems of the Stosch Cabinet*, are of this kind. But we

must strive to understand them ; and a traveller will not be
likely to find them.

16. Much more difficult, however, is the knowledge of art in
the works of the ancients, in which we are continually making
discoveries, even after looking at them a hundred times. Most
persons, nevertheless, think that this knowledge is to be obtained in the same way as they get theirs who gather their
erudition from monthly periodicals ; and they venture to pass
judgment on Laocoön, as the latter do on Homer, even in the
presence of one to whom both have been a study for many
years. Whereas, in reality, they speak, like Lamothe, of the
greatest of poets, and, like Aretino, of the most perfect of
statues. In general, the greater number of writers on these
subjects resemble rivers which rise when their water is not
needed, and remain dry in a period of drought.

17. In this *History of Art* I have exerted myself to discover
the truth, and, as I have had every desirable opportunity of
leisurely investigating the works of the ancients, and have
spared no pains to obtain the requisite kinds of knowledge, I
believed myself competent to undertake it. From youth upward, a love for art has been my strongest passion ; and though
education and circumstances led me in quite another direction,
still my natural inclination was constantly manifesting itself.
All the pictures and statues, as well as engraved gems and
coins, which I have adduced as proofs, I have myself seen, and
seen frequently, and been able to study ; but for the purpose of
aiding the reader's conception, I have cited, besides these, both
gems and coins from books, whenever the engravings of them
were tolerably good.

18. It must not occasion surprise that I have omitted to
notice some few works of ancient art bearing the name of the
artist, and some which have become remarkable from other
circumstances. Those which I have silently passed by are
objects which either afford no help in determining a style or
a period in art, or else they are no longer in Rome, or are
entirely destroyed ; for, in modern times, this misfortune has
befallen very many glorious pieces, — as I have remarked in
several places. I would have described the torso of a statue
with the name Apollonius of Athens, son of Nestor, upon it,
which was formerly in the Massimi palace ; but it is lost. A
painting of the goddess Roma, — not the known one in the

Barberini palace, — which is adduced by Spon, is also no longer in Rome. The Nymphæum described by Holstein has gone to decay, through negligence, it is asserted, and is no longer shown. The relievo on which Painting was making a portrait of Varro, which belonged to the celebrated Ciampini, is likewise no longer in Rome, lost without the slightest further information in regard to it. The Hermæ of the head of Speusippus, the head of Xenocrates, and several others, bearing either the name of the person or of the artist, have had a similar fate. It is impossible to read, without sorrow, notices of so many antique monuments of art, which were destroyed, both in Rome and elsewhere, in the days of our forefathers ; and of many no information even has been preserved. In an unpublished letter of the celebrated Peiresc to the commendator Del Pozzo, I recollect an account of many rilievi in the baths at Pozzuolo, near Naples, which still existed there in the popedom of Julius III., on which were represented persons afflicted with all sorts of diseases, whose health had been restored by these baths. This is the sole notice of them that is to be found. Who could believe that in our day, from the torso of a statue of which the head is in existence, two other statues were made ? Yet this has been the case at Parma, in the very year in which I write, with the colossal trunk of a Jupiter, the beautiful head of which is in the Academy of Painting in that city. The two new figures cut out of the antique one, of a sort that can easily be imagined, stand in the ducal garden. A nose has been affixed to the head in the most bungling manner; and the modern sculptor, intending to improve the forms which the ancient master gave to the forehead, cheeks, and beard, has removed what seemed to him superfluous. I forgot to state that this Jupiter was found in the buried city of Velleia, in the Parmesan territory, of which the discovery has recently been made. Moreover, within the memory of man, indeed since my residence in Rome, many celebrated pieces have been carried to England, where, as Pliny expresses it, they are exiled to remote country-seats.

19. As Greek art is the principal point which this *History* has in view, I have, consequently, been obliged in the chapter upon it to enter more into detail; yet I should have been able to say more if I had written for the Greeks, and not in a modern tongue, which imposes on me certain restrictions. For this

reason, I have, although reluctantly, left out a *Dialogue upon Beauty*, after the manner of the *Phædrus* of Plato, which would have served to elucidate my remarks when speaking of it theoretically.

20. All the monuments of art, whether antique paintings, figures in stone, engraved gems, or coins and vases, which I have introduced at the beginning and end of chapters or their divisions, both for embellishment and demonstration, have never before been published; and I have, for the first time, had drawings and engravings executed from them.

21. I have ventured to present a few speculations of which the proofs may not appear sufficiently strong; but they may, perhaps, help others onward who wish to penetrate into the art of the ancients; and how often it happens that a conjecture is, by a later discovery, converted into a truth! Conjectures — those, I mean, which are attached, at least by a thread, to something firm — are no more to be banished from a treatise of this kind, than hypotheses from natural philosophy. They resemble the frame of a building; they are indispensable indeed, if, in the want of different kinds of knowledge relative to ancient art, we do not wish to make great leaps across many vacant spots. Several of the reasons which I offered in regard to things not so clear as the sun give, when taken separately, only a probability, but collectively and connectedly amount to proof.

22. The list of works which I have prefixed[1] does not include all that I have cited; as, for instance, Nonnus is the sole one among them of the ancient poets, because, in the rare first edition of which I made use, only the verses on each page, and not the books in the poem, are numbered, as is the case with the other poets. Of the ancient Greek historians, the editions from which I have quoted are for the most part those of Robert and Henry Stephens, which are not divided into chapters; on this account I have indicated the lines on each page.

23. My worthy and learned friend, Herr Franke, the very deserving director of the celebrated and superb Bünau library, having taken great interest in the completion of this work, I am bound to express to him publicly the thanks which he deserves; for his kind heart could not have given me any more valuable proof of the friendship existing between us, which

has been fostered by our long-continued and mutual retired habits of life.

24. I cannot omit also — since the expression of gratitude on every occasion is commendable, and cannot be reiterated sufficiently often — to testify anew, in this place, my obligations to my valued friends, Herr Füessly of Zürich, and Herr Wille of Paris. The remarks published by me relative to the discoveries at Herculaneum ought more properly to be attributed to them; for without solicitation, from a voluntary mutual impulse, and a pure love of art and the extension of knowledge, they supported me, — a stranger to them, moreover, — on my first journey to that place, by a generous contribution. Men of this stamp are, for one such act alone, deserving of eternal remembrance, won by their own merit.

25. I, likewise, announce to the public a work, written in the Italian language, which will be published at Rome during the ensuing spring, at my own expense, in royal folio. It is an explanation of antique monuments of all kinds, never before published, especially rilievi in marble. Among them are very many which it was difficult to explain; of the others, some have been pronounced by skilful antiquarians to be riddles, incapable of solution, and some have been explained altogether erroneously. By these monuments the domain of art has been more enlarged than ever before. In them are seen conceptions and images wholly new, of which, in a measure, also, no traces are to be found in the accounts of the ancients; and many passages in their writings, which hitherto have not been understood, and even could not be understood without the help of these works, are explained, and set in a proper light. The volume is composed of more than two hundred engravings on copper, executed by the greatest draughtsman in Rome, John Casanova, a pensioned painter of the king of Poland; so that no work of antiquities can exhibit drawings which have so much correctness, taste, and knowledge of antiquity to recommend them. In regard to the other embellishments of the volume, nothing has been omitted on my part; and all the initial letters are engraved on copper.

The *History of Art* I dedicate to Art and the Age, and especially to my friend, Antonio Raphael Mengs.

ROME, July, 1763.

PREFACE TO THE NOTES.

1. It was not my intention to present these *Notes* in a separate form; but by means of them I expected to be enabled to produce an enlarged and improved edition of the *History of Art*. The large impression of this work, however, and the French translation of it, have induced me to collect the observations which I have from time to time noted down. For, on the one hand, to say what I deemed essential would have necessitated still a long delay; but, on the other hand, as the *History of Art* was becoming more generally known in a strange garb, although awkwardly and ignorantly donned, I esteemed it my duty to make it more complete through the present additions.

2. I do not shrink from acknowledging the deficiencies of the *History of Art;* but as it is no disgrace, when hunting in a wood, not to capture every wild beast, or to make bad shots, I hope to be excused wherever I have failed to mention or observe anything, or whenever I have not hit the mark. On the other hand, I can also assert that much, both here and there, has been intentionally omitted, partly because a notice without engravings would have been either unintelligible or imperfect, and partly because I should have been obliged to enter into learned investigations, which would have led too far from my object. In treatises upon art, learning should constitute the least part; for where it teaches nothing essential, it should be valued at nothing, and regarded — as the cough of shallow speakers or bad lute-players usually is (to make use of an expression of the ancients) — as an indication of poverty. I am also willing to acknowledge that I have occasionally failed to

state a few trifles quite correctly, because one often trusts too much to memory, or wishes to avoid journeys to distant places. This charge, however, would be less serious than that justly brought against Prideaux, that, when he was at Oxford, where the Arundelian marbles stand together in one place, he did not himself examine them for the elucidation of obscure passages.

3. The reader will not, I hope, be displeased, if, in this preamble, — for no future opportunity may perhaps occur, — I point out, for his instruction, the course which I pursued in the investigation of antiquities and works of art.

4. I did not come to Rome at the expense of a court, as persons imagine, and still less under the patronage of the nobleman whom I served in Saxony, — as an ill-informed scribbler asserts, — but supported by a worthy friend, to whom I have publicly expressed my gratitude. I came hither for the purpose of learning, with a view, at the same time, to becoming a teacher; and as I believed that, of the works of ancient art which had been made known, there were few which had been discussed in books in a philosophic spirit and with a well-grounded exposition of the truly beautiful in them, I hoped that my journey would not be entirely fruitless. For this purpose I had made previous preparation, so far as the scanty portion of time of which I was master permitted, and from my meditations at that time proceeded the essay on the *Imitation of the Ancients in Painting and Sculpture.* In pursuit of the objects which I had in view, I rejected every proposal made to me by two well-known cardinals, both before my departure for Rome, and also after my arrival there; for unless I had been my own master, I should have failed in my purpose.

5. During the whole of the first year I looked and contemplated, without forming any definite plan; for although I kept the essential always in view, still it was difficult for me to proceed with the success that I desired, along the untrodden path on which I travelled; many times, indeed, I was led astray by artists, whose judgments contradicted my feelings and my knowledge. But being invincibly firm in the belief that the Good and the Beautiful are the same, and that only one path leads to them, whilst many go to the Evil and the Ugly, I sought to test and establish my observations by a systematic application of knowledge.

6. In the first place, I determined to pay less attention,

at the outset, to the antiquities of places, sites, and regions, and the ancient ruins of buildings, because much is uncertain, and because that which can be known, and that which cannot be known, has been discussed with sufficient fulness by more than one writer. 'Besides, I could not undertake to seek out everything, for I had not the means wherewith to pay those who were able to serve me as guides. Now as this kind of knowledge can be acquired without any talent whatever, I took with me on my expedition no more of it than I could discover and investigate for myself. I compared it to bibliography, which has, not unfrequently, hindered those who have had an opportunity of acquiring it from knowing the contents of books. He who seeks to penetrate into the reality of knowledge has to guard not less against the danger of becoming a man of letters, than against what is commonly understood by the term antiquarian. For of these occupations one is as fascinating as the other, because they flatter our indolence and a sluggish indisposition to think for ourselves. It is, for instance, a pleasing thing to know in what part of Rome the ancient Carinæ were, and to be able to point out almost the exact spot where Pompey dwelt ; and the guide who can show to the traveller these localities does so with acertain self-satisfaction. But when we have seen the latter place, on which there does not remain the slightest trace of an ancient edifice, what more do we know ?

7. For the same reason, I did not trouble myself much about Roman coins, partly because it is difficult at the present day to discover any novelties in them, and partly, also, because I perceived that persons without any learning had acquired great skill in this department. The rarest Roman coins — the medallions excepted, on account of the beauty of their impression — are to be compared to rare books, which have become so because a bookseller would gain nothing by a reprint of them, and a rare Pertinax or Pescennius of silver or gold should not be valued more than one of Giordano Bruno's books. On the other hand, I endeavored to see the coins of Greek lands and cities, for which no particular search is made by the purchasers of coins, because it is not easy to form a series of them, as it is of the Roman. Moreover, in the study of these antiquities, the learner will not waste his thoughts on trifles, if he considers them as the productions of men whose thoughts were of a loftier and more manly strain than ours ; and thus viewed, the investi-

gation of them is able to elevate us above ourselves and above our age. A thinking person, on the shore of the wide sea, cannot occupy himself with low ideas; the illimitable view expands also the bounds of the soul, which, though at first seeming to be lost, returns again enlarged.

8. As I soon made the further discovery that very many works of ancient art were either not known, or had not been understood or explained, I endeavored to unite erudition with art. But the greatest difficulty in things dependent on learning usually is, to know what others have produced, in order not to labor in vain, or say what has been already many times repeated. When, however, I re-examined the works on ancient monuments of art, this apprehension was removed; and I satisfied myself that it was hardly possible to explain correctly, at a distance from Rome, that which has not been interpreted in Rome itself. The free use of the great library of the Cardinal Passionei gave me facilities for this study until I took charge of the library and museum of the Cardinal Alexander Albani; and afterwards, as Greek professor in the Vatican library, I had the privilege of exploring the treasures which it contained subservient to my design.

9. But a critical examination of art continued to be my principal occupation. In such a study, the first step must be skill to distinguish the modern from the ancient, and the genuine from the additions. I soon discovered the general rule, that the detached parts of statues, especially the hands and arms, are for the most part to be looked upon as new, and consequently the emblems also assigned to them. At first, however, it was extremely difficult for me to decide of myself in regard to a few heads. Once, when preparing, with this view, to examine the head of a female statue more nearly, it fell over, and I came nigh being crushed and buried beneath it. Here I must acknowledge, that it is only within a few years that I have discovered an Apollo, wrought in relief, in the Giustiniani palace, to be a modern work, though it is universally regarded as an antique, and has been pronounced by a travelled writer to be the most beautiful piece in the collection.

10. But as it is more easy to find the bad — which is usually the modern addition — than the good, so it was more difficult, far more difficult, for me to discover the beautiful, when it exceeded my knowledge. I did not look upon the works of art as he did,

who, when he saw the ocean for the first time, said, " It is a
pretty sight." 'Αθαυμάσια, or non-wonderment, which Strabo
extols, because it begets composure of mind, I prize highly in
ethics, but not in art : here indifference is prejudicial. The
general celebrity enjoyed by a few works has been occasionally
useful to me, during this investigation, by preoccupying my
judgment : it compelled me to acknowledge something beautiful, at least, in them, and to convince myself of its existence.
The torso of a Hercules, from the hand of Apollonius of Athens,
of which I have given a description, may serve as an instance to
the point. I obtained no light upon this work at my first view
of it ; I could not reconcile the moderate rendering of the parts
in this statue with the strong prominence in other statues of
Hercules, especially the Farnese. On the other hand, I set
before myself the high regard of Michael Angelo, and of all
subsequent artists, for this piece. Their opinion was, necessarily, almost an article of faith with me, yet so qualified that
I could not without reasons yield my approbation. My doubts
were perplexed by the attitude which Bernini and the whole
host of artists have given to this mutilated image, for they
imagine it to be a Hercules spinning. At last, after repeated
contemplation, and after convincing myself that the supposed
attitude of the figure was an erroneous notion, and that in this
case a Hercules reposing, with his right arm placed on his
head, as if occupied in musing on his achievements, has, with
more likelihood, been represented, I believed that I had discovered the ground of the difference between it and other statues
of Hercules. For both attitude and conformation showed it to
be a Hercules who had been received among the gods, and there
had rested from his labors, precisely as a rilievo in the villa of
the Cardinal Alexander Álbani represents him reposing on
Olympus, with the epithet of ΑΝΑΠΑΥΟΜΕΝΟΣ, *The Reposing;* consequently, in the celebrated torso we see an image of
Hercules as a deity, not as a mortal. Having now succeeded in
finding in statues representing him under each form the presumed grounds of the esteem in which they were held, and of
their beauty, I steadily continued so to study the remainder,
that I put myself in the position of one who was going to give
an account of them before an assemblage of connoisseurs ; and I
imposed upon myself the rule of not turning back until I had
discovered some beauty, and the grounds of it.

11. In accordance with some light which I had obtained, I attempted to define the styles of the Egyptian and Etruscan artists, and also to determine the difference between the art of the Etruscans and that of the Greeks. The characteristic marks of Egyptian works seemed to present themselves at once, but I was not equally successful with the style of the Etruscans ; and I do not undertake, even now, to assert, as a matter beyond dispute, that some rilievi which are seemingly Etruscan may not be works of the earliest style of the Greeks. With greater apparent certainty I discovered several periods in Greek works, but some years elapsed before I obtained any proofs of the lofty antiquity of a Muse in the Barberini palace.

12. The study of art had so entirely occupied the first two years of my residence in this city, that I was able to give only a passing thought, as it were, to the knowledge of antiquity derived from books alone. I was, however, put in this direction by the task of preparing a description of the intaglio gems of the Baron von Stosch, — who had died prior to that time, —which I sketched out in the rudest manner during the nine months of my stay at Florence, and afterwards finished at Rome. Here I learnt in regard to engraved gems, that, in every instance, the more beautiful the workmanship, so much the more natural is the representation ; and consequently the explanation is so easy, that those gems upon which are the names of the artists are understood by every one. Further experience satisfied me, that on Greek works of this kind there are fewer obscure images than on the Etruscan, and that the most ancient are usually the most abstruse ; just as the mythology of the earliest Greek poets, of Pamphos and Orpheus, for example, is more obscure than that taught by their successors. Here I came, for the first time, upon the trace of a truth which was afterwards of the greatest use to me in the explanation of the most difficult monuments. This truth consists of the principle, that the images on engraved gems, as well as on rilievi, are very seldom drawn from events occurring posterior to the Trojan war, or later than the return of Ulysses to Ithaca, unless, perhaps, we except those connected with the Heraclidæ, or the descendants of Hercules ; for their history still lies on the borders of fable, and fable was the especial subject of artists. Nevertheless, I know only a single picture taken from the history of the Heraclidæ, — repeated with slight modifications on several antique gems ;

namely, the lot cast by Cresphontes and Temenus, — illegiti-
mate grandsons of Hercules, — and the two sons of their
brother Aristomachus, about the partition of the Peloponnesus,
after they had taken possession of it with the armed hand. This
gem is wrongly explained by Beger and Gori. I was especially
confirmed as to the truth of the principle mentioned above, by
a more frequent examination of twenty-eight thousand impressions in sulphur, made, by direction of the Baron von Stosch,
from every antique gem which he had ever seen, or of which he
had ever heard. As a result of my experience, I came to a
conclusion adverse to the antiquity of all gems on which Roman
incidents are represented, — a conclusion which is obvious to
connoisseurs from the very workmanship of such gems. It is
shown beyond dispute by two cameos in the Strozzi museum, at
Rome, on which Quintus Curtius is engraved in the act of
throwing himself, on horseback, into the chasm. These beautifully executed modern gems have been published and described
by Gori as antique. The remark which I now make in reference to Roman history must not be extended to works in marble
which were executed in Rome, and were public monuments;
for a figure of the same Curtius is found on a small rilievo in
the Campidoglio, and another, of the size of life, in the Borghese villa (1).

13. When, after having finished the *Description* mentioned
above, and completed the *History of Art*, I proceeded to elucidate these monuments of antiquity which had not yet been published, the principle just named was my guide. Although
it explains nothing in itself, nor of itself, still it confines the attention to a more limited range of representation, and the
imagination does not rove about among stories beyond the
mythic circle.

14. In this work I established another test, no less useful;
namely, that the ancient artists have not, especially on rilievi
consisting of several figures, designed any merely ideal pictures,
that is to say, pictures not representing any known history, but
that all are referrible to the mythology either of the gods or of
the heroes. Bacchanalia, dances, &c. are always to be excepted.
If those who have occupied themselves in the explanation of
ancient monuments had taken this principle as a basis, the
knowledge of antiquities would have been far more thorough
and learned. The following examples will illustrate my remark.

Bellori designates a rilievo, engraved by Bartoli, by the title Epithalamium; but he should have investigated whether it might not rather be the marriage of Cadmus with Harmonia, or that of Peleus with Thetis, as the latter has been represented in the Aldobrandini Nuptials, so called. The scene termed by the same author a " Funeral Procession," *Pompa Funeralis*, which is wrought on the cover of a sepulchral urn in the Barberini palace, represents the burial of Meleager, and of his wife, Cleopatra, who dies by her own hand. So too the figures on another funeral urn in the same palace are not to be embraced under the general appellation of a *Passage across into the Elysian Fields, and a Mourning*, but we see therein, quite clearly, the whole history of Protesilaus, as it is told by Homer and other mythic writers. Another work, — of which there are many repetitions, — where Bellori dismisses the reader with the title *A Fearful Deed*, is the death of Agamemnon (2). I have also been convinced, that what has often seemed a riddle beyond solution is not an obscure and far-fetched allegory, in Lycophron's style. Nevertheless, it is not without advantage, when other traces are wanting, to presuppose allegories of such a nature, and to pursue them as far as they go, because we often meet with unexpected things. Such conjectures I have, occasionally, not rejected, but presented them to the reader, when the information conveyed by them is of a rare kind.

15. In the first design of this work I had in view only those monuments which are the most difficult to be explained, and the new course of my reading of the ancient authors was directed entirely to them. But my plan gradually became enlarged by the addition of other remarkable and partly obscure pieces which I found afterwards, and of which I had not thought in my reading, so that my task became laborious, and was doubled. Hence, it happened that I was obliged to peruse anew and repeatedly most of those authors, especially those which promised me any information. How easy to overlook a single word upon which the entire meaning depends! Through the single word ἀροτρεύων, *ploughing*, in the scholiast of Pindar, I found the true signification of the statue of Quintus Cincinnatus, erroneously so called, but properly a Jason, — as I have pointed out in the second part of these *Notes*. If, hereafter, any one should make a gleaning of the ancient monuments which I have left behind, or which have since been discovered,

let him endeavor to improve what I, for want of abilities and
means, have neglected.   Let him not do as I did, and as they
do who erect a building piecemeal, and, as it were, without any
previous plan ; but if he has the means of undertaking a great
work at his own expense, let him beforehand determine precisely all the pieces which he intends to publish, and then, when
he has them perfectly familiar to his memory, let him begin to
read all the ancient authors, without a single exception.   Of
modern authors who might be of immediate assistance in the
elucidation of ancient monuments, I cannot propose any other
than the learned Buonarroti ; but his writings are applicable
merely to points of abstruse learning, and they explain only
coins, — which is not difficult.   In obscure mythology and
heroic history, we must stick to the ancients, for Banier has
not drawn from the original sources ; the principal authority in
his work, as the reader will perceive, is Huet, with his evangelical proof, and under his guidance he has endeavored to derive
everything from the Bible and to trace everything back to it.
But that I may not seem to throw aside all other modern
writers, I recommend, in an undertaking of the kind of which I
now speak, Henning's *Theatrum Genealogicum.*   This rare work,
little known and still less read, especially in Italy, imparts more
information than all the works of all other nations united, —
I mean those which treat of fable and of Greek heroic history.
Neither do I wish to assert that no critical essays upon ancient
authors; and no treatises upon antiquities, may throw any light
on the subject ; but they should, as far as it is possible, be looked
over.

16. My greatest satisfaction in elucidating works of ancient
art has been when they enabled me to explain or amend an
ancient author.   Such discoveries have, for the most part, presented themselves to me unsought, — as the case usually is with
all discoveries, — and may, therefore, be less far-fetched than
many other attempts made by learned men of merit in this
department.   I cannot deny that I once felt the vanity of test-
ing my powers in this way ; but since, in my work now in press,
explaining the unknown monuments of antiquity, I have succeeded in satisfying my desire, I am the more content at not
having wasted the short period of my life on old, worn-out
manuscripts, — for which I had every desirable opportunity.
For the purpose of restraining this itching, I have always had

before my eyes the example of the celebrated Orville, who, during a residence of two years at Rome, went every morning to the Vatican library, for the purpose, partly of collating the Heidelberg Codex of Greek Anthology with the printed copy, and partly of emending and restoring the latter by means of the former. For I hold the time thus passed so much the worse employed, because, at the outset, I undertook the very same task, but relinquished it in season, as I perceived that what is wanting in the printed edition is not worthy of being brought to light. For these epigrams, in every instance in which wit is still to be found, are full of nastiness; and it cannot redound to the honor of him who published, in Holland, a few of them from Orville's manuscripts, — inasmuch as they jest upon unnatural obscenities.

17. To this historical statement of the method which I adopted, I have a few remarks to add upon several points which occurred to me after the discussion in the *Notes*. In the second chapter of the first book of the *History of Art*, I might have made mention of the skill of the ancients in executing mosaic-work in relief. But there is only a single, small piece of the kind known, — representing a young Hercules near the tree of the golden apples in the garden of the Hesperides, — which was taken from Rome to England, in the beginning of the present century, by the distinguished knight, Fountain. The same idea occurred as original to a skilful artist in Rome, a native of Urbino, who had no knowledge of this fact; and he made a happy, successful experiment, which induced the Cardinal Alexander Albani, the great patron and promoter of the arts, to take him into his service; and he has actually begun to execute the five goddesses of the Seasons, as they are called, in the Borghese villa, in this difficult kind of work, compared with which the usual flat mosaic-work may appear exceedingly easy. For, besides the labor of the workmanship, the artist must be skilful in modelling, — which is not necessary in the other case; but the most difficult part of this art consists in the polishing; in the folds of the drapery, indeed, it appears even inconceivable.

18. In the same place, also, I ought to have explained myself more clearly in regard to the forming of ivory figures on a lathe. This, in my opinion, is the art termed by the ancients τορευτικη, in which Phidias was eminently distinguished. It is well known that, in modern days, rilievi of considerable size

have been turned from ivory; but no figures hollowed underneath can be produced in this way, because the tool can act
only on the surface. If any one, therefore, should be disposed
to imagine that the statues which Phidias composed of pieces
of ivory, joined together, were turned upon a lathe, I must
acknowledge that I do not well understand how it can be done,
— for example, in regard to the head of a figure, — by any
skill which the art has attained in modern days. For as the
head, though previously composed of pieces, must be conceived
of as a whole when in the act of being turned, it would be
necessary to presume that it moved steadily under the instrument; hence, the oblique deep parts could not have been executed on the lathe; these must have been done with a chisel.

19. In the same book and chapter might, also, be introduced
a remark relative to the mistake into which others besides
Berkeley have probably fallen, — that the art of painting on
walls was first introduced in the time of Augustus, and that
Ludius was the inventor. The writer just named has drawn
this inference from a misunderstood statement in Pliny; for
Pliny does not say that Ludius was the first in Rome who
painted on walls, but that he was the first to embellish with
landscapes, and similar inanimate objects, the walls of rooms,
on which, prior to his time, none but historical pieces were represented. Gronovius, in his notes to Berkeley, has overlooked
this error; yet he ought to have observed it, because among
the artists who painted on walls he also names Pausias, notwithstanding he lived two hundred years before Augustus; for
he was a pupil of Pamphilus, and the teacher of Apelles.

20. An idea of Dion Chrysostomus, in the fourth chapter of
Art among the Greeks, might, if true, give occasion to further
reflection. This writer, speaking of his own time, under Trajan, says: "Beauty of conformation is less common among
men; of beautiful women there is no lack; but either the
number of handsome men born is very limited, or, if they do
exist, they remain concealed, either because we have ceased to
pay regard to manly beauty, or because we do not know how to
prize it, — as the ancient Greeks did." Notwithstanding, the
same writer says of a young athlete of his time, of very beautiful conformation, that, "if he had not made himself celebrated in bodily exercises, he would have become so solely by
the beauty of his shape."

21. The notes upon drapery, in the same chapter, may recall to the reader's remembrance an unfounded opinion in regard to a clasp, shaped like a cross, upon the straps of the sandals, which I noticed in the *Essay on Allegory*. When I wrote that remark, there was not to be found in Rome on any statue, nor on any of the feet in the notable collection formed by the sculptor Bartolommeo Cavaceppi, a cross of the kind, from which I might have obtained further refutation of that opinion. A short time since, however, the sculptor just named obtained a beautiful foot of a male statue, which must have been far larger than life, on which there is such a cross-clasp. On the same principle, a child's head between two wings, — as we are accustomed to represent angels, — which is the ornament of just such a clasp on the feet of a beautiful Bacchus in the Ludovisi villa, might, if the feet had been found separate from the trunk, have been supposed to indicate a Christian image.

22. In the second part of these *Notes*, — where it has been shown that the period designated by Pliny as the flourishing age of great artists generally corresponds to the cessation of wars, — the reader may notice the Greek proverbial saying, Φειδίας προσήκει εἰρήνῃ, "Phidias belongs to peace." It has been quoted by Suidas, but is not understood by him any better than by others. He explains it in an unintelligible and ridiculous manner, by saying that peace belongs to Phidias, because he is an artist ; for Peace is represented as beautifully shaped. It will easily be perceived from the proofs which I have presented in their proper place, that, if this were actually a proverb, — of which Küster doubts, — it must be understood of a state of peace, in which alone the arts flourish.

23. I have been still more confirmed in my opinion, that the Niobe is to be attributed to Scopas rather than to Praxiteles, by a cast in gypsum of the head of Niobe herself ; and this cast is the only one extant in Rome ; but the head from which it was taken is no longer to be found here. On comparison of the head of Niobe with that single cast, more roundness is observable in the latter, and the mouth also is found to be of a better shape ; hence some persons have inferred a greater probability that the cast was taken from the true head of Niobe, and that the head now on the statue is an antique repetition of the same work, but from the hand of an inferior artist. But they had not reflected upon the nature of the grand style, — of which

roundness had not, as yet, become wholly an attribute, — and that the round manner of forming the eyebrow-bones points to a later age. Furthermore, they had not observed that the mouth of the statue had been much injured, and that the two lips had been badly repaired with gypsum. The head from which the cast was taken, which is truly beautiful, might therefore, on account of its greater softness and roundness, be looked upon as an antique repetition of this work in the beautiful style, and perchance as a copy from the hand of Praxiteles. A comparison of the two heads teaches the distinctive points of the latter as well as of the former style.

24. In those places where I have mentioned the sculptor Ctesias, Ctesilaus must be read. I have spoken of him fully at the beginning of the second part of these *Notes*. From the research made in that place, it appears that the Dying Gladiator, so called, in the Campidoglio, cannot be his work, especially as Pliny speaks of a dying hero, and not of a gladiator.

25. On reconsidering the Farnese Bull, in reference to the names of the two artists by whom the work was executed, which were formerly inscribed on it, but are now no longer to be seen, I find that the inscription may have been engraved upon the trunk of a tree which serves as a support to the figure of Zethus, — for this was the most conspicuous place for it, — and also that the actual trunk is mostly new.

26. In regard to the heroic manner of representing the statue of Pompey, I have expressed my belief that it is the sole statue of a Roman republican which is formed entirely nude. But the supposed statue of Agrippa, — which is likewise treated heroically, — in the Grimani mansion at Venice, might be adduced as proof to the contrary. I might obviate this objection by the consideration, that republican modesty and moderation were no longer sought for, even in art, during the reign of Augustus. But it is not yet proved that this statue represents Marcus Agrippa ; and if there be any resemblance in the head of it to the heads of images of him, then an investigation must be made at the place where the statue stands, for the purpose of ascertaining whether the head belongs to it.

27. Against the appellation of the statue falsely termed Seneca in the Bath, in the Borghese villa, I might have adduced clear proof from a statue of white marble, of the size of life, in the Pamfili villa, which perfectly resembles it even in counte-

nance, and which carries in its left hand a vessel shaped like a basket. Two small statues in the Albani villa are, again, similar to this latter statue, and, like it, they carry a basket. At the feet of one of them is a comic mask ; so that we clearly see that the latter, as well as the former, represent servants in a comedy, who, like Sosias, at the opening of the *Andrias* of Terence, were sent out to buy food.

28. I might have supported my conjecture, — that the Trophies of Marius, as they are called, are rather to be attributed to Domitian, — by adducing a few pieces of other trophies in the Barberini villa, at Castel-Gandolfo, which were disinterred here, where once stood the villa of Publius Clodius, and afterwards of Domitian. The elegance of the workmanship on these fragments does not yield in the slightest degree to the skill displayed by those, and it must be inferred, not without reason, that they are to be esteemed as works of the same period, if not by the same artist. Now, as trophies were raised by Domitian's command in his villa, he may also have ordered them to be erected near an aqueduct on which some improvements had perhaps been made by him.

29. In conclusion, I must lament the fate that has befallen the *History of Art* in the French translation, which has been published at Paris, by Saillant, in two volumes, octavo. On changing the size, it was thought better to set the subject of each section over the section to which it related, instead of placing it in the margin, and to make so many distinct divisions and paragraphs. But this dismemberment breaks the connection ; and as each one portion is thus separated from another, they appear like independent members, — and the more so, as the translator has, in many places, either changed or entirely omitted the connecting words. The size of the volumes might perhaps have been offered as an excuse for not placing the contents in the margin ; but no excuse can be urged for making sections where there are none in the original, and where there ought not to be any, — which is the case at the beginning of the second part. Here the translator has cut up into quite small scraps that part which contains a list of the earliest artists prior to the time of Phidias ; and the brief notices of these artists are again detached, with particular numbers, and translated names, as if he were apprehensive the reader might get out of breath if he did not snip a portion from each end of the connected passage. From one single head he has made twenty-four.

30. But on the translation itself I cannot think without disgust, for I do not believe that it would be easy to treat a work worse, in translating it from its own into another tongue. I began by noticing, on the margin, mistakes in the meaning ; but I became weary of this, because not a single page was free from them. The translator not only shows gross ignorance in the most common acquirements in art, but innumerable passages prove that he does not fully understand German.

31. I should have been ready to revise and correct the translation with the greatest attention, if those interested in it had made me such a request. But I knew nothing about it ; and when I heard, two years ago, — I know not how, — of a translation of this work of mine, I made inquiry concerning it of some persons in Paris whom I knew ; I learnt, however, nothing further. At last, when the rumor in regard to the translation was confirmed, I caused a request to be made to the lieutenant of police at Paris, that it might not pass the censorship until I had examined and approved it ; I believe, however, that the request was made too late. Plato says, that no one is intentionally bad ; the present instance seems to contradict the saying ; for those interested might have furnished a correct translation without expense ; but they did not wish it ; and therefore this monster saw the light.

32. I am now able to announce the publication of my work in the Italian language on the hitherto unpublished monuments of antiquity. It has been printed at my own expense, and without a subscription list, and will appear about next Christmas, in two volumes, large folio. In addition to the ornamental engravings, it contains two hundred and ten plates of the ancient monuments which are explained and illustrated in it, together with a *Full Preliminary Treatise on the Art of Drawing among the Egyptians, Etruscans, and especially the Greeks.*

Rome, September 1, 1766.

HISTORY OF ANCIENT ART.

BOOK I.

THE ORIGIN OF ART, AND THE CAUSES OF ITS DIFFERENCE AMONG DIFFERENT NATIONS.

CHAPTER I.

THE SHAPES WITH WHICH ART COMMENCED.

1. THE arts which are dependent on drawing have, like all inventions, commenced with the necessary; the next object of research was beauty; and, finally, the superfluous followed: these are the three principal stages in art.

2. In the infancy of art, its productions are, like the handsomest of human beings at birth, misshapen, and similar one to another, like the seeds of plants of entirely different kinds; but in its bloom and decay, they resemble those mighty streams, which, at the point where they should be the broadest, either dwindle into small rivulets, or totally disappear.

3. The art of drawing among the Egyptians is to be compared to a tree which, though well cultivated, has been checked and arrested in its growth by a worm, or other casualties; for it remained unchanged, precisely the same, yet without attaining its perfection, until the period when Greek kings held sway over them; and the case appears to have been the same with Persian art. Etruscan art, when in its bloom, may be compared to a raging stream, rushing furiously along between crags and over rocks; for the characteristics of its drawing are hardness and exaggeration. But, among the Greeks, the art of

drawing resembles a river whose clear waters flow in numerous windings through a fertile vale, and fill its channel, yet do not overflow.

4. As art has been devoted principally to the representation of man, we might say of him more correctly than Protagoras did, that "he is the measure and rule of all things." The most ancient records also teach us, that the earliest essays, especially in the drawing of figures, have represented, not the manner in which a man appears to us, but what he is; not a view of his body, but the outline of his shadow. From this simplicity of shape the artist next proceeded to examine proportions; this inquiry taught exactness; the exactness hereby acquired gave confidence, and afterwards success, to his endeavors after grandeur, and at last gradually raised art among the Greeks to the highest beauty. After all the parts constituting grandeur and beauty were united, the artist, in seeking to embellish them, fell into the error of profuseness; art consequently lost its grandeur; and the loss was finally followed by its utter downfall.

The following is, in a few words, the design of this treatise on the History of Art. In the first place, I shall speak, generally, of the shape with which art commenced; next, of the different materials upon which it worked; and lastly, of the influence of climate upon it.

5. Art commenced with the simplest shape, and by working in clay, — consequently, with a sort of statuary; for even a child can give a certain form to a soft mass, though unable to draw anything on a surface, because merely an idea of an object is sufficient for the former, whereas for the latter much other knowledge is requisite; but painting was afterwards employed to embellish sculpture.

6. Art appears to have originated in a similar way among all the nations by which it has been cultivated; and there is no sufficient reason for assigning any particular country as the land of its birth, for every nation has found within itself the first seed of those things which are indispensable; and although Art, like Poetry, may be regarded as a daughter of Pleasure, still it cannot be denied that pleasure is as necessary to human nature as those things are without which existence cannot be continued; and it can be maintained that painting and the forming of figures, or the art of painting and figuring our thoughts, are

older than the art of writing them, — as proved by the history of the Mexicans and other nations. But as the earliest essays appear to have been made on figures of the divinities, the era in which art was invented consequently differs according to the age of each nation, and the earlier or later introduction of religious worship; so that the Chaldæans or Egyptians probably represented for worship, under a material form, the higher powers, whose existence they had imagined at an earlier period than the Greeks. For it is the same in this case as with other arts and discoveries, — take, for instance, the example of the purple color, — which were earlier discovered and practised in the East. The accounts of wrought images, in the Holy Scripture (1), are older than anything that we know of the Greeks. The figures, which were, at the outset, carved from wood, and others that were cast in brass, have each one a special name in the Hebrew language. After a time, the former were gilded, or overlaid with gold-leaf. But those who speak of the origin of a custom, as well as of an art, and their communication from one nation to another, commonly err by confining themselves to isolated points between which there is a resemblance, and drawing from them a general conclusion; just as Dionysius attempts to maintain that the Romans are descended from the Greeks, because the athletes of both nations wore a band about the hips. Even if we were willing to admit that art was introduced from Egypt among the Greeks, we must, at least, also acknowledge that the same thing may have happened to it as to the mythology; for the fables of the Egyptians were seemingly born anew beneath the skies of Greece, and took an entirely different form, and other names.

7. In Egypt art had been flourishing from the remotest periods; and, if Sesostris lived more than three hundred years before the Trojan war, then the tallest obelisks (2) now in Rome, — the work of his reign, — and the largest edifices at Thebes, of which mention has already been made, existed at a time when darkness and obscurity still rested upon art among the Greeks. The causes why art flourished at an earlier date among the Egyptians appear to have been the dense population of the country, and the power of their kings ; the latter was able to carry into execution the inventions growing out of the industrious habits to which the former necessarily gave birth. But the populousness of the country, as well as the power of

its kings, was favored by its position and its climate. The latter, from its uniform temperature and warm skies, enabled the people to pass life, in general, pleasantly, and find support easily ; and propagation was encouraged, because their children went naked until maturity. By the former, that is, the position of Egypt, nature has apparently intended it for a single, indivisible, and consequently mighty kingdom, since it is traversed by one large river, and its boundaries are the sea on the north, and lofty mountains on other sides, — for the river, and the plain surface of the land, were unfavorable to partition ; and if several kings once ruled there at the same time, still it was a condition of things that had but a short duration. Hence, Egypt enjoyed in a greater degree than other kingdoms tranquillity and peace, — by which the arts were brought into being and nurtured. Greece, on the contrary, was divided, even naturally, by numerous mountains, rivers, islands, and promontories, and, in the most remote periods, there were as many kings as cities, the repose of which was disturbed by disputes and wars, to which their proximity gave frequent occasion, — a state of things unfavorable to the increase of population, and consequently also to industry and invention in arts. It is therefore easy to be understood why art should have been cultivated less early in Greece than in Egypt.

8. Among the Greeks, art commenced with the same simplicity as in Eastern lands ; insomuch that they cannot have derived the first seeds of it from any other people : they appear to have been original discoverers. For they had already among themselves thirty divinities, whom they honored under visible forms ; and, not having yet learned to fashion them after the likeness of man, they were contented to signify them by a rude block or square stone, as the Arabians and Amazons did ; and these thirty stones existed in the city of Pheræ, in Achaia, even as late as the time of Pausanias. This was the shape of the Juno at Thespiæ, and the Diana at Icarus. Diana Patroa and Jupiter Milichus at Sicyon were, like the most ancient Venus at Paphos, nothing more than a sort of columns ; Bacchus was worshipped under the form of a pillar ; and even Cupid and the Graces were represented merely by blocks of stone ; hence, the word κίων, *a pillar*, continued to signify a statue even in the best days of Greece. Among the Spartans, Castor and Pollux were in the form of two parallel

PLATE I

blocks of wood, connected by two cross sticks; and this primitive mode of representing the twins is seen in the sign II, by which they were denoted in the zodiac.

9. In course of time, heads were set upon these stones. Among many others, a Neptune at Tricoloni and a Jupiter at Tegea, both places in Arcadia, were of this kind ; for here, more than in any other part of Greece, the people adhered to the most ancient form in art. Even in the time of Pausanius there was still to be found in Athens itself a statue of Venus Urania thus shaped. The first images of the Greeks, therefore, manifest originality in the invention and production of a figure. The Holy Scriptures (3), too, allude to heathen idols which had no other part of the human form than the head. Four-cornered stones with heads on them were termed by the Greeks, as it is well known, Hermæ (4), that is, big stones ; and artists constantly kept a supply of them.

10. The accounts in authors and the ancient monuments will enable us to follow the progressive improvement in the conformation of this rough draught and rude beginning of a figure. At the commencement, there was observable on the middle of these stones with heads merely the difference in sex, which an ill-shaped face probably left doubtful. When, therefore, it is said that Eumarus of Athens first showed in painting the difference of sex, the remark is probably to be understood particularly of the conformation of the face in youth, in which this painter perhaps denoted the sex of young persons by the features and charms peculiar to each. This artist flourished before the age of Romulus, and not long after the restoration of the Olympic games by Iphitus. At last, the upper part of the figure received its form, while the lower portion still retained its previous shape of a Hermes, yet so far modified that the separation of the thighs was denoted by an incision, as we see in a naked female figure of this kind in the Albani villa.[1] I mention this figure, not as being a work of the earliest days of art, — for it was in reality executed at a much later date, — but as a proof that artists were acquainted with such primitive figures, the form of which they intended hereby to represent. We do not know, however, whether the Hermæ designated by the female nature, which were set up by order of Sesostris in those conquered lands that had offered no resistance, were

[1] Plate I.

61440

thus shaped, or whether they bore the sign of a triangle (5), after the Egyptian manner of indicating the female sex.

11. At last, Dædalus, according to the opinion most commonly received, began to separate entirely the lower half of these Hermæ, in the form of legs ; and, as there was not sufficient skill in art at that time to fashion an entire human figure from a single block of stone, he wrought in wood ; and from him the first statues are said to have received the name of Dædali. We can form some idea of his works from the opinion of the sculptors of the time of Socrates, as quoted by him. " If Dædalus," he says, " should live again, and produce works similar to those which pass under his name, he would, as the sculptors say, be an object of ridicule."

12. Among the Greeks the first outlines of these images were simple, and, for the most part, straight lines ; and it is probable, that, in the infancy of art, whether among the Egyptians, Etruscans, or Greeks, there was no difference in this respect ; and this probability is also confirmed by the testimony of the ancient authors.

In regard to Greek art, this method of delineation is visible in one of the oldest Greek figures in bronze, which may be found in the Nani museum, at Venice, — on the base of which is the following inscription, ΠΟΛΥΚΡΑΤΕΣ ΑΝΕΘΕΚΕ, that is, Dedicated by Polycrates, — who was not, probably, the artist of it. To this flat style of drawing is also to be attributed the resemblance of the eyes in heads on the oldest Greek coins, and of Egyptian figures ; in both cases they are without convexity, and somewhat long, — as I shall state more in detail hereafter. It is probable that Diodorus wished to signify such eyes, where he says, in speaking of the figures of Dædalus, that they were made ὄμμασι μεμυκότα, which translators have rendered by luminibus clausis, " closed eyes." This is not probable ; for if he wished to make eyes, it is likely that he made them open. Moreover, the translation is utterly at variance with the proper and invariable meaning of the word μύειν, which means to wink, nictare, in Italian, sbirciare, and must be rendered by conniventibus oculis, "half-shut eyes," just as μεμυκοτα χείλεα means half-opened lips. But the first paintings were monograms, as Epicurus termed the gods, that is, unilinear outlines of the shadow of the human figure.

13. From such lines and forms must, therefore, necessarily

arise a kind of figures which, from their conformation, we are accustomed to call Egyptian ; that is, they are perfectly straight and motionless; and the arms are not detached, but lie close to the sides, precisely in the manner in which a statue of an Arcadian victor in the Games, by the name of Arrhachion, was executed, even as late as the twenty-fourth Olympiad. But this resemblance does not prove that the Greeks learnt their art from the Egyptians. In fact, they had no opportunity of doing so ; for prior to the reign of Psammetichus, one of the last Egyptian kings, foreigners were not allowed to enter Egypt ; but the Greeks had cultivated art long before this time. The voyages to that country by the wise men of Greece — not undertaken, however, until after its conquest by the Persians — were made principally with a view to become acquainted with its form of government, and to penetrate into the secret knowledge of its priests : they had no reference to art. Those who derive everything from Eastern lands would, on the contrary, find greater probabilities on the side of the Phœnicians, with whom the Greeks had commercial intercourse at a very early date, and from whom they are said to have received, through Cadmus, their first letters. The Etruscans, also, who were powerful on the sea, had been allies of the Phœnicians in the remotest times, before the age of Cyrus. One proof of this, among others, may be found in the fact that these two nations equipped a fleet in common to act against the Phocæans.

14. This, however, will not convince those who are aware that a few Greek authors have acknowledged the derivation of their mythology from the Egyptians, and that the priests of this people asserted that they could show the Greek deities in their own, though under different names and a peculiar symbolic form, as Diodorus in particular relates. If this testimony should not be contradicted, I confess that a strong argument against my opinion might be deduced from the alleged communication to the Greeks of the religious system of the Egyptians. For if this communication be assumed as proved, it might be inferred therefrom that the Greeks consequently derived also from the Egyptians the shapes of the gods themselves, and their figures. But I cannot admit this pretension. I am more disposed to believe, that after the conquest of Egypt by Alexander, where his successors, the Ptolemies, reigned, the priests — in order to show their conformity with the Greeks, and in-

duce them to forbearance in regard to their ancient religious
rites — invented the idea of this close relationship between
the deities of the two nations, since they must necessarily have
felt an apprehension of appearing ridiculous in the eyes of their
keen-witted conquerors, on account of the strange shape of
their deities, and, perchance, experiencing a fate similar to that
which happened to them through Cambyses.   This supposition
acquires the greatest probability from the account given us by
Macrobius of the worship of Saturn and Serapis, which was
introduced among the Egyptians by the Ptolemies, not until
after the time of Alexander the Great, with religious services
corresponding to those paid to them by the Greeks of Alexandria.   Now, since the Egyptian priests, and the people too,
were obliged, on the one hand, to acknowledge and honor Greek
deities, the best course, consequently, for them to pursue was
to pretend, on the other hand, that their divinities were not
different from those of the Greeks ; and if the Greeks admitted
this, they must also have admitted the reception of their religious worship from the Egyptians, because they were the older
people (6).   Moreover, it is well known to all, that the Greeks
possessed but little information in regard to the religion of
other nations.   Their ignorance in this respect is proved,
among other instances, by the long list of Persian deities of
which they give us the names ; whereas this people worshipped
one god alone, the Sun, in his emblem of fire.

15. Though this is not the place for me to originate objections which I may find it difficult to answer, still I cannot but
suppose that thoughts of the same kind will suggest themselves
to many of my readers as well as to myself.   If, for example,
any one should see a scarab cut on obelisks, or engraved on the
convex side of Egyptian (7) and Etruscan gems, as an image of
the sun, he might consequently infer that the Etruscans had
borrowed the emblem from the Egyptians, thereby rendering
it probable that they had likewise derived their art from the
same source.   Certainly it must appear strange to us, that an
insect so vile should have become a sacred symbol with the one,
and apparently with the other nation also ; and there is reason
to suppose that even the Greeks attached some peculiar meaning to the beetle.   As Pamphus, one of their earliest poets,
hides his Jupiter in the dung of a horse, we might interpret the
idea to be an image of the presence of divinity in all things,

even the meanest; but it seems to me that this low metaphor may, perchance, be drawn precisely from the scarab, which rakes over, and lives in, horse-dung. But, that I may not enter into any further analysis of this unpleasant image, I am willing to acknowledge that the Etruscans received it from the Egyptians. It is, however, possible that it may have been communicated through a particular channel, not involving the necessity of a visit to Egypt, which, as mentioned above, was a privilege not permitted to foreigners, at the period of which we speak. But the case is different in regard to art; it could not be learnt in any other way than by drawing after their works.

16. The opinion of a few Greek writers, that Greece derived its art from Egypt, will not be regarded as proof of the assertion, even though all of them assented to it, by those who know the fondness of the human mind for everything foreign, — a fondness from which the Greeks were not more exempt than other men; since even the dwellers in the island of Delos alleged that their river, the Inopus, came from the Nile, beneath the sea, and, on reaching them, again burst forth in springs.

17. I might also adduce, in opposition to the common opinion, the different customs of the artists of the three nations of which we now speak; for we know that it was usual among the Etruscans and most ancient Greeks to place the inscription on the figure itself. This is not the case with any Egyptian work; here, the hieroglyphs are on the socle, and on the shaft which serves as a support to the figure (8). Needham attempted to show the contrary by means of a head of blackish stone, in the royal museum at Turin, the face of which was entirely covered with incised unintelligible signs, which were, as he thought, Egyptian letters, and similar to the Chinese (9). But the Turin head has not the least resemblance to other Egyptian heads; and it is wrought from a soft stone, a kind of slate, termed Bardiglio, and must consequently be considered as an imposture.

18. In the course of time, increasing knowledge taught the Etruscan and Greek artists how to forsake the stiff and motionless conformations of their earliest essays, to which the Egyptians adhered, — compulsorily adhered, — and enabled them to express different actions in their figures. But, in art, knowl-

edge precedes beauty ; being based on exact, severe rules, its
teachings at the beginning have necessarily a precise and vigorous definiteness.   Consequently, the style of drawing was
regular, but angular ; expressive, but hard, and frequently exaggerated, — as the Etruscan works show.   This is just the
way in which sculpture has been improved in modern days by
the celebrated Michael Angelo.   Works in this style have been
preserved on rilievi in marble, and on engraved gems, — which
I shall notice in their proper place ; and this is the style which
the writers mentioned above compare with the Etruscan, and
which, as it appears, continued to be a peculiarity of the school
at Ægina ; for the artists of this island, which was inhabited by
Dorians, seem to have adhered to it longer than any others.
Strabo, in the use of the word σκολιός, *distorted* (10), apparently intends to signify that exaggeration which artists still
retained in the position and action of their figures, though
they had forsaken the shapes of the earliest times.   He relates
that there were at Ephesus many temples, some of which had
been built in the most remote periods, and others at a later
date ; that, in the former, there were ancient statues of wood,
ἀρχαῖα ξόανα, but in the others, σκολιὰ ἔργα.   Now it is not
probable that, by the latter expression, he means to say that
the statues in the more modern temples were bad and faulty,
— as Casaubon has understood it, translating σκολιός by *pravus*,
" bad," — because the censure would be far more applicable to
the most ancient figures (11).

19. The word ὀρθός seems to signify just the opposite of
σκολιός, which, where it is applied to statues, — as in Pausanias,
in regard to a statue of Jupiter from the hand of Lysippus, — is
explained by translators to mean an upright posture, whereas
it ought rather to denote a figure in a quiet attitude, without
action.

CHAPTER II.

MATERIALS USED IN STATUARY.

1. THE second chapter of this book treats of the materials in which sculpture executed its works, and also shows the different stages of its development ; in the first of which it wrought in clay; then, carved from wood; next, from ivory; and, finally, applied itself to stone and metal (1).

2. Even the ancient forms of expression point to clay as the earliest material of art ; for the workmanship of the potter, and of the shaper or image-cutter, is denoted by the same word. In the time of Pausanias there were still, in different temples, figures of the divinities, formed of clay, as, for example, at Tritia in Achaia, in the temple of Ceres and Proserpine ; and a clay image of Amphictyon, who hospitably entertained Bacchus together with other deities, stood in a temple of Bacchus at Athens; and in this same city, in the portico named Ceramicus (2), from its works ·in clay, stood Theseus in the act of throwing Sciron into the sea, and also Aurora carrying away Cephalus ; both of these works were in clay. Even in the buried city of Pompeii, four statues of burnt clay have been found, which are now set up in the Herculaneum museum ; two of them, a little less than life, represent comic figures of different sexes, and have masks upon their faces ; the other two, which are somewhat larger than life, are an Æsculapius and an Hygeia. A bust of Pallas, of the size of life, with a small round shield on the left breast, was also discovered there. Images of this kind were occasionally painted of a red color (3), as shown by a male head of clay, which was found in ancient Tusculum ; likewise, by a small figure, clothed as a senator, which is formed in one piece with the socle ; on the back of the socle is the name of the figure, CRVSCVS. The figures of Jupiter, in particular, were said to have their faces painted with this color, and there was one of the kind at Phigalia in Arcadia ; Pan, also, was painted red; and the same thing is done even

now by the Indians (4).   The epithet of Φοινικόπεζα, *Red-footed*, applied to Ceres, is apparently derived from this practice.

3. Even subsequently, not only during the flower of art, but also when that period had passed, clay continued to be the first material employed by artists, partly in rilievi, and partly in painted vases.   The former were not only introduced into the friezes of temples, but they also served the artists as models ; and in order to multiply them, copies were made from a mould, previously prepared.   The numerous fragments of precisely the same representation are a confirmation of what I say.   These impressions were then worked over with the modelling-stick, as can easily be seen.   Occasionally, these models were strung on a cord, and suspended in the workshops of artists ; for in the middle of some of them there is a hole, made for the purpose (5).

4. The ancient artists not only prepared models to assist them in their work, and for the workshop, but they also strove to distinguish themselves, even in the most brilliant period of art, by a public display of works in clay, as well as in marble and bronze.   In fact, the practice of exposing models of this kind to the public gaze was continued even until a few years after the death of Alexander the Great ; that is to say, until the time of Demetrius Poliorcetes.   This exposition occurred sometimes in Bœotia, sometimes in the cities about Athens, and especially in Platæa, at the celebration of the festivals which were held in commemoration of Dædalus, one of the earliest artists.   Besides the emulation in this kind of work which such a public display of models maintained among the artists, it also tended to make the judgment of others as to their skill more correct and thorough, since modelling in clay is to the sculptor what drawing on paper is to the painter.   For as the first gush of the grape-juice from the press forms the finest wine, so in the soft material, and on paper, the genius of the artist is seen in its utmost purity and truth ; whilst, on the contrary, it is concealed beneath the industry and the polish required in a finished painting and a completed statue.   Now as this kind of workmanship continued in high estimation among the ancients, it so happened that, when Corinth rose from her ashes through a colony sent thither by Julius Cæsar, search was made amid the rubbish of the destroyed city, and in its ditches, not less

for works of art fashioned in clay than for those in bronze. This is related by Strabo in a passage which, apparently, has not hitherto been clearly understood. For if Casaubon, his commentator, — whom others have followed, — had formed a distinct idea of his statement, he would not have translated what that writer terms τορεύματα ὀστρακίνα by *testacea opera*, " works in tiles," but by *anaglypha figulina*, " reliefs in clay " ; for τορεύματα, as I shall show hereafter in full, means "raised works." The experience of modern days shows that this esteem for works in clay was well deserved ; and it may be stated, as a general rule, that nothing bad of this kind is ever found, — an assertion that cannot be made of rilievi in marble.

5. The Cardinal Alexander Albani has placed some of the most beautiful fragments in his magnificent villa ; among them is Argos at work upon the vessel of the Argonauts, together with another figure, probably Tiphys, the helmsman of it, and Minerva, who is attaching the sail to a mast. This piece, and two other fragments that were formed in the same mould, together with other sherds of such rilievi in clay, were found in the wall of a vineyard in front of the Porta Latina, where they had served instead of tiles.

6. The usual size of rilievi of this kind is generally that of the large tablets of clay — we cannot call them bricks — that are used in forming arches. They are about three palms (2 ft. 2 in. Eng.) square superficially, and are baked, like the rilievi, in such a manner that, on being struck, they give a sharp ring ; and they are not injured either by dampness, heat, or cold.

7. In this place I cannot forbear to notice a remark by Pliny, from which it would seem as if the ancient artists who worked in bronze prepared the paste of their moulds from a composition of clay and the finest wheaten flour.

The account given by Pliny of the forming of statues in a mould, which the brother of Lysippus is said to have invented, is not credible, in the manner in which he relates it ; for in things relating to art he is not always veracious, and frequently he appears to speak only from hearsay. The portraits of celebrated men which were sent by Varro into all countries, as this same writer mentions, were probably formed of gypsum, like the images of the deities intended for the poor.

8. Of the other kind of monuments of workmanship in clay,

namely, the painted vases of the ancients, several thousands
have been preserved : I shall speak of them more in detail
hereafter. Earthen vessels continued, from the earliest ages,
to be employed in sacred and religious offices, even after the
increase of luxury had driven them out of use among the
burghers. With the ancients, many of them were a substitute
for porcelain, and served for ornament, not for utility, for some
are found which have no bottom.

9. As the edifices of the most ancient Greeks were made of
wood earlier than of stone and marble, so also were statues ;
this was even the case with the palaces of the Median kings.
There are found in Egypt, even at the present day, primeval
figures made of wood, — which is sycamore ; and many museums have such to exhibit. Pausanias enumerates the different
kinds of wood of which the ancient images were carved ; and
according to Pliny the wood of the fig-tree was preferred, on
account of its softness. Even in the time of the former of
these two authors, statues of wood were still to be found in the
most celebrated places in Greece. Among others, there were
at Megalopolis, in Arcadia, a Juno of this kind, an Apollo
with the Muses, likewise a Venus, and a Mercury by Damophon,
one of the most ancient artists ; even the statue of Apollo, at
Delphi, was of wood : it was wrought from a single bole, and
was a gift from the inhabitants of Crete. At Thebes, Hilaira
and Phœbe, together with the horses of Castor and Pollux, of
ebony and ivory, were especially deserving of note, as works of
Dipœnus and Scyllis, scholars of Dædalus ; and at Tegea, in
Arcadia, a Diana of the same kind, executed in the infancy
of art ; at Salamis there was a statue of Ajax, of ebony. Pausanias thinks that statues of wood were called Dædala prior to
the age of Dædalus. At Sais and Thebes, in Egypt, there were
even colossal statues of wood. We find that statues of wood
were still erected to the victors in the Greek public games in
the sixty-first Olympiad, that is to say, in the time of Pisistratus (6) ; even the celebrated Myron made a wooden Hecate
at Ægina ; and Diagoras, who is celebrated among the atheists
of antiquity, cooked his food with a figure of Hercules, because
he had no other wood (7). In the course of time, the practice of gilding such figures was introduced both among the
Egyptians and the Greeks (8) : Gori was the possessor of two
Egyptian figures which had been gilded. A Fortuna Virilis,

which belonged to the age of Servius Tullius, and was probably the work of an Etruscan, was still an object of reverence in Rome under the first Roman emperors. After wood had been, as it were, rejected from statuary, it still continued to be a material in which cunning artists displayed their skill; and we find, for example, that Quintus, the brother of Cicero, ordered a lamp-stand, *lychnuchus,* to be carved, at Samos, for himself; consequently, the artist was celebrated in this kind of work.

10. In the earliest ages, carving in ivory had been practised by the Greeks; and Homer speaks of the handles and sheaths of daggers, even of bedsteads, and many other things, as made from this material. The seats of the first kings and consuls in Rome were also of ivory; and each Roman who attained to that dignity, who enjoyed this honor, had his own ivory seat. Of this kind were the seats on which the assembled Senate sat, when, in the forum at Rome, it listened to a funeral speech from the rostrum. Even the lyres, and the trestles of tables, were made of ivory; and Seneca had in his house, at Rome, five hundred tables of cedar, supported by feet of ivory. On some antique vases of baked clay, in the Vatican library, the pedestals of the stools are painted perfectly white, — probably to denote ivory. In Greece, there were nearly a hundred statues of ivory and gold, the greater number of which belonged to the earlier periods of art, and were larger than life (9); even in a small place in Arcadia there was a beautiful statue of Æsculapius, and in a small temple on the high road to Pellene, in Achaia, there was also an image of Pallas, — both of ivory and gold. A temple at Cyzicum, in Pontus, of which the joints in the stones were ornamented by narrow bands of gold, contained a Jupiter of ivory, upon the head of which an Apollo, in marble, was placing a crown; also at Tibur was a Hercules of this kind. Even the island of Malta possessed a few such statues of Victoria, which, though belonging to the earliest ages, were still executed with great skill. By order of Herodes Atticus, the celebrated and opulent orator of the reigns of Trajan and the Antonines, a chariot with four gilded horses, whose hoofs were of ivory, was placed in the temple of Neptune, at Corinth. With the exception of a few small figures, no trace of ivory statues has yet been found, notwithstanding the many discoveries that have been made, because ivory decomposes in

the earth, like the teeth of all other animals, with the exception of the wolf (10).   At Tirynthus, in Arcadia, there was a Cybele of gold ; all but the face, which was composed of the teeth of the hippopotamus.

11. It seems to have been the practice, in making such stat-ues of different materials, to finish the head first, and then the other parts.   This is an allowable inference from an account, given by Pausanias, of a statue of Jupiter at Megara, designed to be made of ivory and gold ; but the work having been inter-rupted in consequence of the breaking out of the Peloponnesian war, the head was the only part completed ; the remaining parts were moulded of plaster and clay.   I will mention, as some-thing unusual, a small figure of a child in ivory, which was entirely gilded, that is to be found in the museum of Mr. Ham-ilton, Minister Plenipotentiary from Great Britain to Naples.

12. The first stone of which statues were made appears to have been the same with that of which the most ancient edifices in Greece — as, for example, the temple of Jupiter at Elis — were constructed, namely, a kind of tufo, which is of a whitish color : Plutarch mentions a Silenus cut from this stone.   At Rome, the artists also used travertino for the same purpose, and the following figures, formed from it, may be found here ; namely, a consular statue, in the villa of the Cardinal Alexander Al-bani ; another in the Altieri palace, in the quarter named Cam-pitelli ; the latter is seated, and holds on its knee a tablet ; also, a female figure, in the Belloni villa, of the size of life, like the two others, and with a ring on the forefinger.   Figures made from such inferior kinds of stone were usually placed about tombs.

13. At first, the head, hands, and feet of figures in wood were formed of white marble, as was the case with a Juno and Venus executed by that Damophon whose name was mentioned a few pages back ; this sort of statues was still usual at the time of Phidias ; for his Pallas at Platææ was constructed in this manner.   Such statues, of which the extremities only were of stone, were called Acroliths : this is the signification of the word, hitherto undiscovered either by Salmasius or others. Pliny remarks that artists began in the fiftieth Olympiad, for the first time, to work in marble, — a remark which is probably to be understood of entire figures of marble.   Occasionally, marble statues were clothed with real cloth : such was the case

with a statue of Ceres at Bura, in Achaia ; and a very ancient Æsculapius at Sicyon had likewise an actual (11) garment.

14. From the practice just mentioned originated the idea of painting marble figures so as to represent the dress, of which an example is furnished in a Diana found in Herculaneum in the year 1760. It is four palms two and a half inches (36½ in. Eng.) high, and apparently belongs to the earliest period of art. The hair is blond ; the upper garment is white ; so also is the tunic, around the lower part of which run three stripes. The lowest stripe is narrow and gold-colored ; the next is broader, and of a purple color, and ornamented with white flowers and scrolls ; the third is of the same color as the second. The third chapter will give a more circumstantial account of this statue. The statue which Virgil represents Corydon as vowing to Diana was intended to be of marble, but with red buskins. Statues are found wrought from marble of every kind but one, even the variegated ; not one has yet been discovered in the Laconian green marble, named *verde antico,* which was quarried at Tænarus, the celebrated Lacedæmonian promontory. Pausanias speaks of two statues of the Emperor Adrian which were at Athens, one of them being made of stone from the island of Thasus, and the other of an Egyptian stone. By the latter he probably means porphyry ; by the former, a spotted stone, perhaps the same as that which we term *paonazzo.* The heads, hands, and feet were probably of white marble.

15. The artists of every nation in which art has flourished have wrought in marble ; and in the next book, *Art among the Egyptians,* I shall make some special remarks upon the kinds of stone from which the monuments of this nation are sculptured. Among the Greeks, the kinds most celebrated were the Parian and the Pentelic ; and even at the present day two principal varieties of Greek marble are observable in statues. One of them is a fine-grained marble, which appears to be a white, uniform paste ; the other consists of larger grains, mixed with particles which glisten like crystals of salt ; hence it is termed *marmo salino,* " saline marble," and it is probably the Pentelic marble from the Attic territory. It is very hard, harder even than some varieties of the former marble ; and on account of this quality and the irregularity of its grain, is not quite so tractable as the other, which is consequently better adapted for ornaments requiring fine work. Among many other statues

executed from this marble, probably the Pentelic, is the beautiful Pallas in the villa of the Cardinal Alexander Albani. The former kind of marble, apparently the Parian, although found of different degrees of hardness, is yet, on account of the homogeneousness of its substance and its composition, suitable for all sorts of work; and as its color resembles that of a pure white skin, it has for this reason also obtained the preference. Within a few years, veins and strata have been opened in the marble quarries at Carrara, which are not inferior to the Parian marble either in fineness of grain, or color, or softness.

16. If Pausanias is to be credited, statues of bronze must have been made in Italy much earlier than in Greece; for he names, as the first Greek artists in this kind of statuary, a certain Rhœcus, and Theodorus of Samos (12). The celebrated seal of Polycrates, ruler of Samos, was engraved by the latter; he also wrought the great silver cup capable of holding six hundred eimer (149 hogsheads), which Crœsus, king of Lydia, sent to Delphi (13). At the same time the Spartans caused a vessel to be made, as a present to this king, which held three hundred eimer, and was ornamented with figures of all kinds of animals. But at a still earlier date, and prior to the foundation of the city of Cyrene, in Africa, there were three statues of bronze at Samos, each six ells in height; they were in a kneeling posture, and supported a large cup, on which the Samians had expended a tenth part of the gains of their commerce with Tartessus. The first chariot with four horses of bronze was erected by the Athenians before the temple of Pallas, after the death of Pisistratus; that is, subsequently to the sixty-seventh Olympiad (14). The writers of Roman history, on the other hand, relate that, before this time, Romulus had erected a statue of himself, crowned by Victory, and seated on a chariot with four horses, — the whole made of bronze. The chariot and horses were spoil taken from the city of Camerinum. This is said to have been done after his triumph over the Fidenates, in the seventh year of his reign, and consequently in the eighth Olympiad. The inscription on it, according to Plutarch, was in Greek characters; but since the Roman letter resembled the earliest Greek character, as Diodorus mentions on another occasion, that work might have proceeded from the hands of an Etruscan artist. Furthermore,

mention is made of a statue of Horatius Cocles, in bronze, and of another, an equestrian one, which was erected to the renowned Clœlia, in the infancy of the Roman republic ; and when Spurius Cassius was put to death for his attempts against the liberty of his countrymen, a portion of his confiscated property was expended in the erection of statues, likewise of bronze, to Ceres. The little figures of the divinities, in bronze, which are found in great numbers, were used for many purposes. The smallest of them were the travelling-gods, those which the traveller carried with himself, and even on his person ; thus, for example, Sylla carried in his bosom constantly, and in all his campaigns, a small golden image of the Pythian Apollo, and was accustomed to kiss it.

17. The art of engraving gems must be very ancient ; and it was practised even among nations very remote from each other. It is said that, at first, the Greeks used as a seal a piece of wood that had been perforated by worms ; and there is in the former Stosch museum a gem which is cut so as to imitate the grooves in such a piece of wood. In this department of art, the Egyptians, as well as the Greeks and Etruscans, attained to great perfection, — as it will be shown in the following chapters. Even the Ethiopians had seals cut in gems, which were wrought by means of another hard stone. How common this sort of work was among the ancients we may learn, without recourse to other authorities, from the two thousand drinking-vessels, made from gems, which were found by Pompey in the treasury of Mithridates ; and we may infer the host of artists from the incredible number of antique engraved gems which have been preserved, and are still daily disinterred.

18. I will here remark, that in Euripides and Plato a stone set in a ring is termed Σφενδόνη, *a sling* ; the reason of the appellation and the resemblance between the two have, probably, never yet been pointed out. The hoop of the ring resembles the leather in which the stone rests when in the sling, and the two bands by which the body of the sling is suspended and swung. For the very same reason, the Romans afterwards termed a ring with a stone set in it a *funda*, or " sling."

19. Having thus briefly noticed the different materials employed in art by the ancients, I shall close the chapter with

some account of their glass-work, which, from the skill displayed
in it, is also deserving of mention, and the more so, because they
carried this department of art to a higher degree of excellence
than the moderns, — an assertion that might appear unwarrant-
able to those who have not examined their works of this kind.

20. As a general thing, glass was applied to a greater variety
of purposes among the ancients than it has been by the moderns.   Besides its employment for vessels of common use, of
which large numbers are to be found in the Herculaneum
museum, it also served for the preservation of the ashes of the
dead, which were deposited in tombs (15).   Of these vessels,
the two largest are in the possession of Mr. Hamilton, Minister
Plenipotentiary at Naples from Great Britain.   Both are uninjured.   One of them, more than two palms and a half (21 inches
8 lines) high, was found in a tomb near Pozzuoli.   A smaller
vessel, belonging to the same museum, was found in the month
of October, 1767, near Cuma.   It was filled with ashes, and
was protected by a leaden case; but the lead was knocked off
and sold by the finder.   Among some hundred quintals of fragments of vessels for common use which have been dug up in
the Farnese Island, so called, nine miles from Rome, on the
road to Viterbo, and which were sold to the Roman glass-manu-
factories, I have seen a few pieces of drinking-cups that must
have been executed on a lathe; for the ornaments on them,
which were very much raised, and, as it were, cemented upon
them, showed very distinctly the mark of the wheel with which
the artist had begun to polish the corners and edges.

21. Besides the use of glass of a common kind in these vessels, it was also employed in covering the floors of rooms.   For
this purpose, not only glass of a single color was used, but also
a variegated kind, so composed as to imitate mosaic.   Of the
former kind of pavement traces have been found in the Farnese
Island above mentioned, consisting of tablets of a green color
and of the thickness of a medium tile.

22. In the composite variegated kind of glass, two small
pieces which came to light in Rome a few years ago display a
skill that is truly amazing; neither of them is quite an inch
long, or a third of an inch broad.   One of them exhibits on a
dark, variegated ground a bird, resembling a duck, of different
and very lively colors, but painted more after the Chinese manner.   The outline is firm and sharp; the colors are beautiful

and pure, and of very brilliant effect, because the artist has introduced, as the places required it, sometimes translucent, and sometimes opaque glass. The most delicate pencil of the miniature-painter could not have expressed more accurately the circle of the eyeball, and the visibly overlapping feathers on the breast and wings. The fragment is broken off just back of the commencement of the wings. But this piece excites the greatest astonishment in the spectator, when, on looking at the other side of it, he sees the very same bird, without being able to detect any difference in the minutest particular. Hence, we must conclude that the figure of the bird extends through the whole thickness of the glass.

23. On both sides, this painting has a granular appearance; and it seems to be composed of single pieces, in the way in which mosaic is made, yet so exactly joined together, that it was impossible to discover, even with a powerful magnifying-glass, the points of junction. This peculiarity, and the extension of the painting through the whole thickness of the fragment, rendered it difficult to conceive immediately how such a work was executed; and the mode of doing it would have continued a mystery for a long time, if streaks of the same colors as those which appear on the surface, and extending through the whole thickness of the glass, had not been detected on the face of the glass at the point where it had been broken off, and hence leading to the conclusion that the painting had been made by placing threads of glass of different colors in contact with each other, and melting them into union. It is not to be supposed that so much labor would have been expended merely in continuing this image through a thickness so inconsiderable as one sixth of an inch, when it was equally easy to obtain the same effect in the same time, by means of longer threads, through a thickness of many inches. Hence we may conclude that this fragment was a slice from a thicker piece of glass, through which the picture was carried, and that the image could be multiplied just as often as the thickness of the fragment mentioned was contained in the thickness of the piece from which it was separated.

24. The second fragment, which is of about the same size, is prepared in precisely the same way. On it are ornaments in green, yellow, and white, consisting of scrolls, beads, and flowerets, which are represented on a blue ground, and run together

so as to form pyramids. The whole is very clear and distinct, and still so infinitely small, that even a keen eye finds a difficulty in following the extremely fine ends in which the scrolls terminate ; and yet, notwithstanding, all these delicate ornaments are continued, uninterrupted, through the entire thickness of the fragment.

25. The mode of preparing such works in glass is clearly shown in a rod, a span in length, belonging to the museum of Mr. Hamilton, Minister Plenipotentiary at Naples from Great Britain. The outer layer is blue, but the inner part represents a sort of rose of different colors, extending the whole length of the rod, and each one preserving the same place and winding. Now, as glass can be drawn out into threads of any length, and of exceeding fineness, and with equal facility even when many glass tubes are placed together, and then melted, — their relative position not being changed in drawing, just as a gilded piece of silver, when drawn out into wire, remains gilded in the whole length of it, — it is rendered probable that, in such manufactures of glass, larger tubes were reduced, by drawing, to tubes of exceeding fineness.

26. But of all the kinds of ancient glass-work, the most useful to us are the impressions moulded from gems, — some engraved in intaglio, and some in relief, — and rilievi of larger size ; of the latter kind even an entire vessel has been found. The glass casts of gems engraved in intaglio frequently mimic the different veins and stripes in the gem from which they were taken, and many of them, taken from gems cut in relief, are colored precisely in the same way as the original cameo, — a fact to which Pliny also testifies (16). In two very rare pieces of this kind the raised figure is overlaid with thick gold-leaf. One of them displays the head of Tiberius ; it is in the hands of Mr. Byres, a connoisseur in architecture, at Rome. To these casts we are indebted for the preservation of many rare pictures, of which the originals, on engraved gems, are lost. Among others may be mentioned the combat between Pittacus, one of the seven wise men of antiquity, and Phryno, on the promontory of Sigæum : the former entangled his opponent in a net which he threw over his head, and by this means succeeded in mastering him.

27. Of larger pictures, executed in relief on glass, in general only broken pieces are found ; still, these exhibit to us the

singular dexterity of the ancient artists in this department, and perhaps by their size indicate the use to which they were applied. Such pieces were either framed in marble, or even introduced among painted foliage, and arabesques, so called, as ornaments of the walls in palaces. The most valuable of these larger rilievi is a cameo, described by Buonarotti, in the museum of the Vatican library. It consists of an oblong tablet, more than a palm (8.8 in. Eng.) in length, and two thirds of a palm in breadth. The subject is Bacchus lying in the lap of Ariadne, together with two Satyrs. The figures are white, in bas-relief, on a dark brown ground.

28. But the highest work in this art was the splendid vases, ornamented with figures in semi-relief, sometimes pure, but frequently variegated, on a dark ground, just as they appear, in great perfection, on genuine vases cut from sardonyx. Of these vessels, there is probably only a single specimen in the whole world in perfect preservation. It was found in the burial urn of the Emperor Alexander Severus, as it is erroneously termed, filled with the ashes of the deceased ; and it is preserved among the rarities of the Barberini palace. The height of it is about one palm and a half (17). Some idea may be formed of its beauty from the mistake, continued till now, of describing it as a vase of pure sardonyx (18).

29. Such glass-ware cannot but be regarded by connoisseurs of true taste as infinitely more splendid than all the procelain vases so much admired, whose beautiful material has not yet been ennobled by any pure work of art, nor its costly products impressed with any worthy or instructive devices. Most porcelain is formed into ridiculous shapes, from which has sprung a childish taste that has diffused itself everywhere.

CHAPTER III.

INFLUENCE OF CLIMATE ON CONFORMATION.

1. HAVING, in the preceding chapters, adverted to the origin of art, and the materials employed in it, I now proceed to speak of the influence exercised upon it by climate ; and this brings us nearer to the source of the differences observable in it among the different nations by which it has been, and is still, cultivated.

2. By the influence of climate we mean the manner in which the conformation of the inhabitants of different countries, not less than their modes of thought, is affected by their situation, and by the temperature and food peculiar to them. Climate, says Polybius, forms the manners, the shape, and the complexion of nations.

3. In regard to the former, namely, the conformation of man, our own observation convinces us, that as, in general, the soul is expressed in the countenance, so also is the character of a people ; and as Nature has separated great kingdoms and countries from each other by mountains and rivers, so has she also variously distinguished their inhabitants by particular traits, and, in lands widely distant, she displays a marked difference, not in the statue alone, but even in the individual parts of the body. Animals do not vary in their kinds according to the nature of the country in which they live, more than man ; and some persons have even thought that they could discover a similarity between the character of the animals of a country, and that of its inhabitants.

4. The varieties of conformation of the face are not less numerous than languages, than dialects even ; and the differences in the last are immediately dependent upon the organs of speech ; so that, in cold countries, the nerves of the tongue must be more rigid and less active than in those that are warmer. If, therefore, the alphabets of the Chinese and Japan-

ese, of the Greenlanders and different tribes in America, are deficient in certain letters, the explanation is to be found in the reason just mentioned. Hence, it happens that all Northern languages have more monosyllables, and are more burdened with consonants, which other nations find it difficult, partly impossible, indeed, to connect and pronounce.

5. A distinguished writer seeks to explain even the difference in the dialects of Italy by difference in the tissue and conformation of the organs of speech. "For this reason," he says, "the Lombards, who are born in the colder portion of Italy, have a harsh and abrupt utterance; the Tuscans and Romans speak in a more measured tone; the Neapolitans, who enjoy a still warmer climate, pronounce the vowels more fully than the former, and speak with a rounder enunciation." They who are conversant with many nations distinguish them not less correctly or certainly by their conformation of face than by their language; and this difference continues to be observable in the children and grandchildren, although born in other countries to which their parents have removed.

6. The well-known fact of the earlier maturity and puberty of youth in warm countries shows how much more powerful in them is the influence of nature over the complete development of our race; and the brilliancy of the brighter color of the eyes, which are more frequently brown or black than is the case in cold climates, may offer — to those who are unable to pursue the inquiry themselves — additional probability in favor of the superiority of conformation to be found in warm climates. This difference shows itself even in the hair of the head and of the beard, and both, in warm climates, have a more beautiful growth even from childhood, so that the greater number of children in Italy are born with fine curling hair, which loses none of its beauty with increasing years. All the beards, also, are curly, ample, and finely shaped; whereas, those of the pilgrims who come to Rome from the other side of the Alps are, generally, like the hair of their heads, stiff, bristly, straight, and pointed; so that it would be difficult, in the countries of these privileged idlers, to grow a beard like those which we see on the heads of the ancient Greek philosophers. In accordance with this observation, the ancient artists figured the Gauls and Celts with straight hair, as we may see on several monuments, but especially on two seated figures (1) of captive warriors of these

races which are in the villa of the Cardinal Alexander Albani.[1] In connection with these remarks upon the hair, I will observe that fair hair is not of so frequent occurrence in warm as in cold climates ; but still it is common, and beautiful persons with hair of this languishing color are seen in the former as well as in the latter, — with this difference, however, that the color of it never becomes entirely whitish, the usual effect of which is to give to a person an air of coldness and insipidity.

7. Now, as man has been in all ages the principal subject of art, the artists of every land have given to their figures the facial conformation peculiar to their own nation ; and the relation of art to its subject in modern times proves that the different shape in ancient art is to be attributed to the different conformation of its subject, man. For German, Dutch, and French artists, when they do not quit their own land and race, may, like the Chinese and Tartars, be recognized in their paintings ; but Rubens, notwithstanding he resided for many years in Italy, designed his figures, invariably, in the same manner as if he had never left his native land ; and many other examples might be adduced in support of my opinion.

8. The conformation of the modern Egyptians should show itself at the present day, just as it appears in the works of their former art ; but this similarity between Nature and her image is no longer precisely the same that it was. For if the greater number of the Egyptians were as stout and fat as the inhabitants of Cairo are described to be, we could not come to any such conclusion from the ancient figures, for their physical appearance in ancient times appears to have been the opposite of that in modern days : it is to be remarked, however, that the Egyptians have also been described by the ancient writers as corpulent and fat. The climate, indeed, remains always the same ; but the country and its inhabitants may undergo a change of aspect. For if we take into consideration that the modern Egyptians are of foreign origin, — having even introduced their own language, — and that their religious worship, their form of government and mode of life, are entirely different from the system formerly existing, we shall also be able to conceive the difference in their physical conformation. As a consequence of the incredible density of the population, the ancient Egyptians were frugal and industrious ; their principal inter-

[1] Plate II.

PLATE II

est was in agriculture ; their food consisted more of fruits than of meat ; hence their bodies could not be covered with much flesh. The present occupants of the country, on the other hand, seeking only the means of living without labor, are sleeping in sloth ; hence their tendency to corpulence.

9. Precisely the same reflection may be made in reference to the modern Greeks. For — not to mention that their blood during several centuries has been mingled with that of the descendants of so many nations who have settled among them — it is easy to conceive that their present political condition, bringing up, instruction, and mode of thought may have an influence even on their conformation. Notwithstanding all these unfavorable conditions, the Greek race of the present day is still celebrated for its beauty ; on this point all observant travellers agree ; and the nearer we draw to the climate of Greece, the more beautiful, lofty, and vigorous is the conformation of man.

10. For this reason, we seldom find in the fairest portions of Italy the features of the face unfinished, vague, and inexpressive, as it is frequently the case on the other side of the Alps ; but they have partly an air of nobleness, partly of acuteness and intelligence ; and the form of the face is generally large and full, and the parts of it in harmony with each other. The superiority of conformation is so manifest, that the head of the humblest man among the people might be introduced in the most dignified historical painting, especially one in which aged men are to be represented. And among the women of this class, even in places of the least importance, it would not be difficult to find a Juno. The lower portion of Italy, which enjoys a softer climate than any other part of it, brings forth men of superb and vigorously designed forms, which appear to have been made, as it were, for the purposes of sculpture. The large stature of the inhabitants of this section must be apparent to every one ; and the fine development and robustness of their frames may be most easily seen in the half-naked sailors, fishermen, and others whose occupation is by the sea ; and precisely from that circumstance might seem to have originated the fable of the mighty Titans contending with the Gods in the Phlegræan Fields, — which are near Pozzuoli, in the vicinity of Naples. It is asserted that, in Sicily, the handsomest women of the island are found, even at the present day, in ancient Eryx, where the celebrated temple of Venus was situated.

11. He who has never visited these countries can form his own conclusions as to the intellectual organization of their inhabitants, by observing that their acuteness increases as the climate grows warmer. The Neapolitans are still more acute and artful than the Romans; the Sicilians are more so than the Neapolitans; but the Greeks surpass even the Sicilians. Between Rome and Athens there is probably a difference of about one month in the warmth of the season and in the ripening of the fruits, — as the cutting of the honey out of the hives proves; for in the latter place it would happen about the solstice in June; but in the former, on the festival of Vulcan, or in the month of August. In fine, what Cicero says is true here, that "intellects are more acute, the purer and more subtile the air"; for the same disposition seems to prevail with man as with flowers, whose fragrance increases in proportion to the dryness of the soil, and the warmth of the climate.

12. Consequently, that noble beauty which consists not merely in a soft skin, a brilliant complexion, wanton or languishing eyes, but in the shape and form, is found more frequently in countries which enjoy a uniform mildness of climate. If, therefore, the Italians alone know how to paint and figure beauty, as an English author of rank says, the beautiful conformation of the people themselves is, in a measure, the ground of their capability, which the daily view and study of beauty can produce more readily here than elsewhere. Beauty, however, was not a general quality, even among the Greeks, and Cotta in Cicero says that, among the great numbers of young persons at Athens, there were only a few possessing true beauty.

13. The most beautiful race among the Greeks, especially in regard to complexion, must have been beneath the skies of Ionia, in Asia Minor, according to the testimony of Hippocrates and Lucian; and another writer, in order to express manly beauty with one word, terms it Ionic. This province is also productive, even at the present day, in beautiful conformations, as appears from the statement of an observant traveller of the sixteenth century, who finds himself unable to extol sufficiently the beauty of the women there, their soft and milk-white skin, and fresh and healthful color. For in this land, on account of its situation, and in the islands of the Archipelago, the sky is much clearer, and the temperature — which is intermediate between warm and cold — more constant and uniform, than it is

even in Greece, especially in those parts of it lying on the sea,
which are very much exposed to the sultry wind from Africa, like
all the southern coast of Italy, and other lands which lie opposite
to the hot tract in Africa. This wind, which the Greeks termed
λίψ, and the Romans *Africus*, and which is now known as the
Sirocco, obscures and darkens the air with hot, oppressive
vapors, makes it unwholesome, and debilitates all nature, man,
beast, and plant. When it prevails, digestion is retarded ; and
both mind and body are listless and unable to work ; hence it
is very easy to conceive how great influence this wind may
have on the beauty of the skin and complexion. In those who
dwell the nearest to the sea-coast it produces a dull and yellowish color, which is more common with the Neapolitans, especially those of the capital, on account of its narrow streets and
lofty houses, than among those who dwell more inland. The
same complexion may be seen in the inhabitants of places on the
coast of the Mediterranean Sea, in the States of the Church, at
Terracina, Nettuno, Ostia, and towns similarly situated. But the
marshes — which, in Italy, generate a foul and deadly vapor —
cannot possibly have produced in Greece any noxious emana-
tions ; for Ambracia, which was a very well-built and celebrated
city, lay in the midst of marshes, and had only a single avenue
by which it could be entered.

14. The proof, easy to be understood, of the superiority of
shape of the Greeks and the present inhabitants of the Levant,
lies in the fact that we find among them no flattened noses,
which are the greatest disfigurement of the face. Scaliger seems
to have observed that the Jews also have no sunken noses ;
indeed, the Portuguese Jews most generally have hawk-noses ;
hence, a nose of this kind is termed in Portugal a Jewish nose.
Vesalius has noted that the heads of the Greeks and Turks are
of a handsomer oval than those of the Germans and Dutch. It
is also to be taken into consideration, that the small-pox is a
less dangerous disease in warm countries than in cold, where it
is epidemic, and as destructive as the plague. For this reason,
scarcely ten persons out of a thousand are found, in Italy, marked
with a few faint traces of this disease ; but to the ancient Greeks
it was unknown. We are authorized to draw this conclusion
from the silence of the ancient Greek physician, Hippocrates,
and of Galen, his commentator, in regard to it, since they neither
allude to it nor prescribe any directions as to the manner of

treating it.   There is also, of the infinite number of persons of
whose faces we have a description, not one who is characterized
as pock-marked, an appearance which would have furnished an
occasion for laughable jests, especially to an Aristophanes and a
Plautus.   But the special proof that this destructive, fatal poison did not in ancient times display its virulence on the human
race, is afforded by the language itself of Greece, for it contains
no word which signifies small-pox.

15.   At the same time that I acknowledge the superiority of
warmer countries in the more general diffusion of beauty of conformation, I do not therefore deny beauty of shape to colder climates ; I know persons, even of low station, on the other side
of the Alps, in whom Nature has executed her work with the
utmost perfection and beauty ; insomuch, that their development and shape might compare, not only with the handsomest
men of those countries, but have served the Greek artists as
models, not less in single parts than in the whole body, even
for their most lovely and majestic figures.

16.   In the second place, the influence of climate on the mode
of thought of a people — with which external circumstances,
especially education, the form of government, and the manner
of administering it, co-operate — is just as perceptible and conceivable as the influence of the same cause on the conformation.

17.   The mode of thought, as well of Oriental and Southern
nations as of the Greeks, is manifested even in works of art.
The figurative expressions of the former are as warm and ardent as the climate in which they dwell, and the flight of their
thoughts frequently exceeds the limits of possibility.   Hence,
these are the brains which conceived the strange figures of the
Egyptians and Persians, which united in one form creatures of
totally different natures and kinds : and the aim of their artists
was rather to produce the extraordinary than the beautiful.

18.   The Greeks, on the contrary, lived under a more temperate climate and a milder rule, and inhabited a land "which
Pallas," it is said, "assigned to them for their occupancy, as
preferable to all others on account of the moderateness of its
seasons" ; and as their language is picturesque, so also were
their conceptions and images.   Their poets, from the time of
Homer downward, not only speak through figures, but they
produce and also paint images which frequently lie in a single
word, and which have been drawn and sketched, as it were in

living colors, by the sound of that word. Their imagination was not exaggerated like that of the Oriental and Southern nations; and their senses, acting upon a brain of delicate structure through the medium of quick and sensitive nerves, discovered instantly the several qualities of an object, and occupied themselves especially in considering the beauty contained in it.

19. After the migration of the Greeks into Asia Minor, their language became richer in vowels, and consequently softer and more musical, because they enjoyed a still happier climate than the other Greeks. This was the climate that awakened and inspired their earliest poets; on this soil Greek philosophy was formed; here was the birthplace of their earliest historians; and here, beneath the voluptuous skies of this land, Apelles, *the painter of the Graces*, was born. But as they were too feeble to defend their freedom against the power of their neighbors, the Persians, they were unable to erect themselves into powerful free states, like the Athenians; and, consequently, the arts and sciences could not have their most distinguished seat in Ionic Asia.

20. But in Athens, where, after the expulsion of the tyrants, a democratic form of government was adopted, in which the entire people had a share, the spirit of each citizen became loftier than that of the other Greeks, and the city itself surpassed all other cities. As good taste was now generally diffused, and wealthy burghers sought to gain the respect and love of their fellow-citizens by erecting splendid public buildings and by works of art, and thus prepare the way to distinction, everything flowed into this city, in consequence of its power and greatness, even as rivers flow towards the sea. Here the arts and sciences established themselves; here they formed their principal residence; and hence they went abroad into other lands. We may find proof that the causes just mentioned will account for the progress of the arts in Athens, in a similar state of things at Florence, where, after a long interval of darkness, the arts and sciences began, in modern times, to be relumined.

21. We must, therefore, in judging of the natural capacity of nations, and of the Greeks especially, in this respect, take into consideration, not merely the influence of climate alone, but also that of education and government. For external circumstances effect not less change in us than does the air by which we are surrounded, and custom has so much power over us that

it modifies in a peculiar manner even the body, and the very senses with which we are endowed by nature ; thus, for instance, an ear accustomed to French music is not affected by the most touching Italian symphony.

22. The same cause accounts for the difference, even among the Greeks themselves, noticed by Polybius, in regard to their valor and mode of warfare. The Thessalians were good warriors when they could attack with small bands ; but in regular battle-array, they soon gave way. The reverse was the case with the Ætolians. The natives of Crete were excellent beyond comparison in ambush, or on expeditions where craft was required, or in doing an enemy damage in other ways ; but they were of no use in emergencies that must be decided by valor alone ; the Achæans and Macedonians, on the other hand, displayed qualities that were the reverse of these. All the Arcadians were obliged, by the earliest laws of their country, to learn music, and to practise it continually until they were thirty years of age, in order that a soft and loving character might be given to their dispositions and manners, — which the rude climate of their mountainous land tended to make morose and fierce ; and for this reason they were the most honest and the best-mannered men in Greece. The inhabitants of Cynæthium, who alone departed from this regulation, and would not learn and practise music, fell back again into natural wildness, and were held in detestation by all Greece.

23. In lands where some remnant of former freedom co-operates with the influence of climate, the present manner of thinking is very similar to the past. An illustration of my remark is now seen in Rome, where the people, under a priestly rule, enjoy unrestrained freedom. Even at the present day, a band of the most valiant and intrepid warriors might be collected from the midst of them, who, like their forefathers, would bid defiance to death. The women of the common people, with morals less corrupt than those of the ancient Roman women, still display the same courage and spirit, — as I could prove by some remarkable traits, if the design of my work permitted it.

24. The pre-eminent talent of the Greeks for art still shows itself, in modern days, in the great and almost general talent of the inhabitants of the warmest portions of Italy ; and in this admirable capacity for art the imagination predominates, just as reason predominates over the imagination among the sober-

minded Britons. Some one has remarked, not without reason, that the poets on the other side of the mountains speak through images, but afford few pictures. It must even be confessed, that the astonishing, partly fearful pictures, in which Milton's greatness consists, cannot be the subjects of a noble pencil, but are absolutely unfit to be painted. Milton's descriptions, with the single exception of his picture of Love in Paradise, are like Gorgons beautifully painted, similar to each other, and similarly terrible. The images of many other poets are great to the ear, but small to the understanding. In Homer, everything is painted, and devised and created to be painted. The warmer the region is in Italy, the greater are the talents to which it gives birth, and the more ardent the imagination ; and the works of the Sicilian poets are full of rare, new, and unexpected images. This glowing imagination, however, is not of a stimulated and vehement nature : like the temperament of the inhabitants, and the temperature of the country, it is more uniform than in colder climates ; for nature bestows a happy dulness of disposition more frequently on the inhabitants of the latter than of the former.

25. When I speak of the natural capacity, generally, of these nations for art, I do not thereby mean to deny the same capacity to individuals in countries on the other side of the mountains, because experience furnishes striking proofs to the contrary. For Holbein and Albert Dürer, the fathers of art in Germany, have exhibited astonishing talent in it ; and if it had been in their power to study and imitate the works of the ancients, like Raphael, Correggio, and Titian, they would have been equally as great as these ; they might, perhaps, have surpassed them. Even Correggio did not attain his greatness without some knowledge of antiquity, — though it is generally said that he did, — for his master, Andreas Mantegna, was acquainted with it ; and some of his drawings from antique statues are found in the great collection of drawings which passed from the museum of the Cardinal Alexander Albani into that of the king of England. In view of the knowledge which he had of antiquity, Felicianus addressed to him the dedication of a collection of antique inscriptions. But in this notice Mantegna was entirely unknown to the elder Burmann (2). Whether the scarcity of painters among the English, who cannot produce from the past a single one of celebrity, and among

the French, who, with the exception of two, are in a similar condition, notwithstanding their great outlays, proceeds from the causes enumerated, I leave to the decision of others.

26. Meanwhile, by communicating to the reader these general notices on art, and the grounds of its differing in the countries in which it was once practised, and is still practised, I believe that I have prepared him for the discussion on art in each of the three nations which have been celebrated for it.

BOOK II.

ART AMONG THE EGYPTIANS, PHŒNICIANS, AND PERSIANS.

CHAPTER I.

CAUSES OF THE PECULIAR CHARACTER OF EGYPTIAN ART.

1. The Egyptians have not departed much from their earliest style of art; and it could not easily reach the height to which it arrived among the Greeks. The cause may be found partly in the conformation of their bodies; partly in their mode of thought; and not less in their customs and laws, especially those of a religious character; and also in the science of their artists, and the estimation in which they were held. This will be the subject of the first part of this division. The second treats of the original style of their art; that is, of the drawing of the nude figure, and drapery of their earlier figures. The third examines the later style, as well as the imitations of the Egyptian manner executed by Greeks and Romans. The fourth treats of the mechanical part, or the execution, of Egyptian art and works of art, and, in addition to wood and bronze, of the different kinds of stone of which the Egyptians made use.

Of the causes which impressed a peculiar character upon the art of the Egyptians, the first lies in the fact of their conformation; it did not possess those excellences that could stimulate the artist by ideas of high beauty. Though Nature had made the Egyptian women remarkably prolific, she had, in regard to conformation, been less kind to them than to the Greeks and the Etruscans. In proof of this, statues, obelisks, and engraved gems show that the form peculiar to them somewhat resembled that of the Chinese (1) ; and Æschylus says that the Egyptians were, in their shape, different from the Greeks (2).

2. Their artists, therefore, could not seek variety, because it had no existence. In the steady, uniform climate of this land, Nature did not deviate from her extreme conformation ; for as in all things, so also here, she departs from an extreme more reluctantly than from a mean. The very same conformation which Egyptian statues have is observed in the heads of the figures painted on mummies, which, as also with the Ethiopians, were probably accurate likenesses of the deceased ; for the Egyptians, in the preparation of the dead body, sought to retain everything, even the hairs of the eyelids, which would render it of easy recognition. It is probable that the custom among the Ethiopians of painting the figure of the dead upon their bodies was also derived from the Egyptians ; for during the reign of Psammetichus, two hundred and forty thousand persons went from Egypt into Ethiopia, where they introduced their national manners and usages (3). However, as eighteen Ethiopian kings, whose reign occurs in the earliest periods of the country, had ruled in Egypt, the usage of which we speak may have been made by them common to both people.

3. The Egyptians were, besides, of a dark brown complexion, the same which has been given to the heads on painted mummies (4), and hence the word αἰγύπτιασαι signifies "to be burnt by the sun." Now as the faces of the mummies have one and the same color, there is no ground for the assertion made by Alexander Gordon, who maintains that the complexion differed in different provinces.

4. But when Martial expresses a desire for a beautiful boy from Egypt, for sensual purposes, he is to be understood as meaning a boy, not of Egyptian, but of Greek parentage, as the dissolute morals of the youth in that country, and especially of those at Alexandria, are well known (5). The poet, however, adds, that a fair face out of this land of brown skins, *in Mareotide Fusca*, is the more highly to be prized in proportion to its rarity. The celebrated pantomime, Apolaustus, of Memphis, in Egypt, whom Lucius Verus took with him to Rome, and whose remembrance is preserved in several inscriptions, was a Greek of this kind.

5. An attempt has been made, on the authority of a passage in Aristotle to show that the leg-bone of the Egyptians bowed

outwardly. Those who bordered on the Ethiopians probably had, like them, sunken noses; and the Egyptian female figures, however narrow they may be across the hips, have excessively large breasts. Now, as the Egyptian artists imitated nature just as they found it, — according to the testimony of a Church Father, — we might certainly draw a conclusion from their figures as to the female sex in their country. The conformation of the Egyptians is far from being incompatible with a sound state of health, which the inhabitants of Upper Egypt in particular, according to Herodotus, enjoyed far above other nations; and the same conclusion may also be drawn from the circumstance, that, in the countless heads of Egyptian mummies seen by Prince Radzivil, not a tooth was wanting, not even corroded. Moreover, we may find in the mummy at Bologna, mentioned above, proof of what Pausanias has stated in regard to their extraordinary size, since he says that he has seen Celts who were as large as the dead bodies of the Egyptians; and his statement is confirmed by the unusual length of this mummy, which measures eleven Roman palms (that is, eight feet and eight inches English).

6. In the second place, in regard to the disposition and manner of thinking of the Egyptians, they do not appear to have been inclined to pleasure and gayety; for music — by which the earliest Greeks strove to render the laws themselves more acceptable, and in which contests were instituted, even prior to the age of Homer — was not especially cultivated in Egypt; it is, indeed, asserted that it was prohibited; and the same is said also of poetry (6). According to Strabo, no instrument was played either in their temples or at their sacrifices. But this does not exclude music among the Egyptians generally; or it must be understood only of the earliest periods (7); for we know that women conducted Apis with music to the banks of the Nile; and Egyptians are represented playing on instruments, both in the mosaic of the temple of Fortune at Palestrina, and in two Herculaneum paintings.

7. As a consequence of this turn of mind, the Egyptians sought to excite their imaginations and exhilarate their minds by violent means; and their thoughts passed beyond the natural, and were occupied with the mysterious. Hence, the melancholy of this nation produced the first eremites (8); and a modern writer pretends to have discovered somewhere, that, at the

close of the fourth century, there were seventy thousand monks
in Lower Egypt alone (9). Another consequence of this tem-
per of mind was, that the Egyptians were willing to be governed
by severe laws, and positively could not exist without a king;
this is probably the reason why Egypt is termed by Homer
bitter Egypt.

8. In their usages and religious forms, the Egyptians insisted upon a strict observance of the primitive ordinances,
even under the Roman emperors, — not only in Upper Egypt,
but also at Alexandria itself; for as late as the time of
the Emperor Adrian, an insurrection broke out because no
ox could be found to represent the god Apis; indeed, the
enmity of one city towards another, on account of their deities,
was still fresh at that time. The assertion of a few modern
authors, — on testimony falsely attributed to Herodotus and
Diodorus, — that the religious ceremonial of the Egyptians, and
their custom of embalming the dead, had been utterly and forever abolished by Cambyses, is so untrue, that even the Greeks,
at a later date than this, allowed their own dead to be prepared after the Egyptian manner, as I have shown elsewhere,
by that mummy with the word CY $+$ YXI on its breast (10),
which was formerly in the Della Valle mansion at Rome, and
is at present among the antiquities in Dresden. Now, as the
Egyptians, under the successors of Cambyses, revolted more
than once, and elected kings from among themselves, who, by
the aid of the Greeks, were enabled to maintain their authority
for some time, it is probable that, during these intervals, they
also returned back to their former custom.

9. That the Egyptians, under the Cæsars, still adhered to
their ancient religious forms, even the statues of Antinoüs may
testify; two of them stand at Tivoli, and one in the Capitoline
museum, and they are shaped after the manner of Egyptian
statues, and have the form under which he was worshipped
in this country, especially in the city where he lay buried,
which, from him, received the name Antinoëa. A figure in
marble resembling the Capitoline, and, like it, somewhat larger
than life, but without its proper head, is in the garden of the
Barberini palace, and a third, about three palms (2 ft. 2 in.
Eng.) in height, is in the Borghese villa; these have the stiff
attitude, with the arms hanging perpendicularly by the sides,
which belongs to the most ancient Egyptian figures. We see,

therefore, that Adrian was obliged to give to the image of Antinoüs, in order that he might become to the Egyptians an object of reverence, a shape that was pleasing to them, and the only one which was popular (11).

10. The abhorrence felt by the Egyptians for Grecian customs — especially before they fell under the sovereignty of the Greeks — strengthened them in their religious use of the form which they had anciently adopted for the images of their worship ; and this feeling, necessarily, would make their artists very indifferent to the art of other nations ; and, consequently, would check the progress of knowledge as well as of art. As their physicians durst prescribe no other remedies than those recorded in the sacred books, so their artists were not permitted to deviate from the ancient style ; for their laws allowed no further scope to the mind than mere imitation of their forefathers, and prohibited all innovations. Hence, as Plato informs us, statues which had been executed in his time in Egypt did not differ, either in shape or in any other respect, from those which were more than a thousand years old. He is, however, to be understood as speaking of works which were wrought by native artists prior to the era of Greek rule in Egypt. The observance of this law could not be violated, because it, like the entire constitution of the Egyptian form of government, was based on their very religion. For, among the Egyptians, the art of forming figures in human shape seems to have been restricted to their deities, the kings with their families, and the priests, — with the exception of the figures which were carved on public edifices ; that is to say, to a single kind of images (12). But the gods of the Egyptians were kings by whom the country had been governed at some previous time, or at least they were regarded as deities ; so too the earliest kings were priests ; and if statues were erected to any other persons, no one certainly knows the fact, and no writer even mentions it.

11. Finally, one of the causes concurring to produce that condition of art in Egypt which I have noticed lies in the estimation and knowledge of their artists, who were viewed in the light of artisans, and were classed in the lowest rank. No one, from natural inclination, or especial impulse, selected art as his pursuit, but the son followed, as in all crafts and professions, the mode of life of his father, and set his foot in the tracks of his predecessor, so that no one appears to have left a

footprint which strictly could be called his own.   Consequently, there cannot have been different schools of art in Egypt, as there were in Greece.   In such a system of government neither the education nor the circumstances of artists could be of a kind that was able to elevate their minds to venture up the heights of art ; there were, also, neither privileges nor honors to be expected when they had produced anything extraordinary. Hence the word image-cutter applies to the artists of the Egyptian statues in its proper signification ; they chiselled out their figures after an established measure and form, and therefore the law not to depart therefrom was probably not a harsh law to them.   The name of only one Egyptian sculptor has been preserved under a Greek pronunciation ; he was called Memnon, and had made three statues at the entrance of a temple in Thebes, one of which was the largest in Egypt.

12. In regard to science, Egyptian artists must of necessity have been deficient in one of the most important points of art, namely, in knowledge of anatomy, — a science which was not only uncultivated in Egypt, as in China, but was also unknown.   Respect for the dead would by no means have allowed the dissection of a body to be made ; indeed, as we are informed by Diodorus, it was regarded as homicide to make merely an incision into it.   Hence even the Paraschistes, as the Greeks termed him, or he who opened the body by an incision into the side preparatory for embalming, was obliged to flee immediately from the spot after the performance of his duty, in order to save himself from the relatives of the deceased, and from others, by-standers, who followed him with curses and stones.   The slight knowledge of the Egyptian artists in anatomy shows itself, in fact, not only in the incorrect rendering of some few parts, but it might also be inferred from the feeble markings of the muscles and bones.   In Egypt, anatomy did not extend beyond the internal parts or entrails ; and even this limited knowledge, which was transmitted from father to son in the guild of this class of persons, probably remained a secret to others ; for in the preparation of the dead body, no one was present but them.

CHAPTER II.

PRIMITIVE STYLE OF EGYPTIAN ART.

1. THE second portion of this section treats of the ancient primitive style of Egyptian art, and includes the drawing of the nude figure, and the clothing of figures in conformity to it. Considered generally, three varieties, manners, or styles are observable : — the antique style just mentioned ; the later style ; and, finally, that of imitations of Egyptian works, which were probably executed by Greek artists. I will endeavor to show presently, that the genuine antique Egyptian works are two-fold in kind, and that, in their own art, there are two distinct eras. The first lasted until the conquest of Egypt by Cambyses, and the second as long as native Egyptians, under Persian and afterwards under Greek sovereignty, practised sculpture ; but most of the imitations were probably executed during the reign of the Emperor Adrian.

2. In the more ancient style, the drawing of the nude figure has distinct and intelligible characteristics, which distinguish it, not only from the drawing of other nations, but also from their own later style. These qualities exist, and are to be defined, not only in the outline of the whole figure, but also in the drawing and conformation of each particular part.

3. The general and principal characteristic of the drawing of the nude figure in this style is that of forming the contour of it by straight or nearly straight lines, — an attribute which belongs also to their architecture, and their embellishments. Hence on the one hand the Graces — divinities unknown to the Egyptians — are wanting in Egyptian figures ; and on the other, the pic-turesque ; both of which deficiencies Strabo infers from a temple at Memphis. The attitude of the figures is stiff and constrained ; but feet, placed parallel and close together, — which a few ancient writers apparently indicate as a universal mark of distinc-tion of Egyptian figures, and which exist in the earliest Etruscan

figures of bronze, — are found only in seated figures. Feet
which are of genuine antiquity stand parallel, and not outwards ;
but, like produced parallel lines, one is extended before the
other.   In a male figure fourteen palms (10.3 ft. Eng.) in
height, in the Albani villa, the distance between the two feet is
more than three palms (2.2 ft. Eng.).   The arms of male figures
hang straight down along the sides, to which they are united,
as if firmly pressed towards them ; consequently such figures
have no action at all, — action being expressed principally
through the movement of the arms and hands.   The motionless state of these parts is no proof of a want of skill in the
artists, but of a rule established and adopted in statues, according to which they must be executed after one and the same
model ; for action, which they have given to their figures, is
seen on obelisks and other works ; and probably some statues
also have had the hands free, as we might infer from that one
which represented a king holding a mouse in his hand, unless it
was a seated, and not a standing figure.   Of female figures only
the right arm hangs confined to the side ; the left lies across the
body below the breast ; but both arms hang down of those
figures which stand in front near the seat of the statue of Memnon.   Several figures are sitting with their legs crossed under
them, or kneeling on one knee, and for this reason might be
termed Engonases : in this position were the three Dii Nixi,
placed before the three chapels of the Olympian Jupiter at
Rome.

    4. In the great simplicity of drawing of the Egyptian figures,
the bones and muscles are slightly marked ; the nerves and
veins, on the other hand, are not rendered at all ; the knees,
the ankles, and a marking of the elbow, however, are prominently shown, as in nature ; the back is not visible, on account
of the pillar against which their statues are placed, and with
which they form one piece.   The slightly curving outlines of
their figures are, likewise, one cause of the narrowness and contraction of their shapes, — terms by which Petronius characterizes the Egyptian style of art.   Egyptian figures, especially of
the male sex, are also distinguished by the unusual smallness
of the body above the hips.

    5. The foregoing characters and distinguishing marks of the
Egyptian style, namely, the contour and the forms, defined by
nearly straight lines, and the slight marking of the bones and

PLATE III

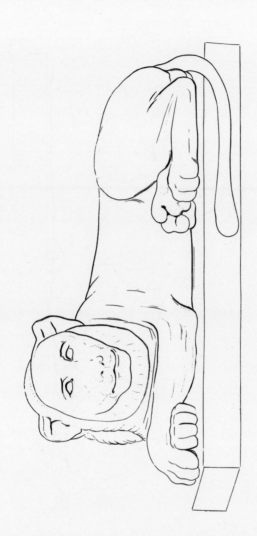

PLATE IV

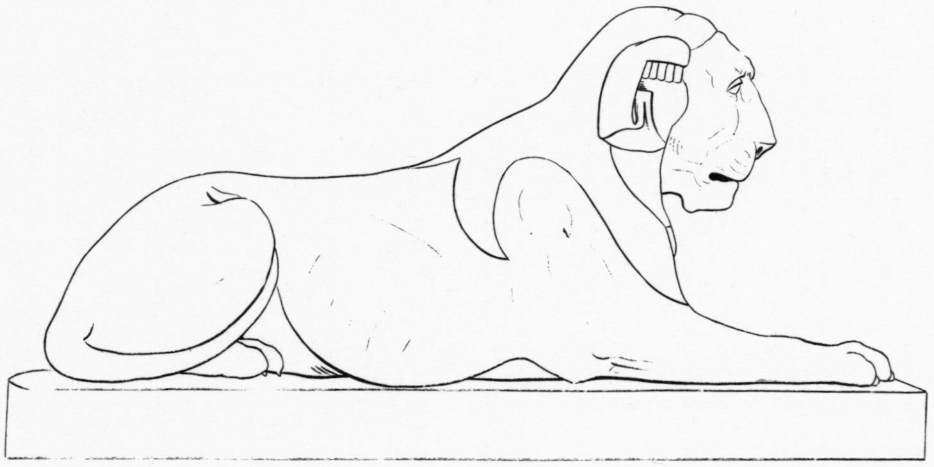

muscles, have an exception in the animals of Egyptian art. Among these are to be particularly noticed a large Sphinx of basalt in the Borghese villa, two lions on the ascent to the Campidoglio,[1] and two others at the Fontana Felice; for they are executed with much understanding, an elegant variety of softly deviating outlines and flowingly unbroken parts (1). The great trochanters, below the hips, which in human figures are passed over undefined, are, together with the bone of the thigh, and other bones, executed in wild beasts with an expressive elegance. And yet the lions by the above-mentioned Fountain are marked with hieroglyphics, which are not found on the other animals named, and show plain indications of being genuine Egyptian works; the Sphinxes by the obelisk of the sun, which lies in the Campus Martius, are in precisely the same style, and the heads evince great skill and much labor.[2]

6. From this difference of style in human figures and the figures of animals, we may conclude that, as the former represent divinities, or persons consecrated to divinities, — among whom I also include kings, in accordance with what I have remarked above, — the conformation of them had been universally determined by the religion of the country, but that, in the formation of animals, the artists were allowed more license for the display of their skill. We may imagine the system of art in Egypt, in regard to the human figure, like the form of government at Crete and Sparta, where it was not allowable to deviate, even by a finger's breadth, from the institutions of their lawgivers; but the figures of animals were not included under this law.

7. In the second place, the extremities, that is, the head, hands, and feet, are the principal points of examination in the drawing of the nude figure.

In the head, the eyes are drawn flat and oblique, and are placed, not deeply, as in Greek statues, but almost on a level with the forehead, so that the upper margin of the orbit, on which the eyebrows are denoted by a sharp prominence, is flat. For in Egyptian figures — the forms of which, though possessing much that is ideal, have no ideal beauty — the artist did not succeed in attaining the ideal and in imparting majesty to this

---

[1] Plates III. and IV.

[2] Plate V. The head of the one given in the plate is more beautifully and carefully executed than that of the other. — FEA.

part of the face ; the Greeks sought and obtained it by setting
the ball of the eye more deeply, thus producing more light and
shadow, and consequently stronger effect, — as I will show hereafter more fully.   The eyebrows, the eyelids, and the edge of
the lips, are generally denoted by incised lines.   The eyebrows
of one of the most ancient female heads, larger than life, of
greenish basalt, in the Albani villa, which has excavated eyes,
are delineated by a raised flat band, of the breadth of the nail
on the little finger; this band extends even to the temples,
where it is cut off at an angle.   From the lower part of the
socket of the eye, a similar band runs in precisely the same way
to the same place, where it terminates in a similar manner.
The Egyptians had no knowledge of the soft profile of Greek
heads, but the depression of the nose is the same as in nature.
The cheek-bones are strongly marked and prominent; the chin
is always somewhat small, and receding, whereby the oval of
the face becomes imperfect.   The section of the mouth, or the
meeting of the lips, which, in nature, at least in Greeks and
Europeans, is drawn rather downwards towards the corners of
the mouth, is, on the contrary, in Egyptian heads drawn upwards; and the mouth is always closed in such a manner that
the lips are separated from each other only by a simple incision ;
whereas the lips of the greater number of Greek divinities are,
on the contrary, opened, — as I shall notice hereafter.   But the
most extraordinary part of the Egyptian conformation would be
the ears, provided they were really situated so high on the head
as they are seen on the greater number of Egyptian figures (2),
and, among others, on the two heads in my own possession.   But
they are placed the highest — so high, indeed, that the lobe of
the ear is almost in the same line with the eyes — on a head
with inserted eyes, in the Albani villa, and on the seated figure
below the point of the Barberini obelisk.

8. The hands have that form which we find in those who
have injured or neglected hands not badly shaped.   The feet
differ from the feet of Greek figures in being flatter and
broader, and by a slight diminution in the length of the toes,
which lie perfectly flat, and, like the fingers, have no markings
of the joints.   Even the little toe is not crooked, nor pressed
inwards, as is the case with Greek feet; consequently it is
probable that the feet of Memnon also have neither the position nor shape with which Pococke allowed them to be drawn.

PLATE V

PLATE VI

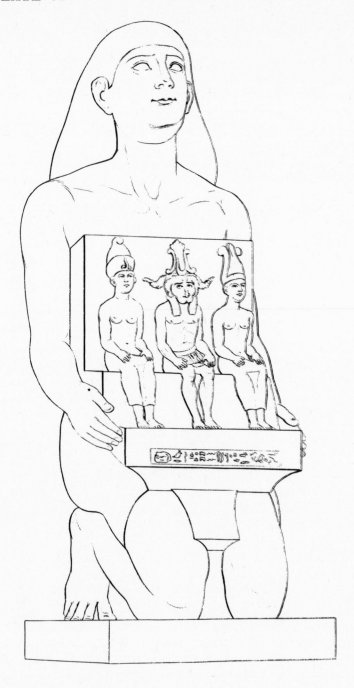

The nails are indicated only by angular incisions, and have neither roundness nor convexity.

9. The feet of the Egyptian statues in the Campidoglio — in those instances in which they have been preserved — are, even as in the Apollo Belvedere and the Laocoön, of unequal length ; the supporting right foot of one of them is about three inches of a Roman palm (2.2 in. Eng.) longer than the other. But this inequality is not without reason ; for it was the intention to give to the foot which stands farther removed from the spectator just as much as it might seem to lose by being withdrawn (3).

The navel, both of men and women, is unusually deep and hollow.

10. By means of the foregoing characteristics of art among this people, it is possible to distinguish each single fragment of a statue, and say whether it is Egyptian or Grecian. A sculptor showed me the thigh, together with the knee of a kneeling figure in greenish basalt, as an Egyptian work ; but I proved to him, by pointing out the markings of the bones and cartilages of the knee, that it was a Greek production, in despite of the Egyptian stone. The figures in a few Herculaneum paintings may also serve to elucidate that passage of Petronius where he speaks of the creeping in of the Egyptian style of art.

I here repeat a remark, which has been stated generally in the Preface, that it is impossible to form an opinion from engravings ; for in the figures in Boissard, Kircher, and Montfaucon, there is not found a single one of the assigned characters of the Egyptian style. It is, moreover, necessary to observe closely what parts of Egyptian statues are really antique, and what are restorations. The lower portion of the face of the supposed Isis in the Campidoglio, which, among the four largest statues there, is the only one of black granite, is not antique, but a modern addition ; the arms and the legs of this statue, and of the two others, of red granite, are also restorations. I mention these restorations particularly, because they are not very apparent. On the other hand, I omit those additions which every one can easily detect ; as, for example, the modern head of the female figure in the Barberini palace, — holding in front of herself a small Anubis in a box, after the manner of a male figure in Kircher,[1] — or the legs of a smaller standing figure in the Borghese villa (4).

[1] Plate VI.

11. Any comments which I might have to make, for the instruction of those who study art, on the singular shape of the figures of Egyptian divinities, and on the attributes assigned to them, should follow, most appropriately in this place, the preceding observations on the drawing of the nude figure. But as this topic has been handled to excess by others, I will confine myself here to some special remarks.

12. Few statues of the divinities to which were given the heads of animals in whose forms they were reverenced by the Egyptians have been preserved; and I believe that only the following are to be found in Rome. The first in the Barberini palace, with the head of a sparrow-hawk, represents Osiris; and the head of this bird is intended, in the figure of Osiris, to typify the Greek Apollo; but according to Homer, the sparrow-hawk was peculiar to the latter, and his messenger, because he is able to gaze at the sun without blinking. The second statue, in the Albani villa, of similar size, with a head which partakes of a lion, a cat, and a dog, is an image of Anubis (5), in whose shape, likewise, there was a mixture of that of the lion, which animal also was reverenced. The third is a small seated figure with a dog's head, in the same villa; the fourth, of precisely the same conformation, is in the Barberini palace; and the fifth, with the head of a cat, is in the Borghese villa. The first four statues are of blackish granite.

13. The head of the second of these figures is covered, on its back part, with the customary Egyptian cap, which, laid in many folds, hangs down in front of a roundish shape, and behind over the shoulders two palms (1 ft. 5 in. Eng.) in length; and on the head, behind, there rises up a round disc, which, if not intended to typify the sun or moon, may be regarded as a Nimbus, so called, which was afterwards given to the images of the deities among the Greeks and Romans and the emperors. Among the Herculaneum paintings, there is a remarkable one of an Osiris, on a black ground, of which the face, arms, and feet have a blue color. A symbolic meaning probably lies concealed herein, since we know that the Egyptians gave to the image of the sun, or to Osiris, more than one color; and blue was intended to denote the sun when it is below our hemisphere. The Anubis of white marble, in the Campidoglio, is a work, not of Egyptian art, but of the age of the Emperor Adrian.

14. Strabo — not Diodorus, as Pococke states — relates of a

temple at Thebes, that no human figures, but merely those of animals, were placed in it, and Pococke pretends to have made the same observation in regard to other temples, preserved there. The statement in Strabo seems to be the ground on which Warburton holds the figures of the Egyptian divinities with the heads of animals to be more ancient than those which are wholly human. Egyptian figures, however, seemingly divinities from the emblems given to them, are now found represented in a form completely human, in greater numbers, than with the heads of animals ; — of this, one proof, among others, is the well-known Isic Tablet in the museum of the king of Sardinia ; — and the statues in which the human form is not disfigured appear to have precisely the same antiquity as those of the other kind. It is impossible to ascribe a less antiquity to the two large female statues in the Capitoline museum ; they are probably images of Isis, although they have no horns on the head (6), which on her denote the waxing and waning of the moon, as shown by a bronze figure of her in the oldest Egyptian style, which has been published in my *Ancient Monuments.* These statues cannot be the statues of priestesses of this goddess, because no woman filled the sacerdotal office in Egypt. The male figures in the same place may even be statues of kings or of high-priests, since they have none of the distinguishing marks of a deity ; for statues of the latter stood at Thebes. Of the wings of Egyptian deities I shall speak in the third chapter of this second book. It may likewise be remarked here, that the Sistrum is not placed in the hand of any figure on any ancient Egyptian work whatever in Rome (7) ; in fact, this instrument is not seen represented at all on them, except on the border of the Isic Tablet ; and they mistake, who, like Bianchini, think that they have found it on more than one obelisk, — a remark which I have already made in another place. The staves in the hands of the male figures generally have, instead of a knob, a bird's head, — which may be seen most distinctly in the case of the seated figures on both sides of a large tablet of red granite, in the garden of the Barberini palace ; and also of those which are cut in the obelisk near to its point. These staves Diodorus seems to have looked upon as ploughs, for he says that the figures of Egyptian kings held a plough ; but it is a staff surmounted by the head of a bird. This bird is either the one which the inhabitants of Egypt termed Aboukirdan,

of about the size of a small crane, or it is the bird Epops
(Hoopoe) of the Greeks, named by the Romans Upupa.　But
here the question arises, What resemblance has this wand to a
plough, and how is it possible for Diodorus to have confounded
one with the other？　In order to explain this, we must suppose
that the meaning given to the afore-mentioned staves was an
invention of his own, inasmuch as he viewed them at a distance,
on the top of the obelisks, and not near by, as it can be done
in Rome, where three of them are lying on the ground.　As
with Diodorus, so it has been with the learned Bianchini, who
explains a staff of this kind, in the hand of the figure on the
apex of the Flaminian obelisk, in the Piazza del Popolo, according to the account given by this historian.　The ancients had
two kinds of ploughs ; one of them, like our own, consisted of
many pieces, and was called $\check{a}\rho o\tau\rho o\nu$ $\pi\eta\kappa\tau\acute{o}\nu$; the other, named
$a\mathring{v}\tau\acute{o}\gamma\nu o\nu$, was made of a single piece ; that is to say, the posterior part — forming the elbow, named $\gamma\nu\acute{\iota}\eta$ by some, and $\mathring{e}\chi\acute{e}\tau\lambda\eta$
by others, and to the under part of which the share is attached
— was of one solid piece with the beam by which the oxen draw.
This is the kind of plough with which the hero Echetlus is
represented on many Etruscan sepulchral urns, hitherto unex-
plained, fighting at Marathon against the Persians.　The bird-
headed staff in the hand of the kings on Egyptian monuments,
when viewed at a distance, has great resemblance to such a
plough ; and this similarity probably explains why Diodorus
mistook one for the other.　The Greeks also carried staves, of
which the top was ornamented by birds.　Among the Assyrians,
according to Herodotus, an apple, a rose, a lily, an eagle, or a
figure of some kind, was carved on the head of them.　The
eagle, therefore, on the head of Jupiter's staff, described by
Pindar, and as it is seen on a beautiful altar in the Albani villa,
is derived from a common custom.

15.　We learn from Porphyry, on the authority of Numenius,
that the Egyptian deities stand, not on the solid earth, but on
a ship ; and that not only the sun, but all souls, according to
the doctrine of the Egyptians, float on the fluid element.　The
author cited has sought to illustrate by this conception the
"moving of the Spirit of God upon the waters," in the Mosaic
account of the creation.　In a similar manner, Thales maintained
that the earth rests like a ship upon the water.　There are a
few monuments in which this belief has been expressed.　In the

Ludovisi villa stands a small Isis, in marble, with her left foot on a vessel; and on two round bases in the Mattei villa, presenting a picture of the Egyptian religious rites adopted by the Romans, is a figure which stands with both feet on a boat. But a still closer approximation to this doctrine of the Egyptians is found in a picture painted on a vessel of terra-cotta in the Vatican library. It represents the sun, together with a personified figure of the moon, standing on a car drawn by four horses, and the whole borne on a ship. This painting has been published in my *Ancient Monuments*.

16. The Sphinxes of the Egyptians are of both sexes; that is to say, they are female in their front parts, with a female head, and male behind, where the testicles are seen. This has hitherto remained unnoticed; and I stated it on the authority of a gem in the Stosch museum, and by it I showed the explanation of the passage, hitherto not understood in the poet Philemon, in which he speaks of male Sphinxes, especially as the Greek artists also formed Sphinxes with a beard, as we see on a rilievo in terra-cotta which stands in the lesser Farnese palace. When Herodotus terms the Sphinxes ἀνδρόσφιγγες, he intends, as I think, to denote their double sex. The Sphinxes on the four sides of the apex of the obelisk of the sun, which have human hands with the sharp claws of rending animals, are particularly deserving of attention.

17. From this investigation of the drawing of the nude figure of the older Egyptian style, I proceed to the dress of figures of this same style. I will remark, in the first place, that it consisted principally of flax, which was abundantly cultivated in Egypt (8), and that the robe, termed Kalasiris, to the lower part of which a ruffled band or hem with many folds was sewed, reached even to the feet. Over this the men threw a white mantle, made of cloth (9). The priests were dressed in white cotton. But all male figures — as well in statues as on obelisks and other works — are naked, with the exception of an apron placed about the hips and covering the abdomen (10). This apron is broken into very small plaits (11). If these figures represent divinities, the practice of figuring them in a nude state may either be an adopted one, — as was the case among the Greeks, — or it may be considered as a representation of the earliest form of dress in Egypt, and which was still existing among the Arabians long after this date; for the latter wore

nothing but an apron about the body and shoes on their feet. But if they are priests, we can conceive of them as we do of the sacrificial priests among the Romans, who were likewise nude as low down as the abdomen, and wore an apron, termed *limus*, bound around them; and thus they slaughtered the victim, as it may be seen on different rilievi. Now, as the Egyptian kings, when one line of them had become extinct, were selected from the body of the priests, and all the kings were consecrated to the priesthood, it might be assumed that it was even in this view that the Egyptian kings have been imaged in such a garb (12).

18. The dress of female figures is signified merely by a prominent or raised border at the legs and neck, as it may be seen on a supposed Isis in the Campidoglio, and on two other figures there. Around the centre of the breasts of one of them a small circle is engraved, and from it proceed many incisions lying close to one another, like the radii of a circle, nearly two fingers broad, and passing round the breasts. This might be regarded as an absurd ornament; but I am of opinion that it was intended to signify by them the folds which would be formed by a thin veil thrown over the nipples. For on the breasts of an Egyptian Isis, but of later style, in the Albani villa, which at the first glance appear to be entirely uncovered, folds of almost imperceptible elevation are drawn, diverging in the same direction from the centre of the breasts. The clothing on the bodies of these figures must be merely imagined; and this may be the reason why Herodotus supposed the twenty female colossal statues of the concubines of King Mycerinus, made of wood, in the city of Sais, to be naked, since they were probably draped precisely in this manner; and this appears so much the more credible, as even the sculptor Francesco Maratti, of Padua, by whom the Capitoline statues were repaired, did not notice the above-mentioned projection, by which alone the dress on them is distinguishable, as I perceive from the neatly executed drawings presented by this artist to Pope Clement the Eleventh. Pococke makes the very same remark in regard to the dress of a seated statue of Isis, which, if it were not for a projecting border above the ankles, would be considered as entirely nude. Hence, he imagines this garment as a fine muslin, of which even now the shifts of the Eastern women are made, on account of the great heat.

19. The figure in the Barberini palace, before mentioned, is dressed in a singular manner. Her robe widens from above downward, like a bell, without folds. An idea of it may be obtained from a figure given in Pococke. The tunic of a female figure of blackish granite, three palms (26 in. Eng.) in height, in the Rolandi museum at Rome, is made precisely in the same manner; but as it is not enlarged below, the lower part of the figure looks like a cylinder, so that the feet are not visible (13). Before her breast she holds a sitting *Cynokephalus*, "a dog-faced baboon," in a casket, on which are four rows, arranged in columns, of what are intended to signify hieroglyphics.

20. The rilievi with painted figures which have been preserved in structures at Thebes, and in other parts of Egypt, are said to be painted, like the dress of Osiris, without gradation of color, and without light and shadow. But this must not surprise us so much as it did the writer who states it, for all rilievi receive light and shadow through themselves, whether they are in white marble or in any other single color; and there would be nothing but confusion produced, if, in painting them over, the high and low parts should be treated the same as in a picture.

21. The dress or covering of the head is of many kinds, and the artist bestowed especial industry on the execution of it. The men, in their every-day life, indeed, usually wore nothing on their heads, and in this respect were the opposite of the Persians, as Herodotus remarks in speaking of the different hardness of the skulls of those who fell on both sides in the battle with the Persians. On the other hand, the male figures in works of art of this first Egyptian style have the head covered either with a hood or a cap, as gods, kings, or priests. With several of them the hood hangs down over the shoulders, as well towards the breast as upon the back, in two broad bands, partly flat, and partly a little rounded on the outside. The cap resembles in a degree a bishop's mitre, and on some few figures the upper part of it is flat, like those caps which were worn two hundred years ago, for example, the cap of the elder Aldus. Animals also have the hood and mitre: the former is seen on the sphinx, the latter on the hawk. A large hawk of basalt, about three palms (26 in. Eng.) in height, with a mitre, is in the above-mentioned Rolandi museum (14). The cap with a

flat crown was tied under the chin by two bands, as, for example, on a seated figure, four palms (33 in. Eng.) in height, of black granite, and the only one of its kind, — in the same museum (15).[1]   This cap enlarges as it rises upwards, like the Modius on the head of Serapis ; and caps of this form, as worn by a few images of the ancient Persian kings in the ruins of Persepolis, are termed by the Arabians Cancal, that is to say, Modius. Similar caps are worn by the seated figures below the pinnacle of an obelisk.   On the front of the cap rises a serpent, just as, on the heads of Phœnician divinities on coins of Malta (16), it rises over the forehead.

22. From a cap of this kind, worn by the figures on obelisks as well as on the Barberini Tablet above mentioned, and also from the cap of the aforesaid figure, and of the figure in the Rolandi museum, rises the ornament supposed by Warburton to be the shrub of which Diodorus speaks, which was a head-ornament of the kings of Egypt.   But as this head-dress on the cap rather resembles an ornament of feathers, and as it is found that the Egyptian deity Cneph, the creative god, bore wings on his head, and royal wings too, that is to say, of the kind which kings are accustomed to wear, it is probable that the ornament in question is not only what it resembles, but we are authorized to infer from it that the wearers represent kings, inasmuch as the divinity named is not otherwise known, whilst such figures are repeated on all the obelisks.

A few figures, both male and female, have four rows, representing gems, pearls, and the like, hanging over the breast like a mantilla.   This ornament is found especially on figures of Canopus and on mummies.

23. The heads of female figures are always covered by a hood, which is sometimes laid in an almost infinite number of small plaits, — as, for instance, on the above-mentioned head of green basalt in the Albani villa.   An oblong gem is represented as being set in the front part of this hood ; and this is the only head on which the roots of the hair on the forehead are indicated.   A few figures of Isis have on their head something which resembles a head-dress of artificial hair ; but in reality, and particularly on the large Isis in the Capitoline museum, it seems to be composed of feathers.   This is rendered more probable by an Isis introduced in my *Ancient Monuments,* upon whose

[1] Plate VII.

PLATE VII

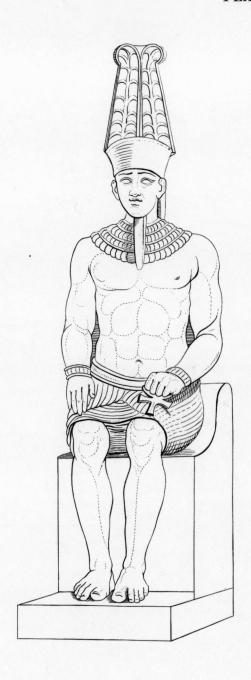

hood sits a Numidian hen, so called, the wings of which hang down by the sides of it, and the tail backwards.

24. Another strange fashion was the single lock of hair, which is seen hanging, near the right ear, from the shaven head of a statue of black marble, in the Campidoglio. This statue will be cited hereafter as an Egyptian imitation. The lock of hair is neither shown in the engraving nor noticed in the description of the figure.[1]   I have spoken of such a lock of hair on the shaven head of a figure of Harpocrates, in the *Description of the Engraved Gems of the Stosch Cabinet,* in which I pointed out, at the same time, this singularity on another figure of the same deity, which was made known by the Count Caylus.   A copper-plate engraving of the Stosch gem has been introduced into my *Ancient Monuments.*   This lock explains Macrobius, who relates that the Egyptians represented the Sun with a shaved head, excepting one lock on the right side of it.   Cuper therefore is not wrong, — although censured for his error by a modern writer, — when he asserts, without however having any knowledge of the preceding statement, that in Harpocrates the Egyptians honored also the Sun.   In the museum of the College of St. Ignatius, at Rome, there is a small Harpocrates, together with two other small genuine Egyptian figures of bronze with this lock.

25. Not a single Egyptian figure has shoes and soles ; and even Plutarch relates that the women in this country went bare-footed.   It must therefore be considered as an exception, that the statue in Pococke, of which mention has been made, has an angular ring below the ankle-bone, from which something like a strap passes down between the great toe and the one next to it, as if for the purpose of fastening the sole (17), though the sole itself is not visible.

26. The Egyptian women, not less than those of other nations, had their ornaments, especially ear-pendants and armlets.   As far as I know, ear-pendants are to be seen only on a single figure, which has been made known by Pococke (18).   The same figure, and the Isis of black granite in the Campidoglio, have bracelets near the knuckles.   If we were to speak accurately, we should say that the ornament in question could not be called an arm-let, for this is placed about the arm of figures of other nations ; but it must denote a ring.   The most ancient nations, especially

[1] In the *Capitoline Museum,*

the Egyptians, apparently wore rings, not on the fingers, but on the hands, — a fact which we might infer from what Moses relates of Pharaoh, that the king drew his ring from his own hand and placed it upon the hand of Joseph. These are the reflections which have occurred to me in regard to the elder style of Egyptian sculpture.

CHAPTER III.

LATER EGYPTIAN STYLE.

1. THE third chapter of this book, — which treats of the following and later style of the Egyptian artists, — like the preceding chapter, has for its objects the drawing of the nude figure in the first place, and, in the second, the dress of figures. An example of each is seen in two figures of basalt, in the Campidoglio; and a figure from the same kind of stone, in the Albani villa, informs us in regard to posture and dress. To the latter, however, the antique head, arms, and legs are wanting.

The face of one of the two former statues seems to deviate somewhat from the usual Egyptian shape; the mouth, however, is turned upwards, and the chin is too short; these are characteristics that belong to the more ancient Egyptian heads. The eyes are excavated; and it is probable that, anciently, the cavities were filled by some foreign material. Though the face of the other statue approaches still nearer to the Greek form, the figure, as a whole, is badly drawn, and the proportion is too short; the hands are more elegant than those of the most ancient Egyptian figures; in shape, the feet are like the most ancient; in position, they differ, being turned a little outwards. The position and action of the former figure, as well as of the third in the Albani villa, perfectly resemble the oldest Egyptian figures; for the arms of both hang perpendicularly and close to their sides, except that the former has an opening drilled between the arms and the sides; at the back of the figures, as in all those of the oldest Egyptian style, there is an angular column against which they stand. The second statue has freer, though not detached arms; and in one hand it holds a horn of plenty, with fruits; the back of this one is free and without a column.

2. These figures, though they are the work of Egyptian artists, were executed when Egypt was under the control of the Greeks, by whom their deities, and consequently also their art,

were introduced into the country, just as they, in their turn, adopted Egyptian customs. Since the Egyptians at the time of Plato, as they from time to time shook off the Persian domination, caused statues to be made, — which is attested by the statement of this writer, above cited, — it is probable that art was also exercised by their own artists in the time of the Ptolemies; and the probability is increased by the continued observance of their religious rites. The figures of this latter style are also distinguishable by bearing no hieroglyphics, which, in the case of the larger number of the most ancient Egyptian figures, are cut sometimes on their base, and sometimes on the column against which they stand (1). But in this case the style alone is the distinctive character, not the hieroglyphics; for although the latter are not found on any imitation of Egyptian figures, — of which I shall speak in the next chapter, — so, on the other hand, there are also genuine antique Egyptian works without the slightest of such signs. Among these are two obelisks, the one in front of St. Peter's church, the other near Santa Maria Maggiore; and Pliny makes the same remark of two others. There are no hieroglyphics on the lions at the ascent to the Capitol, nor on the above-mentioned Osiris in the Barberini palace; and I could adduce other works (2) and figures of the kind.

3. In regard to the dress, we observe on all the three female statues mentioned above a tunic, a robe, and a mantle. But this is no contradiction of Herodotus's remark, that the Egyptian women wear only a single garment, for he probably meant to speak of the robe, or upper garment. The under garment of the two statues in the Campidoglio is laid in small plaits, and hangs down in front as far as the toes, and sideways as far as the base; on the third, namely, the statue in the Albani villa, it is not visible, because the antique legs are wanting. This under garment — to judge from the numerous plaits in which it is laid — apears to have been made of linen; and it covered not only the breast as high as the neck, but also the whole body as low as the feet, and had short sleeves, which reached only to the middle of the upper part of the arm (3). On the breasts of the third statue, this drapery falls into quite slight and almost imperceptible folds, radiating from the nipples in all directions, as I have already remarked.

4. On the first and the third statue the robe is very similar.

It lies close to the flesh, with the exception of a very few superficial folds which extend upwards; and on all the three it reaches only to the lower part of the breasts, where it is drawn up through the mantle, and supported.

5. The mantle is drawn over both shoulders by two of its corners, and by means of them the robe is tied with the mantle beneath the breasts. The superfluous portion of these corners hangs down from the breast, below the tied knot, just as we see it on the beautiful Isis in the Campidoglio, and on a larger Isis in the Barberini palace, where the robe is tied with the ends of the mantle; both are in marble, and of Greek workmanship. By this means the robe is drawn upwards, and the soft folds which form on the thighs and legs are all carried upwards at the same time with it, and from the breast a single straight fold hangs down between the legs even to the feet.

6. The third statue, in the Albani villa, shows a trifling variation; only one of the ends of the mantle passes over the shoulders; the other is drawn round below the left breast, and both are tied between the breasts with the robe. Furthermore, the mantle is not visible, and as it should hang behind, it is seemingly concealed by the column against which this, as well as the first of the three statues, stands; the back of the second is without a column, and detached, and the mantle is drawn round in front of the abdomen. The robes of the aforementioned Greek statues of Isis are trimmed with fringes, like the mantles of the statues of captive kings, apparently for the purpose of denoting by this means a goddess whose worship had been introduced from foreign lands. A garment of this kind was termed Gausapum; it was of a shaggy appearance, and when introduced into Rome, was worn by women in winter.

7. After this peculiarity had attracted my notice, I examined all the figures of Isis relatively to their drapery, and I then observed that all of them, without an exception, wore their mantles in such a manner, and that this fashion is a distinguishing mark of the goddess. By means of it, I recognized an Isis in a torso of a colossal statue which stands against the Venetian palace in Rome, and is called by the people Donna Lucrezia. A beautiful bronze figure of Isis, a palm (8.80 in. Eng.) in height, as well as two or three smaller figures of her in the Herculaneum museum, show the goddess dressed precisely in this way; the attributes of Fortune have been given both to the latter and the former.

8. The second part of this chapter treats of figures which resemble the ancient Egyptian figures more nearly than the latter do, and which were executed neither in Egypt nor by Egyptian artists, but are imitations of Egyptian works, that came into fashion among the Romans contemporaneously with the introduction of the worship of Egyptian deities. The most ancient of such works are, as far as I know, two bas-relief figures of Isis in gypsum, which are to be seen in a small chapel in the front court of the temple of Isis, recently discovered amid the ruins of the buried city of Pompeii. As this calamity befell the city in the reign of Titus, it is probable that these figures are more ancient than the statues of a similar kind which were exhumed at Adrian's villa, in Tivoli. During the reign of the latter emperor, who, with all his acquirements in knowledge, was uncommonly superstitious, reverence for the Egyptian deities appears to have spread more than previously; and his example probably encouraged a belief in this false worship. For he caused a singular temple to be erected in the Tiburtine villa, which he named Canopus; in it he placed numerous statues of Egyptian deities; and the greater number, if not all, of such Egyptian imitations have been taken from it. In some of them he caused the most ancient Egyptian figures to be accurately imitated; in others, he united Egyptian art with the Grecian. Some of both kinds are found, in attitude and adjustment resembling the earliest Egyptian figures; that is, they stand perfectly upright and without action, with arms hanging down straight, and lying close to the sides and hips; their feet are parallel, and, like the Egyptian, they rest against an angular column. Others, however, have the same attitude, but the arms, with which they either carry or point to something, are free. It is a matter of regret that all these figures have not their ancient heads, because the head always affords the principal illustration of the style. It is well to mention the fact, because they who have written about these statues have not, in all cases, been aware of it. Even the Isis quoted above has a modern head, which Bottari holds to be antique. The locks of hair which lie on the shoulders had been preserved, and the hair on the modern head was executed in conformity with the intimation thus given. After the restoration, the genuine antique head was found, and purchased by the Cardinal Polignac, whose museum the king of Prussia bought. This head, and several

others which the same Cardinal also acquired, were found in Adrian's villa, at Tivoli, among many statues broken to pieces by the axe, in a pond the sides and bottom of which were faced with marble. I will notice here the several different kinds of works in this style, and among them the most important pieces, with a criticism upon their drawing and form, and afterwards touch upon the drapery.

9. Of statues, two of reddish granite, which stand near the episcopal residence at Tivoli (4), and the cited Egyptian Antinoüs of marble, in the Capitoline museum, are especially to be noticed. The latter statue is somewhat larger than life; but the two former are nearly twice as large as nature, and have not only the attitude of the earliest Egyptian figures, but, like these, they stand against an angular column; they are, however, without hieroglyphics. The hips and abdomen are covered by aprons; and the hoods have two smooth bands which come forwards, and hang down in front; on their heads they carry baskets, — after the manner of the Caryatides, — made out of the same piece as the figure. Now as the attitude and shape of these statues, generally, perfectly resemble those of Egyptian works of the first style, it has been assumed by all that they are such works; but no careful examination of the form of particular parts was made; if it had been, the contrary would have been shown to be the case. For the chest, which in the earliest male figures of the Egyptians is flat, is, in these examples, strongly elevated, like the breasts of heroes; the ribs beneath the breast, which in the Egyptian are not to be seen at all, here appear distinctly marked; the body above the hips, which is very contracted there, has its right fulness here; the joints and cartilages of the knees are worked out more prominently here than there; the muscles of the arms, as well as of other parts, are plainly visible; the shoulder-blades, which are, as it were, without any indication there, rise up here with a decided rounding, and the feet approach more nearly to the Greek form.

10. But the greatest difference is in the face, which is neither executed after the Egyptian manner, nor similar, in other respects, to Egyptian heads. For the eyes do not lie on the same level with the eyebrow-bones, as they frequently do in nature, and as they always do in Egyptian heads, but they are deeply sunk, after the system of Greek art, for the purpose of project-

ing those bones, and of obtaining light and shade. Besides these
Greek forms, there is plainly to be seen a conformation of face
perfectly similar to that of the Antinoüs : so that I am convinced
that I find in these statues an image of this celebrated young
man (5). In the Egyptian Antinoüs of the Capitoline museum,
of which I have spoken, the blending of the Greek with the
Egyptian style is still more perceptible; moreover, it stands
detached, and not against a column.

11. Among statues of this kind may be included several
Sphinxes; and there are four of them, of black granite, in the
Albani villa, the heads of which have a conformation that cannot, either in design or execution, have been the work of Egyptian artists. Statues of Isis, in marble, do not belong here; for
they are executed altogether in the Greek style, in the days of
the emperors too, and no earlier, because in the time of Cicero
the worship of Isis had not been adopted at Rome.

12. Of rilievi belonging among these imitations is particularly to be mentioned that one of green basalt which stands in
the court-yard of the Mattei palace, representing a sacrificial
procession. Another work of this kind — of which I have also
spoken in another place — is the fragment figured in an engraving in the *Ancient Monuments*, but of which the original is lost.
The Isis on it is winged; and the wings are thrown from behind
forwards and downwards, and cover the whole abdomen.[1] The
Isis on the Isic Tablet, likewise, has large wings; but here they
are placed above the hips, and are expanded forwards, for the
purpose, as it would seem, of mantling the body, — after the
manner of Cherubim. So, too, on a coin of the island of Malta,
are to be seen two figures, shaped like Cherubim, and — what
is remarkable, with the feet of oxen like them — which stand
opposite to one another; and the wings, extended from the
hips, are drawn downwards towards each other. A figure, having wings at the hips, is also found on a mummy; they are
raised for the purpose of overshadowing another deity, which is
seated.

13. I cannot refrain from remarking, that the Isic or Bembo
Tablet, of bronze, with silver inlaid figures, is held by Warburton to be a work that was made in Rome. This assertion, however, appears to have no foundation, and has been adopted
merely in aid of his opinion (6). I have not myself been able

[1] Plate VIII.

PLATE VIII

PLATE IX

to examine the table; but the hieroglyphics on it, which are found on no works imitated by the Romans, give one reason in support of its antiquity, and in refutation of his judgment.

14. The Canopi (7), of which the greater number are wrought from basalt, and the engraved gems, which, like them, are garnished with Egyptian figures and signs, have a place here,[1] with statues and rilievi. Of the Canopi of later times, the Cardinal Alexander Albani possesses the two most beautiful; they are of green basalt; the better one, which was found on the headland of Circe, between Nettuno and Terracina, has already been published. A similar Canopus, of the same stone, stands in the Campidoglio, and, like the other in the Albani villa, was found in Adrian's villa, at Tivoli. In regard to the age of these works, we can draw a conclusion partly from the drawing, and partly from the workmanship, and not less from the absence of hieroglyphs. The drawing, especially of the heads of the Canopi, is altogether in the Greek style; but the rilievi on the abdomen are imitations of Egyptian figures; the work of these figures is raised work, and consequently not done by Egyptian artists, whose raised figures do not project beyond the surface of the stone in which they are cut (8).

15. Among the engraved gems are all those Scarabæi whose high, rounded side presents a beetle, cut in relief, and whose flat side shows an Egyptian deity of later times, cut in intaglio. Writers who hold stones of this kind to be very old, have no other indication of high antiquity than their inelegance, and none at all that they are of Egyptian workmanship. Moreover, all engraved gems with figures or heads of Serapis and Anubis are of the times of the Romans, among whom Serapis, who is the Pluto of the Greeks, as I shall hereafter prove, has nothing Egyptian; and it is also said that the worship of this deity came from Thrace, and was introduced into Egypt by Ptolemy the First. Of gems bearing the image of Anubis, there are fifteen in the former Stosch museum, and all of them are of the later period. The engraved gems, named Abraxas (9), are now everywhere acknowledged as the bungling work of the Gnostics or Basilidians of the earliest Christian periods, and not deserving, in point of art, of being taken into consideration (10).

16. In the drapery of figures imitating the earliest Egyptian, the case is the same generally as with the drawing and form of

[1] Plate IX.

the nude parts of them.   There are a few male figures, girt only
with an apron, like the genuine Egyptian; and the one which,
as I have mentioned, has a lock of hair hanging from its shaved
head on the right side, is entirely naked, — a state in which no
antique male figure of the Egyptians is found (11).   The female
figures are, like the Egyptian, entirely dressed; a few even after
the fashion which I have shown to be the most ancient, in which
the dress is denoted by a slight projection on the legs, and by a
rim around the neck and upper part of the arms.   From the
abdomen of a few of these figures a single fold hangs down between the legs; but, on the body, the dress is merely a thing
of imagination.   Over a dress of this kind other female figures
have a mantle, which, hanging down from the shoulders, is tied
on the chest in front, — precisely in the manner previously noticed by me.   An Isis of marble, in the Barberini gallery, about
which a snake has twined itself, wears a hood, like Egyptian
figures, and a necklace of a few strings of beads or pearls upon
the breast, like the Canopi.   As something singular, I notice a
male figure of black marble (12), in the Albani villa, — the head
of which is lost, — that is dressed precisely in the same manner
as the women; but the sex is distinguishable by the tokens of
it prominent beneath the dress.

CHAPTER IV.

MECHANICAL PART OF EGYPTIAN ART.

1. THE fourth chapter relates to the mechanical part of Egyptian art, — first, in sculpture; secondly, in painting. In both, the kind and mode of execution of their works will be considered, as well as the material in which they are wrought.

2. In regard to the execution, it is related by Diodorus that the Egyptian sculptors, after having applied their established measures to the stone, still in an unwrought state, sawed it through the middle, and that two artists divided between themselves the workmanship of a figure. Telecles and Theodorus, of Samos, are said to have made, in the same way, a wooden statue of Apollo, which stood at Samos, in Greece; — Telecles, one half, at Samos; and Theodorus, the other half, at Ephesus. This statue was divided through the middle below the hips, as low down as the private parts, and afterwards again put together in this place, so that the two pieces fitted to each other perfectly. In no other way than this can the historian be understood (1). For is it credible, as all translators understand it, that the statue was divided from the crown of the head down to the private parts, as Jupiter is said, by the fable, to have cut through the middle, from above downwards, the first generation of double men? The Egyptians would have prized such a work just as little as they did the man whom Ptolemy the First exhibited to them, who, in this way, was half white and half black. In illustration of my explanation, I can adduce the Egyptian Antinoüs of the Capitoline museum, of which mention has been frequently made, as this figure consists of two halves, joined together below the hips, and below the edge of the apron; it would, therefore, be necessary to consider it as an imitation of the Egyptians even in this particular (2). This Antinoüs probably stood among the Egyptian deities in the Canopus, as it was called, in the villa of the

Emperor Adrian, at Tivoli, where it was found. But the mode of working of which Diodorus speaks could not have been adopted except in the case of a few colossal statues, because all other Egyptian statues are formed of a single piece. Diodorus himself, however, makes mention of many Egyptian colossi in one piece, of which a few have been preserved even to the present day : among them was the statue of the King Osymandyas, whose feet were seven ells in length (3).

3. All the Egyptian figures now extant are finished, smoothed, and polished, with infinite pains ; and there is not a single one that has been entirely finished with the chisel alone, as are a few of the best Greek statues of marble, because it was not possible, in this way, to give a smooth surface to granite and basalt. The figures on the points of the lofty obelisks are executed as images are which are designed to be examined within a short distance : this is evident on the Barberini obelisk, and especially on that of the Sun, both of which are lying on the ground. On the latter, the ear, especially, of a Sphinx is elaborated with so much knowledge and delicacy, that a more perfect, finished one is not to be found on Greek rilievi in marble. The same diligence is shown in a really antique Egyptian engraved gem of the Stosch museum, the execution of which does not yield in the least to that of the best Greek engraved gems. This gem, an onyx of extraordinary beauty, represents a seated Isis, and is engraved after the manner of the work on the obelisks ; and as a layer of white lies below the very thin stratum of brownish color, the proper color of the stone, the face, arms, and hands, together with the stool, have been cut so deeply as to reach this layer, for the purpose of having them white.

Occasionally, the Egyptian artists excavated the eyes, for the purpose of inserting eyeballs of a particular material, as may be seen in the above-mentioned Isis of the second style, in the Capitoline museum, in a head in the Albani villa, and in another broken-off head in the Altieri villa. In a head, together with the breast, in the latter villa, the eyes, which are of a different material, are fitted in so accurately, that they seem to have been poured in whilst in a liquid state ; and in the case of another head, in the Albani villa, made of the most beautiful reddish and fine-grained granite, the eyeballs are seen to have been finished by pointed tools, and not smoothed, like the head itself.

4. The other works of Egyptian sculpture consist of figures which are cut into the stone, and likewise raised; that is to say, they are raised of and by themselves, but not in regard to the works on which they are executed; for they lie below the surface of them. But works of the kind which we term rilievi were made by the artists of this nation only in bronze, — being formed in moulds, by casting. Among works of this sort there is a water vessel, or pail with a handle, which was used at sacrifices, and which is termed a *situla* by Roman authors, wherever they mention Egyptian usages; but it has been erroneously pronounced by him who first made it known as the article named *Vannus Iacchi*, the "Fan of Bacchus." It came afterwards into the possession of the celebrated Count Caylus, by whom it has been described: I shall presently have an opportunity to speak of it.

5. But when I assert that Egyptian rilievi, properly so called, were wrought only in bronze, I know very well that rilievi are found in Egyptian stones, as, for example, the above-mentioned Canopi of green basalt. But the reader will remember that I have placed these kinds of figures among the later imitations, which were executed in the time of the Romans. Here an attempt might be made to disprove my opinion by means of a female head of white marble, of the earliest Egyptian art, which is fixed in the wall of the residence of the Senator, on the Campidoglio, because it is apparently executed, not after the Egyptian, but after the Greek manner of forming relief. But if this head be examined through a good telescope, it will be found that it is the sole remaining part of a larger work, which in modern times has been set upon a tablet of marble; it is therefore probable that it also was formerly a rilievo within the marble in which it was executed (4).

6. In the second place, in regard to the material of which Egyptian works are executed, figures are found of burnt clay, wood, stone, and bronze.

Of small figures in burnt clay, a great number, as Count Caylus relates, are found in Cyprus, because this island was subject to the Ptolemies, and therefore probably peopled by Egyptians. Several of such figures, executed in the genuine antique style of their artists, and marked with hieroglyphs, have also been discovered in the temple of Isis at Pompeii; and I myself am the owner of five small priests of Isis of this kind; and several more are to be found in the museum of Mr. Hamilton, Minister Plenipotentiary of Great Britain at Naples. They all resemble each other; and they are coated over with a green enamel or polish. The hands are folded crosswise on the breast; in the left is a staff; in the right, together with the customary whip, is a band, to which is suspended a small tablet behind, on the left shoulder. This tablet, on two of the larger figures of the kind in the Herculaneum museum, is marked with hieroglyphs, — clearly to be discerned.

7. Wooden figures, shaped after the fashion of mummies, are preserved in several museums; three of the kind belong to the museum of the Roman College, one of which is painted.

8. Of Egyptian stones there are several kinds, as it is known; namely, granite, basalt, and porphyry.

9. Granite, which is supposed to be the Ethiopian marble of Herodotus, or the Thebaic stone, is of two kinds; namely, the black and white, and the red and whitish. The former is found in many countries, yet nowhere so perfect in color and hardness as the Egyptian; but the latter comes from Egypt alone. From this kind of granite all the obelisks are hewn; many statues, also, are found wrought from it, — among others, three of the largest in the Capitoline museum (5). The large Isis in the same place is made of a blackish granite; also a presumed Anubis, as large as life, of which mention has already been made, in the Albani villa (6), together with several others. These two are the largest figures of the kind. Granite of a coarser grain was most frequently used for pillars. It is asserted in many books, that one of the corner-pillars of the court of the Pantheon was executed from granite of the island of Elba, by order of Pope Alexander the Seventh; but this is a modern fable, for the column is of red granite, — a variety especially peculiar to Egypt.

10. The common basalt is a stone which may be compared with the lava of Vesuvius, with which all Naples is paved, and also with the pavement-stones of ancient Roman streets (7); to speak properly, basalt is a species of lava of a uniform color, as it is, most frequently, at the present day. But there are two kinds of basalt; namely, the black — the sort more commonly found — and the greenish. Of the former, animals in particular are executed, as, for instance, the Lions on the ascent to the Campidoglio, and the Sphinxes in the Borghese villa. But the

two largest Sphinxes, — the one in the Vatican and the other in the Giulia villa, — both being ten palms (7¼ ft. Eng.) in length, are of reddish granite. Among others, the two statues of the subsequent and later Egyptian style, above mentioned, in the Campidoglio, and a few smaller figures, are also of black basalt. Moreover, that statue of the Emperor Pescennius Niger, which, according to Spartian, was made of black stone, and was sent to him by the king of Thebes, was probably of basalt, and of the commonest sort of it too; it still stood in the days of the writer on the top of the emperor's residence in Rome, and was accompanied by a Greek inscription. The color of the stone pointed symbolically to the name of Niger. Neither Egypt nor Thebes had kings at that time; and therefore the statement cannot be understood in any other sense than as the act of a Roman commander, who was, as it were, in place of the king at Thebes, — as it has already been explained by me. The greenish basalt is found of different shades of green, and also of different degrees of hardness; and both Egyptian and Greek artists have worked in this stone. Of Egyptian figures from this stone, there is a small seated Anubis (8) in the Capitoline museum; also, in the Altieri villa, thighs and crossed legs; and a beautiful base with hieroglyphs, and the feet of a female figure on it, in the museum of the Roman College. These feet indicate that the figure would have been more beautiful than any of the works which we have from Egyptian artists. Heads of this kind of basalt are seen in the Albani and Altieri villas, and I myself possess a head, covered with a mitre, made from it. Of this same material, imitations of Egyptian works, as the Canopi are, were made in later times. Of Greek works, I know a head of Jupiter Serapis, in the Albani villa, wanting the chin, which it has not as yet been possible to restore (9), on account of the difficulty of finding stone of perfectly similar color; also, a head of an athlete with Pancratiast ears, which belongs to the Maltese ambassador now at Rome; and I am the owner of a beautiful, though mutilated, head of the black kind: I shall offer a conjecture in regard to both in another place.

11. Besides these, the usual stones, figures are also found in alabaster, breccia, marble, and the matrix of the emerald. Alabaster was quarried at Thebes in large blocks. In the museum of the Roman College there is a seated Isis with Horus in her lap, about two palms (17½ in. Eng.) in height, and another

smaller seated figure. Of larger statues of this stone, the sole one remaining is the one previously mentioned, which is found in the Albani villa; the upper part of it, having been lost, is replaced by alabaster of this country (10). The alabaster of the lower part, even to the hips, which is whitish, and has veins or layers still whiter, running in a sinuous and undulating direction, must not be confounded with another kind, which was also quarried near Thebes in Egypt, and Damascus in Syria, and by Pliny termed onyx, — not the precious stone of the same name, — which at first was used for splendid vases, but subsequently also for columns. It appears to be the kind of which the layers resemble in a degree those of the agate-onyx; and to this character it probably owes its name. Several vases of this valuable kind, and of different sizes, are contained in the villa of the Cardinal Alexander Albani; a few of them may be as large as an amphora. Pliny calls a vase of this shape *vas amphorale;* and at the time of Cornelius Nepos, it was the largest vessel that had ever been seen. One of the most beautiful of such long vases belongs to Prince Altieri, who found it a few years ago, while making excavations at his villa near Albano. The largest vase of alabaster, though not of the shape of an amphora, but of that of a pear, also not of onyx-alabaster, but rather of the former whiter sort, is in the Borghese villa; it was used to preserve the ashes of the dead, as shown by the following inscription on it : —

P. CLAVDIVS. P. F.
AP. N. AP. PRON.
PVLCHER. Q. QVÆSITOR.
PR. AVGVR.

This inscription is not to be found, at least not in Gruter's work. The individual whose ashes were contained in this splendid vase can be no other than the son of the infamous Publius Clodius or Claudius, — which may be ascertained by examining the register of the Claudian family.

12. Of porphyry there are two kinds found, — the red, termed Pyropœcilon by Pliny (11), and the greenish; the latter is the more rare, and sometimes it seems to be sprinkled with gold; Pliny states this of the Theban stone. Of the latter kind there are, however, no figures remaining, but only columns, and these are of extreme rareness. Two large columns stand outside of the gate of Santo Paolo, in the Church named

Alle Tre Fontane, on the farther side of St. Paul's Church; two others are in the Church of Santo Lorenzo, outside of Rome, but so walled in that only a small portion of them is visible. There were four in the Farnese palace, but they have been carried to Naples, and it is intended to use them in the gallery at Portici; and two smaller ones were taken to Portugal by Fuentes, a Portuguese ambassador to Rome at the beginning of the present century, on his return home. There were formerly in the Verospi palace at Rome two large, badly executed modern vases of this stone, and in the Albani villa a smaller but antique vase.

The extant statues of red porphyry, which, as we are told by Aristides, is quarried in Arabia, — and of which Assemann, custodian of the Vatican library, asserts that there are large mountains between the Red Sea and Mount Sinai, — are to be regarded either as works executed under the Ptolemies by Greek artists in Egypt, — which I shall hereafter adduce proofs to show, — or as made in the time of the Roman emperors; for most of them represent captive kings, with statues of whom the triumphal arches and other public works were ornamented. Two such kings are found in the Borghese villa, and two others in the Medici villa. A seated female figure in the Farnese palace belongs to this same period; the head and hands, which are bad, seem to have been made of bronze by Guglielmo della Porta. The upper part of a statue clad in armor, in the Farnese palace, was executed in Rome; for it was found in its present condition, not wholly finished, in the Campus Martius, as we are informed by the manuscripts of Pirro Ligorio, in the Vatican library. Of a more remote period, and of a higher style of art, are a Pallas in the Medici villa, the beautiful Juno, so called, with the inimitable robe, in the Borghese villa, both of which have heads, hands, and feet of marble, and a torso of a draped goddess, on the ascent to the Campidoglio. All three may, perchance, be works of Greek artists in Egypt, — as it will be shown in its appropriate place. Of the earliest Egyptian figures of porphyry there is only a single one, with the head of a Chimæra, known in our time; but it has been removed from Rome to Sicily. In the Labyrinth at Thebes there were statues of this stone (12).

13. It might be doubted whether porphyry was actually quarried in Egypt, since not a single traveller, so far as we

know, makes mention of quarries of porphyry existing there; and the doubt induces me to enter into a slight examination of this stone, and to state what I hope to prove through the knowledge which I have of granite.

In many countries of Europe, vast mountains of granite are known to exist; and in France houses are frequently built of it; in Spain, indeed, on the road from Alicant to Madrid, nothing but granite is seen. Now, as pieces of white granite, which can be ground to powder, are found beneath the lava of Vesuvius, and as they resemble the fragments of the large column of Antoninus Pius, which has been crumbled by fire, it follows that a granite of this kind from Vesuvius either is not perfectly matured, or, which is the more likely, has been melted by a fresh conflagration of the mountain. If, then, we compare with this fact the account of the burning of the Pyrenees in Spain, from the bosom of which silver is said to have flowed down its sides in streams, at some very early periods, and regard such burning as the fiery eruptions of this mountain, it becomes a probability that the granite of Spain, as well as that of other lands, must be produced by volcanic mountains.

14. This leads us, in the next place, to the origin of porphyry; for it is clear, from what I shall adduce, that it is produced in a similar manner to granite. M. Desmarest, an experienced natural philosopher, and Superintendent of Manufactures in France, has discovered in a few mountain ranges of this kingdom, and especially on a mountain not far from the city of Aix in Provence, red porphyry, though only in small pieces, and enclosed in the granite, as in a matrix; and large specks of the finest porphyry of a greenish-black color are discovered in many fragments of lava similarly disposed; indeed, it is affirmed that red porphyry is found in the mountainous ranges of Dalecarlia, in Sweden.

15. From the rarity of Egyptian figures in porphyry, it might even be conjectured that it is not an Egyptian stone; for during my residence of more than twelve years in Rome, there has been found only a single piece of a small Egyptian figure, made of red porphyry and characterized by hieroglyphics, and this has been removed from Rome, where it lay in the house of a stone-cutter, into the museum at Paris, by M. Desmarest, mentioned above. This doubt was also confirmed by the statement of the learned traveller, Mr. Wortley Montague, that

it was very rare to find a piece of porphyry in Lower Egypt, for the disturbed state of Upper Egypt did not allow him to go there. He wrote to me that, in the ruins of almost countless cities, he had seen only here and there a few small pieces of this stone; but that on the entire route from Cairo to Mount Sinai not a trace of it is to be found. According to his testimony, this stone is produced solely on the mountain of St. Katharine, which is still an hour's travel higher. It may be noticed, however, as the same writer remarks, at the end of three quarters of an hour's travel, though it is not of the best quality, for the red is much brighter than that of the porphyry frequently seen in Rome, and the white is not sufficiently compact, so that holes are visible in the white granules. The mingling of white and red produces a resemblance to those stones on which plants are found figured. This plant-like kind ceases at about half the ascent of this lofty mountain, and the stone becomes more compact and of a better color than it was farther down; but yet it is not to be compared with beautiful porphyry. This traveller, however, did not discover on the whole mountain any traces of a quarry. Finally, we have before us the testimony of Aristides, who says explicitly that porphyry came from Arabia, and we must therefore infer that both the Egyptians and the Romans — the latter especially, who made more frequent use of porphyry — procured this stone from quarries in the mountain ranges of Arabia.

16. If we now assume that granite originated like lava, it follows, from the above-mentioned discovery of porphyry in granite and lava, that porphyry may be produced in a similar way, and that, consequently, where beautiful granite is found, porphyry also may be sought and found; and it may therefore be inferred with great probability, that, as Egypt has sent forth the most beautiful granite, it may furnish porphyry too. The same ranges which produce red porphyry must yield, besides, the far more rare kind of a green color, since veins and large pieces of the latter are found in statues, columns, and tablets of the former. A large piece of green porphyry is observable on the left shoulder of a statue of red porphyry, in the Medici villa, which represents a captive king. Slabs of this sort are found in the church of Santo Lorenzo, in the pavement of the church of Santa Maria Maggiore, in the royal hall, *Sala regia,* so called, of the Vatican palace, in the Borghese villa, and in the Lancellotti

palace. But the clearest proof of the native land of porphyry
is afforded by an uncommonly hard stone of the kind termed
Breccia, of which I shall hereafter speak further.

17. Porphyry, on account of its intractable hardness, cannot,
like marble, be worked with a chisel, *scalpello,* or with the edge
of a broad tool, but it requires to be hammered little by little,
and with great patience, with picks sharpened to a point. In
this work, the progress of which is imperceptible, each blow
strikes out sparks of fire. When at length, after countless
repeated blows with a pick, — for a single year was not sufficient
for the completion of a draped statue, — the deep parts were
got out in the coarsest manner, then it was necessary to reduce
the whole by means of emery ; and this process of rubbing and
polishing required more than another year's time ; for several
artists could not conveniently labor at the same time on the
same statue. Now, as a work executed in this stone demands
infinite time and patience, it cannot but surprise us that skilful
Greek artists were found who were willing to submit to such
toilsome effort and tedious delay, in which the spirit is fettered
and the hand wearied, without enough progress to sustain and
gladden the eye. But in order to explain myself still more
clearly, the labor just noticed is done in the following manner.
The first hand, as the usual expression is, works upon it with
long iron bars hammered square to a point, termed *subbie,*
"chisels," by which pieces imperceptibly small are chipped off.
After the coarsest part is knocked off, a heavy hammer-shaped
tool, pointed at both ends, is next used ; and at last, on the
completion of this second stage, a tool shaped in precisely the
same way, except that it has a broad edge, is substituted ; and
with this the workman goes over the work several times, until
it is in a fit state for polishing. In this way statues and columns are executed ; and the artist, when at work, commonly
wears a particular kind of spectacles, in order to protect his
eyes from the fine dust which flies from the stone. The same
mode of proceeding is adopted with the Egyptian breccia, so
called, though all parts of it are not equally hard.

18. It is necessary to notice this stone, breccia, although
there has been preserved only a torso of a statue made of it.
It is a composite of innumerable other kinds of stone, and,
among them, of fragments of porphyry of each color, — a circumstance which induces me to believe that it was quarried in

Egypt. This stone was included under the generic Italian word *breccia,* a word which neither the Cruscan Academy nor that pitiful Florentine writer, Baldinucci, explains, though it ought to have been defined by both. We understand by breccia a stone which seemingly consists of many fragments of other stones; and this is, as Ménage rightly observes, the ground of its name, which he derives from the German word *brechen,* " to break." Now, as Egyptian stones are more conspicuous than any others in the conformation of this breccia, I have thought that we must give it the name of Egyptian breccia. The ground-color of the stone is green, of which an infinite number of shades and tints are observable in it, insomuch that, as I am assured, neither painter nor colorist has ever produced them; and the blending of them must appear wonderful in the eyes of those who are attentive observers of nature's productions. The torso of the statue mentioned above represents a seated captive king, who is dressed after the manner of barbarian nations; nothing is wanting but the extremities, the head and the hands, which were probably of white marble. It has been set up by the Cardinal Alexander Albani, in a special small edifice belonging to his villa, which is adorned with other works in the same stone. On each side of the statue stands a column, and in front of it a large round cup ten palms (7 ft. 4 in.) in diameter, of the same stone. Besides these pieces, there may be seen in the cathedral at Capua an antique bathing-tub of breccia, which now serves as a baptismal font.

19. The numerous extant works of white, black, and yellowish marble in Egypt, mentioned by writers of travels in this country, show that, besides granite, porphyry, and alabaster, different kinds of marble were also quarried there. The long and narrow passages of the largest pyramid are faced with white marble, which undoubtedly is not Parian marble, as Pliny has allowed himself to state. Even at the present day, fragments of obelisks, statues, and sphinxes of yellowish marble are still to be seen there, one of which is twenty-two feet in length; moreover, colossal statues of white marble. Still, I was for a long time doubtful in regard to Egyptian figures of white marble in Rome, notwithstanding the head on the Campidoglio, wrought in relief, of which mention has already been made; for this might possibly pass for only an imitation of the antique Egyptian style, since it is placed so high as to be beyond the reach

of accurate examination.   My doubts were, however, removed
by a fragment of a genuine Egyptian statue of white marble,
which is marked by hieroglyphs : it belongs to a stone-cutter in
the Campo Vaccino.   But I have been convinced that Egyptian
artists worked in such marble, particularly by the broken slabs
of it in the museum of the Roman College.   These show a
rilievo after the Egyptian style ; that is to say, it does not project beyond the surface of the marble, though it is in relief ; or,
to express myself more perspicuously, the raised work is formed
by cutting into the slabs.   One of the pieces shows the upper
part of the figure, of life-size, as low as the shoulder ; on them,
instead of a human head, are seen the long neck and head of a
bird, from which there rises straight upwards a tuft of feathers ;
the long bill is curved at its tip.   Nevertheless, this figure appears to have its human head, yet in such a manner that it is
entirely covered by the usual Egyptian hood, from which two
bands hang down as low as the breast, and by the neck and
head of the bird, which rise upward in order to conceal the face
of the figure.   A clearer idea of this shape can be formed from
a figure on the Isiac Table, so called, at Turin, which perfectly
resembles the one I am now describing.   Hence I believe that
two similar figures, painted on the first mummy described by
Alexander Gordon, did not have straight bills, as the engraving represents, but bills with the point curving downwards.
He errs, therefore, in common with Pignorius, when he holds
the head of this bird to be that of an ibis or stork, because the
latter has not a curved beak.   I have been told that it is an
African bird, named Acaviac ; this point, however, I leave to be
settled by the natural historians.   The work here described is
evidently a production of the earliest art among the Egyptians.
I am, on the other hand, doubtful as to a small male bust, in
the Herculaneum museum, executed with uncommon care, —
about half a palm (4.4 in. Eng.) in height, wearing a beard, and
made of a white marble called *Palombino*, — because all male
statues of Egyptians show a smooth chin, and also because the
beard is arranged after the fashion of the beard worn by Greek
Hermæ.   A piece of an obelisk of black marble has also been
found.   In the Albani villa there is the upper part of a large
statue in *rosso antico*, "antique red" ; but it was probably made,
as its style indicates, in the reign of the Emperor Adrian, in
whose villa at Tivoli the fragment was discovered.

20. There is only a single small seated figure, so far as we know, made of the plasma of emerald ; the socle as well as the column behind is characterized by hieroglyphs (13). It may be found in the Albani villa, and it is about a palm and a half (13 in. Eng.) in height. This rare stone is commonly regarded as the mother of emerald ; that is, the shell in which the gem is supposed to lie concealed ; but it is harder than any emerald ; whereas the reverse ought to be the case. For it is usually the same with gems as with fruits, whose rind is softer than the fruit which it contains. The opposite of this, however, is also found, since there are large flint-stones which incase petrified muscles, and consequently enclose a softer substance. In the Corsini palace may also be seen a few table-slabs (14), formed by putting together pieces of this rare gem.

21. Besides works in wood and stone by Egyptian artists, a few in bronze have been preserved. They consist of small figures, of the Isiac Table, so called, in the royal museum at Turin, of the sacrificial vessel or water-bucket mentioned above, and of a small oblong square base of about a palm and a half (13 in. Eng.) in length, with engraved figures and characters, in the Herculaneum museum. Of small figures, a multitude were found in the temple of Isis, discovered at Pompeii ; and from another figure, in the museum of Mr. Hamilton, it is seen that these small works were filled internally with lead, in order to make them stand more firmly. The largest of this kind of figures is an Isis with Horus on her lap, which was in the museum of the celebrated Count Caylus. Detached figures of bronze were occasionally coated with gypsum, and gilded, as a small Osiris shows, which was made known by the same writer. The base mentioned above has the true Egyptian form of the simple fluting peculiar to all the bases and structures of this people. On the middle of the front side is represented a long vessel moored by Egyptian rushes, in the middle of which a large bird sits ; on the bow, a figure is seated flat on the floor ; and on the stern stands an Anubis with a dog's head, steering the vessel. On both sides sit female figures with wings stretched forward, which are attached to the hips and cover their feet, — like the figures on the Maltese coins, as well as on the Isiac Table.

22. At the close of this chapter, and of the examination of the mechanical part of sculpture, I shall state what is known to

us of Egyptian painting, in regard to its kind and mode : the reader will easily perceive that I speak of painted mummies in particular.   In the investigation of this kind of painting, I appeal to the immortal Caylus, by whom it has been studied with the utmost diligence, especially in reference to the colors employed, and I have found his observations correct so far as regards the mummies which I have myself seen.

All the colors are dissolved in water, and more or less tempered with gum ; and all of them are laid on unmixed.   They are six in number, — white, black, blue, red, yellow, and green. The red and the blue, however, are those which present themselves most frequently, and they are ground pretty coarsely. The white, which consists of common white-lead (15), forms the coating of the linen cloth of the mummies, and constitutes what modern painters term the priming ; the outlines of the figures are then drawn in black on the white ground, and the ground itself forms the white of those parts which are designed to be of this color.

23. This kind of painting, however, is very unimportant when compared with that of which Norden gives an account.   He states that he found in Upper Egypt entire palaces, and the columns in them, thirty-two feet in circumference, completely covered with ornamental painting, insomuch that walls eighty feet in height were painted, and had colossal figures on them. The colors of these paintings are, as on the mummies, whole and unmixed, and each one is laid on by itself, but on a ground and by means of a cement which have rendered the duration of them everlasting, so that they, as well as the gilding, continue perfectly fresh after the lapse of some thousand years, and cannot be detached from the walls and columns by any violence.

24. I close this treatise upon the art of the Egyptians with the remark, that none of their coins have ever been discovered, by means of which we might have attained a more enlarged knowledge of their skill ; for the known Egyptian coins did not begin until after the time of Alexander the Great.   Hence we might doubt whether the ancient Egyptians had any coins stamped with dies, if some proof of it were not found in writers in regard to the obolus, as it is called, which was placed in the mouths of the dead.   On this account the mouths of the mummies, especially of those that are covered with paintings, like the one at Bologna, are destroyed by persons seeking for the

coins. This was done in the instance of the mummy just mentioned, in presence of the Cardinal Alexander Albani, by the missionary himself who brought it over as a gift to him; for after he had allowed it to be seen in an uninjured state, and to be inspected a long time, he suddenly, and before the by-standers had an opportunity to prevent him, tore open the mouth; he did not find however what he sought. Pococke speaks of three coins, but he does not communicate their age; yet they do not appear from the impression to have been made before the conquest of Egypt by the Persians.

25. In conclusion, let it be considered that a resemblance may be traced between Egyptian art, and the form of the country at the present day; and the history of it may be compared with an extensive desolate plain, which can be overlooked from two or three lofty towers. The entire circuit of ancient Egyptian art has two periods. Works from both are remaining; and from them we can form a reasonable judgment as to the art of the age in which they were executed. On the other hand, Greek and Etruscan art may be compared with the countries of Greece and Etruria, which are full of mountain ranges, and cannot therefore be overlooked; and hence I believe that, in the present treatise, I have thrown upon Egyptian art all the light needed.

CHAPTER V.

ART AMONG THE PHŒNICIANS AND PERSIANS.

HISTORICAL accounts and a few general statements comprise our knowledge of the art of these two nations. We have nothing definite to say in regard to the details of their drawing and figures. There is also little hope that larger and more important works of sculpture will be discovered, from which mcre light and knowledge might be obtained. But as coins by Phœnician artists, and rilievi by Persian, have been preserved, these nations could not be passed by without some mention in this history (1).

1. The Phœnicians inhabited the fairest shores of Asia and Africa on the Mediterranean Sea, besides other conquered territories ; and Carthage, one of their colonies, which according to some had been founded fifty years before the conquest of Troy, was situated in a climate so steadily even, that, by the account of later travellers, the thermometer at Tunis, where that celebrated city formerly had its site, always stands at the twenty-ninth or thirtieth degree (85° or 86° Fahrenheit).

2. Hence the conformation of this people — who, as Herodotus says, were the most healthy of all men — must have been very regular, and the drawing of their figures consequently correspondent to the conformation. Livy speaks of a young Numidian of extraordinary beauty, who was taken prisoner by Scipio in the battle with Asdrubal, near Bæcula, in Spain ; and the celebrated Carthaginian beauty Sophonisba, daughter of Asdrubal, who was first married to Syphax and afterwards to Masinissa, is familiar to all history.

3. The Phœnicians were, as Mela says, industrious, and had signalized themselves in the occupations of war and peace, as well as in the sciences, and in treatises upon them. The sciences were already flourishing among them at a time when the Greeks were an uninstructed people ; and Moschus of Sidon is said to have taught the atomic theory even before the Tro-

jan war. Astronomy and arithmetic, if not invented by them, were carried to a higher degree of excellence than elsewhere. But they are especially celebrated for their many inventions in the arts (2), and for this reason Homer terms the Sidonians great artists. We know that Solomon brought artisans from Phœnicia to build the Temple of the Lord and the house of the king ; among the Romans, too, the best wooden utensils were made by Carthaginian artisans ; hence in their ancient writers mention is made of Punic bedsteads, windows, presses, and hinges.

4. Abundance nurtured the arts ; for it is known what the prophets say of the splendor of Tyre. In this city, as Strabo relates, there were still in his time houses loftier even than those in Rome ; and Appian says that in Bursa, the inner portion of the city of Carthage, the houses were six stories in height. In their temples were gilded statues, as an Apollo at Carthage, for example ; even golden columns and statues of emerald are mentioned. Livy speaks of a silver shield, a hundred and thirty pounds in weight, on which was wrought a portrait of Asdrubal, the brother of Hannibal ; it was suspended in the Capitol.

5. The commerce of the Phœnicians extended through the whole world ; and the productions of their artists were probably circulated in every direction. Even in Greece they had built temples on the islands, of which, in the earliest ages, they were the possessors ; on the island of Thasus, the temple of that Hercules who was still older than the Greek Hercules. It would therefore be probable that the Phœnicians, who introduced the sciences among the Greeks, planted in Greece the arts also, which must have flourished among them at an earlier period, if other accounts, given above, were compatible with such a supposition. It is especially worthy of note, that Appian makes mention of Ionic columns at the arsenal in the harbor of Carthage. The Carthaginians had still greater intercourse with the Etruscans, who were among the number of the allies of the Carthaginians at the time when the latter were defeated on the sea by Hiero, king of Syracuse.

6. Winged deities are common among the Etruscans, as well as among the Phœnicians ; the deities of the latter, however, are winged more after the Egyptian manner, that is to say, the wings are attached to the hips, and overshadow the figures from

that point to the feet, as we see by the coins of the island of
Malta, which belonged to the Carthaginians; so that it might
seem as if the Phœnicians had learned from the Egyptians.
But the Carthaginian artists may also have been instructed,
at a later period, by the Greek works of art which they carried
away from Sicily, and which Scipio, after the capture of
Carthage, caused to be returned.

7. But of works of Phœnician art nothing remains but
Carthaginian coins, which were stamped in Spain, the island of
Malta, and Sicily (3). Of the first kind, ten pieces of the city
of Valencia are found in the Grand-Ducal museum at Florence,
which can bear comparison with the most beautiful coins of
Magna Græcia (4). The coins stamped in Sicily are so exquisite, that they are distinguishable from the best Greek coins
of the kind only by the Punic letters (5); and the Bishop
Lucchesi, at Girgenti, possesses a few of their gold coins; they
are exceedingly rare. Some of the silver coins have on the
obverse the head of Proserpine, and on the reverse a horse's
head together with a palm-tree; on others is the whole figure
of a horse standing by a palm (6). A Carthaginian artist,
by name Boethus, is cited, who executed ivory figures in the
temple of Juno at Elis. Of engraved gems, two only are
known to me; they are heads, and designated by the name
of the individual in Phœnician letters. I have spoken of them
in the *Description of the Engraved Gems in the Stosch Cabinet.*

8. Of the particulars of the clothing of their figures, the
coins give as little information as do writers. As far as I
remember, we do not know much more than that the garments
of the Phœnicians had uncommonly long sleeves; on this
account, an African personage in the comedies at Rome was
represented with such a robe; and it is believed that the
Carthaginians did not wear mantles (7). Striped stuffs must
have been very customary among them, as they were among
the Gauls, as proved by the Phœnician tradesman among the
painted figures of the Vatican copy of Terence. The epithet
discinctus, which the poets apply to the Africans and Lybians,
seems to point to the Carthaginians also, intimating that they
wore their mantles "ungirdled."

9. Of art among the Jews as neighbors of the Phœnicians,
we know still less than of that of the latter. As the Phœnician artists were sent for by the Jews, even in their flourishing

periods, it would seem as if the fine arts, which were regarded by them as a superfluity in the life of man, were also not practised for the very same reason. Sculpture was even forbidden by the Mosaic law, at least in regard to the representation of the deity in human form (8). The conformation of the Jews, like that of the Phœnicians, would, nevertheless, have been suitable for the expression of ideas of beauty.

10. Art must, however, have risen to a certain degree of excellence, I will not say in sculpture, but in drawing and artistic labor, notwithstanding the derogatory idea of it generally entertained among this people ; for Nebuchadnezzar carried away with him, from Jerusalem alone, a thousand artists who made inlaid work ; it will be difficult to find so large a number at the present day in the most populous cities. The Hebrew word signifying artists of this kind is not generally understood ; and it has been absurdly translated and explained by commentators as well as by lexicons, and occasionally even been entirely omitted.

11. Art among the Persians deserves some attention, because monuments of marble, on engraved gems, and of bronze, have been preserved. Those of marble are figures, wrought in relief, on the ruins of the city of Persepolis ; the engraved gems are cylindrical loadstones, and also chalcedonies, having a hole bored through their axis. Besides these, which I have seen in different collections of engraved gems, there are two in the museum of Count Caylus, by whom they have been made known. On one of them five figures are cut ; on the other, two ; on both are ancient Persian letters, arranged under each other in a column. The Duke of Caraffa Noja, at Naples, has four stones of this kind, which were formerly in the Stosch museum ; on one of these is ancient writing, also placed columnar-wise. The letters on the latter, as well as on the former, perfectly resemble those on the ruins of Persepolis. In the *Description of the Stosch Museum,* I have spoken of other Persian gems, and cited the one made known by Bianchini (9). A few gems without any letters on them have been considered as ancient Greek works by those who were ignorant of the style of Persian art ; and De Wilde has supposed that he saw on one of them the fable of Aristeas, and on another a Thracian king.

12. Besides a few antique Persian coins, only a single specimen of Persian works in bronze is known to me ; it is an oblong

square die, an inch in length, in the museum of Mr. Hamilton. It represents a male figure, — whose head as well as face appears to be covered with a helmet, — in the act of thrusting a sword through a lion that is rearing up in front of it ; which is a usual image, also, on the gems above mentioned. A silver coin might likewise be mentioned, on which is a four-horse chariot ; wherein stands a bearded figure wearing the customary Persian cap, together with another figure holding the reins ; on the reverse is a ship with oars, and a few unknown letters ; for this coin is supposed to have been stamped by Persian kings, prior to the age of Alexander the Great.

13. The testimony of the most ancient writers, that the Persians were well-shaped men, is also confirmed by a head, cut in relief, on a glass paste in the former Stosch museum ; it wears a helmet, is of tolerable size, and is surrounded by ancient Persian writing. The conformation of it is regular, and resembles that of the Western nations, as do the heads of the figures, larger than life, wrought in relief, at Persepolis, of which drawings have been made by Bruyn. Consequently, art had every advantage that could be derived from nature. The Parthians, who occupied a large portion of the former Persian kingdom, had a special regard for personal beauty, the possessors of which were placed in authority over others ; Surenas, general of King Orodes, was, in addition to other excellences, celebrated for the beauty of his shape ; notwithstanding, he rouged himself.

14. But it was apparently contrary to Persian ideas of propriety to represent figures in a nude state. Nakedness had a bad signification among them ; for, generally speaking, no Persian was seen without clothing. The same may also be said of the Arabians. The loftiest aim of art, therefore, the conformation of the nude, was not attempted by their artists ; the arrangement of the dress consequently became the object in view with them, not the shape of the nude body, as among the Greeks ; hence it was sufficient to represent a draped figure.

15. The dress of the Persians did not, probably, differ much from that of other Eastern nations. These latter wore an under garment of linen, and over it a woollen robe ; over the robe they threw a white mantle ; and they were fond of wearing figured garments. The robe of the Persians, which was cut square, probably resembled the square robe, so called, of the Greek women ; it had, as Strabo says, long sleeves reaching as far as

the fingers, into which they thrust their hands. But as their figures have no mantles, — the folds of which can be arranged in any desired mode, — perhaps because mantles do not seem to have been a customary garment in Persia, they are shaped, apparently, after one and the same model; those which are seen on engraved gems are perfectly similar to those on their buildings. The robe of the Persian men — female figures are not found on their monuments (10) — is frequently arranged in small folds like steps; and on a gem above mentioned, in the museum of the Duke of Noja, we can count eight such rows of folds from the shoulder to the feet; the cover of the seat of a stool, on another gem in the same museum, also hangs in similar ranges of folds or fringes down upon the trestle of the stool. A garment with large folds would have been looked upon by the ancient Persians as womanish.

16. The Persians allowed their hair to grow; and in some male figures it hangs down in front, over the shoulders, in strings or braids, as in the Etruscan figures; and they generally bound a fine cloth about their heads, a custom which has been perpetuated in the modern turban of Eastern lands. In war they usually wore a hat, shaped like a cylinder or tower; on engraved gems, caps with upturned rims, such as we see on fur caps (11), are also found.

17. Another cause of the slight progress of art among the Persians is their religious service, which was by no means favorable to art; for they believed that the gods could not or must not be figured in human form (12); the visible heavens and fire were the highest objects of their adoration; and the earliest Greek writers even maintained that they had neither temples nor altars. The Persian god, Mithras, can indeed be seen at several places in Rome, as in the Borghese, Albani, and Negroni villas, but we have no knowledge that he was represented in such a manner by the ancient Persians. It is more likely that the figures claimed to be representations of Mithras were executed by Greek or Roman artists, at Rome and during the time of the Cæsars, as the figure and execution prove. For every one sees that the artists of these two people have given to the figure of Mithras long hose and a Phrygian cap, as a distinguishing mark of a foreign divinity, this garb having been adopted in art to denote remote nations, whether to the north or to the south; hose were, it is true, common to the Persians, but not

Phrygian caps, so far as we know (13).   Plutarch relates that
the worship of Mithras was introduced by the Corsairs, — against
whom Pompey made war, and who were ultimately extirpated
by him, — and had continued ever since.   But the explanation
of the symbolic signs of this image has still less connection with
my plan, and, besides, it has been attempted by others.

18. Though religion among the Persians did but little to
stimulate the imagination, still we perceive from their works
that the invention and production of ideal figures was a characteristic of art ; for there are found on Persian engraved gems
beasts with wings and human heads, sometimes wearing serrated
crowns, and other fanciful creations and figures.

19. From the architecture of the Persians we discern that
they loved a profusion of ornaments, whereby the members of
their edifices, splendid of themselves, lost much of their grandeur.   The large columns at Persepolis have forty grooves, but
only three inches in breadth, whereas the Greek columns have
not more than twenty-four, and sometimes fewer, with a breadth
on a few of more than a span ; while those of the temple of
Jupiter at Girgenti were so large, that a stout man could put
himself within them, — an assertion which the ruins confirm
even at the present day.   But the flutes alone did not seem to
the Persians to give sufficient elegance to their columns, as
figures also were wrought in relief on the upper part of them.

20. From the little which has been adduced and said of the
art of the ancient Persians, we can draw this conclusion at least :
that art would not have profited much, even if more monuments
had been preserved.   The Persians themselves seem to have
been aware of the imperfection of their artists ; and this may
have been the cause why Telephanes, a sculptor of Phocis, in
Greece, wrought for the two Persian kings (14) Xerxes and
Darius.

21. At a subsequent period, when Parthia, once a portion of
the Persian empire, became a separate powerful kingdom, ruled
by its own kings, art also assumed a different aspect.   The
Greeks, who before the time of Alexander the Great constituted
the inhabitants of entire cities, even in Cappadocia, and in the
earliest ages had settled in Colchis, where they were called
Scythian Achæans, spread themselves abroad in Parthia also,
and introduced their language into the country to such an extent that Greek plays were performed at court by order of the

kings. .Artabazes, king of Armenia, whose daughter was the wife of Pacorus, the son of Orodes, had even left behind him Greek tragedies, histories, and orations, written with his own hand. The favorable disposition of the Parthian monarchs towards the Greeks and their language extended itself also to their artists ; and the coins of these kings, with Greek writing on them, must have been executed by Greek artists, though probably brought up and instructed in the East ; for in the impression of the coins there is something strange, and, it may be said, barbaric.

22. In conclusion, two general remarks may still be subjoined in regard to the art of the Southern and Eastern nations collectively, of which this second book has treated. If we consider the monarchical form of government among the Egyptians, as well as the Phœnicians and Persians, where the absolute ruler shared the highest honor with not one of the people, we can imagine that no other individual was rewarded by statues for his meritorious services to his native country, as was the case in free states, both ancient and modern ; we cannot, moreover, find any account of such an expression of gratitude having been received by a subject of these kingdoms. Carthage, indeed, was a free state in the country of the Phœnicians, and was governed by its own laws ; but the mutual jealousy of two powerful parties would have contested the honor of immortality to any one citizen. A general stood in danger of expiating each mistake by his head ; and history makes no mention of great testimonials of honor among them. Consequently, art in these nations was mostly dependent on religion, and could derive little advantage and increase from the habits of life of the common people. The artist's conceptions were, therefore, far more limited than among the Greeks, and his genius was tied by superstition to adopted forms.

23. These three people had probably little intercourse with each other in their palmy days (15). We know this to have been the case with the Egyptians ; and the Persians could have had but little commerce with the Phœnicians prior to the time of obtaining a footing on the coasts of the Mediterranean, which did not take place until late ; the letters, also, of the languages of the two people were entirely different from each other. The art, therefore, of each land was probably characteristic. Among the Persians, it appears to have made the least progress ; in

Egypt, it tended to grandeur; while among the Phœnicians elegance of execution was more an object of search, as we may infer from their coins. For with their commerce works of art also probably passed into other lands; it was not so with the Egyptians; and hence we may believe that the Phœnician artists wrought especially in metal, and executed works of a kind which would be generally pleasing. This may be the reason why we look upon a few small works in bronze as Greek (16), which in reality are Phœnician.

24. No antique statues are more shattered than the Egyptian, especially those of black stone. The violence of man contented itself with striking off the heads and arms of Greek statues, and tumbling from its base the remaining portion, which was broken by the fall; but the Egyptian statues, and likewise those executed by Greek artists from Egyptian stones, — as these would have suffered nothing from being thrown over, — were beaten to pieces with great violence; and the heads, which would have remained uninjured by being knocked off and flung away, were found shattered into many fragments. This violence was probably occasioned by the black color of the statues, and the idea, originating therefrom, that they were the works of the Prince of Darkness, and images of evil spirits, whom the imagination pictured as black shapes. It has occasionally happened, especially in regard to buildings, that that portion has been destroyed which, in all likelihood, time itself never would have spoiled; and that which might have suffered damage more easily, through all sorts of accidents, has remained standing, — an observation also made by Scamozzi in reference to the temple of Nerva, so called.

25. Finally, there still remain to be noticed, as something singular, a few small bronze figures, shaped in the Egyptian style, but marked with Arabic letters. Three of them are familiar to me; one of them belonged to the elder Assemann, now dead, custodian of the Vatican library; another is in the gallery of the Roman College; each of them is about a palm (8.8 in. Eng.) in height, and seated, and the latter has Arabic writing on both thighs, on the back, and on the top of the flat cap; the third — which was in the museum of the Count Caylus — is standing, and has Arabic writing on its back. The two former were found among the Druses, a tribe dwelling on Mount Lebanon; and it is probable that the third figure also

may have come from the same place. They are supposed to be descendants of the Franks who took refuge there during the Crusades (17) ; they wish to be styled Christians, but still they worship certain idols, like those mentioned, very secretly, from fear of the Turks; and as they seldom allow the figures to be seen, they are consequently to be regarded as a rarity in Europe.

BOOK III.

ART OF THE ETRUSCANS AND THEIR NEIGHBORS.

CHAPTER I.

PRELIMINARY REMARKS.

AFTER the Egyptians, the Etruscans were the first, of the nations of Europe, to practise the arts, which began to flourish among them even at an earlier date, as it appears, than among the Greeks. Hence, the art of the Etruscans, particularly in regard to its antiquity, merits more than ordinary attention, especially as their earliest works which have been preserved give us an idea of the most ancient Greek works which resembled them, but of which none are in existence.

A thorough consideration of Etruscan art requires, first of all, a brief notice of the earliest history and form of government of this people, as well as of their temperament ; because herein lie the causes of the progress of art among them. In the next place, I shall examine it, in a few of the most remarkable extant works, in reference to the characteristics which they exhibit ; and as the art of the neighboring nations bears a resemblance to that of the Etruscans, whatever we learn in regard to the latter throws light on the former.

1. The first chapter, which touches first upon the earliest history, the characters, and subsequent circumstances of the Etruscans, gives an account of the wandering of the Pelasgi to Etruria ; it then passes on to a comparison of the state of things in this land with that of Greece in the earliest ages. From this comparison, it appears clear that circumstances at that time, among the Etruscans, were far more favorable to art than they

were among the Greeks. But I shall chiefly attempt to show, in the first place, that, if art was not planted by the Greeks among the Etruscans, it had at least been much promoted by them. We infer this, partly from the Greek colonies which established themselves in Etruria, but yet more from the ideas drawn from Greek fable and history, which are represented by the Etruscan artists on the larger number of their works.

2. In regard to the Greek colonies which went to Etruria, we find in the ancient writers an account of two migrations, the first of which took place six hundred years prior to the other. This was the expedition of the Pelasgi who came from Arcadia, and of others who had resided in Athens. They were also called Tyrrhenians by Thucydides, Plutarch, and others, after having mentioned them under the name of Pelasgi. We may therefore infer, that the Tyrrhenians were a people who were embraced under the general name of Pelasgi. When their native land no longer had room for them, they divided into two parts, one of them crossing over to the coasts of Asia, the other to Etruria, principally to the country about Pisa, where they gave to the land which they seized the name of Tyrrhenia. The new-comers, associating themselves with the original occupants of the country, carried on a maritime trade earlier than the Greeks did, and, being jealous of the expedition of the Argonauts to Colchis, opposed them; and having assailed them with a powerful fleet near the Hellespont, a sanguinary battle took place, in which all the Greek heroes, Glaucus excepted, were wounded. This first colony to Etruria was, probably, strengthened by later arrivals, — to say nothing of the Lydians from Asia Minor, who, after the Trojan war, likewise despatched colonies thither. But as the art of drawing does not seem to have been known, during this period, either to the Greeks or to the Etruscans, the first migration of the Tyrrhenians to Etruria is foreign to my purpose.

3. The second migration of the Greeks to Etruria took place about three hundred years after Homer's time, and the same number of years before Herodotus, according to the calculation of time given by this historian himself; that is to say, in the days of Thales and of Lycurgus, the Spartan lawgiver. Strengthened by these fresh accessions, the Etruscans spread themselves throughout Italy, even to the outmost promontories of the land, — which was afterwards named Magna Græcia, as proved by

the coins of that age, in addition to the testimony of authors. Of these, I can mention, among others, one of silver in the museum of the Duke of Caraffa Noja; on one side of it, below the figure of an ox in relief, is stamped the name of the city of Buxentium, TV+OEM, and on the other side, below an ox stamped in deep, is the name of the city of Syrinos, MONZꟼZM, situated on the bay of Heraclea. By the possession of such an extent of territory, the Etruscans enlarged their commerce, and extended it so far as to form an alliance with the Phœnicians. When the Carthaginians, under command of Hamilcar, as allies of the Persians, invaded Sicily, and were defeated by Gelo, king of Syracuse, they united, notwithstanding, with the fleet of the Etruscans, and fell upon the Greeks in Italy, but were repulsed with great slaughter by Hiero, successor of Gelo. It appears from a rare silver coin of the city of Faleria, with the name of the city marked on it in Greek letters, that the Etruscans openly acknowledged its Greek origin. Faleria was one of the twelve chief cities of Etruria, and the site of it could not be a matter of dispute, as Dempster asserts. For the original wall round the town, constructed without mortar, of irregular white stones, as are the ancient fortress of Præneste, and the walls of Fiesole, Terracina, and Fondi, lies about two miles from Città Castellana, and the place is still called Falari.

4. That these new colonies introduced into Etruria their mode of writing with Greek letters, together with their mythology, and instructed the ignorant aboriginal Etruscans in their history unto the end of the Trojan war, and that through them the arts began to flourish in this land, is, in my opinion, manifest from the Etruscan works, most of which, if not all, represent the same mythology and the earliest incidents among the Greeks. For, if the Etruscans had understood the art of writing, they would not have allowed their entire ancient history to sink into oblivion; instead of the events of Greek history, they would have represented on their monuments those of their own land, but, from the want of writing, that is, of annals, they could not have any knowledge of them.

5. In opposition to this opinion, a few Etruscan works might be cited on which the Greek heroic stories are represented in a manner differing somewhat from the way in which they are related in Homer; as, for example, the fates of Hector and Achilles, on an Etruscan patera of bronze, — where the balance

is held, not by Jupiter, as the poet says, but by Mercury, — and several other incidents, of which I have made mention in my *Monuments of Antiquity.* On the patera just mentioned, which has been carried to England, the names of the figures, in the Etruscan language, are placed by them. But this deviation, instead of refuting what I have said, rather gives it additional confirmation, since the traditions of one land usually undergo some change in another; and in regard to the Etruscans, the variation may have been made by one of their poets.

6. The mythology of the Etruscan deities bears a great affinity to the Greek theology of the earliest ages, — as we see from numerous winged figures on Etruscan works. For, on the most ancient Greek representations, wings were given, according to Pausanias, to a far greater number of deities and other figures than was done by the artists of the enlightened ages of Greece. But the Etruscans gave wings not to nine divinities only, as Pliny relates; but it is also shown in my *Ancient Monuments* that they represented almost all the other divinities as winged.

7. But the most ancient and celebrated event, in which the most powerful states of Greece participated, is the league of the Argives against the Thebans, prior to the Trojan war, or the expedition of the seven heroes against Thebes. The recollection of this war, however, has not been preserved in the same manner on Greek as on Etruscan monuments. Five of the seven, and their names in the Etruscan language, are found engraved on a carnelian of the Stosch museum. Tydeus, one of the heroes, likewise with his name in Etruscan letters, may be seen on another carnelian in the same museum. Capaneus, another hero belonging to the expedition against Thebes, is found engraved on more than one gem, — which have not less the appearance of being the workmanship of Etruscan artists, — in the act of being hurled, by a thunderbolt of Jupiter, from the ladder with which he was attempting to scale the walls of Thebes. The other Greek heroes who, with their names, have been imaged on Etruscan gems, are Theseus, when a captive to King Aidoneus, — in the possession of the Baron von Riedesel; Peleus, the father of Achilles, and Achilles himself, in the museum of the Duke of Caraffa Noja, at Naples; and on another gem Achilles and Ulysses, likewise with their names in Etrus-

can letters ; so that we can assert that most of the monuments of Greek art which have been preserved must, in point of antiquity, yield to the Etruscan.　By these representations, drawn from Greek heroic story, the Etruscan artists had not only made it their own, but they also depicted Greek incidents of subsequent periods, — as it is proved by the Etruscan sepulchral urns of later times which have been explained by me in the *Ancient Monuments.*　On them is represented the hero Echetlus, who, during the battle of Marathon, appeared on the field, a stranger to all, and, at the head of the Athenians, slew the Persians with a plough instead of weapons, and hence was called Echetlus, from the portion of a plough named ἐχέτλη, and was honored like other heroes (1).　This image, which is preserved on no Greek monument, proves likewise that the Etruscan arts maintained a constant communication with those of Greece.　It is probable, however, from the primeval style of the engraved gems of which mention has been made, that art flourished even earlier among the Etruscans than among the Greeks themselves.　We may, also, presume this to have been the case by comparing the condition of the Greeks with the circumstances existing in Etruria at the periods subsequent to the second migration above mentioned.

8. From a few brief accounts which authors give us of the form of government of the Etruscans, showing clearly that it was uniform in its nature, we can infer — although we have to regret the loss of their earliest history — that they enjoyed profound peace after the Trojan war, whilst Greece remained in a continual state of distraction.　Etruria was divided into twelve parts, each of which had its special chief, termed Lucumo, and these Lucumons were subject to a common ruler or king, — such as Porsenna appears to have been.　That the constitution of the Etruscan state was of this nature may also be shown by the repugnance displayed towards the kings of other nations.　The dislike went so far, that, when the Veientes, who had previously had a republican government, elected a king, the Etruscans renounced alliance with them, and from friends became enemies.　The government of Etruria appears to have been rather democratic than aristocratic ; for neither war nor peace was negotiated elsewhere than in the public assemblies of the twelve tribes, composing the body of the state, which were held at Bolsena, in the temple of Vulturna.　A government of

this kind, in which each individual of the people participated, must necessarily exert an influence on the intelligence of the whole community, elevate their genius and perception, and render both fit for the practice of the arts. The peace, therefore, which was maintained in Etruria through the union and power of the whole people, whose rule embraced all Italy, was the most prominent cause of the flourishing condition of the arts among them.

9. Greece, on the contrary, with the exception of Arcadia, found itself, at the time of the second migration of the Pelasgi to Etruria, in the most lamentable condition ; rebellions, of frequent occurrence, rent asunder the ancient constitution, and subverted the entire state. The disorder commenced in the Peloponnesus, where the Achæans and the Ionians were the principal tribes. The descendants of Hercules, in order to reconquer this portion of Greece, came with an army, composed mostly of Dorians, who dwelt in Thessaly, and drove out the Achæans, a portion of whom, in return, dispossessed the Ionians. The other Achæans, inhabitants of Lacedæmon, and descendants of Æolus, fled at first to Thrace, and afterwards to Asia Minor, where they gave to the land of which they took possession the name of Æolia, and built Smyrna and other cities. A portion of the Ionians sought safety in Athens ; another portion went to Asia Minor under the lead of Nileus, a son of Codrus, the last Athenian king, and called their settlement Ionia. The Dorians, who were masters of the Peloponnesus, cultivated neither the arts nor the sciences ; they occupied themselves solely with agriculture, — αὐτουργοί τέ γάρ εἰσι Πελοπουνήσιοι, *for the Peloponnesians are tillers of the soil.*[1] But other parts of Greece were devastated and left unimproved ; the sea-coasts, where trade and navigation lay, were constantly visited by pirates ; and the inhabitants saw themselves compelled to remove from the sea, and abandon the fairest portion of the land. The more inland districts shared no better fate ; for the inhabitants mutually drove each other from their possessions ; and hence, as every one was obliged to go always armed, there was no security in cultivating the land, no quiet to think upon the arts.

10. Such was the state of affairs in Greece, when Etruria, tranquil and industrious, won and maintained for herself a

[1] Thucyd. lib. 1, c. 141, p. 93, l. 17.

degree of respect greater than was paid to any other nation of Italy ; and she attracted the entire trade, not only of the Etruscan Sea, but also of the Ionian, which she confirmed by her colonies in the most fertile islands of the Archipelago, and especially in the island of Lemnos. In this flourishing condition of the ancient nation of the Etruscans, united with the Tyrrhenians, the arts were blooming at a time when the first essays in them in Greece had come to naught ; and numerous specimens of their productions plainly show that they were executed before the Greeks themselves were able to produce any work of shapely appearance.

11. This brief sketch of the earliest history of the Etruscans reaches, however, to the period when the arts flourished among them ; and, owing to the favorable external circumstances of which mention has been made, they ought to have attained the highest state of perfection. But as this point was not reached, and as an excessive degree of hardness continued to characterize the drawing of their artists, — which will be shown hereafter, — the cause of the failure apparently lay in the character and temperament of the Etruscans ; at least, we must believe that subsequent circumstances obstructed the further progress of the arts among them.

12. The disposition of the Etruscans appears to have been more tinged with melancholy than was the case with the Greek race, — as we may infer from their religious services and their customs. Such a temperament is fitted to profound investigation, but it gives rise to emotions of too violent a nature, and the senses are not affected with that gentle agitation which renders the soul perfectly susceptible to beauty. This conjecture is grounded, in the first place, on the practice of soothsaying, which was invented, in the West, by this people ; hence Etruria is called the mother and producer of superstition ; and the books in which the art of divination was written filled with fear and terror those who had recourse to them for advice, — so terrible were the figures and words in which they were composed. An idea of their priests may be formed from those who, in the three hundred and ninety-ninth year of the city of Rome, with flaming torches and snakes in their hands, at the head of the Tarquinii, assaulted the Romans. Furthermore, we might infer a temperament of this kind from the sanguinary fights at their burials and on their arenas, which were first practised

among them, and afterwards introduced also by the Romans. These combats were an abhorrence to the refined Greeks (2), as I shall notice more fully in the following book (3). Even the self-inflicted scourging of modern times was an invention of Tuscany. Hence on Etruscan sepulchral urns are commonly seen representations of bloody fights over the dead (4). Roman funeral urns, on the contrary, rather have pleasing images, because the greater number were probably executed by Greeks. Most of them are fables, allusive to human life ; agreeable representations of death, as in the sleeping Endymion on numerous urns ; the Naiades carrying off Hylas (5) ; dances of the Bacchantes, and festivities, as, for example, the beautiful *Marriage of Peleus and Thetis*, in the Albani villa (6). Scipio Africanus desired that his friends would drink at his grave ; and among the Romans (7) dancers preceded the dead body.

13. But the prosperity of the Etruscans did not last long enough to enable them to overcome Nature, and her influence upon art. Soon after the establishment of the Republic at Rome, they were engaged in bloody and unsuccessful wars with the Romans ; and a few years subsequent to the death of Alexander the Great, the entire country was subdued by their enemies ; and even their language, after disguising itself little by little with the Roman, became lost. Etruria was converted into a Roman province after the last king, Ælius Volturinus, fell in battle near the sea of Lucumo, — events which happened in the four hundred and seventy-fourth year of the building of Rome, and in the one hundred and twenty-fourth Olympiad. Shortly afterwards, namely, in the four hundred and eighty-ninth year of the Roman reckoning of time, and in the one hundred and twenty-ninth Olympiad, Volsinium, now Bolsena, "a city of artists," — as the name, by some derived from the Phœnician, signifies, — was taken by Marcus Flavius Flaccus, and from this city alone two thousand statues were carried to Rome ; and it is probable that other cities also were stripped in a similar manner.

14. We may from this fact understand how it happened that Rome, in former times, in addition to an incredible number of Greek statues, was also filled with Etruscan works ; and how it happens that discoveries of such objects are still continually making. Art, however, continued to be practised among the

Etruscans at the time when they were subject to the Romans, as it was among the Greeks, since the latter suffered a common fate with them, as it will be shown hereafter. Of Etruscan artists we find no account by name, with the sole exception of Mnesarchus, the father of Pythagoras, who was a gem-engraver, and is said to have been a native of Thuscia or Etruria.

CHAPTER II.

CONFORMATION OF GODS AND HEROES, PECULIAR TO THE ETRUSCANS.

AFTER these preliminary remarks, I proceed to treat particularly the art of the Etruscans, and, in order to prepare the way for a more exact study and determination of its characteristics, I shall in the first place point out the peculiar conformation of the figures, especially of their deities. In the next place, I shall consider the most remarkable works, and by means of them be enabled to establish two different periods in the style of their artists. The chapter, therefore, is divided into two parts ; namely, one on the images of the deities and heroes, and the other a notice of the principal works.

1. In regard to the configuration and forms, together with the different attributes, of the Etruscan deities, it is not to be denied that the Greeks and the Etruscans agree in the greater number of instances, — a fact which indicates at once that the former colonized among the latter, and that a certain degree of intercourse was constantly kept up between them. There are, however, other conformations of the deities, which are peculiar to the Etruscans.

2. To us the representation of several of the Etruscan divinities appears strange ; but there were strange and extraordinary shapes among the Greeks also, as proved by the figures on the Box of Cypselus, of which Pausanias gives a description. As the heated and undisciplined imagination of the earliest poets sought for strange figures, and those which would make more impression upon the rude men of the times than pictures of beauty and tenderness, — partly to excite attention and wonder, and partly to arouse the passions, — so too, and for the same reasons, Art also in her infancy shaped forms of a similar kind. The conception of a Jupiter, enveloped in the dung of horses and other animals, — as he is represented by

the poet Pampho, who lived before Homer, — is not more strange than is, in the art of the Greeks, the image of Apomyos or Muscarius, whose figure is borrowed from a fly, so that the wings form the beard; the belly forms the face; and on the head, in the place of hair, is the head of the fly. He is represented in this shape on an engraved gem of the former Stosch museum, of which an engraving may be found in the *Ancient Monuments.*

3. The Etruscans formed noble conceptions and figures of the superior deities. I shall speak, in the first place generally, and afterwards particularly, of the attributes assigned to them. Wings are an attribute belonging to almost all the Etruscan divinities. Jupiter, on an Etruscan gem of the Stosch museum, has them; also on a glass paste and on a carnelian of the same museum, when he appears in his glory to Semele. Among the earliest Greeks Diana was winged; so too was she among the Etruscans; and the wings which have been given to the nymphs of this goddess, on a sepulchral urn in the Campidoglio, as well as on a rilievo in the Borghese villa, are probably derived from the most ancient images of them. Minerva, among the Etruscans, has wings not only on the shoulders, but also on the feet; and an English writer mistakes much when he asserts that not a single instance of a winged Minerva is to be found, nor even a mention of one by authors. Venus has, likewise, been represented with wings. The Etruscans attached wings to the heads of other deities, as Cupid, Proserpine, the Furies. Many winged Genii are seen on Etruscan funeral urns, especially of the subterranean graves of the very ancient Etruscan city of Tarquinium, near Corneto, of which I shall give an account hereafter. Among others, we see there a winged Genius, — who stands leaning on a crooked shepherd's staff, in conversation with a clothed female figure, — and two serpents, which raise themselves from the ground towards the Genius. The male figure might denote Tages, who was a Genius, or, as Festus says, a son of a Genius, and who, as the myth of the Etruscans related, sprang forth from a ploughed field. This Tages is said to have taught the Etruscans the art of divination, which they assiduously cultivated earlier than any other people; and the snakes seem to convey an allusion to the same circumstance. I do not, therefore, believe that a bronze child with a bulla about his neck can represent Tages, as

Buonarroti supposes, because he has no wings. It is singular that the Etruscan Genii are nude, with the exception of a cloth which has fallen down upon the hips, and covers the abdomen and the private parts, and half of the thighs. As neither the Genii on Greek works, nor on the Etruscan vases, so called, are thus represented, it may be regarded as one proof that these vases were not pictorially embellished by Etruscan artists. Even cars are found made with wings; but this, too, the Etruscans had in common with the Greeks; for Euripides gives to the Sun a winged car, and on the coins of Eleusis Ceres sits in a car of this kind, drawn by two serpents. Fable also speaks of another winged chariot belonging to Neptune, which Idas received through the aid of Apollo (1), for the purpose of carrying off Marpessa.

4. The Etruscans also armed nine divinities with the thunderbolt, as Pliny informs us; but neither he nor any one since tells who they are. But if we assemble together the deities who were thus fashioned by the Greeks, we shall find the number to be the same. Among the gods, in addition to Jupiter, the thunderbolt was also an attribute of that Apollo who was worshipped at Heliopolis in Assyria; and he is so represented on a coin of the city of Thyrra, in Acarnania. Mars battling with the Titans, on an antique glass paste, and Bacchus on an engraved gem, — both of which are in the Stosch museum, — have the same; with this attribute Bacchus is also seen on an Etruscan patera. Vulcan and Pan, in two small bronze figures, in the museum of the Roman College, and Hercules on a coin of Naxos, have the same emblem. Among the goddesses, the thunderbolt is attributed to Cybele, and to Pallas on coins of Pyrrhus, and also on other coins, and in a small figure of her in marble in the Negroni villa. I might also mention Cupid, on the shield of Alcibiades, holding the thunderbolt.

5. Of unusual modes of representing individual deities, I will mention, among the gods, Apollo with a hat thrown from his head backward upon his shoulders, just as Zethus, the brother of Amphion, is represented on two rilievi in Rome, — probably in allusion to his employment as a shepherd in the service of King Admetus; for those who cultivated the fields or lived in the country wore hats. In this manner the Greeks probably represented Aristæus, the son of Apollo and Cyrene, by whom they were instructed in the management of bees;

for Hesiod terms him the field Apollo. The hats were white. On a few Etruscan works Mercury has a pointed beard, which curves forwards. This is the most ancient form of their beards, — as I will show hereafter, — and Mercury is seen, with a beard so shaped, on a small round altar in the Campidoglio, and on a three-sided one in the Borghese villa.[1] The most ancient Greek statues of Mercury were also probably shaped in this manner; for a beard of this kind, only wedge-like, that is, broad and pointed like a wedge, was continued in their Hermæ. Mercury is also found, on undoubted Etruscan gems, with a helmet on his head. Among other emblems attributed to him is a short sword, shaped like a sickle, and resembling the one generally held by Saturn, with which he emasculated his father, Uranus; and this was the shape of the swords with which the Lydians and Carians in the army of Xerxes were armed. The sword in the hand of Mercury contained an allusion to the decapitation of Argus; for on a gem of the Stosch museum with Etruscan writing, he holds, at the same time, the sword in his right hand, and in his left the head of Argus, from which drops of blood are falling. But a small bronze Mercury, a span high, in the museum of Mr. Hamilton, Minister from Great Britain at Naples, is altogether extraordinary; for it is armed with a coat of mail, which has the usual pendants on its lower edge, but the thighs and legs are bare. This representation, like the helmet on the head of a statue of Mercury at Elis, points to his battle with the Titans, in which, according to Apollodorus, he was armed. Moreover, on a carnelian of the former Stosch museum, this deity is seen with a whole tortoise, which rests on his right shoulder in a manner resembling a hat that has fallen from the head. This image I have published in my *Ancient Monuments*, where I also make mention of a head of the same deity, of marble, which bears a tortoise, partly because a figure with such a covering of the head is likewise found represented at Thebes, in Egypt.

6. Among goddesses, a Juno, on the three-sided altar above mentioned, in the Borghese villa, is especially deserving of note, because she holds with both hands a pair of large tongs (2); and she was thus represented also by the Greeks. The figure is that of a Juno Martialis, a warlike Juno; and the

[1] Plate X.

PLATE X

tongs probably contained an allusion to a particular manner
of forming the order of battle to make an attack, which was
called *forceps;* and it was a saying, " To fight like a pair of
nippers," *forcipe et serra prœliari*, when an army so opened in
fighting as to enclose the enemy between, and was able to execute the same opening, if, whilst engaged in fighting in front,
it should be assailed in the rear. Venus was figured with a
dove in her hand; and in this manner she stands, draped, on
the above-mentioned triangular altar. On the same work is
another figure of a draped goddess, with a flower in her
hand (3), which might indicate another Venus; for she holds a
flower in a round work in the Campidoglio, described below;
she is also represented in this manner on the base of one of the
two beautiful triangular candelabra which were in the Barberini palace; these, however, are Greek productions. But a
statue with a dove, which Mr. Spence thinks he saw in Rome,
not long before my day, is now at least no longer here. He is
inclined to hold it as a Genius of Naples, and quotes two passages from a poet in regard to it. Some one adduces also a
small figure in the gallery at Florence, supposed to be an
Etruscan Venus, with an apple in the hand; perhaps the case
is the same with the apple as with the violin of a small bronze
Apollo in the same gallery, about the age of which Addison
ought not to have been in doubt, for it is evidently a modern
addition. The three Graces are seen draped, as with the earliest Greeks, on the oft-cited Borghese altar; they have taken
hold of each other, and are apparently engaged in dancing.
Gori supposes that he finds them in a nude state on a patera.

7. After these remarks upon the Etruscan images of the
deities, I will endeavor, in the second portion of this chapter,
to designate the principal works of Etruscan art, and thereby
be enabled to form a conclusion as to the drawing itself and
the style of the artists. But I am forced to regret that our
knowledge in this respect is so deficient, that we cannot always
venture to distinguish the Etruscan from the earliest Greek.
For on the one hand we are in doubt on account of the similarity between Etruscan and Greek works; and on the other,
there are a few works, which have been discovered in Tuscany,
that resemble Greek works of a good age (4). It may here be
observed, first of all, that antique Etruscan works differ from
the Greek in this particular; namely, very many of the former,

especially engravings on bronze or gems, have the name placed by the figures, whether the figures be of gods or of heroes, — a practice not usual among the Greeks when the arts were in their bloom. The contrary, indeed, is seen on a few engraved gems; among them I remember a small onyx, in the museum of the Duke of Caraffa Noja, on which, near a figure of Pallas, is written AΘH ΘHA, the goddess Pallas. But the shape of the letters, and the figure itself, point to a period when art was at a very low stage, when artists began to put around figures more than one row of letters.

8. The works to be pointed out consist of figures and statues, rilievi, engraved gems, engraved work on bronze, and paintings.

9. The word *figure*, as used here, includes the smaller images of bronze, and also animals. The former are not rare in museums, and I possess several myself. Among them are found pieces, by their shape and conformation belonging to the earliest age of Etruscan art, as it will be shown in the next section. Of the animals, the largest and most important is a Chimæra,[1] of bronze, in the gallery at Florence, which is composed of a lion of natural size and a goat; the Etruscan writing (5) on it proves it to have been the work of an Etruscan artist.

10. The statues, that is, figures of or under life-size, are some of them of bronze, and some of them of marble. Of bronze, there are two statues which are Etruscan, and two reputed to be Etruscan. The former have indisputable marks of their origin; one of them is in the Barberini palace; it is about four palms (2 ft. 11 in. Eng.) in height, and is probably a Genius (6); hence a cornucopia has been put into the hand in modern times. The second statue, which is in the gallery at Florence, is presumed to be an Haruspex (7); it is dressed like a Roman senator; and on the hem of the mantle is engraved Etruscan writing.[2] The former figure belongs, undoubtedly, to the earliest ages; the latter is of a later date, as we may conjecture from the smooth chin, and understand from the workmanship. We see that it is copied from life, and represents a particular individual; it would, therefore, if it had been made in earlier times, have had a beard (8), since the beard at that time was universally worn among the Etruscans, as it was by the most ancient Romans. The other two statues

[1] Plate XI.   [2] Plate XII.

PLATE XI

PLATE XII

of bronze, in regard to which it would be doubtful to decide between Grecian and Etruscan art, are a Minerva and a presumed Genius, both of the size of life. The lower half of the Minerva is very much injured (9); but the head, together with the breast, is in perfect preservation, and the shape of the head wholly resembles the Greek. The place where it was discovered, namely, Arezzo in Tuscany, is the sole ground for conjecturing it to be the production of an Etruscan artist. The Genius represents a young man of the size of life, and was found in the year 1530, at Pesaro, on the Adriatic (10). Now as this city was a Greek colony, we might suppose that Greek statues would be discovered there rather than Etruscan. Gori, indeed, imagines that he recognizes in the workmanship of the hair an Etruscan artist, and he compares, somewhat inappropriately, the manner in which it lies with that of fish-scales ; but the hair on a few heads of hard stone and of bronze, in Rome, as well as on some Herculaneum busts, is wrought in precisely the same way. This statue is, however, one of the most beautiful of the bronze statues which have come down to us from antiquity.

11. It is not easy to pass a decided opinion upon those marble statues which seem to be Etruscan, because they may possibly belong to the earlier period of Greek art ; and the probability always inclines more in favor of the latter than of the former. Hence an Apollo of this kind in the Capitoline museum, and another statue of the same deity in the Conti palace, — which was discovered about forty years ago, during the popedom of one of this family, in a small temple at the foot of the promontory of Circæum, now called Mount Circello (11), situated between Nettuno and Terracina, — may, with more certainty, be regarded as very ancient Greek productions than as Etruscan (12). These two statues of Apollo are somewhat larger than life, and have quivers which are suspended on the trunks of the trees against which they stand. Both are executed in the same style, with the difference only that the former appears to be more antique ; at least the hair over the forehead is arranged in small ringlets, whereas in the other it is executed with greater freedom. Neither will I undertake to assert that a figure, wrongly called a Vestal, in the Giustiniani palace (13), which probably is among the very oldest statues in Rome, or a Diana in the Herculaneum museum, which has every mark of Etruscan style, was executed by artists of this nation rather than by

Greeks.   In regard to the Vestal, so called, it is scarcely credible that such a figure, of which the feet are not even to be seen, was carried from Greece to Rome, when, from the statements of Pausanias, it is evident that the most ancient works in Greece were left undisturbed.   The Diana of the Herculaneum museum is represented in motion, as are most of the figures of this goddess.   The corners of the mouth are turned upwards, and the chin is rather small; but we see plainly that it is not intended to be a portrait, or to represent any individual, but that it is an imperfect configuration of beauty; nevertheless, the feet are uncommonly elegant, and none of more beauty are found on undoubted Greek figures.   Over the forehead, the hair hangs in small locks; on the temples, it falls in long strings down upon the shoulders; but it is tied behind at a distance from the head, which is surrounded by a diadem, whereon are eight red roses, wrought in relief.   The dress is painted white. The chemise or under-garment has wide sleeves, which are laid in crimped or pinched folds, and the short mantle, as well as the robe, in smoothed parallel folds.   The outer edge of the hem of the mantle is bordered by a narrow golden-yellow stripe, and directly above it passes a broader stripe of an orange color, with white flower-work, to denote embroidery; above this is a third stripe, also orange; and the hem of the robe is painted of the same color.   The strap of the quiver on the shoulder, which passes from the right shoulder across the chest, is red, like the straps of the sandals.   This statue stood in a small temple, belonging to a villa of the ancient ash-buried city of Pompeii.

12. The presumption of Etruscan workmanship would apply with the greatest probability to a statue of a priest, so called, larger than life, and ten palms (7 ft. 3 in. Eng.) in height, in the Albani villa, which has remained uninjured, with the exception of the arms; these are a restoration.   The attitude is perfectly upright, with the feet standing close to each other.   The folds of the robe, which is without sleeves, all lie parallel, and as if they were smoothed upon one another.   The sleeves of the under garment are laid in crimped pressed plaits.   I shall notice this sort of dress at the end of the following chapter, and more fully hereafter, in connection with female dress.   The hair above the forehead lies in small curled ringlets, resembling snail-shells, in the manner in which it is usually executed on the heads of Hermæ; it hangs down in front, over the shoulders on each side,

PLATE XIII

in four long serpentine bands ; behind — where it is cut off perfectly even, and tied at a distance from the head — it falls down below the tie in five long locks, which lie together, and have the shape in some degree of a hair bag, about a palm and a half in length.   A statue in the Mattei villa, which represents a woman far advanced in pregnancy, — probably a patroness of women in pregnancy or labor, as was Juno, too, — is also executed in a style very nearly resembling that of the priest, as it is called. It stands with the feet close together, in a straight direction, and parallel to each other, and supports her belly with both hands crossed.   The folds of the dress run in a straight line, and are not hollowed underneath, as in the Vestal mentioned above, but only denoted by an incision.

13. Of works executed in relief, I will content myself by selecting and describing four monuments, which follow each other step-wise, and according to their ages.   The first and most ancient, not only of the Etruscan, but also of all rilievi in Rome, stands in the Albani villa ; a copperplate engraving of it may be seen in the *Ancient Monuments,* for the first time published by me.   This work in five figures represents the goddess Leucothea,[1] who was called Ino before her deification ; she was one of the three daughters of Cadmus, king of Thebes ; her two sisters were named Semele and Agape.   Semele was, as it is well known, the mother of Bacchus, whose education was undertaken by his mother's sister, Ino ; and the child is here represented standing upon her lap.   She is sitting in a chair which is provided with a back, and also with arms, and to such a seat might even refer the epithet Εὔθρονος, *having a beautiful seat,* which Pindar bestows upon these daughters of Cadmus.   Upon her forehead she has a kind of fillet (diadem) placed, which is shaped like a sling ; that is, the band on the fore part of the head is three fingers in breadth, and is tied about the hair by means of two narrow bands on each side, thereby explaining the Σφενδόνη, in Aristophanes, as a kind of band worn about the head.   The hair is arranged upon the forehead and temples in crimped ringlets, and hangs straight down upon the shoulders and back. Opposite to her stand three Nymphs, by whom Bacchus was reared ; they are of different sizes, and the most forward of them, who is also the largest, holds the walking-strap of the young god.   The heads of all five figures very much resemble those of

[1] Plate XIII.

the Egyptians in the forms of the eyes — which are narrow and turned upwards — and mouth, which likewise is turned up at the corners.   Her garment is grooved with straight parallel folds, denoted by mere incisions (14), so that two lines are continually approximating each other.

14. The second rilievo of Etruscan art, of which a copperplate engraving is to be seen in my *Ancient Monuments,* is a round altar in the Capitoline museum, representing Mercury in company with Apollo[1] and Diana.   The drawing of the figures themselves, and especially the shape of Mercury, appears to leave no doubt in this case as to the Etruscan style.   For only in extant works of the Etruscans has Mercury a beard, and a beard, moreover, of the kind which we term Pantaloon's beard, because the personage so called in our comedies wears a beard, projecting forwards, of such a shape.   Mercury must, however, have been represented in the oldest Greek works also, not only bearded, but even with a beard resembling that on the altar (15) of which I now speak, as may be inferred from the epithet applied to him in the writings of Pollux, which does not signify a " twisted beard," *barba intorta,* as the commentators understand it (16), but a wedge-shaped beard ; and from this primeval form of a Greek Mercury, masks with such a beard seem to have been called Ἑρμώνεια.   If any one should feel disposed, on this account, to remain in doubt, in regard to the workmanship of this altar, between the Etruscan and the earliest Greek style, it does not show that my idea is incorrect; and a knowledge of the Etruscan style can equally well be derived from it, because, as I have already pointed out, the earliest Greek drawing was similar to the Etruscan (17).   The shape of the bow may here receive a passing observation, as it is curved only at the tips, the remainder of its length being almost entirely straight, just as it is shaped also on Greek works where Apollo and Hercules, each with a bow, are found together ; that is, where the latter is carrying off from the former the tripod at Delphos ; Hercules, however, is furnished with a Scythian bow, which was very much crooked (18), like the oldest Greek sigma.

15. The third rilievo is a four-sided altar, — formerly standing in the market-place at Albano, but now to be found in the Capitoline museum, — on which are pictured several of the labors of Hercules.   It might be objected that the parts of this

---

[1] Plate XIV.   See Plate X., Mercury.

PLATE XIV

PLATE XV

Hercules are, perchance, not represented more visibly and prominently than in the Farnese Hercules, and that from this circumstance we cannot infer the Etruscan origin of the work. This I must acknowledge; and I have no other distinctive mark than the beard, which is pointed, and of which, as well as of the hair of the head, the curls are signified by small rings, or rather small balls, arranged in rows, which is the most ancient style in the shape and execution of the beard.

16. The fourth, and a later, work of supposed Etruscan art is likewise found in the Capitoline museum, in the form of a round altar; and it is generally looked upon as such, since at present a large marble vase is firmly set upon it, to which it serves as a base. But in reality it is a well's mouth, *bocca di pozzo*, as is shown by the grooves worn on its inner edge by the rubbing of the cord of the bucket. Of this rilievo, which represents the twelve superior deities (19), there is a copperplate engraving in my *Ancient Monuments*.[1] Besides the style of the drawing, which has all the characteristics of Etruscan art, I thought that I might draw the same conclusion from the figure of a youthful Vulcan, without a beard, who stands in the act of opening Jupiter's forehead with a hammer, in order to hasten the birth of Pallas from his brain; for he is represented at such an age, and without a beard, in the performance of the same office, on undoubted Etruscan gems and sacrificial cups. But this conclusion is not of universal application, since the same divinities have been represented without a beard not by the most ancient Greeks alone; for Vulcan is also seen thus on coins of the islands of Lemnos and Lipari, in the museum of the Duke of Caraffa Noja at Naples, on Roman coins, and on lamps; likewise on a beautiful Greek rilievo in the palace of the Marquis Rondinini, which represents him as having already struck the seated and pregnant Jupiter the blow that is to give birth to Pallas. A copy of the work may be seen on the title-page of the second volume of my *Ancient Monuments*. In view of the drawing, it might be objected, in opposition to such opinion, that, as we know Cicero procured from Athens wells' mouths of this kind for his country residences, the earliest Greek style might have been imitated in this case from a similar work, since the ancients embellished them with rilievi, as it appears from the well near which Pamphus, one of the earliest sculptors, rep-

---

[1] Plate XV.; the upper half of the figure of Juno.

resented Ceres sorrowing over the rape of Proserpine ; and the objection is one not easily answered (20). But I repeat what I have already remarked in reference to the second of these works, that that, as well as this, may, on the same grounds, serve as an example of the Etruscan style.

17. From the engraved gems, I have selected partly the most ancient and partly the most beautiful, in order that the reader may form from them a more correct and thorough judgment. When he has before him works evidently of the highest Etruscan art, and which, with all their beauty, have imperfections, the remarks which I shall make upon them in the next chapter will have so much the greater force if applied to works of less merit. The three gems which I take as the basis of the following argument are, like most of the Etruscan engraved gems, Scarabæi, that is, stones having a beetle wrought on the raised and arched side of them. A hole is bored through them lengthwise ; but it cannot be known whether they were worn as an amulet about the neck, or whether they were set movably in a ring ; the latter is probable, from a golden pivot sticking in the hole of a stone of this kind in the Piombino museum.

18. One of the most antique engraved gems, not only among the Etruscan, but among all that are known, is unquestionably the carnelian in the Stosch museum, of which mention has already been made, representing a council of five of the seven Greek heroes in the expedition against Thebes.[1] As only five heroes appear here, we might believe — in order not to allege the want of space as a reason — that the Etruscan artist had taken a particular account as his guide on this point ; for as, according to Pausanias, there were more chiefs of this army than the seven introduced by Æschylus, so to others a less number than seven may have been known. The names placed by the figures show Polynices, Parthenopæus, Adrastus, Tydeus, and Amphiaraus ; and both the drawing and the letters testify to the remote antiquity of the gem. The figures, in which infinite industry and great delicacy of execution are combined with elegance of form of some parts, as the feet, — which is a proof of a skilful master, — point to an age when the head was, probably, scarcely a sixth part of the height, and the letters come nearer to their Pelasgic originals and to the earliest Greek letters than on other Etruscan works. This gem (21), among

[1] Plate XVI.

PLATE XVI

PLATE XVII

others, is sufficient refutation of a writer who makes the unfounded assertion that the Etruscan monuments of art are
works of their later periods.

19. The two other gems are, probably, the most beautiful of
all the Etruscan gems. One of them, likewise a carnelian, is
also in the Stosch museum; the other, of agate, belongs to Herr
Christian Dehn, in Rome. The former exhibits Tydeus, with
his name, in the act of drawing a javelin from his leg (22), in
which he had been wounded, having fallen into an ambuscade
of fifty Thebans, all of whom he slew with the exception of one.[1]
This figure, in the exactness with which the bones and muscles
are rendered, gives a proof of the correct knowledge of anatomy
possessed by the artist; but also at the same time of the hardness of the Etruscan style (23). The other gem represents
Peleus, the father of Achilles, with his name, in the act of
washing his hair at a fountain, which is intended to signify the
river Sperchius, in Thessaly; for he had made a vow that he
would cut off the hair of his son, and consecrate it to the river,
if he should return in safety from Troy (24). The boys of
Phigalia cut off their hair and consecrated it to the river of the
place; and Leucippus allowed his hair to grow for the river
Alpheus. We notice here, in reference to Greek heroes on
Etruscan works, what Pindar says of Peleus in particular, that
there is no land so remote, and so different in language, that
the fame of this hero, the son-in-law of the gods, has not
reached it.

20. The Etruscan artists, next to their skill in gem-engrav-
ing, have displayed their dexterity in engraving bronze, of
which numerous pateræ give proof. This utensil, which we
term a sacrificial basin, was used in pouring a libation either of
water, or wine, or honey, partly on the altar, and partly on the
victim, and is of different forms. Those which we see figured
in sacrifices, on Roman rilievi, are for the most part proper
round cups without handles; yet on such a work in the Albani
villa a patera is found, shaped after the Etruscan fashion, like
a flat plate, and having a handle; but in the Herculaneum
museum, many pateræ, which are deep cups that have been
hollowed out on a lathe, have a handle, commonly terminating
in a ram's head. The Etruscan pateræ, on the contrary, —
those of them at least on which figures are engraved, — resem-

[1] Plate XVII.

ble a flat dish surrounded by a low rim, and have a handle, of such a kind, however, that it must, in most of the specimens, on account of its too great shortness, have been inserted into a handle of another material. Those pateræ which had ornaments of the plant called *filix*, in Italian *felce*, "fern," are termed *pateræ felicatæ ;* but I know none of this sort. Where the ornaments were of ivy, the vessels were termed *pateræ hederatæ ;* most of them are ornamented in this way ; and I have one of them in my possession. Engraved works like these were termed by the Greeks κατάγλυφα, *kataglyphs.*

21. Of the coins, a few are among the very earliest monuments of Etruscan art ; and I have two of them before me which belong to an artist in Rome who has a museum of curiously rare Greek coins. They are made of a compound whitish metal, and are in very good preservation. On one side of them is an animal, which appears to be a stag ; and on the other are two figures, turned to the front, which resemble each other, and hold staves. These must have been the first essays of their art. The legs are two lines, terminating in round points, denoting the feet ; the left arm, which holds nothing, is slightly crooked, but from the shoulder down, a perpendicular line, and it reaches almost to the feet. The private parts are a little shorter ; they are unusually long in animals also, on the earliest coins and gems. The other coin has a head on one side, and a horse on the other.

22. This notice of Etruscan works according to their kinds, as given above, is the simplest form of classification, and not connected with any system. But in reference to art, and their antiquity, according to which they are to be studied in the next chapter, they should be arranged in the following order. The coins just mentioned, the rilievo of Leucothea, and probably also the cited statue in the Albani villa, likewise the bronze Genius in the Barberini palace, and the pregnant woman in the Mattei villa, appear to belong to the earliest age and to the first style. I consider the three goddesses on a round altar, together with the four-sided base on which are the labors of Hercules, — both in the Campidoglio, — as well as the above-mentioned large three-sided altar in the Borghese villa, and the two figures of Apollo in the Campidoglio and the Conti palace, as works of the next period, and of the second style. I also believe that the engraved gems previously

described are works rather of the second than of the first style, especially if they are compared with the Leucothea. Here, too, I would also place the well-curb, in the Capitoline museum, on which are executed the twelve superior deities, if we are willing to regard it as an Etruscan work. The bronze statues above mentioned, in the gallery at Florence, as well as the greater number, if not all, of the sepulchral urns known, — most of which were discovered at Volterra, — appear, in comparison with the works just designated, to belong to the last period of Etruscan art.

23. Furthermore, Etruscan paintings require some little notice ; but as no others have been preserved than those which were discovered in the ancient tombs of Tarquinii, one of the twelve chief cities of Etruria, it cannot seem a departure from my plan, if I preface it with an account of the last discovered covered tombs themselves.

24. All these tombs are made by digging into a soft stone, named Tufo. They are situated in a plain near Corneto, about three miles from the sea, and twelve miles on the other side of Città Vecchia. The entrance into them is from above through a round vertical shaft, which tapers conically from within outwardly towards the aperture. In this passage-way small holes, almost half the height of a man apart, are dug one over another, that serve as steps by which to enter the excavations ; the number of such steps was usually five. In one of these tombs there is an oblong urn for the reception of the dead body, dug out of the stone itself. The vault, or ceiling, of a portion of these tombs is cut so as to resemble the frame of the ceiling in chambers ; that of another portion resembles sunken squares, which are termed *lacunaria ;* a few of them have ornaments around their borders. In a few others of these tombs the ceiling is cut after the fashion of the ancient pavements, composed of small square slabs of equal sides, set on the narrower edge, in the manner of fish-bones, — a kind of workmanship which is hence termed *spina pesce.* The roof is supported by square pillars, in greater or less number, proportionate to the size of the tomb ; they are cut from the Tufo itself. Although these excavations were not lighted by any opening, — for the entrance from above was closed, — still, they are filled with embellishments, not only on the ceiling, but also on the walls and pillars. Among them may be noticed

the ornaments, called Mæanders.   A few, indeed, have a broad
painted stripe, which, in this case, serves as a substitute for a
frieze, extending around on all sides, and over the columns;
and a few columns are covered, from the bottom to the ceiling,
with large figures.   These paintings are executed on a thick
coating of mortar; a few of them can be discerned tolerably
well ; others, on the contrary, to which moisture or air has had
access, have partly disappeared.

25. The paintings of one of these excavations have been
published by Buonarroti in outlines, badly drawn ; but the
excavations of which I give an account are a later discovery,
and the pictures contained in them are more important.   Most
of the friezes depict fights, or acts of violence against the life of
some persons ; others represent the Etruscan doctrine of the
condition of souls after death.   In these we see, sometimes,
two black, winged Genii, with a hammer in one hand and a
serpent in the other, who are drawing, by the pole, a chariot,
in which sits the figure or soul of the deceased.   Sometimes,
two other Genii are pounding with long hammers a naked
male figure lying on the earth.   Among the class of paintings
first mentioned, we see, at times, regular battles between warriors, three of whom, nude figures, draw close to three others,
place their round shields so as to overlap, and fight in this
manner.   Some warriors have square shields; most of them
are nude.   In other combats, short swords, resembling daggers,
are thrust into the breasts of fallen figures by some above them.
An aged king, with a toothed crown around his head, is running towards such a scene of bloodshed.   It is probably the
oldest dentated royal crown that is found represented on ancient works.   This crown shows, also, the higher antiquity of
the diadem, the first use of it among the Greeks being assigned
by all the more modern writers to a time posterior to the
death of Alexander.   Just such a toothed crown is worn by a
male figure on two Etruscan sepulchral urns, which seems, likewise, to represent a king ; and also by a female figure on a vase
of terra-cotta.   There is also found on a Herculaneum painting
a nude, hovering, youthful male figure, which holds in its hand
a similar crown.   On another frieze, where neither of these
two kinds of conceptions is introduced, we see, among other
figures, a dressed woman, having on her head a cap that widens upwards, over which, as far as the middle of it, her robe is

drawn. Such a cap was termed by the ancient Greeks πυλέων, and it was, according to Pollux, a garb usual with women. The statue of Juno at Sparta had a similar head-dress; it is likewise seen on the Juno of Samos and of Sardis, on coins; Ceres, too, in a rilievo of the Albani villa, wears a similar cap. It may serve for further speculation, if I remark here, that, in the same place, between dancing female figures, a few are represented perfectly stiff, and after the Egyptian style. Probably these are deities, who had this, and no other, accepted shape. I say probably, because the paintings have suffered from mould, and all parts of them are, consequently, not distinguishable.

26. Among the paintings I include painted statues, — like the one in the Herculaneum museum, of which I have given a description, — and painted rilievi on funeral urns, the figures of which are covered with a white color, whereon the other colors are afterwards laid. A few of these have been published by Buonarroti.

An examination of an account of twelve urns of porphyry, which are said to have been at Chiusi, in Tuscany, but are not to be found at present, either there or elsewhere in Tuscany or Italy, will form a supplement to this chapter. They might possibly, if they ever existed, have been made of a stone bearing some resemblance to porphyry, especially as Leander Alberti gives the name of porphyry to such a stone found at Volterra. Gori, by whom the statement is quoted from a manuscript in the library of the Strozzi family, at Florence, also communicates an inscription on one of these urns; but the account seemed to me suspicious, and I therefore procured a perfect copy from the original. The circumstance itself, and the age of the manuscript, create suspicion. It is not credible, that the Grand-Dukes of Tuscany — all of whom have given great attention to everything relating to the arts and antiquity — should have allowed such rare pieces to leave the country, especially as they were probably discovered somewhere about the middle of the previous century. Furthermore, the letters of which the Strozzi manuscript is composed were all written between the years 1653 and 1660; and the one containing this account is of the year 1657, and written by one monk to another. I therefore hold the story to be a monkish legend. Gori himself has made alterations in it. In the first place, he has not given correctly the measures of the urns, as stated.   The letter mentions two braccie in height, and the same in length, — a Florentine braccia contains two and a half Roman palms (1 ft. 10 in. Eng.), — but Gori states only three palms (2 ft. 2 in. Eng.).   In the second place, the inscription in the original does not look very Etruscan; but, in print, this form and appearance have been given to it.

CHAPTER III.

STYLE OF ETRUSCAN ARTISTS.

HAVING, in the preceding chapters, given some introductory information in regard to the external circumstances and sources of Etruscan art, and the manner of representing the gods and heroes, and noticed some of its productions, I now direct the reader's attention to its attributes and characteristics, that is to say, to the style of the Etruscan artists. This will be the subject of the present chapter.

I will here make the general remark, that the characteristics whereby the Etruscan and the most ancient Greek style may be distinguished from each other, — which, apart from the drawing, might be derived from accidental things, as usages and dress, — may be deceptive. The Athenians, says Aristides, formed the arms of Pallas after a design which she had given them; but we cannot infer Greek workmanship from a Greek helmet of Pallas, or other figures. For Greek helmets, so called, are found even on indisputable Etruscan works; as, for example, the one worn by the Minerva on the oft-cited three-sided altar in the Borghese villa, and on a cup with Etruscan letters, in the museum of the College of St. Ignatius, at Rome.

1. The style of the Etruscan artists did not always remain uniformly the same, but, like the Egyptian and Grecian, it had different stages and epochs, from the simple shapes of their earliest periods until the bloom of their art, when, having been subsequently improved by an imitation of Greek works, as it is very probable, it finally assumed an appearance different from that of the earlier ages. These different stages in Etruscan art are to be well noted and accurately distinguished, in order that we may arrive at some degree of systematic knowledge in regard to it. After the Etruscans had been for a considerable time subject to the Romans, their art finally declined, — a decline which is visible in twenty-nine small bronze cups in the museum

of the above-mentioned college.   Of this number, those on which
the writing approximates to the Roman writing and language
are worse drawn and executed than the more ancient ones.   But,
further than this, we do not learn much of a definite nature;
and as art in its decline is of no style in itself, I abide by the
three epochs previously determined.

We can, therefore, fix three different styles of Etruscan art,
as we have already done in regard to Egyptian art, — the more
ancient, the later, and the improved style, or that which has
resulted from imitation of the Greeks.   In all three styles it
would be proper to speak, in the first place, of the drawing of
the nude, and, in the second, of draped figures; but as the dress
does not differ much, in its kinds, from the Greek, the few special remarks which might be needed in regard to it and its ornaments may be grouped together at the end of the chapter.

2.   The most ancient style is of the time when the Etruscans
extended themselves throughout all Italy, even to the outermost
promontories of Magna Græcia; and we can obtain a clear idea
of the drawing of this period from the rare silver coins which
were stamped in the cities of the lower part of Italy, — the
richest collection of which is contained in the museum of the
Duke of Caraffa Noja.

3.   The attributes of the elder and first style of the Etruscan
artists are, in the first place, the straight lines of their drawing,
together with the stiff attitudes and constrained action of their
figures, and, in the second place, their imperfect idea of beauty
of the face.   The first attribute consists in this, that the outline
of the figures sinks and swells but little; the consequence is,
the figures look thin and spindle-like, — notwithstanding Catullus says "the stout Etruscans," — because the muscles are
slightly marked.   This style is, consequently, deficient in
variety.   The cause of the stiffness in the attitudes is to be
found partly in the mode of drawing, but principally in the
ignorance of the earliest ages; for variety in position and action
cannot be expressed and figured without sufficient knowledge of
the body, and without freedom in drawing.   Art, like wisdom,
begins with self-knowledge.

4.   The second attribute, namely, an imperfect conception of
beauty of face, was common to the Etruscans, even as it was to
the Greeks in the infancy of their art.   The form of the head
is an elongated oval, which a pointed chin causes to seem rather

small ; the opening of the eyes is narrow, and turned obliquely upwards ; the eyes lie on a level with the eyebrow-bones ; and the corners of the mouth are likewise turned upwards.

These attributes are precisely the same with those which we defined as belonging to the earliest Egyptian figures ; and, thus, the statements which we made in the first chapter, derived from ancient authors, in regard to the similarity of Egyptian and Etruscan figures, become gradually more intelligible. We must conceive of the figures of this style as of a robe made simply with strait breadths, to which they who made it, and they who wore it, adhered for a long time. The former did not refine upon it ; the latter found it sufficient for a covering. The first artist drew a figure in a certain style ; others followed him. A certain cast of countenances, also, was adopted, from which the artist departed so much the less, that the earliest images were figures of the deities, each one of which must resemble another. Art, at that time, was like a bad system of instruction, which makes blind followers, and admits neither doubt nor inquiry. And drawing was like Anaxagoras's sun, which he and his scholars maintained to be a stone, in defiance of all perceivable evidence. Nature should have taught the artist ; but custom had become nature to him, and hence the difference between art and nature.

5. This first style is found in many small bronze figures, in addition to the coins mentioned ; and some of them perfectly resemble the Egyptian in the arms and feet, the former hanging down close to the sides, and the latter being placed parallel to each other. The statue in the Mattei villa, as well as the rilievo of Leucothea in the Albani villa, has all its characteristics. The drawing of the Genius in the Barberini palace is very flat, and without any special marking of the parts ; the feet stand on an even line, and the excavated eyes are opened flat, and drawn somewhat upwards. The robes of the statue in the Mattei villa, and of the figures on the rilievo, cannot be conceived in a more simple manner ; the folds, which are mere incisions, seem as if they were drawn with a comb. An attentive observer of the essential in antiquities will find this style also in a few other works in Rome, but not located in places equally celebrated and usually visited ; for example, on a male figure, seated on a stool, in a small rilievo in the court-yard of the Capponi mansion.

6. Notwithstanding all this want of skill in the drawing of figures, the earliest Etruscan artists attained, in their vases, to the knowledge of elegance of forms; that is, they had learnt that which is simply ideal and scientific, and had, on the contrary, continued deficient in the excellence acquired by imitation. This fact is shown by many vases, the drawing of the pictures on which indicates the very earliest style; and here I am able to adduce, in particular, a vase in the first volume of the *Hamilton Collection*, the front side of which presents a male figure, in a two-horse chariot, between two standing figures; on the back side, two other figures on horseback are painted. But still more remarkable is a vase of bronze, about a Roman palm and a half (13 in. Eng.) in diameter, which was once gilded, and on the belly of which the most pleasing ornaments are engraved. On the middle of the cover of it stands a nude male figure, half a palm (4.4 in. Eng.) in height, with a discus in the right hand; and on the rim are attached three smaller figures on horseback, one of which is riding, the other two are sitting sidewise on the horses; and both the figures and the horses are executed in the most ancient style. This vase was discovered about five years ago, in the vicinity of ancient Capua. When found it was full of ashes and bones. It is now in the possession of the royal intendant, the Chevalier Negroni, at Caserta.

7. But the Etruscan artists forsook this style, when they had attained a greater degree of knowledge. In the earliest ages they appear to have made more draped than nude figures, like the most ancient Greeks; but they now began to represent more frequently the nude. For it appears from some small figures of bronze, naked as far as the private parts, — which are concealed in a bag, tied by strings about the hips, — that it was considered contrary to decorum to represent figures entirely nude.

8. If we were disposed to judge from the earliest engraved gems of the Etruscans, we should believe that the first style had not been generally adopted, at least among the gem-engravers. For the rendering of figures on gems is knobby and globular, — characteristics which are the opposite of those mentioned as belonging to the first style; but one does not contradict the other. If their gems were engraved on a wheel, in the manner of the present day, as the appearance of them seems to show, then the easiest way of using the lathe was to work out and

produce a figure by spherical forms ; and the most ancient gem-engravers probably did not understand how to work with very pointed tools. Spherical forms, therefore, were not an elementary principle of art, but a mechanical process in execution. The engraved gems of their earliest times, however, are the opposite of their most ancient figures in marble and bronze ; and it is manifest from the former, that the improvement in art commenced with a strong degree of expression, and with a visible marking of the parts in their figures ; this is also evident in some works of marble ; and it is the characteristic of the most flourishing period of their art.

9. We are unable to determine, with any precision, the time when this style was perfectly formed ; but it is probable that it coincided with the improvement of Greek art. For we may look upon the time preceding and during the age of Phidias, as upon the restoration of the arts and sciences in more modern days, which did not commence in one country only, and afterwards spread itself abroad into other lands ; but man's entire nature appeared to be astir, at that epoch, in every land, and great inventions started up at once. In regard to Greece, at the period mentioned, this is true of all kinds of knowledge ; and it seems as if a universal spirit, which exerted an influence especially on art, inspiring and animating it, had also diffused itself, at that time, over other civilized nations.

10. We pass, therefore, from the first and more ancient Etruscan style to the second and subsequent. Its attributes and marks are, in part, a perceptible signification of the joints and muscles, and the arrangement of the hair in rows, and partly a constrained attitude and action, which in some figures is violent and exaggerated. In regard to the first attribute, the muscles are tumidly raised, and lie like hills ; the bones are sharply drawn, and rendered altogether too visibly ; hence, the style is hard and painful. But we must remark, that both modes of this attribute, namely, the strong marking of muscles and of bones, are not found constantly together in all sorts of works. In marble the muscles are not always very artificial because only divine figures have been preserved ; but exaggeration, especially in the drawing of the leg-bone, and a sharp and hard outline of the muscles of the calf of the leg, are visible in all of them.

It may be established as a rule, generally, that the Greeks

studied more the expression and marking of the muscles ; but
the Etruscans, of the bones.   If, therefore, I criticise a rare
and beautifully engraved gem, with this fact before me, and see
bones too strongly rendered, I am inclined to regard it as
Etruscan, although in other respects it would do honor to a
Greek artist.   It represents Theseus, after having slain Phæa,
— of which Plutarch makes mention.   Twenty years ago, this
carnelian was in the royal Farnese museum, at Capo di Monte,
in Naples ; but since that time it has been stolen ; and other
beautiful gems have disappeared, both before and since, from
the same place.   In the Stosch museum there is a carnelian on
which the same conception is engraved ; but the stone is stated
to be a chalcedony.   The former gem can also serve as an
instance of the difficulty of deciding between Etruscan and
Greek works of the elder style.

11. The arrangement of the hair in rows, not of the head
only, but also of the pubis, is found, without an exception too,
on all Etruscan figures, even those of beasts, — as we may notice
on the celebrated she-wolf of bronze, in the Campidoglio, giving
suck to Romulus and Remus.[1]   As this is probably the same
she-wolf which, in the time of Dionysius of Halicarnassus,
stood in a small temple on the Palatine hill, — that is, in the
temple of Romulus, now called Santo Theodoro, in which it
was discovered, — and as it, according to the same writer, was
held to be an ancient work of art, χάλκεα ποιήματα παλαιᾶς
ἐργασίας, it must consequently be regarded as a production of
Etruscan artists, whom the Romans, in their earliest existence,
employed.   Cicero says of a she-wolf of this kind, that it had
been injured by lightning, — an accident which occurred during
the consulship of Julius Cæsar and Bibulus (1) ; and an injury
of such a nature on the hinder leg — where there is a burst
fissure two fingers in breadth — of the animal of which we now
speak, seems to prove it to be the same one.   Dion Cassius
says, indeed, in the passage quoted, that the she-wolf which
was struck by lightning stood on the Capitol ; but this assertion may be a mistake, as the writer lived two hundred years
afterwards.   I wish, however, to observe in this place that
only the she-wolf is ancient ; the two children are a modern
addition.

12. The second characteristic of this style cannot be compre-

[1] Plate XVIII

PLATE XVIII

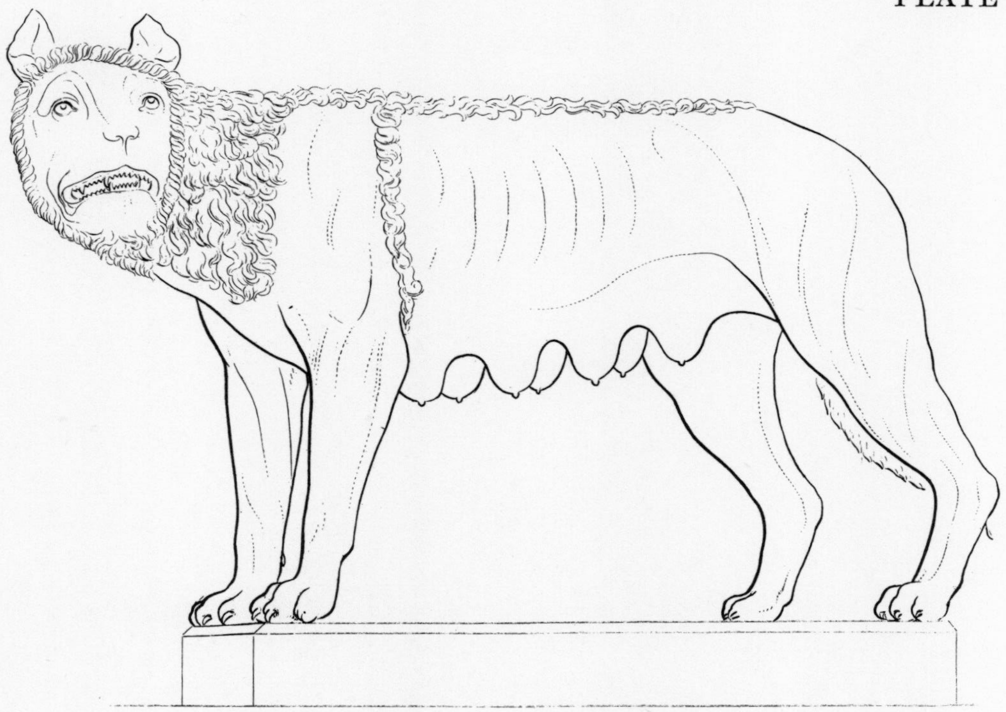

hended in a single idea; for constraint and violence are not one
and the same. The latter relates not only to attitude, action,
and expression, but also to the movement of all parts; the former
may, it is true, be said of the action, but it also consists with
the quietest position. Constraint is the opposite of naturalness; and violence is the reverse of decency and decorum.
The former is an attribute also of the first style; but the
latter belongs particularly to the second. Exaggeration in
attitude flows from the first attribute; for, in order to obtain
the desired strong expression, and the visible marking of the
bones and muscles, the figure was placed in attitudes and
actions in which they could be most strikingly manifested; and
the artist chose exaggeration instead of repose and stillness;
and feeling was, as it were, blown up, and swelled to its utmost
limits.

13. The remark which I have just made in general terms
may be illustrated, particularly, by individual figures and
works; and I refer the reader especially to Tydeus and Peleus,
and also to a bearded Mercury on the oft-mentioned Borghese
altar, who has the muscles of a Hercules. The collar-bones of
these small figures, the ribs, the cartilages of the elbow and
knees, and the joints of the hands and feet, are rendered as
prominently as the bones of the arms and legs; in regard to
Tydeus, even the point of the breast-bone is made visible. All
the muscles are in the most violent action, even those of
Peleus, in whose case there is less reason for it than with
Tydeus, of whom even the muscles under the arm are not forgotten. The constrained position shows itself on the round
altar before mentioned, in the Capitoline museum, and in several figures on the Borghese altar. Here, the feet of the goddesses placed in front are set close and parallel to each other;
and the feet of those who are seen sidewise stand in a straight
line one behind the other. The action of the hands, generally
of all figures, is constrained and unlearned, so that, when anything is held in the fore-fingers the others stick out stiff and
straight. Notwithstanding the great knowledge and skill in
execution possessed by the Etruscan artists, they were deficient
in conceptions of beauty; for the head of Tydeus is designed
after a common conformation, and the head of Peleus, not finer
in form, is twisted as much as his body out of its natural
shape.

14. The remark made by Pindar in regard to Vulcan, "that he was born without grace," might be applied, in some measure, to the figures of this style as well as of the first. Generally, this second style, compared with the Greek style of a good period, might be looked upon as a young man who has not enjoyed the advantages of a careful education, and whose desires and exuberant spirits, which impel him to acts of excess, have been left unchecked, — as such one, I say, when compared with a beautiful youth in whom a wise education and skilful instruction will control the ardor of the passions, and impart, by refinement of demeanor, greater elevation even to the admirable conformation of nature. This second style is, also, to be termed mannered, as we now say, — an expression which means nothing else than a constant uniformity of character in all sorts of figures; for Apollo, Mars, Hercules, and Vulcan, on Etruscan works, do not differ in drawing. Now, as a character always one and the same is no character, we might apply to the Etruscan artists the censure which Aristotle made of Zeuxis, namely, that they had no character; and we find the same fault to censure in the eulogies of celebrated persons, written in the modern style, in the histories of our time, — being usually composed in so indefinite and general a manner, that they might be attributed to a hundred others.

15. These characteristics of the ancient Etruscan artists still show forth, in modern days, in the works of their descendants, and to the eyes of impartial connoisseurs manifest themselves in the drawings of Michael Angelo, the greatest among them. Hence some one says, not without reason, that whoever has seen one figure by this artist, has seen them all. This mannerism also, is unquestionably, one of the imperfections of Daniel da Volterra, Pietro da Cortona, and others.

16. In regard to Etruscan dress I have nothing but this to remark, that in marble figures the mantle is never cast freely, being always placed in parallel folds, which run either vertically or diagonally. A free cast of the mantle is, however, seen in the case of two of the five Greek heroes; consequently, no general conclusion can be drawn from those works. The sleeves of the female under-garment are often broken into quite small crimped plaits, after the manner of the Italian surplice, *rocchetto,* of the cardinals and canons of some churches; but persons in Germany can form an idea of what I wish to signify, from the

round lanterns, made of paper, which are arranged in such folds, for the purpose of drawing them out and closing them again. A male figure also, namely, the statue noticed as being in the Albani villa, has sleeves of precisely the same kind. The hair of most male as well as female figures is so divided, that the portion which comes down from the crown of the head is tied behind, while the other portions fall in strings upon the shoulders, and hang down in front of them, — according to the usage of older times even among other nations. The same custom has been previously pointed out as existing among the Egyptians, and it will also be noticed of the Greeks, in one of the following books.

17. Hitherto, and in the first and second style, we have considered art under that form which was peculiar to the Etruscans, and prior to their attainment of a more intimate knowledge of Greek works ; that is to say, before the Greeks had acquired possession of the lower portion of Italy and of other lands on the Adriatic Sea, and compressed the Etruscans within narrower limits. After they had seized upon the most beautiful part of Italy, and founded powerful cities, the arts began to flourish among them, at an earlier date even than in Greece itself, and to diffuse light among their neighbors, the Etruscans, who still maintained themselves in Campania. Now as the latter, in the earliest ages, had represented the history of the Greeks on their monuments, and consequently recognized them as their teachers, the path was thus prepared for receiving instruction from them in art also. That this actually was the case is rendered probable by coins of most of the cities in Campania, which, according to their names in Etruscan letters, were stamped at the time when the cities were still inhabited by Etruscans ; for the heads of the divinities on them perfectly resemble the heads on Greek coins, and of Greek statues, so that even Jupiter, on Etruscan coins of the city of Capua, has the hair on the forehead arranged just as the Greeks fashioned it, in the manner which will be pointed out in a subsequent chapter.

18. This, therefore, is the third Etruscan style; and it is the style of the greater number of works of Etruscan art, especially the sepulchral urns of white alabaster of Volterra, which were all discovered in the year 1761, near the above-named city ; four of them are in the Albani villa. These urns are only three palms (26 in. Eng.) long, and one palm (8.80 in. Eng.) broad,

and consequently can have served for the preservation only of
the ashes of the dead.   A figure on the cover represents the deceased, half life-size, with the body raised and supporting itself
on one arm.   Three of such figures hold a cup, and one, a drink-
ing-horn.   It seems as if the feet had been sawed off because
there was not space enough on the cover.

CHAPTER IV.

ART OF THE NATIONS BORDERING ON THE ETRUSCANS.

THIS chapter contains a review of the art of the nations bordering on the Etruscans, — which I here embrace in one group, — namely, of the Samnites, Volsci, and Campanians, and of the latter especially; for among them art flourished not less than among the Etruscans. The chapter concludes with an account of some figures that were discovered in the island of Sardinia.

1. Of the works of art of the Samnites and Volsci, nothing, so far as we know, has been preserved (1), with the exception of a couple of coins; but of the Campanians, we have coins and earthen painted vases. I can, therefore, give only general accounts of the form of government and mode of life of the former, from which conclusions might be drawn in regard to art among them : this is the first part of the present chapter; the second treats of the works of art of the Campanians.

2. It is probably the same with the art of the two former nations as with their language, which was the Oscic. It would at least not differ much from the Etruscan, even if it is not to be regarded as one of its dialects. But as we do not know the difference in dialect of these two nations, so are we also deficient in that knowledge which would enable us to point out the characteristics of their coins or engraved gems, if perchance any of them have been preserved.

3. The Samnites were fond of splendor, and, although a warlike people, were very much devoted to the pleasures of life. In war, their shields were inlaid, some with gold, others with silver; and at a time when the Romans did not, apparently, know much of linen fabrics, the picked men of the Samnites, even when in the field, wore linen robes; and Livy relates that the entire camp of the Samnites, in the war with the Romans under the Consul Lucius Papirius Cursor, which embraced a

square of two hundred paces on each side, was enclosed by linen-cloths (2). Capua — which was built by the Etruscans, and, according to Livy, was a city of the Samnites, that is, as he states elsewhere, had been taken from the former by the latter — was celebrated for its voluptuousness and effeminacy.

4. The Volsci, like the Etruscans and other neighboring nations, had an aristocratic form of government. On this account, they elected a king or leader only on the breaking out of war ; and the organization of the Samnites resembled that of Sparta and Crete. The frequent ruins of destroyed cities on hills situated near to each other still testify to the numerous population of this nation ; and the history of their many sanguinary wars with the Romans, who did not succeed in subduing them until after twenty-four triumphs, tells of their strength. A numerous population and a love of show excited intellectual and bodily activity, and freedom elevated the soul : these are circumstances very favorable to art.

5. In the most remote periods, the Romans employed the artists of both nations. Tarquinius Priscus procured from Fregellæ, in the country of the Volsci, an artist, named Turrianus, who made a statue of Jupiter, of terra-cotta ; and from the great similarity of a coin of the Servilius family of Rome to a Samnite coin, it has been conjectured that it was stamped by Samnite artists. On a very ancient coin of Anxur, a city of the Volsci, now Terracina, there is a beautiful head of Pallas.

6. The Campanians were a people to whom the soft climate which they enjoyed, and the rich soil which they cultivated, imparted voluptuous tastes. The country occupied by them, as well as that of the Samnites, was, in the earliest times, included in Etruria ; but the people did not belong to the Etruscan state ; they had an independent existence. Afterwards, the Greeks came, settled in the country, and also introduced their arts, — proof of which can still be found, apart from the Greek coins of Naples, in the coins of Cumæ, which are yet more ancient.

7. I do not wish to show, here, that Cumæ was a more ancient city than Naples, because both were built at the same time, — the former by Megasthenes, the latter by Hippocles. The two sailed simultaneously from Cumæ in Eubœa, their native land, with a company formed of the surplus population of the city, and sought their fortunes elsewhere ; this has been

proved by Martorelli more clearly than it was previously
known. But coins of Cumæ, older than any of Naples, have
been preserved ; and my intention is to remark that both cities
were founded in the most remote ages, though we cannot state
the exact date ; Strabo says that Cumæ was the oldest Greek
city of all those in Sicily and Italy. Citizens of Chalcis, the
capital city of Eubœa, settled on an island, not far from Naples,
which was then called Pithecusæ, the Ischia of modern days ;
but they forsook it on account of the frequent recurrence of
earthquakes and volcanic eruptions, one portion of them building Naples on the neighboring coast, and another going further
towards Vesuvius, where they founded Nola ; hence, the coins
of this city are impressed with Greek letters. I omit several
other Greek cities, — as Dicæarchea, afterwards called Puteoli,
— which were built by Greeks at a later period, because the
whole shore of the country was then inhabited by them ; consequently, they also practised their arts here at an early date,
and at the same time, probably, taught their neighbors, the
Campanians, who dwelt in the heart of the land. We understand, therefore, by what nation a portion of the vases of terra-
cotta which have been frequently disinterred in Campania, and
especially about Nola, from the tombs there, were executed
and painted. But if we are willing to relinquish to the Campanians the honor of many of these productions, it cannot be
derogatory to them if we regard them as scholars of the Greek
artists. No proof of this would be requisite, if it be true, as
Diodorus asserts, that the Campanians did not begin until the
eighty-fifth Olympiad to be a distinct nation.

8. We must, unquestionably, regard as Campanian works,
peculiar to this people, the coins of those cities which lay in
the heart of the land, — whither the Greeks led no colonies, —
as Capua, Teanum, now Tiano, and other places, because they
are marked with the letters of the Campanian language, which,
from its resemblance to the Etruscan, has been held by some
of the learned to be Punic, as, for example, by Bianchini in
regard to a coin of Capua ; but Maffei acknowledges his ignorance of the signification of the letters on the same coin. The
letters on a coin of Tiano are held to be Punic in the book of
Pembroke coins. Now, as the writing is a proof that it was
adopted by the Campanians from the Etruscans, so, on the
other hand, the impress of the coins does not show the style of

Etruscan art, — which perhaps had been, at some former time, that of the Campanian artists, — but seems to confirm, by the drawing, exactly what I have already asserted to be the case. The head of a young Hercules on coins of both cities, and the head of Jupiter on those of Capua, are drawn after the highest idea of beauty; and a Victoria, standing on a four-horse chariot, on coins of the latter city, is not distinguishable from a Greek impression.

9. The coins, however, of the Campanian cities are few in number compared with the above-mentioned painted vases, which have been discovered at all times in this district, and which are commonly, though erroneously, called Etruscan, in accordance with the opinions of Buonarroti and Gori, by whom copies of them were, for the first time, made known. Being Tuscans, they sought, for the honor of their country, to appropriate these works to the Etruscans.

10. The grounds of this claim are in part the accounts of the vases, once so popular, which were made in Tuscany, and especially at Arezzo, an Etruscan city, and in part the similarity between many pictures on those vessels and the representations engraved on the bronze Etruscan sacrificial basins. The figures of Fauns with horses' tails, in particular, are cited on this point, because the tails of Greek Fauns and Satyrs are short, and resemble the tails of goats. They might also have appealed to the birds, of unknown kinds, which are painted on some of the vessels, because Pliny says that, in the soothsaying books of the Etruscans, there were representations of birds with which he was totally unacquainted. I must, however, remark in this place, that a large unknown bird is also found on a vase, marked with the most ancient Greek writing, and exhibiting a chase, in the museum of Mr. Hamilton, minister from Great Britain at Naples, which has been frequently cited by me. It resembles a bustard, — a bird which was known to the ancient Romans, but in modern days, in the warmer parts of Italy at least, is quite a stranger. I omit here the unimportant comments of Buonarroti concerning crowns and vases in the hand of Bacchus, playthings, and instruments, and square caskets, some of which he has not seen at all on Greek works, and some of which he has seen of a different form. But he had far too much experience to assert what Gori positively, though wrongly, imputes to him, that the divinities and the fabulous history which are rep-

resented on vases of this kind are very different from the same
representations in Greek pictures; for the contrary could have
been demonstrated to him.   The opinion of Gori himself, on the
other hand, is absolutely of no weight in this instance, since he
was never out of Florence, and consequently has no personal
knowledge of that larger portion of antiquities and ancient works
of art which exists outside of his native city.   But, finally, —
as it cannot be denied that the greater number of the vases made
known by those learned men were discovered in the kingdom of
Naples, — they had recourse, in behalf of their presumed native
land, even to the earliest period of history, and to times when
the Etruscans were spread throughout all Italy, not considering
that the drawing of most of these paintings pointed to far later
times, and to those in which art had either attained its perfection, or was beginning to approach it, according as the vases are
more or less ancient.   An account of vases of this kind, actually
exhumed in Tuscany, would have been no weak ground on which
to uphold the common opinion in favor of the Etruscans; but
of these no one has made mention.

11. I am willing to acknowledge that some few vases of this
kind, which are exhibited in the Grand-Ducal gallery, were found
in Tuscany, though it cannot be proved.   I also know that small
fragments of vessels, made of terra-cotta, have been discovered
near the Etruscan tombs in the vicinity of Corneto.   On the
other hand, it is not to be denied that all the large collections
existing in Italy, as well as those pieces which have been removed to the other side of the Alps, were discovered in the kingdom of Naples, principally near Nola, and extracted from the
ancient tombs of this city.   Still, the unquestionable certainty
of this fact does not determine everything that is required in
order to understand and form a judgment of these vessels, since
we know, — as I have but recently cited a passage to show, —
that Nola was a colony of the Greeks, and that a large portion
of those known to us are painted with Greek drawings, and a
few have Greek letters on them, — as I shall point out more
clearly.   If, therefore, we deny that the artists of Etruria proper
had any share in the production of these vases, whose style,
notwithstanding, is distinctly shown in very many of them,
whilst, on the contrary, others manifestly proceed from Greek
artists, our judgment hangs suspended between the Campanians
and the Greeks; and hence a clearer explanation is requisite.

12. It is very probable that vases by Campanian artists are found among this painted pottery, inasmuch as the earthen vessels of Campania, *Campana supellex,* are mentioned even by Horace; he speaks of them, however, only in making mention of his household articles of trifling value. But this conclusion may be formed with more certainty from the style of drawing on some few of the pieces, which, as I have said, resembles Etruscan drawing; and there may be the same ground for the similarity as for the possession by the Campanians of a sort of Etruscan writing. As the Tyrrhenians or most ancient Etruscans had spread themselves throughout Campania, even into the land which was afterwards called Magna Græcia, and the Campanians, consequently, are to be regarded as their descendants, the letters introduced by them, and also the drawing of their artists will, in this way, have been preserved here. Even the artisans of the Campanians wrought differently from the Greeks and Sicilians, as Pliny remarks of the cabinet-makers, in particular, among them.

13. But, to conclude, the principal proof against the Tuscans is furnished partly by the most beautiful of the vases of this kind, which were discovered and collected in Sicily, and which, according to the account of my friend, the Baron von Riedesel, — who, as a connoisseur of antiquities and arts, travelled throughout Sicily and Magna Græcia, — perfectly resemble the most beautiful vases that are contained in the museums at Naples; and partly by the Greek writing on several of them.

14. Three vases, marked with Greek writing, are contained in the Mastrilli collection at Naples, which were made known, for the first time, by the Canon Mazzochi, badly drawn, and worse engraved; but they appeared afterwards more correctly drawn, at the same time with the *Hamilton Vases.* Another vase, with the inscription ΚΑΛΛΙΚΛΕΣ ΚΑΛΟΣ, " The Beautiful Kallicles," is contained in the same collection; there is, moreover, to be seen there a cup of terra-cotta, with Greek letters on it. But the most ancient writing of all is on the above-mentioned vase belonging to Mr. Hamilton; and in the following chapter I shall make mention anew of these, as well as of other pieces marked with Greek writing. Now, as not a single one of these works with Etruscan writing on it has hitherto been discovered, it follows of course that the letters, no longer to be distinguished, on two beautiful vases in the collection of Signor

Mengs, at Rome, are not Etruscan, but Greek : one of them I have published in my *Ancient Monuments* (3). On a vase in the Vatican library, which I have likewise published and explained, the name of the painter may be seen signed in the following form : ΑΛΣΙΜΟΣ ΕΓΡΑΨΕ, " Alsimos painted it." This inscription has been erroneously read by others, ΜΑΞΙΜΟΣ ΕΓΡΑΨΕ ; and Gori, to whose system the writing is hostile, boldly pronounces it a deception, without having seen the vase itself.

15. The proof which arises from the writing, as well as from the style of the drawing, extends also to other vases without any writing, and warrants the ascription of them to Greek artists ; and is confirmed, as I have already mentioned, by vases of a like kind and workmanship, found in Sicily. I shall notice the collections of them, after having previously given an account of those which were partly formed in the kingdom of Naples, and a portion of which are to be found at the present time in the city of Naples.

16. The first and oldest collection formed there is, so far as I know, the one which adorns the Vatican library. We are indebted for it to the Neapolitan jurist, Joseph Valetta ; it was purchased from his heir by the senior Cardinal Gualtieri ; and after his death it was incorporated into the library mentioned (4). The same Valetta bequeathed to the library of the Theatines in the church of the Santi Apostoli, at Naples, some twenty vases of a similar kind, which are there exhibited.

17. Not inferior, at least in size, is the collection made by the Count Mastrilli, of Naples. It was enlarged, a few years ago, by a considerable number which had been collected by another member of the same family residing at Nola. Both collections, united together, are now in possession of their heir, the Count Palma, of Naples.

18. Together with this collection is to be noticed the one contained in the Porcinari mansion. It consists of nearly seventy pieces, one of the most beautiful of which represents Orestes, pursued by two figures, and kneeling with the left knee on the cover of the tripod of Apollo. The cover, ὅλμος, is hung with something, of which I shall speak at a fitting time, in the third volume of my *Ancient Monuments*. This vase, together with a pair of others in the same cabinet, appears in the *Hamilton Collection*.

19. A short time ago, the Duke of Caraffa Noja, a passionate

lover of antiquities, began to collect, together with other ancient works, vases also, of which engravings will soon be published. The most beautiful, and at the same time the most learned piece represents, in some twenty figures, the fight of the Greeks and Trojans over the body of Patroclus ; the latter are distinguished from the former by their helmets, which have some resemblance to a Phrygian bonnet.

20. At last, and subsequently to all the lovers of such earthen productions just named, Mr. Hamilton, of whom I have made frequent mention, collected a still larger, and a more select, number of them, which have been published by M. d'Hancarville, together with the choicest specimens of the Mastrilli and Porcinari collections, in four splendid volumes of the largest folio size. This work surpasses in magnificence all engraved works of the ancient monuments hitherto published ; for, together with the shape of the vessels, and their measured solid contents, each one is presented in several different plates ; the ornaments on them, but still more the figures, are accurately copied with the utmost care, and with a true understanding of the drawing of the ancients ; and, besides, each vase has been struck off with its own proper color ; so that in these volumes we have a treasure of Greek drawing, and the clearest evidence of the perfection of Greek art. The worthy possessor of this collection can boast of being able to show, in two vases, not only one of the most ancient monuments of Greek art, but also the most perfect in drawing and beauty, which the world knows, — as I will prove concerning both.

21. Among some other collections, also emanating from the kingdom of Naples, one of the most considerable is that which has been formed by Signor Raphael Mengs, during his residence there ; five, quite singular pieces, from the collection, have been published in my *Ancient Monuments*. There are, besides these, yet other vases among them not less deserving of publicity, as, for instance, the one which represents an Amazon on horseback, her hat thrown down upon her shoulder, in combat with a Hero. The Hero is probably Achilles, and the Amazon, Penthesilea, because the use of a hat is an invention attributed to her.

22. To conclude, I must not forget to cite, amongst the vases whose native land is the country about Naples, the one which was purchased at Rome, by his Serene Highness, the reigning Prince of Anhalt-Dessau, — on account of a peculiarity hitherto

unobserved on other vases. We see painted on it a female draped figure, which stands in front of a winged Genius, and holds before herself a round mirror, grasped by its handle, in which we see the profile of the face of the figure, drawn, not in color, but with a shining glaze, which appears of a lead tint. I presume that the larger portion of vases of this kind to be found in different cities of Italy, the collections of which are noticed by Gori, originate from the same places.

23. I have had frequent opportunities to examine, at my leisure, all the collections previously mentioned; and I should have liked to examine for myself, and not with the eyes of others, the vases that are to be found in Sicily, because all the arts flourished in this island not less than in Magna Græcia. On this account, I must confine myself to a bare notice of the places in which the greater number of them have been collected; these are Girgenti and Catania.

24. In the former place, several adorn the museum of Lucchesi, the bishop of the city, who likewise possesses a beautiful cabinet of coins; and I shall hereafter cite from his museum two very ancient golden cups. One of the most beautiful vases is found in the scribe's office of the cathedral church. It is five Roman palms (3 ft. 8 in. Eng.) in height; the figures, as usual, are yellow, on a black ground; and the style of the drawing, as I have been assured, conforms to the idea which we have of the grandest epoch in art.

25. The Benedictines of the latter city have in their museum more than two hundred of these vases; and the Prince Biscari, a worthy man and a lover of the arts, is the possessor of a collection not less considerable. In the latter, as well as the former, are all possible forms of such vases, and on them may be seen depicted (5) rare incidents in heroic history.

26. I am well aware that the list, just presented, of existing celebrated collections of vases ought to have been placed at the close of the remarks which still remain to be introduced in regard to such works, and that the uses to which they were applied in ancient times, not less than the drawing and painting on them, should have been first discussed, because information of the latter kind relates to that which is essential in them, more than the former, which is merely an historical notice. But the reason which induced me to prefer the one to the other was, that the collections mentioned, having been made in lands

inhabited by the Greeks, are able to furnish proof in refutation of the erroneous opinion, that such vases were executed by Etruscan artists. I have, therefore, precisely through their aid, endeavored to establish a correct name for them, — which must be the first point in all subjects of discussion.

27. In the first place, — in regard to the use made of such vases, — they are found of every kind and shape, from the smallest, which must have served as playthings for children (6), to those of three, four, five palms in height; the varied forms of the larger ones are seen in books, containing engravings of them. They were used in various ways. Earthen vessels continued to be employed at sacrifices, especially those of Vesta. Some served for the preservation of the ashes of the dead, the greater number of them having been found in tombs buried in rubbish, and in graves, particularly near the city of Nola, not far from Naples. It is asserted that several of these vases, belonging to the Castellan at Caserta, were found enclosed in a common stone; and a vase, which I have published in my *Ancient Monuments* (7), is said to have been discovered in a similar envelope. The very shape of the vase itself is painted on the stone, and it stands seemingly on a hill, which is probably designed to denote a grave, of the kind usual in the most ancient times. On each side of this vessel stands a young male figure, which is nude, with the exception of a robe hanging from one shoulder, and which has a sword under the arm pointing upward, after the manner of heroic figures; — the sword, in such cases, is termed ὑπωλένιος; — and it is my opinion, that these figures represent Orestes and Pylades at the tomb of Agamemnon.

28. Vases of this kind were found even in the tombs situated in the midst of the Tiphates mountains, ten miles above the ancient city of Capua, near to a place called Trebbia, which is reached by untrodden and toilsome paths. Mr. Hamilton, the Minister from Great Britain to Naples, caused these tombs to be opened in his presence, partly for the purpose of seeing the mode of their construction, and partly for the purpose of ascertaining whether vases of the kind would be found in tombs located in places so difficult of access. On the discovery of one of these tombs, a drawing of it was made on the spot by this amateur and connoisseur of the arts, of which a copperplate engraving may be seen in the second volume of the large collection of his vases. The skeleton of the deceased lay

stretched upon the bare earth, the feet turned towards the entrance of the tomb, and the head near the wall, into which six short, flat iron rods, spread out like the sticks of a fan, were driven by means of the nail about which they are enabled to turn. In the same place, and by the head, stood two tall, iron candelabra, corroded by rust. But, at some height above the head, vases hung from bronze nails driven into the wall; one stood near the candelabra; and two others were placed at the right side of the skeleton, near the feet. On the left side, near the head, lay two iron swords, together with a *colo vinario*, "wine-strainer," of bronze, which is a deep cup, pierced with holes like a sieve, and furnished with a handle; this cup fits nicely into another cup, not perforated, and it served, as it is known, for the filtering of wine. For since wine could be kept in the large *doliis*, "casks" of burnt earth, longer than in tuns formed of wooden staves, and was, consequently, thicker than our wine, which is commonly drunk soon after the vintage, such a wine seemed to require filtration. On the same side, at the feet, stood a round bronze cup, in which was a *simpulum*, that is, a smaller round cup with a long handle, the upper extremity of which is bent like a hook, and which was used to dip wine from the casks, in order to taste it, and also for the purpose of pouring into a larger cup the wine of libation, at sacrifices. Near the cup lay two eggs and a grater, resembling a cheese-grater.

29. I cannot refrain from subjoining a few observations in relation to this discovery, although they lead me somewhat from my point; I shall, however, return to it again presently, when I come to speak generally of the vases in tombs. That the dead were entombed with the feet turned towards the entrance of the sepulchre is known also through other sources; but it must have been a custom peculiar to the dwellers in this land to place the body, not in a coffin, but on the bare earth, since it might have been put, without much expense, in an oblong box, — many of which are found with their bodies. The pieces of iron, spread out in the shape of a fan, close to the head of the skeleton, seem to have represented an actual fan, and to refer to the custom of driving away with a fan the flies from the face of the dead. The cup or crater, and grater, together with the eggs, are to be regarded as symbols of the food and drink which were left behind for the soul of the de-

ceased, since we know that, among the last appeals to the dead, they were reminded to drink to the welfare of those who remained behind.   On a round sepulchral urn in the Mattei villa, among others we read

HAVE. ARCENTI. TV. NOBIS. BIBES.

"Farewell to thee, Arcentes!   Mayest thou drink to us!"

The suspended vases cannot be regarded as for the ashes of the dead, any more than those which stood near the skeleton ; partly because, as we see, it was either not a general custom, in that place, to burn the dead, or because it was not agreeable to the owner of the tomb in question ; and partly, also, because only a single body was entombed here ; and, finally, because all these vases were open and uncovered, whilst, on the contrary, all jars intended for the ashes of the dead have a cover.

30. It is singular, however, that the ancient writers make no mention, anywhere, of vases being deposited in tombs for other purposes than that of holding the ashes of the dead ; for a vase with oil, which, according to Aristophanes, was placed near the corpse, does not seem to be intended in this case.

31. Not less familiar is the use made of such vases in the public games of Greece, where, in the earliest ages, a mere earthen vase was the prize of victory, as is indicated by a vase on coins of the city of Tralles, and on many engraved gems. The custom had been retained, even to later periods, in Athens, where the prize in the Panathenæa was precisely such vases, which were filled with oil pressed from olives consecrated to Pallas ; and to it the vases on the summit of a temple at Athens are allusive.   They were embellished with painting, as Pindar indicates (8) in a passage which is so interpreted also by the scholiast of the poet.   To this custom the pictures on several of the largest vases, both in the Vatican and Hamilton collections, appear to allude ; for sometimes they represent Castor, at others, Pollux, in a temple, the latter standing, and with a horse, the former sitting, with a pointed helmet in his hand, of the form of the cap usually worn by him.   Castor would be an image of horse-racing ; and in Pollux, as a celebrated athlete, the other games would be denoted.

32. Moreover, many of these vases, if not the most of them, must have served instead of our porcelain, and have been executed for the ornamentation of the places in which

they were put. This may be inferred, in the first place, from the painting, as it is commonly finished better on one side than on the other, so that the inferior side was placed against the wall. But the make of some of these vases renders such use of them unquestionable, for they have no bottom, nor ever have had one, as some of the largest pieces in the Hamilton collection are found to be thus shaped (9). From the numerous figures which hold a *strigilis*, a bathing-scraper, it would seem as if many of them had been made with the view of being placed in bathing-houses.

33. The chief purpose of the present treatise, however, is neither to discuss the shape of these vases, nor to define their uses, but to consider the paintings or drawings executed on them, the greater number of which may, from their character-istics, be ascribed to Greek artists, and, consequently, may be to our artists a worthy subject of study and imitation. We often perceive in drawings, more distinctly than in finished pictures, the spirit of the artist, his thoughts, together with his manner of designing them, as also the freedom with which the hand was capable of following and obeying the understanding. This is the object which should be kept in view in the forma-tion of valuable collections of drawings. Now this purpose will be attained in a still nobler way by means of such painted vases, since these are actual drawings, and, together with four marble slabs in the Herculaneum museum, — of which I shall make mention hereafter, — are the sole drawings that have come down to us from ancient times. For the figures, here, are given merely in outline, as drawings must be; that is to say, not only the exterior outlines of the figures, but also all parts of them, together with the cast and folds of the garments, as well as the ornaments on them, are rendered, but they are rendered by means of lines and strokes, without light and shade. We term them paintings, therefore, not in the proper meaning of the word, it is true, but because they are drawings laid on with colors, though this is a usual practice even in drawings; and we can designate these vases as painted vases, without any misapplication of the term, just as we call that an engraving on copper which in reality is only an etching.

34. In most specimens, the figures are painted with a single color only; or, to speak more correctly, the color of the figures is the true ground of the vases, or the natural color of the very

fine, burnt clay itself; but the field of the picture, or the color
between the figures, is a shining blackish color, with which
the outlines of the figures are painted on the reddish-yellow
ground (10). Of vases painted with more than one color, several are found in the collections. One of them, and likewise
one of the learned vases in the museum of Signor Mengs, at
Rome, presents a parody of the fable of Jupiter and Alcmena;
that is, it is turned into ridicule and represented in a comic
way; or we might say, that it is a picture of the principal
scene of a comedy, such as the Amphitryon of Plautus (11).
Alcmena is looking out of a window, as they did whose favors
were venal, or who wished to play the prude, and enhance their
price; the window is placed high in the wall, after the custom
of the ancients. Jupiter is disguised by a bearded white mask,
and, like Serapis, wears on his head the Modius, which is of one
piece with the mask. He is carrying a ladder, between the
rounds of which he sticks his head, as if he had the intention of
climbing to the chamber of his love. On the other side is Mercury, with a big belly, figured as a servant, and disguised like
Sosia in Plautus. In his left hand he holds his wand downward, as if he was desirous of concealing it, in order that he
may not be recognized; in the other, he carries a lamp, which
he raises towards the window, either for the purpose of lighting
Jupiter, or to signify the intention of using the axe and the
lamp, as Delphis in Theocritus says to Simætha; that is, to express the idea in a corresponding phrase of our day, to employ
force with fire and sword, if his beloved should deny him admission. He wears a large priapus, which, even here, has its significance; and in the comedies of the ancients, the actors tied
a large member of red leather in front. Both figures have
whitish hose and stockings of one piece, which reach to the
ankles, like the seated comic actors, with masks before their
faces, in the Mattei and Albani villas; for the actors in the
comedies of the ancients could not appear without hose. The
nude of the figures is flesh-colored, even to the priapus, which
is a dark red, as is also the clothing of the figures; the robe of
Alcmena is marked with little white stars. Garments, wrought
with stars, were known among the Greeks in the earliest ages;
the hero, Sosipolis, in a very ancient picture, had such a one;
and Demetrius Poliorcetes wore one of the same kind.

35. The drawing on most of the vases is of such a quality,

that the figures might deservedly have a place in a drawing by Raphael; and it is remarkable, that no two are found with pictures of precisely the same kind; and of the many hundreds which I have seen, each one has its peculiar representation. Whoever studies and is able to comprehend the masterly and elegant drawing on them, and knows the mode of proceeding in laying the colors on baked works of a similar kind, will find in this sort of painting the strongest proof of the great correctness, and dexterity too, of the artists in drawing. For these vases are painted not otherwise than our pottery, or the common porcelain, when the blue color is laid on it, after it has been baked, as the term is. Painting of this kind requires to be executed dexterously and rapidly; for all burnt clay instantly absorbs the moisture from the colors and the pencil, even as a parched and thirsty soil absorbs the dew, so that, if the outlines are not drawn rapidly with a single stroke, nothing remains in the pencil but an earthy matter. Consequently, as breaks, or lines joined and again commenced, are not generally found, every line of the contour of the figure must be drawn with an unbroken sweep; this must seem almost miraculous, when we consider the quality of the figures. We must also reflect, that, in this sort of workmanship, no change or amendment is possible; as the outlines are drawn, so they must remain. As the smallest, meanest insects are wonders in nature, so these vases are a wonder in the art and manner of the ancients; and as, in Raphael's first sketches of his ideas, the outline of a head, and even entire figures, drawn with a single unbroken sweep of the pen, show the master to the connoisseur not less than his finished drawings, so the great facility and confidence of the ancient artists are more apparent in the vases than in other works. A collection of them (12) is a treasure of drawings.

36. However much I might say of many such vases, I should not believe that I had done anything, unless I again placed before the reader a description of a part of the most beautiful vase in the Hamilton collection; I mean only that representation which is painted on the upper part of the curve of the belly, below the mouth, — omitting the painting on the belly of the vase, which depicts the love of Jason and Medea. I confine myself to this picture especially, because it may be pronounced the very highest specimen of drawing which has been preserved to us in the works of the ancients; but the meaning of the figures is somewhat obscure.

37. My first thought fell upon the chariot-race which Œno-maus, king of Pisa, had established for the suitors of Hippo-damia, and in which Pelops obtained the victory and a bride. This conjecture seemed to be supported by the altar in the middle; for the course extended from Pisa to the altar of Nep-tune at Corinth. But there is no token of this divinity here, and as Hippodamia had only a single sister, named Alcippa, the other female figures would be imaginary.

38. Afterwards, I thought of the race which Icarius proposed to the suitors of his daughter Penelope, at Sparta, who should fall to the lot of him who outstripped the others. Ulysses obtained the prize. It would, therefore, be necessary to imag-ine him in the figure of the young hero embracing a youthful beauty, who strives to escape from him. The image of the goddess, who, in this case, seems to designate the place, would be that of Juno at Sparta, which wore a similar broad-topped hood, named πυλεών, — of which I have previously spoken in the second chapter of this book, and more in detail in the *Ancient Monuments*.

39. But as Penelope had only two sisters, Erigone and Iph-thime, who had no share in the race, the contest arranged by Danaus, at Argos, for the marriage of his forty-eight daughters, seemed to be more pertinent here. As they, with the sole excep-tion of Hypermnestra, had murdered in one night, by their father's command, the same number of sons of Ægyptus, their uncle, a general feeling of indignation was excited against them by the deed. Their father, therefore, offered to bestow his daughters in marriage without demanding a dowry, so that they might select among the young men, each the one who pleased her most. But as many suitors did not present themselves, Danaus arranged a race, in which the winner should make the first choice among his daughters; and so on, one after another. We do not know, however, who of the suitors was the first; neither is it known who were the subsequent ones.

40. The figure of the goddess might be Juno at Argos, if we regarded only the hood, which likewise resembled that of the figure on the vase; but the thing which she holds in her hand does not correspond with the emblems attributed to that god-dess. It would be appropriate to Rhea, because it resembles the stone which she offers, wrapped up like a child, to Saturn, on a four-sided altar in the Capitoline museum.

41. To see two female figures on a chariot will not surprise those who know that the Venus of Homer rode on a chariot together with Iris, who holds the reins, and who remember, in Callimachus, that Pallas was accustomed to take with her on her chariot Chariclo, who afterwards became the mother of Tiresias; it is known, indeed, that Cynisca, the daughter of the Spartan King Archidamus, obtained the victory in the chariot-race of the Olympic games.

42. The chariots, in this scene, are carved as they were — I will not say in the time of Danaus, but — at a very early date; for Euripides gives to the son of Theseus, in the expedition of the Greeks against Troy, a chariot which was ornamented with an image of Pallas.

43. It seems to me to be the most appropriate place, at the conclusion of this chapter, to say a few words in regard to some bronze figures, discovered in the island of Sardinia, which, from their conformation and remote antiquity, deserve a certain degree of attention. A short time ago, two other similar figures from this island were made known; but those of which I speak are in the museum of the College of Saint Ignatius, to which they were sent, as a gift, by the Cardinal Alexander Albani. They are four in number, and of different sizes, varying from half a palm to two palms (16.8 in. Eng.). The form and configuration of them are altogether barbarous, and at the same time offer the clearest indications of the remotest antiquity in a land wherein the arts never flourished. Their heads are elongated, eyes unusually large, members ill-shaped, and necks long and stork-like, in the style in which some of the ugliest of the small Etruscan figures of bronze are formed.

44. Two of the three smaller figures appear to be soldiers, but without helmets; both of them have a short sword, hanging upon the front of the chest, and from right to left, by a belt, thrown over the head. On the left shoulder is suspended a short mantle, — which is a narrow strip of cloth, — that reaches half down the thigh. It is apparently a four-cornered cloth, capable of being folded up; on one side, the inner, it is edged with a narrow raised border. This singular sort of garment may, perhaps, be the garb called Mastruca (13), which belonged exclusively to the Sardinians. One figure holds in its hand a plate, apparently containing fruits.

45. The most remarkable of these figures is a soldier,[1] almost two palms in height, with a short doublet, and, like the former, having hose and greaves to the lower part of the calf of the leg, — being the reverse of other examples of greaves; for whilst those worn by the Greeks covered the front part of the leg, these lie over the calf of the leg, and are open in front. In this manner the legs of Castor and Pollux may be seen protected on a gem in the Stosch museum, in the description of which I have cited the former figure as an illustration. This soldier holds with the left hand, before his body, but at some distance from it, a round shield, and beneath it three arrows, the feathers of which rise above the shield ; in his right hand he holds the bow. The breast is protected by a short cuirass, as also are the shoulders with capes, — a sort of shoulder-armor which is seen on a vase of the former Mastrilli collection at Nola, and on another vase in the Vatican library. A gladiator, in a monument made known by me, likewise wears a similar piece of armor on his shoulder ; the piece in this case, as well as on the figures of the vases before mentioned, is square ; but in the Sardinian figures, of which we now speak, it is shaped like the capes worn by our drummers on the shoulders of their uniforms. I have since learned that this mode of protecting the shoulders was also customary among the Greeks of the earliest periods; for, among other pieces of armor which Hesiod assigns to Hercules, he gives him this; and the scholiast of the poet terms it Σωσάννιον, from σώζειν, *to protect.* The head is covered with a flat cap, from the sides of which two long horns, like teeth, project forwards and upwards. On the head lies a basket with two shaft-handles, which is supported on the horns, and can be taken off. On his back he carries the body of a wagon with two small wheels, the pole of which is stuck into a ring on his back, so that the wheels project above his head.

46. This arrangement informs us of an unknown custom of the ancient nations, in war. In Sardinia, the soldier was obliged to carry his rations with him ; but he did not carry them on his shoulders, as the Roman soldiers did, but drew them after him on a frame, on which the basket stood. When the campaign was ended, and the soldier had no further need of his light wagon, he stuck it in the ring which was fastened on his back, and set the basket on his head above the two horns. The

[1] Plate XIX

PLATE XIX

soldier probably went even into battle with all this apparatus, as we see it, and was constantly provided with every appurtenance.

47. To bring this chapter to a complete close, I submit it to the consideration of the reader, who might desire more light on many particulars, that, in comparing these ancient nations in Italy with the Egyptians, I am like some persons who are less learned in their mother tongue than in a foreign language. Hence we are able to speak with more certainty of the art of the Egyptians, than of the art of those people whose lands we traverse without any impediment, and even dig over. We possess a multitude of small Etruscan figures, but not statues enough to enable us to arrive at a fully correct system of their art ; and after a shipwreck, no safer bark can be constructed from a few planks. Most of them consist of engraved gems, which are like the small bushes of a cleared wood, wherein only detached trees are still standing as evidence of the destruction. The misfortune is, that we have little hope of discovering works produced in the flourishing periods of these nations. The Etruscans had, in their territory, the marble-quarries of Luna (14), — now Carrara, — which was one of their twelve capital cities ; but the Samnites, Volsci, and Campanians found no white marble in their lands, and consequently most of their works were made of baked clay, or of bronze. The former are broken in pieces ; the latter are melted ; and herein lies the cause of the rareness of works of art of these nations. Since, however, the Etruscan style resembled the older Greek style, the present treatise may be regarded as a preparation for that which follows, — to which the reader is referred.

Volume II

BOOK IV.

ART AMONG THE GREEKS.

CHAPTER I.

GROUNDS AND CAUSES OF THE PROGRESS AND SUPERIORITY OF GREEK ART BEYOND THAT OF OTHER NATIONS.

1. The same remark is applicable to the study of Greek art, as to that of Greek literature. No one can form a correct judgment of either, without having read, repeatedly, every thing in the latter, and without having seen and investigated, if possible, all that remains of the former. But as the study of Greek literature is made more difficult than that of all other languages united, by the great number of its authors and commentators, so the countless multitude of the remains of Greek art renders the investigation of them far more laborious than that of the remains of other ancient nations; no one individual can possibly observe them all.

2. Greek art is the principal purpose of this history, and, from the innumerable beautiful monuments of it which remain, it is the worthiest object of study and imitation; it therefore demands a minute investigation, consisting, not in notices of imperfect characteristics, and in explanations of the conceptions which it embodies, but in information as to its essential; an investigation in which not merely facts are communicated for instruction, but also principles for practice. The treatise in which we have discussed the art of the Egyptians, the Etruscans, and other nations, may enlarge our ideas, and lead to correctness of judgment; but this on Greek art will attempt to base

them on the Unity of Truth (the one and the true), as a standard of opinion and a rule in execution.

3. The work will be divided into four parts. The first, which is introductory, will treat of the grounds and causes of the advancement and superiority of Greek art over that of other nations; the second, of its essential; the third, of its rise and fall; and the fourth, of the mechanical part of art. This chapter will close with a consideration of the paintings which have come down to us from antiquity.

4. The superiority which art acquired among the Greeks is to be ascribed partly to the influence of climate, partly to their constitution and government, and the habits of thinking which originated therefrom, and, in an equal degree also, to respect for the artist, and the use and application of art.

5. The influence of climate must vivify the seed from which art is to be produced; and for this seed Greece was the chosen soil. The talent for philosophy was believed by Epicurus to be exclusively Greek; but this preëminence might be claimed more correctly for art. The Greeks acknowledged and prized the happy clime under which they lived, though it did not extend to them the enjoyment of a perennial spring; for, on the night when the revolt against the Spartan government broke out in Thebes, it snowed so violently as to confine every one to the house. Moderateness of temperature constituted its superiority, and is to be regarded as one of the more remote causes of that excellence which art attained among the Greeks. The climate gave birth to a joyousness of disposition; this, in its turn, invented games and festivals; and both together fostered art, which had already reached its highest pinnacle at a period when that which we call Learning was utterly unknown to the Greeks. At this time they attached a peculiar signification to the honorable title of Author, who was regarded with a certain degree of contempt; and Plato makes Socrates say, that distinguished men, in Greek cities, had not drawn up or left behind them any writings, for fear of being numbered among the Sophists.

6. Much that might seem ideal to us was natural among them. Nature, after having passed step by step through cold and heat, established herself in Greece. Here, where a temperature prevails which is balanced between winter and summer, she chose her central point; and the nigher she approaches it, the more genial and joyous does she become, and the more gen-

eral is her influence in producing conformations full of spirit and wit, and features strongly marked and rich in promise. Where clouds and heavy mists rarely prevail, but Nature acts in a serene and gladsome atmosphere, such as Euripides describes the Athenian, she imparts an earlier maturity to the body; she is distinguished for vigorous development, especially of the female form; and it is reasonable to suppose that in Greece she perfected man to the highest degree; — for what the Scholiasts assert respecting the long heads or long faces of the inhabitants of the island of Eubœa is an absurd dream, devised for the sole purpose of finding the derivation of the name of a people there, called Μάκρωνες.

7. The Greeks were conscious of this, and, as Polybius says, of their superiority generally to other nations; and among no people has beauty (1) been prized so highly as among them. In a very old ode, — ascribed by an unpublished Scholiast to Simonides or Epicharmus, the first of the four wishes, of which Plato quotes only three, is to be healthy; the second, beautiful, καλὸν γενέσθαι, or φυὰν καλὸν γενέσθαι, as, according to the Scholiast above referred to, the words properly signify; the third, to be rich honestly, ἀδόλως πλουτεῖν; and the fourth, not mentioned by Plato, to be gay and merry with one's friends, ἡβᾶν μετὰ φίλων; — this signification of the word in this place may, by the way, serve to eludidate Hesychius.

8. Since, therefore, beauty was thus desired and prized by the Greeks, nothing was concealed which could enhance it. Every beautiful person sought to become known to the whole nation by this endowment, and especially to please the artists, because they decreed the prize of beauty; and, for this very reason, they had an opportunity of seeing beauty daily. Beauty was an excellence which led to fame; for we find that the Greek histories make mention of those who were distinguished for it. Some persons were even characterized by a particular name, borrowed from some beautiful portion of the body; thus, Demetrius Poliorcetes was named, from the beauty of his eyelids, χαριτοβλέφαρος, that is to say, "on whose lids the Graces dwell." It appears, indeed, to have been a belief, that the procreation of beautiful children might be promoted by the distributiou of prizes for beauty, as there is reason to infer from the contests of beauty which were instituted in the remotest ages by Cypselus, king of Arcadia, in the time of the Heraclidæ, on the banks

of the river Alpheus, in Elis; and also from the fact, that, at
the festival of the Philesian Apollo, a prize for the most exquisite kiss was conferred on the youthful.   Its assignment was
subject to the decision of a judge, as was probably also the case
at Megara, at the tomb of Diocles.   At Sparta, and at Lesbos,
in the temple of Juno, and among the citizens of Parrhasia, the
women contended for the prize of beauty (2).   The regard for
this quality was so general and so strong, that, as Oppian declares, the Spartan women placed in their sleeping-rooms an
Apollo, or Bacchus, or Nereus, or Narcissus, or Hyacinthus, or
Castor and Pollux, in order that they might bear beautiful children.   If it is true, what Dion Chrysostom asserts of his own
time and that of Trajan, that manly beauties had ceased to be
an object of regard, that people no longer knew how to prize
them, then this very disregard may be considered as one cause
of the decline of art at that time.

9. To the same influence, in an equal degree, which the
atmosphere and climate exercised upon the physical conformation, — which, according to the testimony of all travellers, is of
superior excellence even among the Greeks of the present day,
and could inspire their artists in former times, — are to be
ascribed their kindly natures, their gentle hearts, and joyous
dispositions, — qualities that contributed fully as much to the
beautiful and lovely images which they designed, as nature did
to the production of the form.   History convinces us that this
was their character.   The humanity of the Athenians is as well
known as their reputation in the arts.   Hence a poet says, that
Athens alone knows the feeling of pity; for it appears that,
from the times of the oldest wars of the Argives and Thebans,
the oppressed and persecuted always found refuge and received
help there.   This same genial disposition was the origin of
theatrical representations, and other games, — for the purpose,
as Pericles says, of chasing sadness from life.

10. This is more easily understood by contrasting the Greeks
with the Romans.   The inhuman, sanguinary games, and the
agonizing and dying gladiators, in the amphitheatres of the
latter, even during the period of their greatest refinement, were
the most gratifying sources of amusement to the whole people.
The former, on the contrary, abhorred such cruelty; and, when
similar fearful games were about to be introduced at Corinth,
some one observed, that they must throw down the altar of

Mercy and Pity, before they could resolve to look upon such horrors. The Romans, however, finally succeeded in introducing them even at Athens.

11. The humanity of the Greeks and the fierceness of the Romans are, moreover, manifest from the mode in which they respectively conducted their wars. With the latter it was almost imperative, not only to cut down every human being in captured cities, on first entering them, but also to rip open the dogs' bellies, and hack to pieces all other animals; and this even Scipio Africanus the elder permitted, when Carthage was taken by storm. We observe the reverse of this in the Athenians. They had resolved, in public assembly, to order the commander of their fleet to put to death all the male population of Mitylene, in the island of Lesbos, because this city had thrown off its allegiance, and been the leader in the rebellion of the whole island against their supremacy. But scarcely had the order been despatched, when they repented of it, declaring it to be an inhuman decree.

12. The contrast between the dispositions of the Romans and Greeks is especially manifested in the wars of the latter. The Achæans conducted them with so much humanity, that they agreed among themselves neither to carry nor to use weapons which might be discharged from a distance or from an ambush, but to fight hand to hand with the sword. Indeed, when the Olympic games occurred, at which all Greece harmoniously assembled to share in the general hilarity, all hostilities ceased and were forgotten for some days, even in times of the greatest exasperation. In remoter and less civilized times, during the obstinate Messenian wars, the Spartans made a truce of forty days with the Messenians, on the occurrence of the festival celebrated by the latter in honor of Hyacinthus. This event took place in the second Messenian war, which terminated in the twenty-eighth Olympiad.

13. The independence of Greece is to be regarded as the most prominent of the causes, originating in its constitution and government, of its superiority in art. Liberty had always held her seat in this country, even near the throne of kings, — whose rule was paternal, — before the increasing light of reason had shown to its inhabitants the blessings of entire freedom. Thus, Homer calls Agamemnon a shepherd of his people, to signify his love for them, and his solicitude for their welfare.

Although tyrants afterwards succeeded in establishing themselves, still they did so in their own territories alone ; the nation, as a whole, never recognized a common ruler ; and, prior to the conquest of Naxos by the Athenians, no free state in Greece had ever subjugated another. Hence, no individual possessed the sole prerogative of greatness in his own country, and the power of gaining immortality for himself to the exclusion of all others.

14. Art was, indeed, employed very early, to preserve the remembrance of individuals ; and such a mode of commemoration was free to every Greek. It was even allowable to set up in the temples the statues of one's children, which we know was done by the mother of the celebrated Agathocles, who devoted to a temple an image of him in his childhood. The honor of a statue was, in Athens, what an empty, barren title, or a cross upon the breast, the cheapest of all royal rewards, is in our day. The Athenians, therefore, acknowledged the praise which Pindar, in one of his odes, still extant, merely incidentally bestowed upon them, not by a courteous expression of thanks, but by erecting to him a statue in a public place, before the temple of Mars. But as the more ancient Greeks far preferred natural advantages to learning, so the earliest rewards were conferred on bodily exercises ; and we find mention made of a statue which had been erected, at Elis, to a Spartan athlete, named Eutelidas, as early as the thirty eighth Olympiad ; and this probably was not the first instance. In the lesser games, as at Megara, a pillar was set up with the name of the victor upon it. Hence, the most celebrated men among the Greeks sought, in their youth, to distinguish themselves at these games. Chrysippus and Cleanthes were famous here, before they were known by their philosophy. Plato himself appeared among the combatants in the Isthmian games at Corinth, and in the Pythian at Sicyon. Pythagoras won the prize at Elis, and was the teacher of Eurymenes, who was also victorious in the same games. Even among the Romans, bodily exercises were a path to fame. Papirius, who avenged on the Samnites the disgrace of the Romans at the Furculæ Caudinæ, is less known to us by this victory than by the name of "the Runner," which is also given to Achilles by Homer. Not only were the statues of the victors formed in the likeness of those whom they represented, but even the images of the successful

horses in the chariot-races were copied after life, as we are particularly informed with respect to the horses of Cimon, the
Athenian.

15. Next to these causes, the reverence for statues may be
regarded as among the most prominent. For it was maintained that the oldest images of the deities — the artists of
which were unknown — had fallen from heaven, Διϊπετῆ ; and
that not only these, but every sacred statue, whose sculptor
was known, was filled with the godhead which it represented.

16. Besides this superstitious belief, the gayety of the
Greeks had also an influence upon the general progress of art.
The artist, even in the earliest ages, was occupied in executing
statues of the victors in the numerous games then celebrated,
which he was required to make in the likeness of the individuals, and not above the size of life ; upon these points the
judges in the games, Ἑλλανοδίκαι, strictly insisted.

17. The portrait-statue of a victor, being erected on the
holiest spot in Greece, and gazed at and honored by the whole
nation, presented a powerful inducement to excellence in its
execution, not less than to effort for its attainment. Never,
among any people, from that time to the present, has the artist
had such an opportunity to distinguish himself; to say nothing of the statues in the temples, — not of the gods only (3),
but also of their priests and priestesses. The highest honor
among the people was to be an Olympic conqueror ; it was
regarded as the height of felicity ; the city to which he belonged considered that good-fortune had befallen it. He was
therefore supported from the public revenues, and sumptuously
buried by his native city ; the demonstrations of respect were
extended even to his children. Statues were erected to the
conquerors in the great games, — and to many of them in proportion to the number of their victories, — not only on the
spot where the games were celebrated, but also in their native
land ; since, to speak correctly, the city of the victor, not the
victor himself, was crowned. His fellow-citizens, consequently,
participated in the honor of his statue, for which they paid,
and the artist had the whole nation for judges of his work.
To Euthymus, of Locri, in Italy. — who, with one exception,
had invariably conquered at Elis, — the Olympic oracle, indeed,
ordered sacrifices to be offered even during his life, as well as
after death. Meritorious citizens also obtained the honor of a

statue ; and Dionysius makes mention of the statues of those
citizens of Cumæ, in Italy, which Aristodemus — the tyrant of
this city, and the friend of Tarquin the Proud — caused to be
removed from the temple in which they stood and thrown into
unclean places, in the twenty-second Olympiad.   To certain
victors in the Olympic games at an early date, before the arts
had yet attained to excellence, statues were erected long after
their death, to perpetuate their memory : thus, upon one Œbo-
tas, who lived during the sixth Olympiad, this honor was first
conferred in the eighteenth.   It is singular that any one (4)
should have permitted his statue to be made before obtaining
the victory ; yet it was done by one individual, such was his
confidence of success. , At Ægium, in Achaia, a hall, or covered
gallery, was appropriated to a certain conqueror, for whom it
had been built by his native city, in which to practise his gymnastic exercises.

It appears to me not to be out of place to make mention here
of a beautiful, but mutilated, nude statue of a slinger, which it
is proved to be by the sling, with the stone in it, resting on the
right thigh.   It is not easy to say on what grounds a statue had
been erected to such a person.   The poets have not represented
any hero with a sling ; and slingers (5) were very unusual among
the Greek warriors ; wherever found, they were always rated
lower than any other portion of an army, and, like the archers,
were light-armed troops, γυμνῆτες.   It was so likewise among
the Romans ; and whenever it was intended to inflict a severe
punishment on a soldier belonging to the cavalry or heavy-armed
infantry, he was degraded to the slingers.   Now, as the statue
of which we speak must represent some particular individual of
antiquity, and not merely a slinger, one might say that Py-
ræchmes, the Ætolian, is intended by it ; for, on the return of
the Heraclidæ to the Peloponnesus, he was the champion in
the single contest which was to determine the possessor of the
territory of Elis ; and his skill lay in the use of the sling.

18. The thoughts of the whole people rose higher with freedom, just as a noble branch rises from a sound stock.   As the
mind of a man accustomed to reflection is usually more elevated in the broad fields, on the public highway, and on the
summit of an edifice, than in an ordinary chamber, or in a confined space, so, also, the manner of thinking among the free
Greeks must have been very different from that of nations liv-

ing under more arbitrary forms of government. Herodotus shows that freedom alone was the basis of the power and superiority to which Athens attained; since this city previously, when obliged to acknowledge a sovereign, was unable to keep pace with its neighbors. For the very same reason, eloquence did not begin to flourish among the Greeks prior to their enjoyment of perfect independence; hence, the Sicilians attributed to Gorgias the invention of oratory. It might be maintained, from coins of the cities of Sicily and Magna Græcia, that the arts began to flourish in this island and in the lower part of Italy sooner even than in Greece, just as the other departments of knowledge, generally, were cultivated there at an earlier date than in Greece. This we know to have been the case with the art of oratory, in which Gorgias, of Leontium, in Sicily, first distinguished himself, and who, when sent as ambassador from this city to Athens, attracted universal attention. Even philosophy received a systematic form in the Eleatic or Italian school, and in that founded by Pythagoras, sooner than among the other Greeks.

19. The freedom which gave birth to great events, political changes, and jealousy among the Greeks, planted, as it were in the very production of these effects, the germ of noble and elevated sentiments. As the sight of the boundless surface of the sea, and the dashing of its proud waves upon the rocky shore, expands our views and carries the soul away from, and above, inferior objects, so it was impossible to think ignobly in the presence of deeds so great and men so distinguished. The Greeks, in their palmy days, were a thinking people. At an age when we do not generally begin to judge for ourselves, they had already exerted their reasoning faculties for twenty years or more; they employed their intellectual powers at the period when they are brightest and strongest and are sustained by the vigor and sprightliness of the body, which, among us, is ignobly nourished until it decays.

20. The youthful understanding, which, like the tender bark, retains and enlarges the incisions made in it, was not amused by mere sounds without ideas; nor was the brain — like a waxed tablet, which can contain only a certain number of words or images — filled with dreams, to the exclusion of truth. To be learned, that is to say, to know what others have known, was the ambition of a later period. In the best days of Greece,

it was easy to be learned, in the signification of the word at that time ; and every one could be wise. For there was one vanity less in the world at that time than at present, namely, that of being conversant with many books, — since the scattered fragments of the greatest of poets were not collected until the sixty-first Olympiad. These the child learned ; the youth thought as the poet thought ; and when he had achieved any meritorious act, he was numbered among the first men of his nation.

21. With the advantages of such an education, Iphicrates, when in his twenty-fourth year, was elected by his fellow-citizens of Athens commander-in-chief of the army. Aratus was scarcely twenty years old, when he freed his native land, Sicyon, from the rule of tyrants, and, soon afterwards, became the head of the whole Achæan league. Philopœmen, though a mere boy, had the greatest share in the victory which Antigonus, king of Macedonia, aided by the members of the Achæan league, gained over the Lacedæmonians, and which made them masters of Sparta.

22. A similar education produced, among the Romans also, that early maturity of intellect which we see manifested, among other instances, in Scipio the younger and Pompey. The former, in his twenty-fourth year, was sent to Spain, at the head of the Roman legions, for the express purpose of restoring the discipline of the army in that country, which had become impaired; and Velleius says of the latter, that, in his twenty-third year, he levied an army at his own expense, and, without any public authority, followed his own counsels. When Pericles stepped forward, and said, what we are permitted scarcely to think of ourselves, — "Ye are angry with me because I believe myself inferior to no one in the knowledge of what may be required, or in the ability to speak about it," — he did so in reliance upon the elevated habits of thought created by such an education, and common to a whole nation, and upon the ardent desire for glory which was felt by every individual of it. Their historians speak with no less frankness of the virtues of their own people than of the faults of other nations.

23. A wise man was the most highly honored ; he was known in every city, as the richest is among us ; just as the younger Scipio was, who brought the statue of Cybele to Rome. The artist also could attain to this respect. Socrates, indeed, pro-

nounced the artists the only truly wise, as being actually, not apparently so; it was probably from this conviction that Æsop constantly associated with sculptors and architects. At a much later period, Diognetus, the painter, was one of those who taught Marcus Aurelius philosophy. This emperor acknowledged that he had learned of him to distinguish truth from falsehood, and not to regard follies as merits. The artist could become a lawgiver, for all the lawgivers were common citizens, as Aristotle testifies. He could command an army, like Lamachus, one of the neediest citizens of Athens, and see his statue placed beside those of Miltiades and Themistocles, and even near those of the gods themselves. Thus, Xenophilus and Strato placed statues of themselves, in a sitting posture, close to their statues of Æsculapius and Hygeia, at Argos; Chirisophus, the sculptor of the Apollo at Tegea, stood in marble near his work; the figure of Alcamenes was wrought in relief on the summit of the temple at Eleusis; and Parrhasius and Silanion, in their picture of Theseus, were honored together with the hero himself. Other artists put their names upon their works, — as Phidias, for example, at the feet of the Olympian Jupiter. The names of the artists also appeared on different statues of the victors at Elis; and on the chariot with four bronze horses, which Dinomenes erected to his father Hiero, king of Syracuse, was an inscription in two lines, to the effect that Onatas was the artist. Still, however, this custom was not so general, that the absence of the artist's name upon admirable statues proves them, conclusively, to be works of later times (6). Such an inference was to be expected only from those who had seen Rome in dreams, or, like young travellers, in one month.

24. The reputation and success of artists were not dependent upon the caprice of ignorance and arrogance, nor were their works fashioned to suit the wretched taste or the incompetent eye of a judge set up by flattery and fawning; but the wisest of the whole nation, in the assembly of united Greece, passed judgment upon, and rewarded, them and their works; and at Delphos, as well as at Corinth, contests in painting, for which judges were specially appointed, were instituted in the time of Phidias. The first contest of the kind was between Panænus, the brother, or, as others have it, the nephew, of Phidias, and Timagoras of Chalcis, in which the latter won the prize. Before such judges Aetion appeared with his picture of Alexander and

Roxana: the presiding judge, named Proxenides, who pronounced the decision, bestowed his daughter in marriage upon the artist. We also see that the judges were not so dazzled by a brilliant reputation in other cities, as to deny to merit its rights; for at Samos, the picture by Timanthes, representing the decision upon the arms of Achilles, was preferred to that of Parrhasius.

25. The judges, however, were not unacquainted with the arts; for there was a time in Greece when its youth were taught in the schools of art as well as philosophy; Plato learned drawing at the same time with the higher sciences. The design was, as Aristotle says, that they might acquire a correct knowledge and judgment of beauty.

26. Hence, the artist wrought for immortality; and the value set upon his works placed him in a position to elevate his art above all mere mercenary considerations. Thus, it is known that Polygnotus gratuitously embellished with paintings the Portico at Athens, and also, as it appears, a public edifice (7) at Delphos, in which he represented the taking of Troy. Gratitude for the latter work seems to have induced the Amphictyons, or national council of the Greeks, to award to the noble-minded artist the honor of being entertained at the public expense throughout Greece.

27. In general, excellence in art and handiwork of every kind was particularly prized; the best workman in the most humble craft might succeed in rendering his name immortal; and we are told that the Greeks were accustomed to pray the gods that their memories might never die. We know, even at this day, the name of the architect of an aqueduct on the island of Samos, and of him who constructed the largest vessel there; also the name, Architeles, of a famous stone-cutter, who excelled in working columns. The names of two weavers or embroiderers, who wrought a mantle for the Pallas Polias, at Athens, are known; likewise the name, Parthenius, of a maker of very correct balances, or balance-scales (8); the name is also preserved of the saddler, as we should call him, who made the leathern shield of Ajax; even a certain Peron, who prepared a fragrant ointment, was noticed in the works of different distinguished men. Plato himself has immortalized in his works Thearion, a baker, on account of his skill in his handicraft, as well as Sarambus, a clever innkeeper. With this view, the

Greeks appear to have named many excellent articles after the persons by whom they were made, and the articles were always known by those names. Thus, the vessels that were fashioned in a form similar to those made by Thericles, of burnt clay, in the time of Pericles, received their name from this artist. Wooden candelabra were made at Samos, which were much valued ; Cicero pursued his nightly studies, at his brother's country-seat, by the light from such candlesticks. In the island of Naxos, statues were erected to him who first wrought the Pentelic marble into tiles, for the purpose of covering the roofs of buildings, and merely on account of this invention. Superior artists were distinguished by the surname Godlike, — as Alcimedon, for instance, by Virgil: this was the highest praise among the Spartans.

28. The uses to which art was applied sustained its greatness. Being consecrated to the gods, and devoted only to the holiest and best purposes in the land, at the same time that economy and simplicity characterized the abodes of the citizens, the artist was not cramped in the grandeur of his subject or of his conceptions to suit the size of the dwelling or gratify the fancy of its proprietor, but his work was made to conform to the lofty ideas of the whole nation. We know that Miltiades, Themistocles, Aristides, and Cimon, the leaders and deliverers of Greece, resided in no better houses than their neighbors. The dwellings of the opulent differed from ordinary houses only in having a court, called αὐλή, which was enclosed by the building, and in which the master of the family was accustomed to sacrifice. Tombs were regarded as sacred edifices ; we must not, therefore, be surprised that Nicias, the celebrated painter, was willing to be employed in embellishing with his pencil a tomb before the city of Tritia, in Achaia. We must also consider how much emulation in art was fostered, when cities rivalled each other in the endeavor to obtain a beautiful statue, and when a whole people defrayed the expense of statues, not only to the gods, but also to the victors in the public games. Some few cities were known, even in ancient times, merely through one exquisite statue, — as Aliphera (9) by a Pallas in bronze, executed by Hecatodorus and Sostratus.

29. The arts of sculpture and painting attained among the Greeks a certain excellence earlier than architecture, because the latter has in it more of the ideal than the two former ; it

cannot be an imitation of anything actual, and must therefore, of necessity, be based on the general principles and rules of proportion. The two former, which originated in mere imitation, found all the requisite rules determined in man; whereas, architecture was obliged to discover its own rules by repeated trials, and establish them by general approval.

30. Sculpture, however, outstripped painting, and, like an elder sister, served as a guide to the younger. Pliny, indeed, is of opinion that painting had no existence at the date of the Trojan war. The Jupiter of Phidias and the Juno of Polycletus, the most perfect statues of antiquity, were in being before light and shadow had been introduced into painting. Apollodorus (10), and especially Zeuxis, his scholar, who were celebrated in the nineteenth Olympiad, are the first in whose pictures this improvement appears. Prior to this time, one must represent to himself the figures in paintings as statues placed near one another, which, except in the action of standing opposite to each other, appeared as single figures, without being grouped so as to compose a whole, exactly in the style of the paintings on the (so called) Etruscan vases of burnt clay. According to Pliny, Euphranor, who was contemporary with Praxiteles, and therefore later still than Zeuxis, introduced symmetry into painting.

31. The reason of the slower growth of painting lies partly in the art itself, and partly in its use and application. Sculpture promoted the worship of the gods, and was in its turn promoted by it. But painting had no such advantage. It was, indeed, consecrated to the gods and temples; and some few of the latter, as that of Juno at Samos, were Pinacothecæ, or picture-galleries; at Rome, likewise, paintings by the best masters were hung up in the temple of Peace, that is, in the upper rooms or arches. But paintings do not appear to have been, among the Greeks, an object of holy, undoubting reverence and adoration. There is not, at least, among all those noticed by Pliny and Pausanias, a single one which obtained this honor, unless, perchance, an allusion to such a picture may be discovered in the passage from Philo in the note (11). Pausanias merely mentions a picture of Pallas in her temple at Tegea, which represented a Lectisternium (12) to the goddess.

32. Painting, however, is very much indebted to the custom among the ancients of embellishing their rooms with the pencil.

This also was one of the causes to which the art owed its improvement in Italy, in our forefathers' times, before tapestry, a less costly covering of the walls, had displaced painting. The ancients likewise decorated their rooms with geographical charts, — a mode of embellishment of which one may obtain an idea from the long and splendid topographical hall of the countries of Italy, in the Vatican.

33. Painting and sculpture stand to each other in the same relation as oratory and poetry. As the latter was regarded as more sacred than the former, was employed in religious offices, and specially remunerated, it arrived earlier at perfection ; and this is partly the reason why, as Cicero says, there have been more good poets than orators. But we find that painters were also sculptors ; as, among others, an Athenian painter, Mico, who made the statue of Callias of Athens ; the distinguished painter, Euphranor, the contemporary of Praxiteles ; Zeuxis, whose works in burnt clay stood at Ambracia ; and Protogenes, who wrought in bronze ; even Apelles made a statue of Cynisca, the daughter of Archidamus, king of Sparta. Sculptors have also been no less celebrated as architects. Polycletus built a theatre, at Epidaurus, which was dedicated to Æsculapius, and which stood within the enclosure of his temple.

34. All Greece may rightly be called the land of art ; for though its favorite seat was in Athens, yet it was, nevertheless, practised also at Sparta. This city, in the oldest times, and prior to the Persian wars, sent to Sardis to purchase gold to gild the face of a statue of Apollo.

Such were the advantages which Greece had over other nations in art, and only such a soil could produce fruits so splendid.

CHAPTER II.

THE ESSENTIAL OF ART.

1. WE now pass from the first to the second division, that is, from the introductory notices, to the essential itself, of art among the Greeks, — just as their young men, after days of preparatory training for the great games, presented themselves in the Stadium before the eyes of the assembled nation, — not without anxious fears for the result. What has been said of the Egyptians and Etruscans, in the preceding books, may, indeed, be considered only as the prelude to the proper contest of the Stadium.

2. I imagine myself, in fact, appearing in the Olympic Stadium, where I seem to see countless statues of young, manly heroes, and two-horse and four-horse chariots of bronze, with the figures of the victors erect thereon, and other wonders of art. Indeed, my imagination has several times plunged me into such a reverie, in which I have likened myself to those athletes, since my essay is to be regarded as no less doubtful in its issue than theirs. I cannot but think of myself thus, when venturing on the enterprise of elucidating the principles and causes of so many works of art, visible around me, and of their lofty beauties ; in which attempt, as in the contests of beauty, I see before me, not one, but numerous enlightened judges.

3. I would not, however, wish this imaginary flight to Elis to be regarded as a mere poetic fancy. It will, on the contrary, be seemingly realized, if I conceive all the statues and images of which mention has been made by authors, and likewise every remaining fragment of them, together with the countless multitude of works of art which have been preserved, as present before me at the same time. Without collecting and uniting them so that a glance may embrace all, no correct opinion can be formed of them ; but when the understanding and the eye assemble and set the whole together in one area, just as the

choicest specimens of art stood ranged in numerous rows in the Stadium at Elis (1), then the spirit finds itself in the midst of them.

4. But as no intelligent man in modern days has ever penetrated to Elis, — to avail myself of the words which a skilful and learned antiquarian employed to stimulate me to this journey, — so writers upon art do not seem to have prepared themselves, as they should have done, to appear in the Stadium there, willing to give a well-grounded explanation of everything, before a Proxenides. This censure I can maintain before those who have read the authors to whom I allude.

5. But how has it happened, that, whilst well-grounded elementary treatises on all other departments of knowledge exist, the principles of art and of beauty have been so little investigated? The fault, reader, lies in our innate indolent unwillingness to think for ourselves, and in scholastic philosophy. On the one hand, the ancient works of art have been regarded as beauties which one can never hope fully to enjoy, and which on this account easily warm some imaginations, but do not touch the heart; and antiquities have given occasion for the display of reading only, but have ministered little nutriment, or absolutely none at all, to the understanding. On the other hand, philosophy has been practised and taught principally by those who, from reading the works of their gloomy predecessors, have but little room left for the feelings, over which they have, as it were, drawn an insensible cuticle, and we have consequently been led through a labyrinth of metaphysical subtilty and wordiness, which have principally served the purpose of producing big books, and disgusting the understanding.

6. For these reasons, art has been, and still is, excluded from philosophical consideration; and the great general truths which lead pleasantly to the investigation of beauty, and thence upward nearer to its source, not having been applied to and explained by the beautiful in particulars, have been lost in profitless speculation. How can I judge otherwise, even of treatises which have selected the highest object after the Deity, namely, Beauty, for their subject? I have meditated long upon it, but my meditations commenced too late, and in the brightest glow of mature life its essential has remained dark to me; I can speak of it, therefore, only feebly and spiritlessly. My exertions,

however, may be an incentive to others to propose doctrines, not only more profound, but breathing the inspiration of the Graces.

7. It is my intention to treat first of the drawing of the nude figure, — which also comprehends that of animals; then of the drawing of clothed figures, and in particular of female drapery. The delineation of the nude figure is grounded on the knowledge and conceptions of beauty. These conceptions consist partly in measure and relations, and partly in forms, the beauty of which was the aim of the first Greek artists, as Cicero[1] says; the latter give shape to the figure, the former determine its proportions.

8. I shall, in the first place, speak of beauty in general, not only of forms, but also of attitude and gesture, together with proportion; and then of the beauty of single parts of the human body. In the general consideration of beauty, I shall, in some preliminary remarks, venture on an unusual view of it, that is, consider its negative character; and then present some definite ideas of it. It is, however, easier to say what it is not than what it is, as Cotta, in Cicero,[2] says of God. There is nearly the same relation between beauty and its opposite, as there is between health and disease; we feel the latter, but not the former.

9. Beauty, as the loftiest mark and the central point of art, demands some preliminary discussion, in which I should wish to satisfy both myself and the reader; but this is a wish of difficult gratification in either respect. When, after some general observations upon the art of design among the Greeks, I sought to advance farther into the examination of it, Beauty seemed to beckon to me, — probably that same Beauty which exhibited herself to the great artists, and allowed herself to be felt, grasped, and figured, — for I have sought and longed to recognize her in their works. I cast my eyes down before this creation of my imagination, — as did those to whom the Highest appeared, — believing that I saw the Highest in this vision of my fancy. At the same time, I blushed for the confidence which had emboldened me to pry into her mysteries, and to treat of the loftiest conception of humanity, as I recalled to mind the fear which this undertaking formerly caused me. But the kind reception which my reflections have met encour-

[1] De Finib., lib. 2, cap. 34, *in fine*.   [2] De Natura Deor., lib. 1, cap. 21.

ages me to follow that invitation, and meditate further on beauty. With an imagination warmed by the desire of assembling all the single beauties which I had observed, and uniting them in one figure, I sought to create a poetic Beauty, and place her before me. But in this second trial and exertion of my powers, I have been again convinced that this is still more difficult than to find in human nature perfect beauty, if such can exist. For beauty is one of the great mysteries of nature, whose influence we all see and feel; but a general, distinct idea of its essential must be classed among the truths yet undiscovered. If this idea were geometrically clear, men would not differ in their opinions upon the beautiful, and it would be easy to prove what true beauty is; still less could there be one class of men of so unfortunate sensibility, and another of so perverse self-conceit, that the former would create for themselves a false beauty, and the latter refuse to receive a correct idea of true beauty, and say with Ennius, *Sed mihi neutiquam cor consentit cum oculorum adspectu,* " But my heart does not assent to what my eyes behold."[1] It is less difficult to instruct the former than to convince the latter, whose doubts, being intended rather for the display of ingenuity, than carried to the extent of denying the reality of beauty, have, consequently, no influence upon art. These a glance should enlighten, especially in the presence of more than a thousand ancient works which have been preserved; but there is no remedy for insensibility, and we have no rule and canon of beauty according to which, as Euripides says, ugliness may be judged; and for this reason we differ about that which is beautiful, just as we differ about that which is truly good.

10. It ought not to create surprise, that our ideas of beauty are, as I have already observed, very different from those among the Chinese and Indian nations, when we reflect that we ourselves rarely agree in every particular respecting a beautiful face. Blue eyes are generally attracted by brown eyes, and brown eyes charmed by blue; and opinions differ about a beautiful person, just as inclinations differ in preferring fair or dark beauty. He who prefers dark to fair beauty is not on that account to be censured; indeed, one might approve his choice, if he is attracted less by sight than by the touch. For a dark-complexioned beauty may, perhaps, appear to have a softer skin

[1] Cic. Lucull., cap. 17.

than one of a fair complexion, because the fair skin reflects more rays of light, and of course must be denser, thicker, and consequently harsher, than a brown skin. Hence, a brown skin is to be regarded as the clearer, because this color, when natural, is occasioned by the blood showing through it, and from this very cause it is tanned more quickly than a fair skin ; this is also the reason why the skin of the Moors is far softer to the touch than ours. A brown complexion in beautiful boys was, with the Greeks, an indication of courage ; those of fair complexion were called children of the gods.

11. This difference of opinion is shown still more strongly in the judgment passed upon the beauties impersonated by art, than upon those in nature itself. For since the former excite less than the latter, so will they also — when they are designed after ideas of elevated beauty, and are more serious than gay — be less pleasing to the uninstructed mind than an ordinary pretty face which is lively and animated. The cause lies in our passions, which with most men are excited by the first look, and the senses are already gratified, when reason, unsatisfied, is seeking to discover and enjoy the charm of true beauty. It is not, then, beauty which captivates us, but sensuality. Consequently, young persons, in whom the passions are in a state of excitement and ferment, will look upon those faces as divine, which, though not strictly beautiful, have the charm of tender and passionate expression ; and they will be less affected by a truly beautiful woman, even with the shape and majesty of Juno, whose gestures and actions evince modesty and decorum.

12. The ideas of beauty with most artists are formed from their first crude impressions, which are seldom weakened or destroyed by loftier beauties, especially when they cannot improve their minds by recurring to the beauties of the ancients. For it is with drawing as with writing ; few boys who learn to write are taught how the beauty of the letters consists in the nature of the strokes, and in the light and shadow in them, but they get a copy to imitate, without any further instruction, and the handwriting is formed before the pupil attends to the principles on which the beauty of the letters is founded. Most young persons learn to draw in precisely the same manner ; and, as the writing-strokes remain in adult years just as they were formed in youth, so the designer's conceptions of beauty are commonly pictured in his own mind as his eye has been

accustomed to observe and copy it; but they will be incorrect, because most artists draw from imperfect models.

13. It is also very probable that the idea of beauty, with artists as with all other men, is conformable to the texture and action of the nerves of sight. From the imperfect and frequently incorrect coloring of the painter, one must infer, in part, that the colors are so represented and pictured in his eye; for, in this particular, the conclusion at which the sect of Skeptics in philosophy arrived is not groundless, who argued, from the diversity in the color of the eyes both in beast and man, that our knowledge of the true colors of objects is uncertain. As the color of the humors of the eye might be regarded as the cause of this defect, so the different ideas of the forms which constitute beauty are probably dependent on the nature of the nerves. This is conceivable from the innumerable kinds of fruits and the innumerable varieties of the same fruit, whose different shape and taste are elaborated through divers filaments, by the interlacing of which the tubes are woven, within which the sap ascends, is purified, and ripened. Now since there must exist a cause for the many different impressions made even upon those who are occupied in delineating them, the foregoing supposition may by no means be rejected.

14. In others, the climate has not allowed the gentle feeling of pure beauty to mature; it has either been confirmed in them by art, — that is, by constantly and studiously employing their scientific knowledge in the representation of youthful beauties, — as in Michael Angelo, or become in time utterly corrupted, as was the case with Bernini (2), by a vulgar flattery of the coarse and uncultivated, in attempting to render everything more intelligible to them. The former busied himself in the contemplation of lofty beauty; this is evident from his poems, some of which have been published; in them his thoughts relative to it are expressed in elevated language, worthy of the subject. In powerful figures he is wonderful; but, from the cause before mentioned, his female and youthful figures are, in shape, action, and gesture, creatures of another world. Michael Angelo, compared with Raphael, is what Thucydides is to Xenophon. The very course which led Michael Angelo to impassable places and steep cliffs plunged Bernini, on the contrary, into bogs and pools; for he sought to dignify, as it were, by exaggeration,

forms of the most ordinary kind. His figures are those of vulgar people who have suddenly met with good fortune, and their expression is oftentimes opposed to the action, as when Hannibal laughed in the extremity of his grief. Yet this artist long held undisputed sway, and homage is paid to him even now. The eye also is as incorrect in many artists as in the uninstructed, and they do not depart from the truth in imitating the colors of objects, more than in the conformation of the beautiful. Baroccio, one of the most celebrated painters, who studied after Raphael, is distinguishable by his drapery, but still more by his profiles, in which the nose is commonly very much sunken. Pietro da Cortona is known by the chin of his heads, which is somewhat small, and flat at its lower part; and yet these are painters of the Roman school. In other Italian schools still more imperfect conceptions are observable.

15. Individuals of the second class — namely, those who question the correctness of all conceptions of beauty — found their doubts principally on the notions of the beautiful existing among remote nations, which must be different from ours, in conformity to the difference in the shape of their faces. Since many nations compare the complexion of their beauties with ebony, as we do with ivory, — and a dark-colored skin is more brilliant than a white skin, just as ebony has more gloss than any other wood, — so, it is argued, will they probably compare the forms of the face with the corresponding parts in beasts, which to us would appear deformed and ugly. I acknowledge that, even in the faces of Europeans, forms similar to those of brutes can be found; and Otto van Been, the master of Rubens, has, according to Porta, written a special treatise in exposition of the fact. But it must also be conceded, that, the more striking this similarity in some few parts, so much the more does their form differ, partly by variation and partly by excess, from the characteristics of our race, thereby destroying the harmony, unity, and simplicity, in which beauty, as I shall show hereafter, consists.

16. The more oblique, for example, the eyes, as in cats, so much the more does their direction deviate from the fundamental form of the face, which is a cross, whereby it is divided equally, in length and breadth, from the crown of the head downward, since the perpendicular line passes through the middle of the nose, and the horizontal line through the orbits of

the eyes. If the eye is placed obliquely, then the face is divided by a line oblique to the vertical line passing through the nose. This at least must be the true cause of the unseemliness of an obliquely situated mouth ; for, if of two lines one deviates from the other without reason, a disagreeable impression is produced. Such eyes, therefore, when found among us, and in Chinese, Japanese, and some Egyptian heads, in profile, are a departure from the standard. The flattened nose of the Chinese, Calmucks, and other distant nations, is also a deviation, for it mars the unity of the forms according to which the other parts of the body have been shaped. There is no reason why the nose should be so much depressed, should not much rather follow the direction of the forehead ; just as, on the other hand, it would be an exception to the variety displayed in the human conformation, if the forehead and nose were formed by one straight bone, as in beasts. The projecting, swollen mouth which the negro has, in common with the monkey of his land, is a superfluous growth, caused by the heat of the climate, just as among us the lips swell up from heat, or a humid and harsh, salt air, and in some men, indeed, from violent anger. The small eyes of extreme northern and eastern nations make a part of the incompleteness of their growth, which is short and small.

17. Nature effects such conformations more generally, the nigher she approximates her extremes, and the more she has to contend either with heat or cold. Her productions, in the former case, are characterized by excess and prematureness ; in the latter, her growths of every kind are immature. A flower withers beneath an excessive heat, and, in a cellar into which the sun never penetrates, it remains without color ; indeed, plants degenerate in a close, dark place. But, in proportion as nature gradually draws nigher to her centre in a temperate climate, her productions are marked by more regularity of shape, as it has been shown in the third chapter of the first book. Consequently our ideas and those of the Greeks relative to beauty, being derived from the most regular conformation, are more correct than those that can possibly be formed by nations which, to adopt the thought of a modern poet, have lost one half of their likeness to the Creator ; for, as Euripides says, what is not beautiful in itself can be beautiful nowhere.

18. But we ourselves differ as to beauty, — probably more than we do even in taste and smell, — whenever our ideas respecting it are deficient in clearness.   It will not be easy to find a hundred men who would agree as to all the points of beauty in any one face, — I speak of those who have not thought profoundly on the subject.   The handsomest man that I have seen in Italy was not the handsomest in the eyes of all, not even of those who prided themselves on being observant of the beauty of our sex.   But those who have regarded and selected beauty as a worthy subject of reflection cannot differ as to the truly beautiful, for it is one only, and not manifold ; and when they have studied it in the perfect statues of the ancients, they do not find, in the beautiful women of a proud and wise nation, those charms which are generally so much prized, — because they are not dazzled by the fairness of their skin.   Beauty is felt by sense, but is recognized and comprehended by the understanding, which generally renders, and ought to render, sense less susceptible, but more correct.   Most nations, however, and among them the most cultivated, not only of Europe, but of Asia and Africa, invariably agree as to the general form ; consequently their ideas of it are not to be considered as arbitrarily assumed, although we are not able to account for them all.

19. Color assists beauty ; generally, it heightens beauty and its forms, but it does not constitute it ; just as the taste of wine is more agreeable, from its color, when drunk from a transparent glass, than from the most costly golden cup.   Color, however, should have but little share in our consideration of beauty, because the essence of beauty consists, not in color, but in shape, and on this point enlightened minds will at once agree.   As white is the color which reflects the greatest number of rays of light, and consequently is the most easily perceived, a beautiful body will, accordingly, be the more beautiful the whiter it is, just as we see that all figures in gypsum, when freshly formed, strike us as larger than the statues from which they are made.   A negro might be called handsome, when the conformation of his face is handsome.   A traveller assures us that daily association with negroes diminishes the disagreeableness of their color, and displays what is beautiful in them ; just as the color of bronze and of the black and greenish basalt does not detract from the beauty of the antique heads.   The beautiful female head (3) in the latter kind of stone, in the villa

Albani, would not appear more beautiful in white marble. The head of the elder Scipio, of dark-greenish basalt, in the palace Rospigliosi, is more beautiful than the three other heads, in marble, of the same individual. These heads, together with other statues in black stone, will meet with approbation even from the unlearned, who view them as statues. It is manifest, therefore, that we possess a knowledge of the beautiful, although in an unusual dress and of a disagreeable color. But beauty is also different from pleasingness or loveliness. We term a person lovely or pleasing, who, without being beautiful, has the power to charm by demeanor, conversation, and understanding, also by youth, skin, and complexion. Aristotle calls such persons ἄνευ κάλλους ὡραῖοι, *charming without beauty ;* and Plato says, ὡραίων προσώποις, καλῶν δὲ μή, *of pleasing, but not beautiful faces.*

20. Thus far, then, we have, as proposed, treated of beauty negatively ; that is, by showing that the conceptions entertained of it are incorrect, we have separated from it attributes which it does not possess. A positive idea of it requires a knowledge of its essence, into which, except in a few cases, we have no power to look. We cannot proceed here, as in the greater number of philosophical investigations, after the mode used in geometry, which advances and concludes from generals to particulars and individuals, and from the nature of things to their properties, but we must satisfy ourselves with drawing probable conclusions merely from single pieces. But fear lest the following considerations upon beauty may be misconstrued must not disturb him who desires to instruct ; for, as Plato and Aristotle, the teacher and scholar, entertained precisely opposite opinions as to the aim of tragedy, — the latter commending it as a purifier of the passions, and the former, on the contrary, describing it as a stimulus to them, — so it is possible that a harsh judgment may be pronounced on the most innocent intentions even of those who think correctly. I make this remark especially in regard to my treatise on the *Capability of the Perception of the Beautiful in Sculpture,* which suggested to some few individuals an opinion that certainly never entered into my thoughts.

21. Wise men who have meditated on the causes of universal beauty have placed it in the harmony of the creature with the purposes of its being, and of the parts with each other and

with the whole, because they have investigated it in the works
of creation, and have sought to reach even the source of the
highest beauty.   But, as this is synonymous with perfection,
of which humanity is not a fit recipient, our idea of universal
beauty is still indefinite; and it is formed within us by single
acquisitions of knowledge, which, when they are collected and
united together, give us, if correct, the highest idea of human
beauty, — which we exalt in proportion as we are able to elevate ourselves above matter.   Since, moreover, this perfection
has been bestowed by the Creator on all his creatures, in a
degree suitable to them, and every idea originates from a cause
which must be sought, not in the idea itself, but in something
else, so the cause of beauty cannot be found *out* of itself, since
it exists *in* all created things.   From this circumstance, and —
as all our knowledge is made up of ideas of comparison — from
the impossibility of comparing beauty with anything higher
than itself, arises the difficulty of a general and clear explanation of it.

22. The highest beauty is in God; and our idea of human
beauty advances towards perfection in proportion as it can be
imagined in conformity and harmony with that highest Existence which, in our conception of unity and indivisibility, we
distinguish from matter.   This idea of beauty is like an essence
extracted from matter by fire; it seeks to beget unto itself
a creature formed after the likeness of the first rational being
designed in the mind of the Divinity.   The forms of such a
figure are simple and flowing, and various in their unity; and
for this reason they are harmonious, just as a sweet and pleasing tone can be extracted from bodies the parts of which are
uniform.   All beauty is heightened by unity and simplicity, as
is everything which we do and say; for whatever is great in
itself is elevated, when executed and uttered with simplicity.
It is not more strictly circumscribed, nor does it lose any of
its greatness, because the mind can survey and measure it with
a glance, and comprehend and embrace it in a single idea;
but the very readiness with which it may be embraced places
it before us in its true greatness, and the mind is enlarged, and
likewise elevated, by the comprehension of it.   Everything
which we must consider in separate pieces, or which we cannot
survey at once, from the number of its constituent parts, loses
thereby some portion of its greatness, just as a long road is

shortened by many objects presenting themselves on it, or by many inns at which a stop can be made. The harmony which ravishes the soul does not consist in arpeggios, and tied and slurred notes, but in simple, long-drawn tones. This is the reason why a large palace appears small, when it is overloaded with ornament, and a house large, when elegant and simple in its style.

23. From unity proceeds another attribute of lofty beauty, the absence of individuality ; that is, the forms of it are described neither by points nor lines other than those which shape beauty merely, and consequently produce a figure which is neither peculiar to any particular individual, nor yet expresses any one state of the mind or affection of the passions, because these blend with it strange lines, and mar the unity. According to this idea, beauty should be like the best kind o water, drawn from the spring itself; the less taste it has, the more healthful it is considered, because free from all foreign admixture. As the state of happiness — that is, the absence of sorrow, and the enjoyment of content — is the very easiest state in nature, and the road to it is the most direct, and can be followed without trouble and without expense, so the idea of beauty appears to be the simplest and easiest, requiring no philosophical knowledge of man, no investigation and no expression of the passions of his soul.

24. Since, however, there is no middle state in human nature between pain and pleasure, even according to Epicurus, and the passions are the winds which impel our bark over the sea of life, with which the poet sails, and on which the artist soars, pure beauty alone cannot be the sole object of our consideration ; we must place it also in a state of action and of passion, which we comprehend in art under the term *Expression.* We shall, therefore, in the first place, treat of the shape of beauty, and in the second place, of expression.

25. The shape of beauty is either *individual,* — that is, confined to an imitation of one individual, — or it is a selection of beautiful parts from many individuals, and their union into one, which we call *ideal,* yet with the remark that a thing may be ideal without being beautiful. The form of the Egyptian figures, in which neither muscles, tendons, nor veins are indicated, is ideal, but still it shapes forth no beauty in them ; neither can the drapery of Egyptian female figures — which

can only be imagined, and consequently is ideal — be termed beautiful.

26. The conformation of beauty commenced with individual beauty, with an imitation of a beautiful male form, even in the representation of the gods ; and, in the blooming days of sculpture, the statues of goddesses were actually made after the likeness of beautiful women, even of those whose favors were venal (4) ; such was Theodote, of whom Xenophon speaks. On this point the ancients thought differently from us, insomuch that Strabo calls those women holy who had devoted themselves to the service of Venus on Mount Eryx ; and an ode by the lofty Pindar, — in praise of Xenophon of Corinth, a thrice-crowned Olympic conqueror, — which was intended to be sung by young women dedicated to the public service of Venus, commences thus : — " Ye much-delighting maids, and servants of persuasion in rich Corinth." [1]

27. The gymnasia and other places where the young exercised naked in athletic and other games, and which were the resort of those who desired to see beautiful youth, were the schools wherein the artist saw beauty of structure ; and, from the daily opportunity of seeing it nude and in perfection, his imagination became heated, the beauty of the forms he saw became his own, and was ever present to his mind. At Sparta, even the young virgins exercised naked, or nearly so, in the games of the arena.

28. To each age, even as to the goddesses of the seasons, there belongs its peculiar beauty, but differing in degree. It is associated especially with youth, which it is the great effort of art to represent. Here, more than in manhood, the artist found the cause of beauty, in unity, variety, and harmony. The forms of beautiful youth resemble the unity of the surface of the sea, which at some distance appears smooth and still, like a mirror, although constantly in movement with its heaving swell. The soul, though a simple existence, brings forth at once, and in an instant, many different ideas ; so it is with the beautiful youthful outline, which appears simple, and yet at the same time has infinitely different variations, and that soft tapering which is difficult of attainment in a column is still more so in the diverse forms of a youthful body. Among the innumerable kinds of columns in Rome, some appear pre-emi-

[1] Athen., lib. 13, cap. 4, p. 574.

nently elegant on account of this very tapering; of these I
have particularly noticed two of granite, which I am always
studying anew : just so rare is a perfect form, even in the
most beautiful youth, which has a stationary point in our sex
still less than in the female.

29. The forms of a beautiful body are determined by lines
the centre of which is constantly changing, and which, if continued, would never describe circles. They are, consequently,
more simple, but also more complex, than a circle, which, however large or small it may be, always has the same centre, and
either includes others, or is included in others. This diversity
was sought after by the Greeks in works of all kinds; and
their discernment of its beauty led them to introduce the
same system even into the form of their utensils and vases,
whose easy and elegant outline is drawn after the same rule,
that is, by a line which must be found by means of several
circles, for all these works have an elliptical figure, and herein
consists their beauty. The greater unity there is in the junction of the forms, and in the flowing of one out of another,
so much the greater is the beauty of the whole.

30. From this great unity of youthful forms, their limits
flow imperceptibly one into another, and the precise point of
height of many, and the line which bounds them, cannot be
accurately determined. This is the reason why the delineation
of a youthful body, in which everything is and is yet to come,
appears and yet does not appear, is more difficult than that of
an adult or aged figure. In the former of these two, the adult,
nature has completed, and consequently determined, her work
of formation; in the latter, she begins again to destroy the
structure; in both, therefore, the junction of the parts is clearly
visible. In youth, on the contrary, the conformation is, as it
were, suspended between growth and maturity. To deviate
from the outline in bodies having strongly developed muscles,
or to strengthen or exaggerate the prominence of muscles or
other parts, is not so great an error as the slightest deviation
in youthful figures, in which even the faintest shadow, as it is
commonly said, becomes a body, just as a rule, though shorter
or narrower than the requisite dimensions, still has all the
properties of a rule, but cannot be called so if it deviates from
a straight line; whoever misses the centre-white has missed as
much as though he had not hit the target at all.

31. This consideration will establish the correctness of our opinion, and teach the ignorant better, who, in general, admire the art more in a figure where all the muscles and bones are distinctly shown, than in the simplicity of youth. Convincing proof of what I maintain is found in the engraved gems, and the copies from them, by which it is seen that aged heads are imitated by modern artists better and much more accurately than beautiful young heads. A connoisseur might probably doubt, at the first glance, as to the antiquity of an aged head upon an engraved gem ; but he will be able to decide with more confidence upon the copy of a youthful ideal head. Although the celebrated Medusa in the museum Strozzi, at Rome, — which is, moreover, not a figure of the highest beauty, — has been copied, even in size, by the best modern artists, still the original can always be recognized. This is true, likewise, of the copies of the Pallas of Aspasius, though it has been engraved by several artists, and by Natter of the same size as the original.

32. It may be observed, that I speak here merely of the perception and impersonation of beauty in its strict sense, not of science in design and skill in execution. In respect to the latter, more science can exist in, and be introduced into, vigorous than tender figures. The Laocoön is a much more learned work than the Apollo. Agesander, the sculptor of the principal figure in the group of the Laocoön, must, therefore, have been a far more skilful and complete artist than it was requisite for the sculptor of the Apollo to be. The latter, however, must have possessed a more elevated mind and more tender sensibilities ; the Apollo has a sublimity which was not possible in the Laocoön.

33. But nature and the structure of the most beautiful bodies are rarely without fault. They have forms which can either be found more perfect in other bodies, or which may be imagined more perfect. In conformity to this teaching of experience, those wise artists, the ancients, acted as a skilful gardener does, who ingrafts different shoots of excellent sorts upon the same stock ; and, as a bee gathers from many flowers, so were their ideas of beauty not limited to the beautiful in a single individual, — as at times are the ideas of both ancient and modern poets, and of the majority of artists of the present day, — but they sought to unite the beautiful parts of many beautiful

bodies; this we learn also from the dialogue between Socrates and the celebrated painter Parrhasius. They purified their images from all personal feelings, by which the mind is diverted from the truly beautiful. Thus, personal affection makes Anacreon fancy that the eyebrows of his mistress, which are to be imperceptibly separated from one another, are beautiful, like the joined eyebrows (5) of her whom the Daphnis of Theocritus loved. One of the later Greek poets, in his *Judgment of Paris*, has probably from the passages just quoted derived the idea of this form of the eyebrows, which he assigns to the most beautiful of the three goddesses. The conceptions of the beautiful entertained by our sculptors, and even by those who pretend to imitate the antique, are individual and limited, when they select, as a model of great beauty, the head of the Antinoüs, in which the eyebrows are turned downwards, imparting to his face a somewhat harsh and melancholy expression.

34. Bernini expressed a very superficial opinion, when he pronounced the story of the selection of the most beautiful parts, made by Zeuxis from five beautiful women of Crotona, on being employed to paint a Juno there, an absurd invention, because he fancied that a particular part or limb would suit no other body than that to which it belonged. Others have been unable to think of any but individual beauties; and their dogma is, that the antique statues are beautiful because they resemble beautiful nature, and nature will always be beautiful whenever she resembles those beautiful statues. The former position is true, not singly, but collectively; the second, on the contrary, is false; for it is difficult, indeed almost impossible, to find in nature a figure like that of the Apollo of the Vatican.

35. This selection of the most beautiful parts and their harmonious union in one figure produced ideal beauty, — which is therefore no metaphysical abstraction; so that the ideal is not found in every part of the human figure taken separately, but can be ascribed to it only as a whole; for beauties as great as any of those which art has ever produced can be found singly in nature, but, in the entire figure, nature must yield the palm to art.

The conception of high or ideal beauty is, as I have observed, not equally clear to all, and one might suppose, from remarks made on the Ideal, that it can be formed only in the mind. By the Ideal is to be understood merely the highest possible beauty of the whole figure, which can hardly exist in nature in the same high degree in which it appears in some statues ; and it is an error to apply the term to single parts, in speaking of beautiful youth. Even Raphael and Guido seem to have fallen into the mistake alluded to, if we can judge from what both have expressed in their letters. The former when about to paint the Galatea, in the palace Farnesina, writes to his friend, the distinguished Count Balthazar Castiglione, in the following terms: — " In order to select a beautiful woman, one must see those who are more beautiful ; but, as beautiful women are rare, I make use of a certain image supplied by my imagination." But the conception of the head of his Galatea is common ; women of greater beauty are to be found everywhere. Moreover, the figure is so disposed, that the breast, the most beautiful part of the naked female form, is completely covered by one arm, and the knee which is in view is much too cartilaginous for a person of youthful age, to say nothing of a divine Nymph. When Guido was preparing to paint his Archangel Michael, he wrote to a Roman prelate, — " I should like to give to the figure I am about to paint beauty such as that which dwells in Paradise, irradiated by the glories of heaven ; but I have not yet been able to rise so high, and I have sought it in vain on earth." Nevertheless, his Archangel is less beautiful than some young men whom I have known, and still know. But if Raphael and Guido failed of finding beauty, — the former in the female, and the latter in the male sex, — such as they deemed worthy of the Galatea and the Archangel, as appears from the autograph papers of those artists, then I do not hesitate to say that the opinion of both was the result of inattention to that which is beautiful in nature. I am, indeed, bold enough to assert that I have seen faces quite as perfect in conformation as those which our artists regard as models of lofty beauty.

36. The attention which the Greek artists paid to the selection of the most beautiful parts from numberless beautiful persons did not remain limited to male and female youths alone, but their observation was directed also to the conformation of eunuchs, for whom boys of handsome shape were chosen. Those equivocal beauties effected by the removal of the seminal vessels — in which the masculine characteristics approximated, in the superior delicacy of the limbs, and in greater plumpness and roundness generally, to the softness of the female sex —

were first produced among the Asiatics, for the purpose, as Petronius says, of retarding the rapid career of fleeting youth. Among the Greeks in Asia Minor, boys and youths of this kind were consecrated to the service of Cybele, and the Diana of Ephesus. The Romans also attempted to check the appearance of the garniture of manhood by washing the chin and other parts with a decoction of hyacinth roots made by boiling them in sweet wine.

The ancient artists must have observed this ideal development of youth piecemeal in eunuchs, since their conformation varies according to the earlier or later age at which they are removed into that state of ambiguous nature. Their form is, nevertheless, always distinct, as well from that of man, as that of woman ; it is intermediate between the two. This difference is fully apparent in the hands of these persons, which, when they are beautifully formed by nature, have a shape that merits the attention of him who studies beauty in all parts. It would not be possible, however, to point it out by description, except very imperfectly. It is, on the other hand, more manifest in the hips and back. The former, as well as the latter, are feminine ; that is, the hips are fuller and have a greater breadth, and the spinal column lies less deeply, than with males, so that fewer muscles are distinguishable ; and hence the back shows more unity in its shape, as with women. As in women, so in eunuchs, the region over the *os sacrum*, termed the posteriors, is large, broad, and flat.

37. The ancient sculptors denoted the eunuch form, in the hitherto unobserved figures of the priests of Cybele, by the female hips just mentioned. This breadth of hip is distinguishable even beneath the drapery of a figure of this kind, of the size of life, which has been sent to England. It represents a boy of about twelve years of age, with a short vest. The Phrygian cap led some persons to believe that they recognized in it a Paris, and, when it was repaired, an apple was placed in its right hand as a characteristic symbol. An inverted torch, and of the very kind which was used at sacrifices and in religious offices, rests at the feet of the figure, against a tree, and appears to indicate its true signification. The shape of the hips of another priest of Cybele, on a mutilated work in relief, is feminine to such a degree, that the most skilful sculptor in Rome was led, from this circumstance alone, to regard this figure as

belonging to the female sex. But the whip in its hand indicates a priest of Cybele, because these emasculates scourged themselves ; and the figure in question stands before a tripod. These figures, and a relievo at Capua representing an Archigallus, that is, the superior of the eunuch-priests here referred to, will give us some notion of the celebrated picture by Parrhasius, which was a portrait of a person of this description, and was therefore called Archigallus. The priests of Diana at Ephesus, also, were eunuchs, but not one of them, so far as it is known, has been found represented on the ancient works.

38. In this respect the ancient artists have risen to the ideal, not only in the conformation of the face, but also in the youthful figures of certain gods, as Apollo and Bacchus. This ideal consists in the incorporation of the forms of prolonged youth in the female sex with the masculine forms of a beautiful young man, which they consequently made plumper, rounder, and softer, in admirable conformity with their ideas of their deities. For to some of these the ancients gave both sexes, blended with a mystic significance in one, as may be seen even in a small Venus of bronze, in the museum of the Roman College. This commingling is especially peculiar to Apollo and Bacchus.

39. Art went still farther; it united the beauties and attributes of both sexes in the figures of hermaphrodites. The great number of hermaphrodites, differing in size and position, shows that artists sought to express in the mixed nature of the two sexes an image of higher beauty ; this image was ideal. Without entering into any inquiry how hermaphrodites may be constituted, on the supposition of the actual existence of creatures called by this name, — like the philosopher Favorinus, of Arles, in France, according to Philostratus, — every artist cannot have an opportunity of seeing so rare a deviation of nature; and hermaphrodites, like those produced by sculpture, are probably never seen in real life. All figures of this kind have maiden breasts, together with the male organs of generation ; the form in other respects, as well as the features of the face, is feminine. Besides the two recumbent statues of hermaphrodites (6) in the grand-ducal gallery at Florence, and the still more celebrated and beautiful one in the villa Borghese, there is a small upright figure, not less beautiful, in the villa Albani, of which the right arm rests upon the head. In selecting the most beautiful parts from the ancient statues, one would have to

PLATE I

PLATE II

take a female back from the beautiful hermaphrodite in the villa Borghese.

40. Next to the selection and harmonious union and incorporation of single parts, of superior beauty, from different conformations of the human figure, the study of artists in producing ideal beauties was directed to the nature of the nobler beasts, so that they not only instituted comparisons between the forms of the human countenance and the shape of the head of certain animals, but they even undertook to adopt from animals the means of imparting greater majesty and elevation to their statues. This remark, which might at first sight seem absurd, will strike profound observers as indisputably correct, especially in the heads of Jupiter and Hercules. For, on examining the conformation of the father and king of the gods, it is seen that his head has the complete aspect of that of the lion, the king of beasts, not only in the large round eyes (7), in the fulness of the prominent, and, as it were, swollen forehead, and in the nose, but also in the hair, which hangs from his head like the mane of the lion, first rising upward from the forehead, and then, parting on each side into a bow, again falling downward.[1] This is not such an arrangement of the hair as belongs to man ; it is peculiar to the animal in question. In the statues of Hercules, the make of a powerful bull is seen in the relation of the head to the neck ; the former is smaller, and the latter larger, than is usual in the human figure, and they stand just in that proportion to each other which the head of a bull bears to the neck, — in order to express in this hero a preternatural vigor and strength. One might, indeed, say, that even the short hairs on the forehead of Hercules, as an allegorical figure, may have been copied from those on the forehead of that animal.

[1] Plates I. and II. represent the eyes, forehead, and arrangement of the hair of Jupiter. The head from which Plate I. was engraved formerly adorned the façade of the villa Medici; it was afterwards carried to Florence, to be set up in the garden Boboli. — GERM. ED.

The engraving of Plate II. was executed by Mr. J. Andrews of this city, from a drawing, also by himself, of a cast in the Boston Athenæum, which is supposed to be a Jupiter of Phidias. The engravings of the Jupiter of Otricoli in the *Pio-Clement Museum* (Vol. VI., Plate I.) and in the *Musée François* did not satisfy my wishes, and any reader who will take the trouble to make a comparison will, I think, concede the superiority in breadth of outline, nobleness of forms, and majesty of expression, to the engraving before him. — TR.

BOOK V.

ART AMONG THE GREEKS (*continued*).

CHAPTER I.

THE CONFORMATION AND BEAUTY OF THE MALE DEITIES AND HEROES.

1. THE most beautiful forms, thus selected, were, in a manner, blended together, and from their union issued, as by a new spiritual generation, a nobler progeny, of which no higher characteristic could be conceived than never-ending youth, — a conclusion to which the consideration of the beautiful must necessarily lead. For the mind, in rational beings, has an innate tendency and desire to rise above matter into the spiritual sphere of conceptions, and its true enjoyment is in the production of new and refined ideas. The great artists among the Greeks — who regarded themselves almost as creators, although they worked less for the understanding than for the senses — sought to overcome the hard resistance of matter, and, if possible, to endue it with life, with soul. This noble zeal on their part, even in the earlier periods of art, gave rise to the fable of Pygmalion's statue. For their hands produced those objects of devout respect, which, to inspire veneration, must necessarily appear to be images taken from a more elevated order of beings. The first founders of the religion — who were poets — attached to these images exalted ideas, and these in their turn excited the imagination to elevate her work above herself, and above sense. To human notions, what attribute could be more suitable to sensual deities, and more fascinating to the imagination, than an eternal youth and spring-time of life, when the very remembrance of youth which has passed away can gladden us in later years ? It was

conformable to their idea of the immutability of the godlike nature ; and a beautiful youthful form in their deities awakened tenderness and love, transporting the soul into that sweet dream of rapture, in which human happiness — the object and aim of all religions, whether well or ill understood — consists.

2. Among the female divinities, constant virginity was attributed to Diana and Pallas, and the other goddesses could obtain it again when once lost, — Juno, for instance, as often as she bathed in the fountain of Canathus. Hence the breasts of the goddesses and Amazons are like those of young maidens whose girdle Lucina has not loosed, and who have not yet gathered the fruits of love; I mean to say, that the nipple is not visible (1), unless the goddesses are repesented in the act of giving suck, as, for example, Isis suckling Apis; but the fable says, that, instead of the breast, she placed her finger in the mouth of Orus, and she is actually represented in this manner, on an engraved gem in the Stosch museum, probably in conformity to the idea above stated. The nipples would, also, probably be visible on the breasts of a sitting statue of Juno suckling Hercules, in the Papal garden, if they were not covered by the head of the child and the hand of the goddess. An explanation of this statue, with an engraving, has been brought to notice in my *Monuments of Antiquity* (2). In an old picture, in the palace Barberini, which is supposed to represent a Venus, of the size of life, the breasts have nipples; this is a good reason why the figure may not be a Venus.

3. The spiritual nature of divinities is likewise represented in their gliding gait. Homer compares the swiftness of Juno in walking with the thought of a man, which passes through many distant countries that he has visited, and says at one and the same instant, " I have been here; I was there." The running of Atalanta is an example of this; she sped so swiftly over the sand as to leave no impress of her foot behind; and just so light appears the Atalanta on an amethyst in the Stosch museum. The step of the Vatican Apollo floats, as it were, in air; he touches not the earth with the soles of his feet. Pherecydes, one of the oldest Greek poets, seems to have intended to express this light and gliding movement in the snake-form which he gave to the deities, in order to describe figuratively a mode of progression of which it is not easy to discover any trace.

4. The youth of the deities has, in both sexes, its different degrees and periods, in the representation of which sculpture sought to display all their beauties. This youth is an ideality, adopted partly from the bodies of beautiful males, and partly from the nature of beautiful eunuchs, and elevated by a conformation surpassing that of humanity. Hence Plato says, "that not the true proportions, but those which seemed to the imagination most beautiful, were given to statues of the divinities."

5. The first, or male ideal, has its different degrees. It begins in the young Satyrs or Fauns, as humble conceptions of divinities.[1] The most beautiful statues of Fauns present to us an image of ripe, beautiful youth, in perfect proportion. They are distinguished from young heroes by a common profile, and a somewhat sunken nose, — so that they might, for this reason, be called Simi, flat-nosed, — not less than by a certain innocence and simplicity, accompanied by a peculiar grace, of which I shall speak hereafter in discussing Grace. This was the general idea which the Greeks had of these deities (3).

6. Now, since more than thirty statues of young Satyrs or Fauns are to be found in Rome, resembling each other in attitude and features, it is probable that the original of them was the celebrated Satyr of Praxiteles, which was in Athens, and was regarded by the artist himself as his best work (4). The next most distinguished artists in this kind of figures were Pratinas and Aristias (5) of Phlius, not far from Sicyon, together with one Æschylus. Sometimes these Satyrs had a laughing countenance, and warts pendant beneath the jaw (6), like goats.[2] Of this kind is one of the most beautiful heads of antiquity (7), in respect to execution; it was formerly in the possession of the distinguished Count Marsigli, but now stands in the villa Albani. The beautiful Barberini sleeping Faun is no ideal, but an image of simple, unconstrained nature. A modern writer (8), who sings and speaks of painting in poetry and prose, could never

---

[1] Plate III., A, B. A is the profile of a young Faun of the noblest kind. It is engraved from an admirable statue of white marble in the gallery at Dresden.

B is the profile of a Faun of common character. The statue is in the Capitoline museum. There is a figure almost exactly like it, of red marble, in the Pio-Clement museum, and another in the miscellaneous room of the Capitoline museum. They are works of the time of Adrian, and were excavated at his villa near Tivoli. — GERM. ED.

[2] Plate III., a, a.

PLATE III

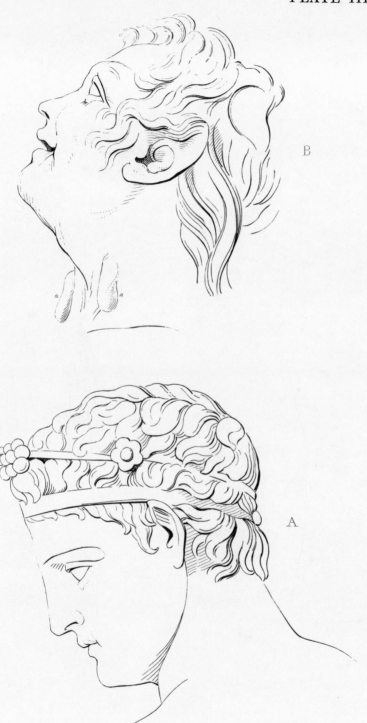

PLATE IV

have seen an antique figure of a Faun, and must have been ill informed by others, when he states, as a well-known fact, that the Greek artists selected the shape of the Fauns for the purpose of representing heavy and sluggish proportions, and that they may be known by their large heads, short necks, high shoulders, small and narrow chests, thick thighs and knees, and misshapen feet. Is it possible that any one can form notions so low and false of the sculptors of antiquity? It is a heresy in art, first hatched in the brain of this author. I do not know that he was obliged, like Cotta, in Cicero, to say what a Faun is.

7. The young Satyrs or Fauns are all beautiful, without exception, and so shaped, that each one of them, if it were not for the head, might be mistaken for an Apollo, especially for that Apollo called Σαυροκτόνος (Lizard-killer), the position of whose legs is that common to the Fauns. Among the many statues of this kind, two in the palace Ruspoli have been preserved uninjured. In one head of a young Faun, the artist has risen above the usual idea, and given an image of high beauty, over which an inexpressible sweetness is diffused. He appears to be in a quiet rapture, which shows itself particularly in the half-closed mouth. The upper part of the ears, which should be pointed, is concealed by the hair; this likewise has not the usual stiffness, but is disposed in lovely waves. A Faun would never have been recognized in this head, if it had not been for the addition of small horns, which are beginning to shoot forth on both sides of the forehead. If the arrangement of the hair warranted it, this image might represent a young Bacchus with horns. This head, of which mention has been made in the accounts of the latest discoveries at Herculaneum, is now in the author's possession.

8. The older Satyrs or Sileni, and that Silenus in particular who educated Bacchus, have, in serious figures, not a single trait inclining to the ludicrous, but they are beautiful bodies in the full ripeness of age, just as the statue of Silenus holding the young Bacchus in his arms (9), in the villa Borghese, represents them.[1] This figure is precisely similar to two others, in the villa Ruspoli, of which only one has an antique head. Silenus either has a joyous face and a curly beard, as in the statues just

[1] Plate IV. This engraving is made after a statue in the Pio-Clement museum, which is exactly like that in the Borghese villa (10). — Tr.

mentioned, or, as in other figures, he appears as the teacher of
Bacchus, in philosophic form, with a long and venerable beard,
which falls in soft waves down upon his breast, just as we see
him in the oft-repeated reliefs known under the highly erroneous appellation of the " Repast of Trimalchion."   I have presented this idea of Silenus, confined exclusively to serious
figures, for the purpose of obviating the objection which might
be made, that he is uncommonly corpulent, and rides reelingly
upon an ass, and is thus represented on different raised works.[1]

9. As the common idea entertained of the Satyrs or Fauns
is usually erroneous, so it has happened with Silenus; I should
say, with the Sileni, for the ancients said Σιληνοί, in the plural
number.   Since one generally thinks of Silenus as an old,
exceedingly corpulent, and slouching personage, always intoxi-
cated, sometimes reeling, and sometimes sinking down and falling from his ass, und usually leaning for support upon Satyrs,
as he is ordinarily represented, it has been found difficult to
reconcile with such a figure the foster-father and instructor of
Bacchus, which he actually was.   This misconception is the
reason why the statue of Silenus with the young Bacchus in his
arms, standing in the villa Borghese, has been supposed to be a
Saturn, because the figure resembles an ancient hero; yet its
true signification ought to have been recognized by the pointed
ears, and the ivy about the head.

10. The principal of these deities of a lower order is Pan.
Pindar calls him the most perfect of the gods.   Of the conformation of his face we have hitherto had either no idea at all, or
a very erroneous one.   I believe, however, that I have discovered it, in a head crowned with ivy, on a beautiful coin of Antigonus the First.   The countenance is serious, and the beard
full and shaggy, resembling the hair of a goat; hence Pan is
called Φριξοκόμης, "bristly-haired."   Of this coin I will give
some further account hereafter (in the second chapter of the
tenth book).   Another head of this deity, not more known, but
executed with greater skill, is to be found in the Capitoline
museum (12).   He is more easily recognized by the pointed
ears in this than in the former figure.   The beard, on the other
hand, is less stiff; it resembles that on some heads of philosophers, the deeply thoughtful expression of whose faces lies par-

---

[1] Plate V. This engraving is also made after a statue in the Pio-
Clement museum (11). — TR.

PLATE V

ticularly in the eyes, — which are sunken, after the manner of those of Homer. An engraving of this head will appear in the third volume of my *Ancient Monuments*. The god Pan was not always represented with the feet of a goat, for a Greek inscription mentions a figure of him, of which the head resembled the usual one with goat's horns, whilst the body and chest were shaped in imitation of those of Hercules, and the feet were winged like Mercury's.

11. The highest conception of ideal male beauty is especially expressed in the Apollo, in whom the strength of adult years is found united with the soft forms of the most beautiful spring-time of youth. These forms are large in their youthful unity, and not those of a minion wandering about in cool shades, and whom Venus, as Ibycus says, has reared on roses, but befitting a noble youth, destined to noble purposes. Hence Apollo was the most beautiful among the gods. Health blooms in his youth, and strength manifests itself, like the ruddiness of morning on a beautiful day. I do not, however, mean to say that all statues of Apollo possess this lofty beauty, for even the Apollo of the villa Medici (13), so highly prized by our sculptors, and so frequently copied, too, in marble, is, if I may make the remark without offence, of a beautiful shape, as a whole, but in single parts, as the knees and legs, is inferior to the best.

12. I could wish, in this place, to describe beauty, the like of which can hardly have had human origin. It is a winged Genius (14), in the villa Borghese, of the size of a well-made youth. If the imagination, filled with the single beauties everywhere displayed in nature, and occupied in the contemplation of that beauty which flows from God and leads to God, were to shape during sleep a vision of an angel, whose countenance was brightened by the divine effulgence, and whose form was seemingly an effluence from the source of the highest harmony, — in such a form let the reader set before himself this lovely image. It might be said, that nature, with God's approval, had fashioned it after the beauty of the angels (15).

13. The most beautiful head of Apollo, next to that of the Belvedere, as it appears to me, belongs to a sitting statue of this god, larger than life, in the villa Ludovisi. It is quite as uninjured as that of the Belvedere, and more conformable to our idea of Apollo, as a benignant and gentle deity. This

statue, which has been but little noticed, deserves remark, as the only one having a shepherd's crook, an emblem ascribed to Apollo. It lies on the stone on which the figure is sitting, and shows that Apollo the shepherd, Νόμιος, is represented here, — with especial reference to his service, in this capacity, with Admetus, king of Thessaly.

14. From the head of a statue of Apollo in the villa Belvedere, at Frascati, likewise from the bust with the uninjured head in the galleries of the Conservatori of the Capitol (16), and also from two other heads of the same deity, — one of which is in the Capitoline museum, and the other in the Farnesina, — one can get an idea of that style of arranging the hair which the Greeks termed κρωβύλος, and of which there remains no clear description. This word, when applied to young men, has the same signification as κόρυμβος in the case of young maidens, that is, hair collected in a knot on the back part of the head. With young men, the hair was smoothed upwards around the head, and then gathered together on the crown, without any visible band to confine it. The hair is knotted together in precisely the same manner on the head of a female figure, — in one of the most beautiful of the pictures from Herculaneum, — which is resting on one knee, near a tragic personage, and writing on a tablet.

15. This similarity of head-dress, in both sexes, may be some excuse for those who have given the name of Berenice to a beautiful bust of Apollo, of bronze, in the Herculaneum museum, which has the hair thus smoothed upward, and perfectly resembles in idea the four heads of Apollo just mentioned, — especially since these last could not have been known to them ; but the ground for the appellation — namely, a medal of this Egyptian queen, on which is an impression of a female head with the hair thus arranged, together with the name of Berenice — is not sufficient. For all heads and statues of Amazons, all figures of Diana, indeed all figures of virgins, have the hair smoothed upward. Now, as the braids on the hinder part of the head on the medal are twisted into a knot, after the invariable custom of virgins, it is impossible that a married queen can be represented by it. I am, therefore, of opinion, that the head on the coin is a Diana, notwithstanding the name Berenice stamped around it.

16. The youth which is so beautiful in Apollo advances to

PLATE VI

maturer years in other youthful gods, and becomes manly in Mercury and Mars. Mercury [1] is distinguished by a particular delicacy of countenance, which Aristophanes would have called Ἀττικὸν βλέπος, an Attic look, and his hair is short and curly. Mention has already been made of figures of him with a beard, on Etruscan works, and by the earliest Greek artists (17).

17. The modern artist who restored the head and a portion of the chest of another Mercury (18), of the size of life, embracing a young maiden, in the garden behind the palace Farnese, has given him a strong beard. For a long time this circumstance surprised me, as I could not imagine whence he got the idea. It cannot be supposed, that, even if he had been acquainted with the Etruscan manner of representing him, he would have been willing to introduce such a scrap of antique erudition in an enamored Mercury. I rather believe that he was induced to it by some learned scholar, who used the occasion to realize his understanding of the word ὑπηνήτη, in Homer, which he erroneously supposed to mean, " having a strong beard." The poet says, that Mercury, when about to accompany Priam to Achilles, assumed the form of a young man, πρῶτον ὑπηνήτη, which signifies " the age when the covering of the chin first begins to show itself," and can be predicated of a young man in the brightest bloom of life, that is, when the down first appears on the cheeks, which Philostratus, in speaking of Amphion, calls ἴουλον παρὰ τὸ οὖς, " the down beside the ear." Mercury is also represented in the same manner by Lucian. The young maiden with whom he is dallying does not appear to be Venus, who, according to Plutarch, is usually represented near this god, — in order to signify that the enjoyment of the pleasures of love must be accompanied by gentle words. On looking at the tender age of this figure, it might rather be supposed to be either Proserpine, who had three daughters by Mercury; or the nymph Lara, mother of the two Lares; or perhaps Acacallis, daughter of Minos; or Herse, one of the daughters of Cecrops, by whom also Mercury had children. I am inclined to favor the last conjecture, because I suppose that this group was discovered on the Appian Way, together with the two celebrated columns which stood by the

[1] Plate VI. From a bust in white marble, of about the size of life, and the loveliest and most beautiful of all the heads of this deity yet known. It is probably to be found among the antiques of the Duke of Buccleuch. — GERM. ED.

tomb of Regilla, wife of Herod Atticus, on the same spot, and which were formerly in the palace Farnese. The ground of my conjecture is the inscription on the tomb, which is now in the villa Borghese, in which it is stated that Herod Atticus derives his descent from Ceryx, son of Mercury and Herse ; I believe, therefore, that this group stood in that tomb. — I take this occasion to remark, that the only statue of Mercury, in which the usual antique purse in the left hand has been preserved, lies in the cellar of the palace of the villa Borghese (19).

18. Mars is commonly found represented as a young hero, and without beard, as one of the ancient authors also testifies. But it never occurred to any sculptor of ancient times to represent him as the writer[1] whom I have already censured would have him represented, that is, as one in whom every fibre, even the smallest, may express strength, boldness, and the fire which animates him. Such a Mars is not to be found in the entire range of antiquity. The three figures of him that are best known are a sitting statue (20), with Cupid at its feet, in the villa Ludovisi, — in which, as in all figures of deities, there is neither sinew nor vein visible, — a small figure on one of the bases of the two beautiful marble candelabra which were in the palace Barberini (21), and a third on the round work in the Capitol, described in the second chapter of the third book. The last two are standing. All three are of youthful age, and in a quiet position and action. He is represented as such a young hero on medals and engraved gems. But, if a bearded Mars (22) is to be found on other medals and gems, I should be almost of opinion that this latter figure may represent that Mars whom the Greeks call Ἐνυάλιος ; he was distinct from the other, and was his inferior and assistant.

19. Hercules is likewise represented in the most beautiful youth, with features which leave the distinction of sex almost doubtful (23), as the beauty of a young man should be, according to the opinion of the complaisant Glycera. He is represented in this manner, in an engraving on a carnelian belonging to the Stosch museum. But, generally, his forehead projects with a roundish fat fulness, which arches,[2] and, as it were, puffs

[1] Watelet, Art de Peindre, chant 1, p. 13.

[2] Plate VII., A, is intended, as far as an outline can, to give an idea of the forms of the forehead and the arrangement of the hair of that head of Hercules of which mention is made in note 27 ; in the marble, however, the forms are more blended, and the transitions softer. — GERM. ED.

PLATE VII

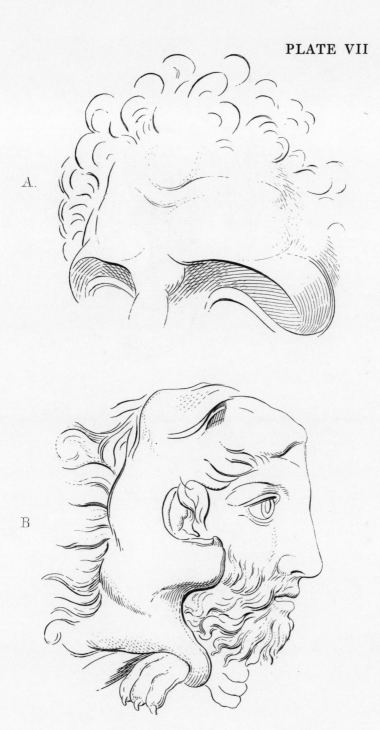

A.

B

PLATE VIII

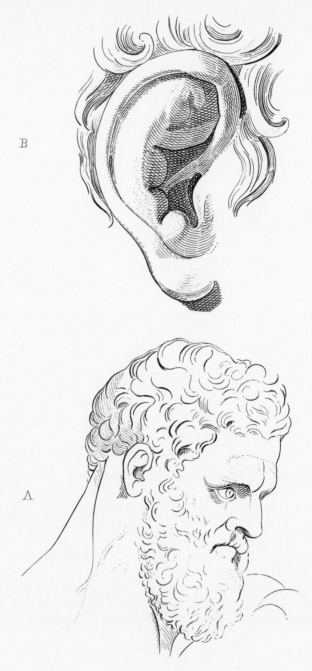

B

A

out, the upper bone of the socket of the eye, — to signify his strength, and his constant toil in sadness which, as the poet says, makes the heart swell.

20. Hercules is distinguishable particularly by his hair, which is short, curly, and smoothed upwards over the forehead. This characteristic is especially useful in a young Hercules; for I have remarked that, by the absence of such a disposition of the hair, the heads of young heroes, which might otherwise have been taken for heads of Hercules, have been instantly distinguished. From my observation of the hair generally, and particularly over the forehead of Hercules, I cannot consent to call by this name the fragment of a small figure which, on account of some similarity in the heads, is now in process of restoration as a Hercules. But since this single head cannot be an exception to the general rule, I should be inclined to regard the figure, inasmuch as it has the ears of a Pancratiast,[1] as representing a philosopher who had been an athlete in his younger days, as Lycon was. This admirable work, which was carried to England some years ago, and again brought back to Rome, was repaired for General von Wallmoden, of Hanover.

21. The second kind of ideal youth is drawn from the conformation of eunuchs. It is represented, blended with masculine youth, in Bacchus.[2] He appears under this form, at different ages, until he attains his full growth, and, in the most beautiful statues, always with delicate, round limbs, and the full, expanded hips of the female sex, for, according to the fable, he was brought up as a maiden. Pliny, indeed, mentions a statue of a Satyr holding a figure of Bacchus clothed as a Venus; hence Seneca also describes him, in shape, gait, and dress, as a disguised virgin. The forms of his limbs are soft and flowing, as though inflated by a gentle breath, and with scarcely any indication of the bones and cartilages of the knees, just as these joints are formed in youths of the most beautiful shape, and in eunuchs. The type of Bacchus is a lovely boy who is treading the boundaries of the spring-time of life and adolescence, in whom emotions of voluptuousness, like the tender shoots of a plant, are budding, and who, as if between sleeping and wak-

[1] Plate VIII., B. See Book V., ch. v., § 30.

[2] See frontispiece, and Plate IX., a profile of the head in the frontispiece. Note 25 gives a further account of this lovely head. — GERM. ED.

ing, half rapt in a dream of exquisite delight, is beginning to collect and verify the pictures of his fancy; his features are full of sweetness, but the joyousness of his soul is not manifested wholly upon his countenance (24).

22. The ancient artists have retained this quiet joyousness in Bacchus, even when represented as a hero or warrior, on his Indian campaigns, as it appears from an armed figure of him, on an altar in the villa Albani, and on a mutilated relievo in my possession. It is from this consideration, probably, that this deity is never represented in company with Mars, — for Bacchus is not one of the twelve superior deities; and hence Euripides says, that Mars is unfriendly to the Muses, and to the merriment of the festivals of Bacchus. It may be observed in this connection, that Apollonius gives a coat of mail even to Apollo, as the Sun. In some statues of Apollo, his conformation is very similar to that of Bacchus; of this kind is the Apollo negligently leaning, as if against a tree, with a swan below him, in the Campidoglio, and three similar, yet more beautiful, figures in the villa Medici; for, in one of these divinities, both were occasionally worshipped, and one was taken for the other.

23. Here I can scarcely refrain from tears, when I think of a Bacchus, once mutilated, but now restored, in the villa Albani, originally nine palms high (6½ ft. Eng.), to which the antique head, breast, and arms are wanting. He is draped from the middle of the body to the feet, or, to speak more correctly, his garment or mantle, which is ample, has fallen down, and is gathered in rich folds about his hips, and that portion of it which would otherwise lie upon the ground is thrown over the branch of a tree, about which ivy has crept, and a serpent is twisted. No single figure gives one so high an idea of what Anacreon terms a belly of Bacchus.

24. The head of Bacchus which possesses the highest beauty belongs to a restored statue, somewhat larger than nature, which has gone to England. The face exhibits an indescribable blending of male and female beautiful youth, and a conformation intermediate between the two sexes, which will be perceived by an attentive observer. This head will be recognized, by any one who looks for it in its present location, by a fillet around the forehead, and by the absence of the usual crown of vine-leaf or ivy.

PLATE IX

PLATE X

B

A

B.

One cannot but be astonished that the best artists, even in Rome, after the restoration of art, entertained so erroneous ideas of the person of Bacchus. The best painter now living in Rome, when he was asked how this deity appeared to Ariadne, represented him of a brownish-red color (25).

25. Bacchus was worshipped not only under a youthful form, but also under the form of manhood. The latter, however, is distinguished solely by a long beard, so that the countenance in its hero-expression, and softness of features, presents an image of the joyousness of youth. The intention of the artist, in representing him in this form, was to show him as on his campaign in India, when he suffered his beard to grow ; and such an image of him presented an opportunity to the ancient artists to exhibit, partly, a peculiar ideal, — manliness blended with youth, — and partly, their art and skill in the execution of the hair. Of the heads and busts of this Indian Bacchus the most celebrated are those crowned with ivy, on silver coins from the island of Naxos,[1] the reverse side of which represents Silenus with a bowl in his hand ; and, in marble, a head in the palace Farnese, which passes very erroneously under the name of Mithridates. But the most beautiful of these heads is a Hermes (26), belonging to the sculptor Cavaceppi, the hair and beard of which are executed with infinite skill.

26. The full-length figures of the Indian Bacchus, when in an upright position, are always draped, even to the feet ; they have been represented on works of every kind, and, among others, on two beautiful marble vases ornamented with raised work, of which the smaller is to be found in the palace Farnese ; the larger and more beautiful one in the Herculaneum museum. But these figures are still oftener seen represented on engraved stones, and on vases of burnt clay, of which I will mention here one from the Porcinari collection, at Naples ; an engraving of it may be seen in the first volume of the Hamilton work ; it exhibits a sitting bearded Bacchus, crowned with laurel, as a conqueror, in an elegantly embroidered dress.

27. Ideal beauty, however, exists not only in the spring-time of life, and in youthful or female figures, but also in manhood, to which the ancient artists, in the statues of their deities, imparted the joyousness and freshness of youth. In Jupiter,

[1] Plate X. See note 25. Figures B, B, represent the eyes of Bacchus, denoting the effeminacy of his character. — GERM. ED.

Neptune, and an Indian Bacchus, the beard and venerable head-hair are the sole marks of age ; it is not denoted either by wrinkles, projecting cheek-bones, or hollow temples.   The cheeks are less full than in youthful divinities, and the fore-head is usually more rounded.   This conformation is in keeping with their admirable conception of the divine nature, which neither suffers change from time, nor passes through gradations of age, and in regard to which we must think of existence without succession.   Such elevated ideas of the godhead ought to be peculiar to our artists, rather than to the ancients ; and yet, in most of the figures of the Eternal Father, — according to the Italian manner of speaking of the Deity, — we see an aged man, with a bald head.   Even Jupiter himself is represented by the scholars of Raphael, in the *Feast of the Gods*, in the Farnesina, with the hair of the head, as well as of the beard, snow-white ; and Albano has expressed the same idea in a similar manner, in his Jupiter, on the famous ceiling painted by him in the palace Verospi.

28. The beauty of deities of a manly age consists in a com-bination, uniting the robustness of mature years with the joy-ousness of youth, which in them, as in the images of more youthful divinities, is denoted by the concealment of muscles and sinews, which, in the spring-time of life, make but little show.   Together with these characteristics there is also to be seen an expression signifying the all-sufficiency of the divine nature to itself, that it has no need of those parts which are destined to the nutrition of human bodies.   This elucidates a passage from Epicurus, relative to the shape of the gods, to whom he gives a body, but only an apparent body, and blood, but only apparent blood, — a sentence which Cicero finds obscure and incomprehensible.   The presence or the absence of these parts distinguishes the Hercules who had to contend against monsters and fierce men, and had not yet reached the end of his toils,[1] from him whose body had been purified by fire, and who had been raised to the enjoyment of the happiness of Olympus.   The former is represented in the Hercules Far-

[1] Plate VIII., A, Hercules Farnese. Plate VII., B, Hercules deified These two heads are introduced here, in order to show the difference between the more common and the nobler ideal of Hercules. The head, B, was taken from a silver coin, which is ascribed to Amyntas II., king of Macedonia ; it is, consequently, a monument of the high style of Greek art. — GERM. ED.

PLATE XI

PLATE XII

nese, and the latter, in the torso of the Belvedere (27). It becomes evident, from these characteristics, whether statues — which, through the loss of heads, and other marks of distinction, might be doubtful — represent a god or a mortal. This consideration should have taught those better, who converted a sitting statue of Hercules, above the size of life, into a Jupiter, — by the addition of a new head and appropriate emblems. Through such ideas nature was elevated from the sensual to the uncreated, and the hand of the artist produced beings which were purified from human necessities : figures which represent humanity in a higher scale of excellence appear to be merely the veil and vestment of intelligent spirits and heavenly capacities.

29. The conformation of face of all the deities is so fixed and invariable, that it seems modelled by Nature's self. It is still more apparent in the gods of manly age than in the youthful divinities, that the face of each always retains the same character, — as may be seen in numberless images ; so that their heads, from Jupiter to Vulcan, are not less easily recognized than the likenesses of distinguished individuals of antiquity ; and, as Antinoüs is known by the lower portion of his face, and Marcus Aurelius by the hair and eyes of a mutilated cameo, in the museum Strozzi, at Rome, so would Apollo be known by his forehead, or Jupiter by the hair of his forehead, or by his beard, if heads should be found of which these parts alone remained.

30. Jupiter was figured with a countenance always serene (28) ; and they mistake, who wish to find a statue of Jupiter with the epithet of " the Terrible " in a colossal head of black basalt (29), in the villa Mattei, which bears a great resemblance to the Father of the gods, but has a stern countenance.[1] They did not observe that the head in question — as well as all those supposed heads of Jupiter which have not a kind and benevolent expression — wears, or has worn, the Modius ;[2] nor did

[1] Plate XI.

[2] Plate XII., Jupiter Serapis, with a Modius, A, on the head. Plate XIII., another head of Jupiter Serapis. The former is from a colossal bust in the Pio-Clement museum. It is a valuable monument of ancient art, and one of the best of those images which represent this Egypto-Grecian divinity. Though the Modius and rays are modern restorations, they are justified by marks which show them to have been there anciently. The latter is a small head, formerly in the collection of the poet Goethe. — GERM. ED.

they recollect that Pluto, according to Seneca, resembles Jupiter " the Thunderer," and, like Serapis, wears the Modius, — as may be seen on the seated statue, among others, which was formerly in his temple at Pozzuoli, and is now to be found at Portici, and likewise on a relief in the bishop's residence at Ostia. It has, moreover, not been observed with respect to this figure, erroneously assumed to be a Jupiter " the Terrible," that Pluto and Serapis are one and the same deity, who is distinguished by the Modius on his head. Besides, these heads may be known from those of Jupiter by the hair, which hangs down over the forehead, whilst that of Jupiter is carried upward from the forehead. Consequently, such heads represent, not Jupiter under any name, but Pluto; and since neither statues nor heads of the latter deity, of the size of life, have been known until now, the number of forms under which the deities have been represented has been increased by the characteristics just mentioned. It follows, therefore, from this well-established observation, that a large head of white marble (30), with a Modius head-dress, in the villa Pamfili, likewise represents a Pluto (31).

Hitherto no notice has been taken of this characteristic of the countenance; and modern artists have, consequently, supposed that they could designate Pluto in no other way than by a two-tined sceptre, or rather by a fork. The fire-forks with which devils in hell are usually painted appear to have suggested the first idea of this fork. On ancient works, Pluto holds a long sceptre, like the other gods, — as may be seen, among other examples, in the piece at Ostia just mentioned, and on a round altar, belonging to the Marquis Rondinini, in which he has Cerberus on one side, and Proserpine on the other.

31. Jupiter is distinguished from other deities of mature age and with a beard, — from Neptune, Pluto, and Æsculapius, — by his forehead, beard, and hair, not less than by the serenity of his expression. The hair is raised upward on the forehead, and parted; it then describes a short curve, and again falls down on each side, as shown in a copperplate engraving, copied from a head of him, cu in relief on an agate. This arrangement of the hair has been considered as so essential a characteristic of Jupiter, that it has been used to indicate the resemblance of the sons of this god to their father, — as one may readily perceive in the heads of Castor and Pollux, the two colossal statues

PLATE XIII

on the Campidoglio, especially in the head of the former, which is antique; that of the latter is a restoration.

32. On the forehead of Æsculapius, the hair is usually carried upwards in a similar, though somewhat different, manner, and, having formed an arch on each side, again falls downward. In this particular, therefore, there is no special difference between the Father of the gods and his grandson,—which can be proved by the most beautiful head of this divinity, on a statue above the natural size, in the villa Albani (32), and by many other images of him, and, among them, a statue of burnt clay, in the Herculaneum museum. But Æsculapius is distinguished by smaller eyes and older features, by the other part of his head-hair, and by his beard, especially on the upper lip, which has more of a bow-shape, whilst the moustache of Jupiter turns down at once about the corner of the mouth, and unites with the beard on his chin. This strong resemblance between grandchild and grandfather might even be grounded on the fact, that the child oftentimes less resembles his father than his grandfather. Experience, drawn from the observation of beasts, and especially horses, has shown that Nature, in the conformation of her creatures, occasionally takes such skips. In a Greek epigram, it is said of the statue of Sarpedon, son of Jupiter, that the race of the Father of the gods was manifest in the countenance; but, according to the foregoing remark, we must believe that the likeness could not have been denoted by the eyes, as it is there stated, but that the hair on the forehead was the distinctive mark of his origin.

33. The arrangement of the front hair on heads of Serapis or Pluto is the reverse of that of Jupiter. It hangs down on the forehead, in order to impart to the countenance a sadder and sterner expression,— as is shown by a superb, but imperfect, head of Serapis, of the most beautiful greenish Egyptian basalt, in the villa Albani, by a colossal head of marble, in the villa Pamfili, and another of black basalt, in the villa Giustiniani. On a head of Serapis, cut in very high relief on an agate, in the royal Farnese museum,[1] at Naples, as well as on a head of marble, in the Capitoline museum, we see the beard parted on the chin, in addition to the characteristic just mentioned; this, however, may be noticed as a singularity. I will here remark, that not one of all the heads and figures of Se-

[1] Now called Museo Nazionale. — Tr.

rapis can have been executed before the time of Alexander the Great, for Ptolemy Philadelphus first brought this divinity from Pontus to Egypt, and introduced his worship there.

34. The arrangement of the front hair of the Centaurs brings them within the scope of the remark in the thirty-second paragraph. It is almost precisely the same as that of Jupiter, probably for the purpose of signifying their relationship to him, since, as the fable says, they were begotten by Ixion and a Cloud, which had assumed the form of Juno. I am very well aware that the hair is not arranged in this manner on the forehead of the Centaur Chiron, in the Herculaneum museum, whose figure is of sufficient size to admit the representation of this peculiarity; but, as my observation is made on the Centaur in the villa Borghese, and on the more ancient of the two Centaurs in the Capitoline museum, I imagine that the relationship in question will account for the hair being thus arranged.

35. Jupiter is distinguished from those gods who resemble him in the arrangement of their front hair, by the hair which hangs down from his temples, and completely covers his ears. It is longer than on other deities, and arranged, not in curls, but in softly waving lines, and resembles, as I have before remarked, the mane of a lion. This resemblance, and the shaking of the lion's mane, as well as the motion of his eyebrows, appear to have been in the poet's mind, in his celebrated description of Jupiter, who shakes Olympus by the waving of his hair and the movement of his eyebrows.

36. The beautiful head of the unique statue of Neptune,[1] at Rome, in the villa Medici (33), appears to differ from the heads of Jupiter only in the beard and hair. The beard is not longer, but curly, and is thicker on the upper lip. The hair is curled in locks, and rises upward on the forehead in a manner different from its usual arrangement with Jupiter. An almost colossal head, with a garland of sedge, in the Farnesina, cannot, therefore, represent a Neptune; for the hair of the beard, as well as of the head, hangs directly down in waves; and its aspect is not serene, as in the statue; consequently, a sea-god, or river-god, must be here figured.

37. A passage in Philostratus, which has been misunderstood,

[1] Plate XIV., a. This statue was afterwards carried to Leghorn. The nose is probably modern. — GERM. ED.

PLATE XIV

A

B

ΣΟΝΥΝΟΙ

PLATE XV

occurs to me at this moment. He says, describing a picture of Neptune and Amymone, Κῦμα γὰρ ἤδη κυρτοῦται ἐς τὸν γάμον, γλαυκὸν ἔτι, καὶ τοῦ χαροποῦ τρόπου, πορφυροῦν δὲ αὐτὸ ὁ Ποσειδῶν γράφει, "Already the wave is arching for the nuptials; though green still, and of an azure hue, yet Neptune is painting it purple." Olearius, in his commentaries on this writer, has understood the last clause of the quotation as applying to a golden light which surrounds the head of Neptune, and censures, on this occasion, the scholiast of Homer, who interprets the word πορφύρεος by *obscurus*, "dark." He is wrong on both points. Philostratus says, "The sea begins to be arched," κυρτοῦται, "and Neptune is painting it purple." This remark is derived from observation of the Mediterranean Sea after a calm; for, when it begins to be agitated, it presents in the distance a red appearance, so that the waves appear purple-colored.

38. This is the most appropriate place to notice the facial conformation of the other, inferior sea-deities, though it is entirely different from that of Neptune. It is the most strongly marked in two colossal heads of Tritons, in the villa Albani, if we except a bust in the Capitoline museum : an engraving of one of them may be found in my *Ancient Monuments*. They are distinguished by a sort of fins, which form the eyebrows,[1] and resemble the eyebrows of the marine god Glaucus, in Philostratus, — ὀφρῦς λάσιαι συνάπτουσαι πρὸς ἀλλήλας, "his shaggy eyebrows joining each other." These fins pass again over the cheeks, nose, and even round the chin. Tritons of this form are found on divers burial urns, one of which is in the Capitoline museum.

39. As the ancients had mounted gradually from human to divine beauty, each of the steps of beauty remained through which they passed in their ascent.

Near the divinities stand the Heroes and Heroines of fable. To the artist, the latter as well as the former were objects of beauty. In Heroes, that is, in men to whom antiquity attributed the highest excellence of human nature, he advanced even to the confines of the divine nature, without passing beyond them, and without blending the very nice distinctions which separated the two. Battus, on medals of Cyrene, might easily be made to represent a Bacchus, by a single expression of ten-

---

[1] Plate XV., head of a Triton, in the Pio-Clement museum (34). — Tr.

der delight, and an Apollo, by one trait of godlike nobleness.
Minos, on coins of Gnossus, if it were not for a proud, regal look,
would resemble a Jupiter, full of graciousness and mercy.

40. The artist shaped the forms of Heroes heroically, and
gave to certain parts a preternatural development; placed in
the muscles quickness of action and of motion; and in energetic
efforts brought into operation all the motive powers of nature.
The object which he sought to attain was variety in its utmost
extent; and in this respect, Myron exceeded all his predecessors.
It is visible even in the Gladiator, erroneously so called, of Agasias of Ephesus, in the villa Borghese, whose face is evidently
copied after that of some particular individual. The serrated
muscles on the sides, as well as others, are more prominent,
active, and contractile than is natural. The same thing is yet
more clearly seen, in the same muscles, in the Laocoön, — who
is an ideally elevated being, — if this portion of the body be
compared with the corresponding portion in deified or godlike
figures, as the Hercules and Apollo of the Belvedere. The
action of these muscles, in the Laocoön, is carried beyond truth
to the limits of possibility; they lie like hills which are drawing themselves together, — for the purpose of expressing the
extremest exertion in anguish and resistance. In the torso of
Hercules deified, there is a high ideal form and beauty in these
same muscles; they resemble the undulations of the calmed
sea, flowing though elevated, and rising and sinking with a soft,
alternate swell. In the Apollo, an image of the most beautiful
of the gods, these muscles are smooth, and, like molten glass
blown into scarce visible waves, are more obvious to touch than
to sight.

41. In all these respects, beauty was uniformly the principal
object at which the artist aimed, and both fable and the poets
justified him in representing even young heroes with such a
conformation of face as to leave the sex doubtful, — as I have
already remarked of Hercules; and this might easily be the
case with a figure of Achilles, who, from the charms of his face,
assisted by female dress, lived undetected with the daughters
of Lycomedes, as their companion. He is thus represented on
a relievo in the villa Belvedere, at Frascati, — which is placed
over the preface to my *Ancient Monuments,* — and also on
another raised work in the villa Pamfili.

On first looking at the relievo which represents the recognition of Telephus by his mother, Auge, at the moment when she is about to kill him, I was in some doubt as to the sex of his figure. The face of the young hero is perfectly feminine, when looked at from below upwards; but viewed from above downward, it has something masculine blended with it. This relievo, in the palace Ruspoli, which has never before been explained, may be ranked among the most beautiful in the world: it may be seen among my *Monuments of Antiquity.* Beauty of the same equivocal kind would be found in Theseus also, if he should be figured as he came from Trœzene to Athens, dressed in a long robe reaching to his feet. The workmen on the temple of Apollo looked upon him as a beautiful virgin, and were astonished to see one, whom they supposed to be a handsome girl, going into the city unattended, contrary to the usual custom of that day.

42. No regard has been paid either to this idea of beauty, or to the age of Theseus, in a picture in the Herculaneum museum, in which the ancient painter has represented him with the Athenian boys and maidens kissing his hand, on his return from Crete, after slaying the Minotaur. But Nicholas Poussin has deviated still farther from the truth, and from the beauty of youthful age, in a picture (35) belonging to Lewis Vanvitelli, royal architect at Naples, in which Theseus, in presence of his mother, Æthra, discovers his father's sword and shoe concealed beneath a stone. This event took place in the sixteenth year of his age; but, in the picture, he is represented as already having a beard, and of a manly age, divested of all youthful roundness. I will say nothing of the edifice and triumphal arch, which are wholly incongruous with the times of Theseus.

43. The reader will pardon me, if I am obliged once more to direct the attention of that poetical writer on painting [1] to his erroneous prejudices. Among many absurd characteristics of the shape of heroes and demigods, as he terms them, he enumerates meagre limbs, lean legs, small head, narrow hips, sunken abdomen, smallish feet, and hollow soles to the feet. Where in the world did he meet with these appearances? Would that he had written of what he better understood!

44. Modern artists ought to have formed their figures of the Saviour conformably to the ideas which the ancients entertained of the beauty of their heroes, and thus made him correspond

[1] Watelet, L'Art de Peindre.

to the prophetic declaration, which announces him as the most beautiful of the children of men. But the idea of most figures of him, beginning with Michael Angelo, appears to be borrowed from the barbarous works of the Middle Ages, and there can be nothing more ignoble than the face in such heads of Christ. How much more noble the conceptions of Raphael are may be seen in a small original drawing, in the Royal Farnese museum at Naples, which represents our Saviour's burial, and in which his head exhibits the beauty of a young hero without beard. Annibal Caracci is the only one, so far as I know, who has imitated his example, in three similar pictures of the same subject, one of which is in the museum just mentioned, another in Santo Francesco *a ripa* at Rome, and the third in the family chapel of the palace Pamfili. But if such a face should possibly appear to the artist a scandalous innovation on the customary representation of the Saviour with a beard, then let him study the Saviour of Leonardo da Vinci, and, in particular, a wonderfully beautiful head from the hand of the same master, in the cabinet of Prince Wenzel von Lichtenstein, in Vienna. This head, notwithstanding the beard, expresses the highest manly beauty, and may be commended as the most perfect model.

45. If one will now reascend the steps from heroes to gods, which we have just descended from gods to heroes, pursuing exactly the gradation by which deities have been formed from heroes, it will appear that the effect has been produced rather by subtraction than by addition, that is to say, by the gradual abstraction of all those parts which, even in nature, are sharply and strongly expressed, until the shape becomes refined to such a degree that only the spirit within appears to have brought it into being.

CHAPTER II.

THE CONFORMATION AND BEAUTY OF THE FEMALE DEITIES AND HEROINES.

1. IN the female, as in the male divinities, different ages, and even different ideas of beauty, are observable, at least in their heads, for Venus is the only goddess who is entirely nude. In regard to forms and development, however, there are not so many gradations of difference in the figures of beautiful females, because that development is varied only according to their age. The limbs are equally rounded and full in heroines as in goddesses, — for even the former are found represented, as well as the latter; and if the artist had imparted a more marked development to certain parts in heroines, he would have deviated from the characteristics of their sex. For the same reason that I find less to notice in the beauty of the female sex, the study of the artist in this department is much more limited and easy; even Nature appears to act with more facility in the formation of the female than of the male sex, since there are fewer male than female children born. Hence Aristotle says, that the operations of Nature tend to perfection, even in the formation of human beings; but if a male cannot be produced, owing to the resistance of matter, then a female is the result. There is also another reason, not less easy to be understood, why the consideration, as well as the imitation, of beauty of shape in female statues may require less labor, which is, that most of the goddesses, as well as all the heroines, are draped, — an observation which is repeated in the dissertation on Drapery; whilst, on the contrary, the greater number of statues of the male sex are in a nude state.

2. I would observe, however, that my remark as to the similarity of the nude parts of female figures is to be understood only of the shape of the body, and does not exclude a distinctive character in their heads. This has been strongly expressed

in each goddess as well as in the heroines, so that both superior and inferior goddesses can be distinguished, even when the emblems usually adjoined to them are wanting. Each goddess had her peculiar aspect, as well as each god ; and the ancient artists constantly adhered to it. With this characteristic individual expression of the face they also endeavored to associate beauty in its highest degree, but they did not stop here ; they impressed similar beauty likewise upon the female masks.

3. Among the goddesses, Venus stands fairly preëminent, not only as the goddess of beauty, but because she alone, with the Graces, and the Seasons or Hours, is undraped (1), and also because she is found represented more frequently than any other goddess, and in different ages. The Medicean Venus, at Florence, resembles a rose which, after a lovely dawn, unfolds its leaves to the rising sun ; resembles one who is passing from an age which is hard and somewhat harsh — like fruits before their perfect ripeness — into another, in which all the vessels of the animal system are beginning to dilate, and the breasts to enlarge, as her bosom indicates, — which, in fact, is more developed than is usual in tender maidens. The attitude (2) brings before my imagination that Laïs who instructed Apelles in love. Methinks I see her, as when, for the first time, she stood naked before the artist's eyes. In the Capitoline museum there is a statue of Venus (3) that stands in precisely the same attitude, and is in a state of better preservation than most of these figures, for one finger only is wanting, and there are no fractures in it ; in the villa Albani is another ; there is still another (4), copied by one Menophantus from a Venus which stood at Troy (5). The last differs from the others in that the right hand is nearer the bosom, the second finger resting upon the centre of it ; the left hand supports a drapery. But both are represented in a riper age, and even larger than the Venus de' Medici. A shape of beautiful maidenhood, resembling hers, may be seen in the half-draped Thetis, of the size of life, in the villa Albani, who appears here of the age when she was given in marriage to Peleus : this statue will be described hereafter, in the second chapter of the twelfth book.

4. The celestial Venus (6), daughter of Jupiter and Harmonia, is different from the other Venus, who is the daughter of Dione. She is distinguished by a high diadem of the kind peculiar to Juno ; a similar diadem is also worn by a Venus

PLATE XVI

B

A

C

victrix, *victorious.* The most beautiful known statue of her was discovered in the theatre of the ancient city of Capua ; the arms are wanting, and her left foot rests upon a helmet. It is now in the royal palace at Caserta. A diadem of the same kind may also be seen, in some reliefs which represent the rape of Proserpine, on the head of a draped Venus, who is gathering flowers in company with Pallas, Diana, and Proserpine, in the fields of Enna, in Sicily. But it can be observed the most distinctly on two sepulchral urns in the palace Barberini. This head-ornament has been given to no other goddesses than these, with the exception of Thetis, who bears it on her head in a painting on a beautiful vase of burnt clay in the Vatican library, of which an engraving may be seen in my *Ancient Monuments.*

5. The celestial, not less than the Medicean Venus, has in her softly opened eyes that expression of tenderness and love which the Greeks term τὸ ὑγρόν, "liquid" ; it is owing entirely to the lower eyelid being somewhat elevated,[1] as I will point out hereafter in my remarks on the beauty of the eyes. This look is, however, entirely free from wantonness, for Love was regarded by the ancient artists and intelligent philosophers as, in the words of Euripides, the associate of Wisdom ; yet certain modern sculptors have imparted an expression of this sort to their statues of Venus, with the design of showing thereby what goddess they intended to represent.

6. When I remarked that Venus, with the Graces and Hours, is the only one of the goddesses who is not draped, I did not mean to be understood to say that she is uniformly represented nude, because we know the contrary of the Venus of Praxiteles, at Cos. There is also a beautiful draped statue of this goddess, which was formerly in the palace Spada, but has since been sent to England ; and she is thus represented in a relief on one of the two beautiful candelabra which were formerly in the palace Barberini, and now belong to the sculptor Cavaceppi.

7. As a wife and goddess, Juno is seen preëminent above the other goddesses in development as well as regal pride. She may be known, not only by her lofty diadem, but by her

[1] Plate XVI., B and C. Two eyes of Venus Urania. The former is copied from the beautiful fragment in the Dresden collection. The latter is after a head of the same goddess, which was formerly in the museum at Cassel, where it bore the name of Juno — GERM. ED.

large eyes, and an imperious mouth, the line of which is so characteristic, that one can say, simply from seeing such a mouth in a mere profile, — the sole remains of a female head on a mutilated gem cut in high relief, in the museum Strozzi, — that it is a head of Juno. The beauty in the expression of her large, roundly arched eyes is of an imperious character, like that of a queen who wills to rule, and who cannot fail to command respect and inspire love. The colossal head of this goddess (7) in the villa Ludovisi [1] is the most beautiful head of her ; another, smaller head may also be found there, which merits the second rank. The most beautiful statue is in the palace Barberini,[2] in which there is, besides, a colossal head of her ; but it does not equal in beauty the one first mentioned.

8. Pallas, on the contrary, is always a virgin, of mature form and age.[3] She and Diana are always serious. The former, in particular, who appears to have divested herself of all feminine weakness, and even to have conquered Love himself, is an image of maiden modesty. Hence the eyes, more especially of Pallas, explain the name which was given by the Greeks and Romans to the pupil of the eye : the latter terming it pupilla, *young virgin ;* the former, κόρη, which had the same signification. Her eyes are moderately full, and less open than those of Juno. Her head is not carried proudly erect, but her look is rather cast slightly downward, as if she was in quiet meditation. The contrary is observable in the heads of Roma (8), who, as the mistress of so many kingdoms, bears a regal boldness in her aspect. Like Pallas, however, she wears a helmet. But I must observe here, that the face of Pallas, on Grecian silver coins of the city of Velia in Lucania, on which her casque has wings on both sides, exhibits the reverse of what I have remarked in statues and busts ; for there her eyes are large, and her look is directed forwards or upwards, and her hair is gathered into a knot, a style which, the poet [4] says, speaking of Pallas and Diana, can belong only to the latter. For Pallas generally wears her hair knotted together at a distance from

[1] Plate XVI., A. Profile of the colossal head of Juno in the villa Ludovisi. — GERM. ED.

[2] Now in the Pio-Clement museum

[3] Plate XVII. Profile of the Pallas of Velletri, so called because it was found at Velletri, in 1797. It is a statue of colossal proportions, and is almost entirely uninjured. — GERM. ED.

[4] Statius, Theb., l. 2, v. 237.

PLATE XVII

S. A. Schoff. sc.

PLATE XVIII   B

A

S.A.Schoff. sc.

her head, and it then hangs down, beneath the fillet that binds it, in rows of long locks. From this arrangement of the hair, which is peculiar to her, she has received the name, but little known, of παραπεπλεγμένη. Pollux explains this word by ἀναπεπλεγμένη, but without making the idea clearer. It is an epithet which probably signifies hair thus disposed ; the mode of its arrangement would therefore illustrate the writer mentioned above. As she wore her hair longer than other goddesses, this may be the reason for swearing by her hair. On a medallion of Adrian, in the Vatican library, and on a rilievo in the Campidoglio, representing a sacrifice by Marcus Aurelius, she sits near Jupiter on the summit of the temple of this god, with her right hand placed on her helmeted head, — which is an unusual position. The most beautiful statue [1] of her is in the villa Albani (9).

9. Diana has, in a greater degree than any other of the superior goddesses, the shape and carriage of a virgin. Endowed with all the attractions of her sex, she appears to be unconscious of them herself. Her look is not downcast, like that of Pallas, but frank, sprightly, and cheerful. It is turned towards the source of her enjoyments, the chase, — especially as she is generally represented in running or walking, — so that it is directed straight forwards, and away into the distance, beyond all near objects. Her hair is smoothed upwards on all sides around her head, and then gathered into a knot behind, on the crown of the head, just above the neck, after the manner of virgins, or even at a distance from her head. She is without diadem or other ornaments, which have been given to her in modern times. Her figure is lighter and more slender than that of Juno, and even of Pallas. A mutilated Diana would be as readily distinguishable among the other goddesses as she is in Homer among all her beauteous Oreads. She generally wears a dress which is tucked up, and descends no lower than the knee ; but she is also represented in longer garments ; and is the only one of the goddesses who, in some figures, has her right breast bared (10).

10. Ceres (11) is nowhere represented more beautiful than on a silver coin of the city of Metapontus, in Magna Græcia,

[1] Plate XVIII., A. Profile of the glorious statue of Pallas, in the high style, in the villa Albani. B. Front view of the mouth of the same statue, of the size of the original. — GERM. ED.

which is in the museum of the Duke Caraffa Noia at Naples ;
on its reverse is stamped, as usual, an ear of wheat, on which a
mouse is seated.   In this, as in other images of her on coins,
the veil or drapery is drawn to the back part of the head ; and
a diadem, like that of Juno, together with ears and leaves of
wheat, is placed just above the front hair, which lies scattered
about on the forehead in sweet disorder.   This discomposure of
the hair was probably intended to signify her grief at the abduction of her daughter, Proserpine.

11. In the head of Ceres, and likewise that of her daughter,
the cities of Magna Græcia and Sicily endeavored to represent on their coins the highest beauty.   It will be difficult
to find more beautiful coins, even as respects the impression,
than those of Syracuse, which, on their obverse, exhibit the
head of Proserpine, and on the reverse a conqueror in a four-
horse car.   The drawing and engraving of this coin, in the collection belonging to the cabinet of Pellerin, ought to have been
better executed.   She is there represented as crowned with
long, pointed leaves, similar to those which, with the wheat-ears,
surround the head of her mother, Ceres.   Hence I am of opinion that the leaves on the head of Proserpine are leaves of
the wheat stalk, and not sedge, as they have been regarded by
others, who, on this assumption, wish to find the likeness of the
nymph Arethusa in the head on these coins.

12. Figures of Hebe are more rare than those of any other
goddess.   On two rilievi, only the upper part of her body is
visible ; and on one of them, in the villa of the Cardinal Alessandro Albani, which represents the *Reconciliation of Hercules*,
her name is near her.   There is another figure, perfectly similar
to this, on a large marble cup in the same villa.   This cup will
appear in the third volume of my *Ancient Monuments* (12).
These figures, however, give no particular idea of Hebe, because
they have none of the attributes ascribed to her.   On a third
rilievo, in the villa Borghese, — in which she is seen, as a sup-
pliant, on her knees, because her office was taken from her and
conferred on Ganymedes, — the subject of the marble enables
us to recognize her, even although other indications had been
wanting by which she might be distinguished.   But her dress is
tucked up high, after the manner of the boys who attended on
sacrifices, *Camilli*, and of servants who waited at table, and thus
distinguishes her from other goddesses.

13. Of the inferior and subordinate goddesses, I shall mention particularly the Graces, Hours, Nymphs, Muses, Parcæ, Furies, and Gorgons.

14. The Graces were the nymphs and playmates of Venus, and in the most ancient times were, like her, represented fully draped. As far as I know, however, only a single monument remains which exhibits them in this manner, namely, the triangular Etruscan altar, in the villa Borghese, to which reference has already been frequently made. In the palace Ruspoli there are figures of nude Graces, about half the size of life. They are the largest, most beautiful, and best preserved of all that remain. The heads, in this instance, are the original heads of the statues, whereas those of the Graces in the villa Borghese are modern and ugly ; our judgment will consequently be based upon the former. They are entirely without ornament ; the hair is confined by a fine cord passing round the head, and in two of the figures it is gathered together behind, near the neck. Their countenances express neither gayety nor seriousness, but a quiet contentment, appropriate to the innocence of their years.

15. The Hours, Ὧραι, are the companions and attendants of the Graces, — that is, they are the goddesses of the seasons and of natural beauties, and daughters of Themis by Jupiter, or, according to other poets, daughters of the Sun. In the earliest periods of art, they were represented by two figures only ; but their number was afterwards increased to three, because the year was divided into three seasons, spring, autumn, and winter ; their names are Eunomia, Dice, and Irene. They are generally represented dancing, by poets as well as artists, and, in most works by the latter, as being of the same age. Their garments are short, reaching only to the knee, as dancers were accustomed to wear theirs ; and their heads are crowned with a wreath of upright palm-leaves, as they may be seen on a three-sided base in the villa Albani, which is engraved in my *Ancient Monuments.* When, after a time, four seasons were established, four Hours were also introduced into art, as may be seen on a sepulchral urn in the same villa, of which an engraving is given in the work just mentioned. In this instance, however, they are represented of different ages and in longer vestments, and also without the garland of palm-leaves, so that Spring resembles an innocent virgin at that age when her shape has attained what

an epigram terms the growth of the Spring-Hour, and the three other sisters ascend in age by a regular gradation. When more than four figures appear in the dance, as in the well-known relief in the villa Borghese, then we have the Hours in company with the Graces.

16. In regard to the Nymphs, it may be said that each one of the superior divinities, as well of the male as of the female sex, had special Nymphs; even the Muses were ranked among them, as the Nymphs of Apollo. But those with whom we are most familiar are, in the first place, the Nymphs of Diana, or the Oreads, and the Nymphs of the trees, or the Hamadryads; and, in the second place, the Nereids, or Nymphs of the sea, and the Sirens.

17. The Muses may be seen represented, on different monuments, with far greater diversity of countenance, as well as of position and action, than any other Nymphs; for the tragic Muse, Melpomene, is distinguishable, even without her emblems, from the comic Muse, Thalia, and this latter — it is unnecessary to mention the names of the others — from Erato and Terpsichore, who presided over dancing. The peculiar characteristic of the two last-named Muses was forgotten by those among the moderns who placed a garland in the left hand of the celebrated lightly draped statue in the court of the palace Farnese, — which holds up its under-dress with the right hand, after the manner of dancing-girls, — and then imagined that, by this means, they had made a Flora of it, the name by which alone it is known at the present time. The consequence has been, that the same appellation is now extended, without further consideration, to all female figures whose head is crowned with flowers. That the Romans had a Flora, I know well; but no such goddess was known to the Greeks, whose skill executed the statues which we admire. Different figures of the Muses, much larger than life, are to be found; among them is one, in the above-named palace, which has been converted into a Urania; I am therefore confident that the statue called Flora is wrongly named, and is either an Erato or a Terpsichore. As to the Flora in the Capitoline museum, whose head is crowned with flowers, I find no ideal beauty in it; and, in my opinion, it is the likeness of some unknown beautiful individual, who, by means of this garland, is made to represent one of the goddesses of the seasons, namely, Spring. In the description of this Muse,

the remark, that she holds a bunch of flowers in her hand, ought at least to have been omitted, because the hand, as well as the flowers, is a modern addition.

18. Catullus describes the Fates as old, wrinkled, and bent with years, with trembling limbs and harsh countenances; but they are represented, on more than one ancient monument, in a manner which is the very reverse of this description. They are generally found present at the *Death of Meleager*, where they appear as beautiful young virgins, sometimes with, and sometimes without, wings on their heads, and distinguished by their appropriate emblems; one is always writing with a pen on a scroll. At times there are only two Parcæ, as there were but two statues of them in the porch of the temple of Apollo, at Delphi.

19. Even the Furies are represented as beautiful young virgins (13), either with or without snakes about their heads. Sophocles calls them "virgins ever young." On a vase in the Porcinari collection, at Naples, of which an engraving has been published in the second volume of the *Hamilton Vases*, there is a painting which represents them with snakes, and blazing torches, and bared arms, seeking vengeance on Orestes. These avenging goddesses appear, likewise, young and beautiful on different reliefs in Rome, descriptive of the same incident in relation to this hero.

20. The Gorgons, the last named of the inferior goddesses, are, with the exception of the head of Medusa, not represented on any antique work. But, if images of them had been preserved, their shape would have been found not to correspond to the description given of them by the most ancient poets, in which they are armed with long teeth, like tusks; since Medusa, one of the three sisters, has been to artists an image of high beauty, and fable also presents her to us in a similar aspect. According to some accounts, which are quoted by Pausanias, she was the daughter of Phorcus. After her father's death, she assumed the government of his dominions, which bordered on Lake Tritonis, in Africa, and even led her subjects in war. She was slain in an attack upon the army of Perseus, against whom she had marched. The hero, astonished at the beauty displayed even by her lifeless body, cut off her head, for the purpose of showing it to the Greeks. The most beautiful head in marble of a dead Medusa (14) is that in the hand of a much

repaired statue of Perseus, in the palace Lanti. One of the most beautiful heads on gems is a cameo in the royal Farnese museum, at Naples; another, on carnelian, is in the museum Strozzi. Both of these are of a loftier character than the more celebrated one in this same museum, marked with the name of Solon.[1] This last celebrated Medusa is cut on a chalcedony. It was found in a vineyard, near the church of Saints John and Paul, on Mount Cœlius, by a gardener, who offered it for sale to a purchaser of things of the kind, which we call antiques, who kept on the square Montanara, near the theatre of Marcellus. This man, who could have no particular knowledge of such articles, wished to take an impression from the stone, on wax. It happened to be winter, and early in the morning; the wax of course was not sufficiently soft, and the stone was broken into two pieces. The finder received two sequins (four dollars) for it. From the buyer it passed into the possession of Sabattini, a practical antiquarian of some note, who purchased it for three sequins. He had it set in gold, and sold it for five sequins to the Cardinal Alessandro Albani, — who at that time had not assumed the clerical profession. He exchanged it again with this same Sabattini for other antiquities, at an estimated value of fifty scudi (fifty dollars). If it were not for the preceding authentic account of it, I should be unable to divest myself of a suspicion that the figure might be the work of a more modern hand, — an opinion which I entertained for some time (15). However, this Medusa has obtained the utmost celebrity; it is selected by our artists for imitation, and has been frequently cut on stone; yet the above-mentioned head on carnelian is far more deserving of such preference.

21. With the goddesses I associate the Heroines or Amazons (16), as ideal images. They all resemble each other in conformation, even to the hair of the head; and their countenances appear to have been executed after one and the same model. Among the Heroines, the Amazons are the most celebrated; and they are represented in many statues, and on rilievi. Their look is serious, blended with an expression of pain or sorrow, for all these statues have a wound in the breast; this must have been the case with those, also, of which only the heads remain. The eyebrows are defined with an energetic sharpness; now, as this manner was usual in the more ancient

[1] Plate XIV., B.

style of art, as I shall hereafter show, it is an allowable supposition, that the Amazon of Ctesilaus, which received the prize over the Amazons of Polycletus and Phidias, may have served as a model to succeeding artists. The look of the Amazons is neither warlike nor fierce, but serious, even more so than that of Pallas is wont to be.

22. There are six entire Amazon statues, known as such, in Rome. The first is in the villa Mattei, and is the only one which has a helmet lying at its feet. The second is in the palace Barberini. The third, in the Capitoline museum, bears the name of the artist, Sosicles. The fourth is in the court of the palace Verospi. The fifth and sixth are likewise in the Capitol; but their heads — one of which is antique, and the other modern, and covered with a helmet — do not belong to them; and neither corresponds to the statue upon which it is placed. The restorers of the last two statues did not understand that the heads of the Amazons are characterized by a definite idea, and to such a degree, that those of the four first-mentioned statues appear to be the heads of sisters, and taken, as it were, from the same mould. There is no difference even in the hair, either in its arrangement or execution; the countenance of all expresses what the word *virago* signifies. There are, however, in the Capitoline museum two heads perfectly similar to the others, and very well preserved, which, if they had been recognized, might have been placed upon those statues of Amazons which have not their original heads, for these supplemental heads are not in keeping with the rest of the body. No heads would have furnished to our artists better models for figures of the Holy Virgin than these, if the idea of using them for this purpose had ever occurred to any one.

In the villa Pamfili is an Amazon (17), above the size of life, — as these figures always are, — which the process of restoration has converted into a Diana, though the drapery and head ought to have pointed out its true character. The sight of a single head of an Amazon would have removed all the doubts of a certain author (18), who finds himself unable to decide whether a head crowned with laurel — on the coins of the city of Myrina, in Asia Minor, which was built by the Amazons — represents an Apollo, or one of these heroines. I will not again repeat here what I have already remarked in more than one place, that, among all the statues of Amazons, there is not a single instance in which the left breast is wanting.

23. In the heads of particular individuals the ancient artists approximated as closely to the ideal as it could be done without injury to the resemblance.   These heads show with how much good judgment certain details which do not add to the likeness are passed over.   Many of those wrinkles which are the necessary accompaniments of age are omitted; those which detract nothing from our conception of beauty are expressed, — as, for instance, beneath the chin and on the neck.   The precept of the ancient sage was observed here, namely, to make the good as good as possible, but to conceal and diminish the bad.   On the other hand, those parts of the face of an individual which are beautiful, but which neither add to nor detract from the likeness, may be brought particularly into view.   This rule has been judiciously observed in the heads of Louis the Fourteenth, on his coins, as is evident from a comparison of them with Ranteuil's beautifully engraved heads of this monarch.

24. As animals cannot be excluded from our observations on beauty, a few remarks relative to them will be subjoined.   It has been observed of horses, by critics who can speak knowingly upon the subject (19), that those which remain to us in marble and bronze are copied from a coarse breed of the animal.   In confirmation of their assertion, they point especially to the supposed clumsy make of the parts between the neck and spine, at the place where the shoulder-blades are situated in man, which in horses is called the withers.   In the Arabian, Spanish, Neapolitan, and English horses this part is finer, lighter, and more flexible.   Some other animals, especially lions (20), have received from the ancient artists an ideal shape, — a piece of information for those to whom lions in marble appear different from lions in life.   The same remark may be made, yet more strongly, of the dolphin; it cannot be found in nature as it is represented on antique works; yet its imaginary form has been adopted by all modern artists as a reality.[1]

[1] The paragraphs 23 and 24, which are inserted here, are taken from the Notes to the History of Art.   It is true that their insertion here interrupts in some degree the connection between 22 and 25; but, as the author's remarks upon the portrait-figures of the ancients and the ideal conformation of animals could not find a more appropriate place, we thought it better to disturb the connection a little, rather than banish them from the text to find a place among the notes. — GERM ED.

25. Whilst on the subject of female ideal beauty, I cannot refrain from mentioning the Masks of this sex. Among them are to be found faces of the highest beauty, even on works of indifferent execution; such, for instance, is a procession of Bacchus, in the palace Albani, in which are two female Masks that give me renewed pleasure every time I look at them, — a hint for the information of those who have supposed all the ancient Masks to be of a frightful character.

26. I close these general remarks on beauty of shape and forms with some observations on the beauty of Masks. The term Masks appears to convey an idea of disguise and deformity. When, therefore, we see the beauty of conformation which is displayed in works seemingly scarce worthy of such elegance, not less than in those of a loftier character, we can the more readily infer how generally the principles of beauty must have been known, and how common was the representation of beautiful forms. This inference gains strength when we consider that the procession above mentioned, in which Masks are introduced, was taken from a sepulchral urn, the most ordinary class of antique works. Of all the reflections contained in this history, no one can be brought to the proof more generally than the foregoing, because it can be tested everywhere, even at a distance from the treasures of antiquity; whereas those investigations which relate especially to expression, action, drapery, and style, can be carried on only with the ancient works before one's eyes. Coins and engraved gems, or impressions from them, are to be obtained even in lands which have never seen any admirable work from a Greek chisel, and from these the whole world can form an idea of the lofty conceptions expressed in the heads of the divinities. A head of Jupiter on the coins of Philip of Macedon, on those of the first Ptolemies, and likewise those of Pyrrhus, is not inferior in majesty of conformation to his image in marble. The head of Ceres, on silver coins of the city of Metapontus, in Magna Græcia, and the head of Proserpine, on two different silver coins of Syracuse, in the royal Farnese museum at Naples, surpass anything that can be imagined. The same remark might be made of other beautiful female figures, on numerous coins and engraved gems.

27. Nothing mean or ordinary, indeed, could be introduced into the images of the deities, because their conformation was

so universally settled among Greek artists as apparently to
have been prescribed by some law. The head of Jupiter on
coins of Ionia, or stamped by Doric Greeks, is perfectly similar
to that of the same god on coins of Sicilian or other cities.
The heads of Apollo, Mercury, Bacchus, Liber Pater, and Hercules, either in youthful or more manly age, are, on coins and
gems, as well as statues, designed after one and the same idea.
The law referred to was found in the most beautiful of the
images produced by the most celebrated artists, to whom the
gods were believed to have manifested themselves in special
visions. Thus, Parrhasius boasted that Hercules had appeared
to him in the very form in which he had painted the hero.
This appears to have been the idea of Quintilian, where he says
that the statue of Jupiter from the hand of Phidias had done
much to awaken a greater degree of reverence towards this god.
The Jupiter of Phidias, the Juno of Polycletus, the Venus of
Alcamenes, and afterwards the Venus of Praxiteles, were the
noblest prototypes of these deities to all succeeding artists, and,
thus embodied, they were adopted and worshipped by all Greece.
However, the highest beauty cannot be imparted in an equal
degree to every one, even among the deities, as Cotta remarks
in Cicero, any more than to all the figures in the most beautiful
picture ; indeed, this is not more admissible than it would be to
introduce only heroes in a tragedy.

CHAPTER III.

THE EXPRESSION OF BEAUTY IN FEATURES AND ACTION.

1. NEXT to a knowledge of beauty, expression and action are to be considered as the points most essential to an artist, just as Demosthenes regarded action as the first, second, and third requisite in an orator. Action alone may cause a figure to appear beautiful; but it can never be considered so, if the action is faulty. An observance of propriety in expression and action ought, therefore, to be inculcated at the same time with the principles of beautiful forms, — because it is one of the constituents of grace. For this reason, the Graces are represented as the attendants of Venus, the goddess of beauty. Consequently the phrase, *to sacrifice to the Graces*, signifies among artists to be attentive to the expression and action of their figures.

2. In art, the term *expression* signifies imitation of the active and passive states of the mind and body, and of the passions as well as of the actions. In its widest sense it comprehends action; but in its more limited meaning, it is restricted to those emotions which are denoted by looks and the features of the face. Action relates rather to the movements of the limbs and the whole body; it sustains the expression. The censure which Aristotle passed on the pictures of Zeuxis — namely, that they had no ἦθος, *expression* — can be applied either to expression or action. I will explain myself on this point hereafter.

3. Expression, in its limited as well as more extended signification, changes the features of the face, and the posture, and consequently alters those forms which constitute beauty. The greater the change, the more unfavorable it is to beauty. On this account, stillness was one of the principles observed here, because it was regarded, according to Plato, as a state intermediate between sadness and gayety; and, for the same

reason, stillness is the state most appropriate to beauty, just as it is to the sea. Experience also teaches that the most beautiful men are quiet in manners and demeanor. In this view, even abstraction is required in an image not less than in him who designs it; for the idea of lofty beauty cannot be conceived otherwise than when the soul is wrapt in quiet meditation, and abstracted from all individuality of shape. Besides, a state of stillness and repose, both in man and beast, is that state which allows us to examine and discover their real nature and characteristics, just as one sees the bottom of a river or lake only when their waters are still and unruffled, and consequently even Art can express her own peculiar nature only in stillness.

4. Repose and equanimity, in their highest degree, are incompatible with action. The most elevated idea of beauty, therefore, can neither be aimed at, nor preserved, even in figures of the deities, who must of necessity be represented under a human shape. But the expression was made commensurate, as it were, with the beauty, and regulated by it. With the ancient artists, therefore, beauty was the chief object of expression, just as the cymbal guides all the other instruments in a band, although they seemingly overpower it. A figure may, however, be called beautiful even though expression should preponderate over beauty, just as we give the name of wine to a liquor of which the larger portion is water. Here we also see an indication of the celebrated doctrine of Empedocles relative to discord and harmony, by whose opposing actions the things of this world are arranged in their present situation. Beauty without expression might properly be termed insignificant, and expression without beauty, unpleasing; but, from the action of one upon the other, and the union of the two opposing qualities, beauty derives additional power to affect, to persuade, and to convince.

5. Repose and stillness are likewise to be regarded as a consequence of the propriety which the Greeks always endeavored to observe both in feature and action, insomuch that even a quick walk was regarded as, in a certain measure, opposed to their ideas of decorum. It seemed to involve a kind of boldness. Demosthenes reproaches Nicobulus with such a mode of walking; and he connects impudent talking with quick walking. In conformity to this mode of thinking, the ancients regarded slow movements of the body as characteristic of great minds. I find it hardly necessary to remark, that a posture which

denotes servitude is different from one that conforms to propriety and good manners. In this attitude a few statues of captive kings are represented ; they stand with their hands crossed one over the other, — an act indicative of the deepest submission, — in the manner in which Tigranes, king of Armenia, caused himself to be served by four kings who were his vassals.

6. The ancient artists have observed this sort of propriety even in their dancing figures, with the exception of the Bacchantes. It has been thought by some, that the action of these figures was measured and regulated by a style belonging to dances of a period anterior to that in which they were executed, and that, in subsequent dances of the ancient Greeks, they in their turn were adopted as a standard by which female dancers so governed themselves as not to overstep the limits of modest propriety. The proof of this can be seen in many lightly dressed female statues, of which the greater portion have no girdle, wear no emblems, and are represented as if engaged in a very modest dance. Even where the arms are wanting, it is apparent that one was occupied in supporting the dress upon the shoulder, and the other in slightly raising it from below. This action gives to these figures significance, and at the same time serves to explain their true character. As several of them have ideal heads, one of the two Muses who specially presided over dancing, namely, Erato and Terpsichore, may be represented by them. Statues in this attitude are to be found in the villas Medici, Albani, and elsewhere. Two figures in the villa Ludovisi, of the size of life, and similar to these, and a few among the Herculaneum statues, have not ideal heads. One of those in the villa Ludovisi has a head of high beauty, but the hair is deficient in that simplicity which is usual in ideal heads ; it is artistically twisted together and braided, so as to resemble a fashion of our day. Another, which stands over the entrance to the palace Caraffa Colubrano, at Naples, has a head of high beauty, encircled by a garland of flowers (1). It may, therefore, be the case that these statues were actually erected to beautiful female dancers, for the Greeks conferred on them this undeserved honor, and several Greek epigrams on such statues are still extant. Some of these statues have one breast bared : it is a sure sign that neither of the two Muses above mentioned is intended, because such exposure in them would be a violation of decency.

7. The highest conception of these principles, especially of repose and stillness, is embodied in the figures of the divinities, which, from the Father of the gods down to the inferior deities, show no trace of emotion. Thus, Homer pictures to us his Jupiter as shaking Olympus solely by the bending of his eyebrows and the waving of his hair. Most of the images of the gods are equally tranquil and passionless. Hence, the high beauty exhibited by the Genius, in the villa Borghese, could be expressed only in such a state.

A serene, quiet look has been imparted, not only to figures of the superior divinities, but also to those of the subordinate marine gods. From some epithets of the poets, we should form an idea of the Tritons different from that usually entertained. In our view, the Greek artists appear to have intended them as images of the calmness of the sea, when it resembles a greenish-blue sky, — an idea which is admirably expressed in two colossal heads of Tritons in the villa Albani, of which mention has already been made.[1] An engraving of one of them may be seen in the *Ancient Monuments.*

8. Jupiter himself is not uniformly represented with the same degree of serenity. He has a disturbed look on a rilievo, belonging to the Marquis Rondanini, in which he is represented immediately after having received a blow on the head, with a wooden mallet, from Vulcan, who stands near, full of expectation, to see Pallas spring forth from his brain. Jupiter sits as if stunned by the blow, and seemingly suffering the pains of parturition, which, through the birth of this goddess, are to introduce into the world all sensual and spiritual wisdom. A copperplate engraving of this work is on the title-page of the second volume of the *Monuments.*

9. The Vatican Apollo was intended to represent this deity in a state of anger over the serpent, Python, slain by his arrows, and at the same time with a feeling of contempt for his victory, which to a god was an easy achievement. As the skilful artist wished to personify the most beautiful of the gods, he expressed only the anger in the nose, — this organ, according to the old poet being its appropriate seat, — and the contempt on the lips. The latter emotion is manifested by the elevation of the lower lip, by which the chin is raised at the same time ; the former is visible in the dilated nostrils.

[1] Plate XV.

10. As the position and action usually correspond to the passions expressed in the face, both are made to conform to the divine excellence, in statues and figures of the gods. The union of these two qualities may be termed *Decorum*. There is not a single instance in which a god of mature age stands with his legs crossed. A statue of a hero with the legs crossed would have been censured by the Greeks; for such a posture would have been considered unseemly in an orator, as it was, among the Pythagoreans, to throw the right thigh over the left. I therefore do not believe that the statue at Elis — which stood with its legs crossed, and leaned with both hands on a spear — represented a Neptune, as Pausanias (2) was made to believe. Apollo, Bacchus, and Mercury are the only deities thus represented: the first, to personify frolicsome Youth; the second, Effeminacy. There are, however, but few statues of the kind. An Apollo in the Capitoline museum, a few similar figures of him in the villa Medici, and one other in the palace Farnese, stand in this position; the last surpasses all the others in the beauty of its shape and of its head. In one of the paintings from Herculaneum his attitude is precisely the same. Among the figures of Mercury, there is only a single one known to me which stands thus, namely, a statue in the grand-ducal gallery at Florence, upon which the Mercury in bronze, of the size of life, in the palace Farnese, was moulded and cast. This position is peculiar to Meleager and Paris; the statue of the latter, in the palace Lancelotti, stands in this manner. The young Satyrs or Fauns — two of the most beautiful of which are in the palace Ruspoli — have one foot awkwardly, and, as it were, clownishly, placed behind the other, to denote their character. This is precisely the attitude of the young Apollo Σαυροκτόνος, *the Lizard-killer*, of whom there are two figures in marble in the villa Borghese, and one in bronze in the villa Albani. They probably represent him during the period of his servitude, as herdsman to king Admetus. Of the female divinities I know not one that is represented in this attitude, which would be less becoming in them than in the gods; I therefore leave it undecided, whether a coin of the Emperor Aurelian, on which is a figure of Providence with crossed legs (3), is an antique. This position may, however, befit Nymphs; one of them, of the size of life, which formerly belonged to the family Giustiniani, stands thus; also one of the three Nymphs who are

carrying off Hylas, in the palace Albani. From observation of
these particulars, I believe myself authorized to doubt the antiquity of an engraved gem on which is represented the (so
called) Minerva Medica, — holding a staff entwined by a serpent, and having one leg thrown over the other, — more especially as the figure in question has the right breast bared, an
exposure which is not to be found in a single figure of Pallas.
This fact recurred to my recollection when a similar figure on a
gem was shown to me as an antique work; but, for the reasons
just mentioned, I recognized it as not being such. This attitude
was regarded as appropriate to persons in grief; for thus, in a
picture described by Philostratus, the weeping warriors stood
around the body of Antilochus, son of Nestor, and bewailed his
death; and in this attitude Antilochus communicates to Achilles the death of Patroclus, as seen on a relief in the palace
Mattei, and also on a cameo, — both of which have been published in my *Ancient Monuments,* — and in a picture from Herculaneum.

11. The ancient artists displayed the same wisdom in their
conception of figures drawn from the heroic age, and in the
representation of merely human passions, the expression of
which always corresponds to what we should look for in a man
of disciplined mind, who prevents his feelings from breaking
forth, and lets only the sparks of the fire be seen, who seeks
to penetrate the latent motives of him who comes to honor
him, or to play the spy. The manner, also, in which such a
man expresses himself conforms precisely to this idea. Hence,
Homer compares the words of Ulysses to flakes of snow, falling
abundantly, but softly, upon the earth. Moreover, the Greek
artists were convinced that, as Thucydides says, greatness of
mind is usually associated with a noble simplicity. Even Achilles presents himself to us in this aspect; for, though prone to
anger and inexorable in wrath, his character is ingenuous, and
without dissimulation or falseness. The ancient artists accordingly modelled the faces of their heroes after the truth thus
taught them by experience. No look of subtlety is there, nor
of frivolity, nor craft, still less of scorn, but innocence is diffused over them, blended with the calmness of a trustful nature.

12. In representing heroes, the artist is allowed less license
than the poet. The latter can depict them according to their
times, when the passions were as yet unrestrained by social

laws or the artificial proprieties of life, because the qualities ascribed to a man have a necessary relation to his age and standing, but none necessarily to his figure. The former, however, being obliged to select the most beautiful parts of the most beautiful conformations, is limited, in the expression of the passions, to a degree which will not conflict with the physical beauty of the figure which he models.

13. The truth of this remark is apparent in two of the most beautiful works of antiquity. One of them is a representation of the fear of death; the other, of extreme suffering and pain. The daughters of Niobe, at whom Diana has aimed her fatal shafts, are represented in that state of indescribable anguish, their senses horror-struck and benumbed, in which all the mental powers are completely overwhelmed and paralyzed by the near approach of inevitable death. The transformation of Niobe into a rock, in the fable, is an image of this state of deathlike anguish; and for this reason Æschylus introduced her as a silent personage in his tragedy on this subject. A state such as this, in which sensation and reflection cease, and which resembles apathy, does not disturb a limb or a feature, and thus enabled the great artist to represent in this instance the highest beauty just as he has represented it; for Niobe and her daughters are beautiful according to the highest conceptions of beauty (4).

14. Laocoön (5) is an image of the most intense suffering. It manifests itself in his muscles, sinews, and veins. The poison introduced into the blood, by the deadly bite of the serpents, has caused the utmost excitement in the circulation; every part of the body seems as if straining with agony. By this means the artist brought into action all the natural motive powers, and at the same time displayed the wonders of his science and skill. But in the representation of this intense suffering is seen the determined spirit of a great man who struggles with necessity and strives to suppress all audible manifestations of pain, — as I have endeavored to show, when describing this statue, in the second part of this work.

15. Even Philoctetes,

"Quod ejulatu, questu, gemitu, fremitibus,
Resonando multum, flebiles voces refert,"
Ennius *apud Cic. de Fin.*, B. 2, ch. 29,

Whose shrieks and groans, wide echoing through the air,
Combine with tearful words of wan despair,

has been represented by these judicious artists more in accordance with the principles of wisdom than with the description of
the poet, — as is shown by the figures of this hero in marble
and on engraved gems, which have been published in my *Ancient Monuments*.   The frantic Ajax of the celebrated painter
Timomachus was not represented in the act of slaughtering the
rams, under the impression that they were the chiefs of the
Grecian forces, but after it was completed, and when, restored
to the possession of his senses, and overwhelmed by despair,
and buried in the deepest sadness, he sat and brooded over his
offence.   In this manner he is figured in the (so called) "Trojan Tablet," in the Capitoline museum, and on several engraved
gems.   There is, however, an antique cast in glass, taken from
a cameo, which represents Ajax as Sophocles has done, in his
tragedy of *Ajax*, that is, killing a large ram, while two herds-
men and Ulysses are standing near, to the latter of whom
Pallas is showing this display of rage on the part of his enemy.
This rare piece will appear in the third volume of the *Ancient
Monuments*.

16. In women, particularly, artists followed the fundamental principle, — taught by Aristotle, and observed in all the
tragedies of the ancients which are known to us, — never to represent women in such a way that they shall violate the characteristics of their sex, or appear excessively daring and fierce.
For this reason, the rilievo which represents the murder of
Agamemnon shows Clytemnestra as at a distance from the
scene of blood, and in another chamber, merely holding a torch
to light the assassin, not laying hands herself on her husband.
A similar circumstance is observed in a picture by the above-
mentioned Timomachus, in which the children of Medea are
smiling while the dagger of their mother is suspended over
them, so that her fury is mingled with compassion as she looks
upon their innocence.   The representations of this same deed,
in marble, present Medea as if still hesitating in the execution
of her revenge.

17. In accordance with similar principles, the wisest among
the ancient artists strove to avoid the representation of whatever conflicted with beauty.   They much preferred to deviate
from truth, rather than from beauty, in their figures, — as may
be seen, among other instances, in the Hecuba, on a rilievo in
my *Ancient Monuments*.   Though this aged queen of Troy

is generally represented with a countenance very much wrinkled, — especially in the statue of her in the Capitoline museum, and on a mutilated relief in the abbey of Grotta Ferrata, — and with long, flaccid, and pendulous breasts on another marble, in the villa Pamfili, which will also be published in the third volume of the *Ancient Monuments;* still, on the work first mentioned, she is figured as a woman who has scarcely passed the maturity of her charms. In judging the figure of Medea on the very beautiful earthen vessels of the Hamilton collection, we must not lose sight of the principle mentioned above, for she is there represented as not older than her daughter.

18. Distinguished men, and rulers, are conceived and represented in a manner worthy of them, and as they would appear before the eyes of the whole world. The statues of the Roman empresses resemble Heroines; displaying no artificial graces, either in feature, position, or action ; we see in them, as it were, that social propriety which, in the opinion of Plato, is no object of sense. Even as the two celebrated schools of ancient philosophers placed the greatest good in a mode of life which conformed to nature, but the Stoics, in decorum and propriety, so, in this case, also, the observation of artists was directed to the workings of nature when left to herself, unchecked, and when controlled by the observance of decency.

19. On public monuments, the Roman emperors always appear as principal citizens among their fellows, exhibiting nothing of the pride of sovereigns, and seemingly having no prerogatives greater than the by-standers, ἰσόνομοι. The surrounding personages are apparently equal to their ruler, who is distinguished as such from the others only by the principal action being given to him. No one who offers anything to the emperor does so on bended knee, and no one, with the exception of captive kings, bows his body or head when addressing him. Although adulation was carried to great excess, — since we know that the Roman Senate fell at the feet of Tiberius, — yet Art still held herself as proudly erect as when in the height of her glory at Athens. I have observed that captive kings are an exception to the general application of my remark, even when limited to the monuments which remain to us ; but we also know that kings, not conquered, showed to Roman generals this mark of submission, as Plutarch informs us of Tigranes, king of Armenia. When this despot went to visit Pompey, he dismounted

from his horse in front of the Roman camp, unbuckled his sword, and delivered it to the two lictors who advanced to meet him; on coming into Pompey's presence, he laid his cap at his feet, and prostrated himself before him.

20. Among other examples which I might adduce to show the degenerate tone of thought, and the extent to which violation of the principle in question has been carried in modern times, is a large rilievo on the fountain of Trevi at Rome, which was executed a few years ago. It represents the architect of this aqueduct presenting, on his knees, the plan of it to Marcus Agrippa. I will simply remark that the long beard (6) of this distinguished Roman is in contradiction to every known likeness of him, whether on coins or in marble.

21. When I reflect on the fundamental principles of decency entertained by the ancient artists, I cannot persuade myself that it is the Emperor Adrian who is represented among the figures on the pediment of the temple of Pallas at Athens, because, as Pococke assures us, the figure in question is embracing another, a female figure. Such an act would have been regarded as offending against the dignity of an emperor, and the sanctity of the place. I do not believe, therefore, that either Adrian, or his wife Sabina, is here impersonated, as Spon claims to have discovered; for I do not so far confide in this author's knowledge of such subjects as to take all his assertions upon trust.

22. It must also be considered here, that, in general, all excess in the passions was rigorously excluded, especially from public works of art, and that the representation of them on public monuments was not allowable, even in a degree which might be very proper and decent in other works, not public. If this be assumed as proved, it may also serve as a principle by which to distinguish counterfeit from genuine objects of antiquity, — a test which may be applied to a coin, in Occo and Mezzabarba, which exhibits an Assyrian man and woman bound to a palm-tree, and tearing the hair from their heads, with the inscription, — "ASSYRIA. ET. PALAESTINA. IN. POTEST. P. R. REDAC. S. C." A connoisseur in coins is obliged to seek the proof that this coin is a counterfeit (7) in the word *Palaestina*, which, according to his showing, is not found on a single Latin-Roman coin; but the same conclusion at which even this learned inquiry arrives might have been drawn from

the foregoing remark. I do not pretend to decide whether a person, not of the male, but of the female sex, could with propriety be represented in a picture as rending her hair in the extremity of her grief and despair; but such an act would have been considered as great a violation of decency in a symbolical figure on a coin, as though it were on a public monument, a triumphal car, and associated with the principal figures on it; it would be inconsistent with the dignity of its place; it would, as the Greeks say, not be κατὰ σχῆμα, *appropriate.* It is this principle which governed the representation of Hecuba on the rilievo at Grotta Ferrata, just mentioned. Her head is bowed down, and her right hand pressed upon her forehead, in token of the fulness of her sorrow, — according to the instinctive promptings of grief or deep thought. In the bitterness of her anguish, while sitting by the dead body of her son, Hector, she sheds not a tear; for tears are crowded back upon their source when grief is choked by despair, as Seneca makes Andromache to say : —

> " Levia perpessæ sumus, si flenda patimur."
>
> No heavy ills are ours, when tears can flow.

23. The wisdom of the ancient artists in regard to expression becomes more clearly manifest when we contrast their works with those of most artists of modern days, in which much is not signified by little, but little by much. The ancients would have termed the latter mode παρένθυρσος; and their commentators would have explained it by τὸ παρὰ πρέπον, or παρὰ σχῆμα, θύρσῳ χρῆσθαι, that is, *an unseasonable use or introduction of the Thyrsus,* namely, on the stage, since tragic personages only were accustomed to carry it. The expression, consequently, signifies *the magnifying of trifles into undue importance.* I introduce this explanation here, because I do not think that the precise meaning of the word παρένθυρσος has been given by commentators on Longinus. It would, however, exactly designate the faults in expression committed by most modern artists. For, as regards action, their figures resemble the comic performers of the ancient amphitheatres, who were obliged to violate the truth of nature by exaggeration, in order to make themselves intelligible, in the broad light of day, to the most ordinary classes of the people on the outermost rows of seats; whilst, in the expression of their faces, they are like the ancient masks, for the distortion of which we may find an explanation in the cause just stated.

This exaggerated style of expression is even inculcated by Charles le Brun, in his *Treatise on the Passions*, — a work in the hands of most young students of art. In his illustrative drawings, the passions are not only represented, in the face, in an extreme degree, but in several instances the expression of them amounts even to frenzy. It is supposed that expression is taught on the principle by which Diogenes lived; "I imitate musicians," said he, "who strike a higher note in the scale than the one upon which they wish to fall." But, as the impetuosity natural to the young rather disposes them to adopt extremes than a mean, they will in this way hardly acquire the right tone, from the difficulty of keeping it when once struck. There is an analogy in this case with the passions themselves, which, as Chrysippus the Stoic taught, resemble the passage down a steep, precipitous descent; if a traveller thereon once gets to running, he can neither stop himself, nor yet turn back. Horace says, that the Shades in the Elysian Fields listen less attentively to the tender odes of Sappho than to the lyrics of Alcæus, who sings of battle, and tyrants deposed; and so it is, that, from youth upward, we are more captivated by wild tumults and dread alarums than by peaceful incidents and wisdom's tranquil life. Hence, the youthful designer is more readily guided by Mars into the battle-field, than by Pallas to the calm society of the wise. The doctrine of repose and stillness, in the drawing of his figures, is as repugnant to his feelings, but yet as necessary, as precepts of virtue are to all youthful persons. As, according to Hippocrates, the cure of the foot depends on repose, so also must improvement with such artists commence in repose.

24. Moreover, we do not find in those figures of the ancients which are in a still position any of that meretricious, artificial grace so common among the moderns; to mention one instance of it, the hinder foot is frequently made to rest upon the toes alone. Now the ancients gave this position to the foot only when the action represented running or walking, — never when a figure was in repose. It is true that a rilievo in my possession, and copied into the *Ancient Monuments*, shows Philoctetes with his right foot thus placed; but the position of the foot, in this instance, expresses the pain endured by the hero from the serpent's bite, which disabled him from bearing his weight on it.

25. These explanations and reflections, in relation to action,

deserve more attention, on some accounts, from those who are beginning to study works of art, than even conceptions of beauty, because they are more readily comprehended, and also better appreciated, by those who do not possess a quick perception of the beautiful. On comparing ancient and modern works, the difference in this particular is so striking, that the latter appear to be the reverse of the former. Every one perceives that the greater number of modern artists, especially sculptors, have been governed by principles of an entirely different spirit from those just considered. They confidently believed that art was capable of improvement by such principles, and imagined that, like several other arts, it had not yet attained the highest degree of excellence in action. For this reason, the successors of Raphael deserted him ; and the simplicity of his manner, in which he imitated the ancients, was termed a marble manner, that is, one in which the repose resembles death. This corruption advanced with steady and gradual increase from the time of Michael Angelo to that of Bernini ; and although the constant tendency of the manners and customs of social life to become more and more natural and unrestrained threw light upon this portion of art, still a trace of the new school was always perceptible. One of the most distinguished painters now living, in his picture of *Hercules between Virtue and Pleasure,* — which has recently been sent to Russia, — supposed that Virtue was not represented sufficiently beautiful under the shape of Pallas, unless her right, forward foot was made to rest upon the toes only, — just as if she were about to crack a nut. Such an elevation of the foot would have been considered by the ancients a sign of pride ; or, according to Petronius, of shamelessness ; according to Euripides, this was the attitude of the Bacchantes.

26. He who desires to institute a comparison between ancient and modern sculptors must reflect upon what I have said of beauty generally, and of action in particular. If a certain learned member of the French Academy had had any knowledge of the works of the ancients, he would not have ventured to say that modern, meaning thereby French, sculptors had finally succeeded, not only in equalling, but even in surpassing, the finest productions of Rome and Athens.[1] To convince one

---

[1] Burette, Diss. sur les Effets de la Musique, dans les Mém. de l'Acad. des Inscript., T. v., p. 133.

who expresses such opinions of their incorrectness is always a
difficulty; but, in the following instance, it seemed to me an
impossibility; — a Russian nobleman, whilst preparing for his
third journey to Italy, said to me, in the presence of other persons, that he regarded all statues, the Apollo, the Laocoön, the
Farnese Hercules, as nothing, when compared with the Mercury
of Pigalle, in the Sans-Souci, near Potsdam.

27. Others, who appear more modest in their opinions, and
believe that a Michael Angelo, a Puget, a Fiammingo, need not
shrink from comparison with an Apollonius or an Agasias, may
take beauty as the touchstone of their comparative merit.   Let
us commence by offering to their view the best heads by the
heroes of modern art; let us place before them the finest figure
of Christ, by Michael Angelo, the celebrated head of Prudence (8)
on the monument of Paul III., in St. Peter's church, by Guglielmo della Porta, the scholar of Michael Angelo, then the
much-admired head of St. Susanna (9) by Fiammingo, and that
of St. Bibiana (10) by Bernini : I name the last statue, because
it is always selected by those who wish to extol the artist.   If
any one should think me too severe, when I assert, in another
place, that Michael Angelo originated and promoted this corruption of taste, even in sculpture, let him consider, among
other examples, a rilievo by him, in marble, in the possession of
the sculptor Bartolommeo Cavaceppi.   This work, which represents Apollo flaying Marsyas, is in the very reverse of good
taste.   I can, moreover, justify my assertion by reference to
the sketches of this great artist, of which the sculptor above
mentioned has a rare collection.   These manifest the spirit of
his genius in the clearest light, and the wildness of it is everywhere visible.   What imperfect ideas of youthful beauty the
celebrated Algardi had is proved by his well-known rilievo of
St. Agnes, in the church of St. Agnes, on the Piazza Navona.
Her figure is rather ugly than beautiful; and the head is absolutely drawn awry.   And yet a copy of this piece, in gypsum, is
suspended as a study in the French Academy at Rome.

28. It is found, on comparing modern with ancient painting,
that the result of the comparison is less unfavorable to it than
to modern sculpture.   The reason probably is, that painting,
since its restoration, has been more practised, and consequently
has furnished greater facilities than sculpture for the formation
of eminent masters.   Leonardo da Vinci and Andrea del Sarto,

who saw but few works of the ancients, thought and toiled as we cannot but imagine the Greek artists did. The *Christ and the Pharisees* from the hand of the former, (11) and the *Madonna del Sacco* of the latter, (12) at Florence, are worthy of antiquity. Indeed, there is so much of innocent and innate grace in the heads of Andrea, that a Pythagorean would say, the soul of Protogenes or Apelles had found a dwelling-place in his body. It may be said, generally, that the spirit of grace manifested itself more fully to those painters who flourished in the golden age of the art, at the commencement of the sixteenth century, than to their successors. After a long interval, it reappeared in Annibal Caracci. The *Dead Christ*, (13) in the Royal Farnese Gallery at Naples, is one, among others of his imperishable works, which testifies how worthily his conceptions corresponded to the dignity of his subject. The altarpiece in the house-chapel of the palace Pamfili, on the Corso at Rome, appears to be a repetition of the same picture, by the artist himself. In it he has figured the Saviour as a beardless young hero, and imparted to him an ideal elevation, adopted from the most beautiful of the ancient heads, for the purpose of representing the fairest among the children of men. Guercino has given a similar heroic face, without beard, to his dead Christ, in a beautiful picture in the palace Pamfili, on the Piazza Navona; it puts to shame the mean and vulgar countenance which Michael Angelo has given to his heads of the Saviour.

29. To the honor of the present age, however, it must be conceded, that in it the diffusion of knowledge in regard to beauty has kept pace with the general cultivation of the intellect. This remark is true in an especial manner of sculpture. The modesty of our Roman artists will not admit of a comparison between themselves and a Buonarotti; but, though difficult, it is not impossible to attain a similar superiority in scientific knowledge. There are, on the contrary, a few of them, who, in beautiful conformations, forms, and conceptions, far surpass all their predecessors in modern times. The reason is to be found in a more attentive study of the works of antiquity, which, during the few years that have elapsed since the veil fell from the eyes of our sculptors, have become the object of their imitation. A love for art — which, in England, has become an impulse to ambition, and, in Germany, exists even on the throne

— has, in conjunction with good taste, been the most efficient promoter of this result. For our artists, having been required to make copies of antique works, have consequently been more confined to an imitation of the style of the ancients; whereas, prior to this time, art was almost exclusively devoted to churches and monasteries, where the style of Algardi and Bernini was regarded as the evangelical law, from which there was to be no deviation.

CHAPTER IV.

PROPORTION. — COMPOSITION.

1. NEXT to the consideration of beauty in general, I proceed to speak first of the proportion, and then of the beauty, of single parts of the human body. Indeed, it is impossible to conceive of beauty without proportion; the latter is the basis of the former. Single portions of the body, however, can be beautiful in shape, yet not beautiful in their relation to the whole figure. It is appropriate, therefore, to make some special remarks upon proportion, as a distinct idea, and unconnected with the spiritual attributes of beauty. These remarks, with a few thoughts on grace, I append as supplementary to the general consideration of beauty.

2. As health, without any other enjoyment, seems to be no great blessing, so exactness in proportion is not of itself sufficient to make a figure beautiful. Science being entirely distinct from good taste and sensibility to beauty, the proportions of a figure which are founded on science may be faultless, and yet the figure itself not be beautiful. Many artists are skilled in proportion; but few have produced beauty, because soul and feeling, rather than intellect, are required in its creation. The ideal part of beauty was always regarded by the ancient artists as the higher part of it; they therefore made accuracy of proportion subordinate, and adjusted, as it were, proportion to beauty with a freedom which is justifiable, when warranted by good reasons. Thus, for example, the length of the chest from the neck-pit to the pit of the stomach ought to be only one face; yet it is generally an inch, and frequently more than an inch, longer, that the chest may have a grand arch. So, likewise, the distance between the pit of the stomach and the navel — the usual length of which is one face — was increased when the artist wished to give slimness to his figure: this deviation is actually found in the shape of fine, well-built men.

3. The structure of the human body consists of triads. Three is the first uneven number, and the first number of relation, for it contains in itself the first even number, and another which unites the two together. Two things, as Plato says, cannot exist without a third. The best band is that which binds together most securely itself and the thing bound, in such a manner that the first is related to the second as the second is to the intermediate. Hence the number three contains in itself beginning, middle, and end. It was regarded as the most complete of all numbers, and by it, according to the doctrines of the Pythagoreans, all things were determined. Even the stature of our bodies bears a relation to this number ; for it has been observed, that, in the third year of life, man attains one half of his height.

4. The body, as well as its principal members, is composed of three parts. The body consists of trunk, thighs, and legs ; the lower extremity, of thighs, legs, and feet ; and a similar disposition is true of the arms, hands, and feet. The same construction can be shown in other organs which are not so evidently composed of three parts. The relation existing among these divisions is the same in the whole body as in its parts. The head and body of a well-built man will have the same relation to his thighs, legs, and feet, as his thighs have to the legs and feet, and as the upper arm has to the fore-arm and hands. The face, likewise, has three parts, namely, thrice the length of the nose ; but the head does not contain four lengths of the nose, as a certain author,[1] very erroneously, wishes to make it out. The upper portion of the head — namely, the distance from the roots of the hair, on the forehead, to the crown of the head, measured perpendicularly — contains only three fourths of a nose-length ; that is to say, the length of this part is to that of the nose as nine is to twelve.

5. Vitruvius was of opinion, that, in architecture, the proportion of columns is adopted from the proportion of the human body ; and that the diameter of their lower extremity is to their height as the length of the foot is to that of the whole body. His assumption, however, is not borne out by nature, though it might be true of figures formed by art. This proportion is not to be found in the oldest columns, either in Magna Græcia and Sicily, or in Greece proper ; the height of most of them is scarcely five

[1] Watelet, Réflex. sur la Peint.

diameters of the lower extremity of the shaft. As the proportion of the head to the entire figure on some very ancient Etruscan works is less than we usually find it in nature, — as I have mentioned in the second chapter of the third book, when speaking of the gem on which are engraved the five chiefs who went against Thebes, — one must either say that the proportion of columns has not been determined from nature, or that the assertion of Vitruvius is not correct: I am of the latter opinion. If he had studied the proportion of the oldest Doric columns, — of which, however, he makes not the least mention, notwithstanding their importance, — he would himself have perceived that his comparison of columns with the human body is arbitrary and unfounded. For the purpose of lending at least some degree of probability to his hypothesis, I supposed that it might be based on the proportion of some ancient figures of which the head constitutes a larger portion than it does in nature. But even this supposition is not generally true ; indeed, the more ancient the figures, the less ground there is for it ; for in the most ancient, small Etruscan figures of bronze, the head is scarcely the tenth part of their whole height.

6. It is generally the case, that the side of the head which is averted is made flatter than the other. This is very evident in the heads of Niobe, but even more so in some few almost colossal heads, — for example, the portrait-head belonging to the sculptor Cavaceppi. It was a remark of the celebrated Count Caylus, that the heads of antique figures are generally very large and coarse ; but, so far as I can judge, there is no ground for this censure, which was suggested by Pliny's criticism of Zeuxis and Euphranor, who are said to have formed their figures with big heads and joints. The distinguished Count ought to have let this criticism pass without any comment, as one of little or no meaning, since the reverse of it is apparent to every one who attentively observes the works of antiquity. Whence, do you suppose, originated the absurd notion, that the head of the Hercules Farnese was found some miles apart from the body ? Simply from the fact, that, to the vulgar conception of a Hercules, the head seems rather small. Such critics as these would find a similar occasion for censure in more than one Hercules, especially if they were to examine the figures and heads of the hero engraved on gems. The reverse of Caylus's opinion is far more susceptible of proof. We

can form an idea of the proportion observed in this particular
by the ancient artists, from the proportion of the Ionic capital,
which, in columns of this order, was regarded as the head (1).
Now, as modern artists have far exceeded the ancient proportion in the Ionic capital, we are at liberty to infer that they
have also erred by making the heads of their figures too large.
It is impossible for me, therefore, to subscribe to the opinion
either of the ancient or the modern writer. For the proportion
of the head to the neck and the rest of the body was better
known to the ancients, and especially to artists like Zeuxis,
than to us, — which is apparent, among other examples, from
a passage in the hymeneal song by Catullus, on occasion of the
marriage of Peleus and Thetis. "The nurse," says the poet,
"when she sees Thetis on the day following her bridal night,
will no longer be able to make the thread meet around her
neck." By consulting the commentators on this passage, the
reader can see whether it has been made perfectly clear. The
custom to which allusion is made is not unknown, even at the
present day, in some parts of Italy, and may serve as an illustration of the passage in question. The neck of a marriageable
youth or maiden is measured with a thread or ribbon. A
string of double the length is then taken, and the two ends
are brought together, and the middle of it is held between
the teeth. If, now, it is sufficiently long to be carried from the
mouth over the head without difficulty, it is a sign that the
person is still a virgin ; but if not, the contrary (2) may be
inferred. I have made this trial on some young persons, and,
as it has seemed to me, successfully.

7. It is probable that the Grecian, like the Egyptian, artists
had rules by which not only the greater, but the smaller, proportions of the body were accurately determined ; and that the
length, breadth, and circumference of parts suitable to each
age and station were laid down with precision, and taught in
the writings of those artists who treated of symmetry. The
accuracy with which these proportions were established is likewise the reason why the same system of art is found in all,
even ordinary, figures by the ancient artists. For, notwithstanding differences in execution which had become a subject
of observation even to the ancients, as early as the works of
Myron, Polycletus, and Lysippus, still all the old works appear
to have been executed by followers of one and the same school.

As a connoisseur would recognize in different violin-players who had been taught by one master the style of their teacher, so the same general principles are visible in the drawing of the ancient sculptors, from the greatest to the least. Departures from them, it is true, are occasionally observed. This is the case with a small, beautiful torso of a nude female figure, belonging to the sculptor Cavaceppi, the body of which, from the navel to the privates, is unusually long. It is probable that this figure was copied from a living individual in whom the part was thus shaped. I do not wish, however, to palliate in this way actual errors ; for, if the ear is not parallel with the nose, as it should be, but is placed as it is on an Indian Bacchus, in the possession of the Cardinal Alessandro Albani, it is an inexcusable fault.

8. It must be acknowledged that the ancient artists have at times erred in proportion, — an instance of which occurs to me in a beautiful rilievo in the villa Borghese ; one of the arms of the female figure to whom Auge hands the youthful Telephus, in swaddling-clothes, is too long. Errors of proportion occur even in beautiful heads, as may be seen in the head of the laughing Leucothea (3), in the Campidoglio ; the ears, which should be parallel with the nose, fall below it. Incorrect drawing may also be observed in a head of Venus, which is a beautiful head in other respects, in the villa Albani ; the outline of it is the most beautiful that can be imagined, and the mouth is most lovely ; but one eye is awry. Two female figures, in two Herculaneum paintings, are manifestly faulty in every proportion, and much too long. In the *History of Art* [1] I remarked that, in an Egyptian statue and the Apollo Belvedere, the retreating foot is larger than that which is stationary. I am now convinced, more than ever, that its increased size was intended to compensate for what it might apparently lose by being drawn back. I have remarked, in the Laocoön, the same inequality in the size of the feet. The left leg, in fact, of the Apollo, which is the retreating leg, is longer than the right by a couple of inches (4). It would be possible for me to strengthen this opinion by additional examples.

9. The rules of proportion, as adopted in art from the proportions of the human body, were probably first established by sculptors. Afterwards, they became canonical in architecture

[1] Vol. I., Book 2, chap. 2, § 8. — Tr.

also. Among the ancients, the foot was the standard of all
large measurements, and by its length sculptors determined
the height of their statues, giving to them, as Vitruvius states,
six lengths of the foot; for the foot has a more determinate
length than the head or the face, from which modern sculptors
and painters generally deduce the proportions of their figures.
Hence, Pythagoras calculated the height of Hercules from the
length of his foot, with which he measured the Olympic stadium at Elis. We are, however, by no means authorized to conclude from this, as Lomazzo has done, that the length of his
foot was one seventh of his whole height. The statements of
this writer, relative to the proportions established by the ancient artists for the different divinities, — such as ten faces to
the height of a Venus, nine to a Juno, eight to a Neptune, and
seven to a Hercules, — made by him with all the confidence of
an eye-witness, and with a trustful reliance on the credulity of
his readers, are imaginary and false.

10. This relation of the foot to the whole body strikes a
certain learned scholar as absurd and inconceivable; and Per-
rault absolutely rejects it. It is, however, grounded on observation of nature, even in persons of a slender make, and is
found not only in Egyptian figures, on accurate measurement
of them, but also in Grecian statues, as most of them would
show, if their feet had been preserved. Any one can convince
himself of the existence of this proportion in the figures of divinities, although a greater length than is natural has been
given to some few parts; thus, for instance, in the Apollo, who
was a little more than seven heads high, the foot upon which
he stands is one quarter of a Roman palm ($2\frac{1}{5}$ in. Eng.) longer
than his head. Albert Durer has given precisely the same
proportion to his figures, eight heads tall; he makes the length
of the foot one sixth of their height. The shape of the Venus
de' Medici is uncommonly slender; and yet, notwithstanding
her head is very small, her height does not contain more than
seven heads and a half; her foot is a palm and half an inch in
length (9.30 in.), and her whole height, six palms and a half
(4.76 feet).[1]

---

[1] It seems as though there must be some mistake here, for the height
assigned differs from that usually given to the Venus de' Medici. In
the Guide-book of Florence the height is stated at 4. 9. 8 ft., French
measure, which is equivalent, in English, to 5.122 ft. — Tr.

11. That portion of the body which extends from the pit of the stomach to the navel usually contains, as modern artists say, only one length of the face; they therefore commonly request their pupils to notice that the ancient sculptors made it, in the figures of divinities, longer than nature by half a length of the face. This is also an error; for whoever has an opportunity to see nature in beautiful slender men will find this region formed as in those statues.

12. A minute detail of the proportions of the human body would have been a very easy matter in this treatise on Greek drawing of the naked figure. But mere theory without practical instruction would afford just as little information, in this work, as it does in others into which it has been largely introduced, without even the assistance to be derived from illustrative figures. Attempts have been made to subject the proportions of the body to the rules of abstract harmony and music; such endeavors, however, offer but feeble hopes of instruction to the designer and those who are seeking to acquire a knowledge of the beautiful. Investigations to determine the proportions of the body, in numbers, would be of less assistance, on this occasion, than the instructions of the fencing-school on a battle-field.

13. But, that I may not leave those who are beginning to draw entirely without practical information on this point, of Proportion, I will mention at least the proportions of the face, taken from the finest antique heads, and likewise from beautiful life, as an infallible rule by which to work, and to test the works of others. This rule has been expressed with more accuracy and precision than ever before, by my friend, Antony Raphael Mengs, the most accomplished instructor in his art; and he has probably hit upon the exact method observed by the ancients. Draw a vertical line, and divide it into five equal parts; the uppermost fifth is for the hair. Again divide the remainder of the line into three equal parts. Draw a horizontal line through the lower extremity of the first of these three divisions, forming with the perpendicular line a cross. The horizontal line must be as long as two of the three parts into which the length of the face is divided. Let curved lines be drawn from the extreme points of this line to the upper extremity of the fifth part originally set off; these form the smaller end of the oval of the face. Now divide one of the three

parts of the length of the face into twelve equal portions. Let three of them, that is, a fourth of one of these three divisions, or one twelfth of the length of the face, be measured off on both sides of the point of intersection of the horizontal and perpendicular lines; these two portions indicate the space between the eyes. Let three other portions be measured off on both outer extremities of the horizontal line. The space which now remains, included between the quarter at the outer end of the horizontal line and the quarter at the point of intersection of the two lines, is equal to two quarters or six of the twelve portions mentioned above, and gives the length of an eye. One quarter is the width of the eye, and also the distance from the tip of the nose to the opening of the lips, and from this point to the curvature of the chin, and thence to the tip of the chin. The breadth of the nose to the wings of the nostrils contains just a quarter. The length of the mouth requires two quarters; it is therefore equal to the length of the eyes, or to the height of the chin from its point to the line of junction of the lips. One half of the face, measured from the roots of the hair, gives the length from the chin to the pit at the lower extremity of the neck. This method of drawing a face will, I think, be intelligible without a plate, and whoever observes it cannot fail to draw a face of true and beautiful proportion (5).

14. To these remarks upon proportion I will annex a few observations upon Composition. The principal rules of the ancient artists on this point were, first, fewness of figures; second, repose in action. It was a rule of the drama, first introduced by Sophocles, not to allow more than three persons to be present on the stage at one time. It appears from a very large number of ancient works, that the same principle was adopted and observed also in art (6). We find, indeed, that the ancient artists strove to express much, an entire action, in fact, in a single figure, — as the painter Theon attempted in his figure of a warrior, to which he gave the attitude and expression of one repelling an assault, though no assailants were represented. As they all drew their subjects from the same source, namely, Homer (7), they were in fact limited to a certain number of figures, because in a great many of the scenes in that poet only two or three persons are engaged : such, for example, is the celebrated interchange of arms by Glaucus and Diomedes, so frequently repre-

sented in ancient times; also the enterprise of Ulysses and Diomedes against the Trojan camp, together with the death of Dolon, and numberless other incidents formerly represented. It is the same with heroic history anterior to the Trojan war, as every one knows; most of its incidents were fully comprised and completed in three figures.

15. As regards repose in composition, the works of ancient artists never present, like those of modern times, an assemblage of persons, all seeking to be heard at the same time, or resembling a crowd hastily gathered together, in which each one is straining to look over his neighbor's shoulder. No; their images resemble an assemblage of persons who inspire and demand respect. They understood very well what we call *grouping;* but we must not expect to find composition of this kind on that class of rilievi with which one most frequently meets, because these are all taken from sepulchral urns (sarcophagi), the narrowness of whose shape would not always admit of it. The composition of some of 'them, however, is rich, crowded with figures; as, for instance, the *Death of Meleager*, which is published in the *Ancient Monuments.* But, whenever the space was ample enough to allow the figures to be arranged in a variety of positions, then even these urns may serve as models in composition, as it is manifest from the antique paintings in my *Monuments*, and from numerous paintings brought from Herculaneum.

16. Of Contrast, as it is termed by modern artists, I shall say nothing. Every one will acknowledge that it was as well known to the masters of antiquity as to those of the present day; not less familiar to them than Antithesis — which is Contrast in art — was to the poets and orators of Greece. Contrast, therefore, like antithesis in writing, ought to be easy and unaffected, and not to be regarded as an important or elevated point of knowledge in one art more than in the other; though modern artists value it as a substitute for every excellence, and an excuse for every fault. On this principle Chambray justifies Raphael for having, in his design of the *Massacre of the Innocents*, engraved by Marco Antonio, made his female figures stout, and the murderers lean. He says that it was done for the purpose of contrast, that the murderers might thereby be rendered still more horrible.

CHAPTER V.

BEAUTY OF INDIVIDUAL PARTS OF THE BODY.

1. NATURE is the best teacher as to the beauty of single parts of the body. In particulars she is superior to art, but in generals art can soar above her. This is true, especially in regard to sculpture, which cannot represent life in those points in which painting is able to approach it very closely. But since some few parts, a soft profile, for instance, are seldom found in perfection, even in the largest cities, we must, for this very reason, study them — to say nothing of the nude parts — in the ancient figures. A description of particulars is at all times difficult, and consequently is so in this instance.

2. In considering beauty I have proceeded analytically, that is, from the whole to its parts. Equal benefit, however, might be derived from teaching it synthetically, and studying it as a whole after having examined its parts separately. The latter method is perhaps preferable in oral instruction, imparted by means of questions, in which the teacher requires from his pupils some account of the form of single parts, and thus tries and proves their knowledge of the beautiful. But, as a knowledge of general principles must, in every regular system, be presumed before any particular observations are made, although the former have grown out of the latter, I have given a preference to the analytical mode of proceeding.

3. In considering those parts which individually constitute beauty, attention must be especially directed to the extremities of the human figure, not only because in them reside life, motion, expression, and action, but also because their configuration is the most difficult, and principally determines the peculiar difference which distinguishes the beautiful from the ugly, and modern from ancient works. In drawing, head, hands, and feet, are the principal points; they must, therefore, be the parts first taught.

4. In the conformation of the face, the Greek profile, as it is called, is the first and principal attribute of a high style of beauty. This profile consists in a nearly straight or slightly depressed line which the forehead and nose describe in youthful heads, especially of the female sex. It is of less frequent occurrence in cold (1) than in mild climates, but, wherever it exists, the form of that face may be beautiful : for grandeur is produced by straightness and fulness ; but tenderness, by gentle inflexions of the forms. That this kind of profile is a source of beauty is proved by its opposite ; for the more the nose is depressed, the greater is the deviation of the line of the face from the form of beauty ; and if a face, when viewed sideways, shows a bad profile, it is useless to look for beauty in it. The nose of Egyptian figures, which is very much depressed, — in opposition to the straight outlines of all other parts, — proves that, if any form in works of art does not conform to the straight lines of the most ancient style, sufficient reasons can be assigned for the deviation. The old writers make use of the term *square* nose. It is not probable that they understood by it a full nose, as Junius explains the word, for this gives no idea of its shape, but that they applied it to the slightly indented profile just mentioned. We might give another explanation of the word, and understand it to mean a nose with a broad, flat back, and sharp edges, of the kind which may be seen in the Pallas, and the Vestal, as she is called, of the Giustiniani palace (2). This form, however, is found only in statues, like these, of the most ancient style, — indeed, in these two alone.

5. Having thus noticed the beauty of the profile, that is to say, the beautiful form of the whole face, I will now examine it in detail, commencing with the head. One of the principal points of a beautiful face consists in the conformation of the forehead, which should, above all things, be low. Our own observation in part, and partly the remarks of the ancient writers, teach us this ; a high forehead was even regarded by the ancients as ugly. Yet a high, open forehead is not ugly, but rather the reverse. This, though seemingly a contradiction, is very easily explained. The forehead should be low in youth. It generally is low in the bloom of life, before the hair which covers it falls off, and leaves it bare. Nature herself has endowed the age of beauty with this characteristic ; the absence of it, therefore, will always detract from the beauty of form of the face.

It would, consequently, be a violation of the characteristics of youth, to give to it the high, open forehead which belongs to manhood. We can easily convince ourselves of this by covering with the finger the front hair of a person who has a low forehead; the additional height thus given to it will show the inharmoniousness of proportion, if I may so express myself, and enable us to understand on what principle a high forehead is unfavorable to beauty. Even the Circassian women know this; and, for the purpose of making the forehead seem still lower than it really is, they comb down the frontal hair, cut short for the purpose, so that it reaches nearly to the eyebrows. It may be inferred from what Arnobius says, that women who had a high forehead placed a band over it, with the design of thereby making it seem lower.

6. When Horace sings the praises of *insignem tenui fronte Lycorida,* he means to say, " Lycoris, celebrated for her low forehead." He was at least so understood by the old commentators, who explained the expression *tenui fronte* in the following manner : — *Angusta et parva fronte, quod in pulchritudinis forma commendari solet,* "A narrow and small forehead, which is usually commended in a beautiful form." But Erizzo did not understand the passage; for on the words *tenui fronte* he remarks as follows : — *Tenuis et rotunda frons index est libidinis et mobilitatis simplicitatisque, sine procaci petulantia dolisque meretricis,* " A low, round forehead denotes sensuality, fickleness, and simplicity, unaccompanied by wanton forwardness or meretricious arts." Francis Junius, likewise, has not understood the meaning of the word *tenuis* in this passage; he explains *tenuem frontem* by ἁπαλὸν καὶ δροσῶδες μέτωπον from Anacreon, " the soft and dewy forehead," i. e. of Bathyllus. In Martial, instead of *frons tenuis,* " low forehead," we have *frons brevis,* " short forehead," — a point of beauty which he wishes to see in a handsome boy.

7. The lower the forehead, the shorter is the hair on it; and the points of the lowest and shortest hairs usually curve forwards over it. We observe this forward curve of the hair on all beautiful heads of Hercules, both in his youth and manhood; and it is, in a measure, so characteristic of them, that it not unfrequently enables us to detect a modern head on engraved gems. Petronius represents Circe with precisely such hair; but the beauty of it has not been understood either by his transcribers or commentators. For, in the following passage,

Frons minima et quæ radices capillorum retroflexerat, " A very low forehead, on which the roots of the hair turned backward," we must unquestionably substitute for the word *radices,* "roots," the word *apices,* " points," namely, of the hair, or some word of similar meaning, since *apex* signifies the point of a thing. How can the roots of the hair curve forward? The French translator of Petronius has, in his remarks on this passage, supposed an artificial head-dress, beneath which the natural roots of the hair were visible. Can any thing be more absurd? The meaning of the phrase, *frons minima,* "a very low forehead," which is mentioned by Petronius in his description of the form of Circe, is not expressed by *front petit,* "small forehead," as the French translator has rendered it, because the forehead may be broad and at the same time low.

8. A low forehead is so peculiar to the ideas which the ancient artists had of a beautiful head, that it is a characteristic by which an antique can frequently be distinguished from a modern work. Many heads, which I could not approach sufficiently near to examine, I have either recognized to be modern, solely by the high forehead, or else this conformation first excited doubts as to their age, which were afterwards verified by further investigation.

9. To complete the beauty of a youthful head, the frontal hair should grow in a curve down over the temples, in order to give the face an oval shape. Such a forehead is to be found in all beautiful women; and this form of it is so peculiar to all ideal and other youthful heads of the ancients, that we do not see on any figures, not even those of mature manhood, the receding, bare corners over the temples, which usually enlarge as life advances beyond that age when the forehead is naturally high. Few modern sculptors have noticed this peculiarity; and wherever new youthful male heads are placed upon antique statues, the hair is carried obliquely over the forehead, and strikingly displays the faulty conception of modern days in regard to the natural beauty of its disposition. Some of our artists have made portrait-figures of young persons of both sexes, with whom I am acquainted, and who have low foreheads; yet they have given so little attention to the beauty of which I now speak, that they have added to the height of the foreheads, and made the growth of hair commence farther back, with the presumed intention of forming an open forehead. Bernini belongs

to this class; but in this particular, as in many others, he has
mistaken the reverse of beauty for beauty's self.   Baldinucci,
his panegyrist, wishing to adduce a very striking example of
his fine taste, says that, when he modelled from life a statue
of Louis XIV., then in the prime of youth, he smoothed the
hair away from his forehead.   In this instance, as in many
others, the babbling Florentine revealed the poverty of his own
knowledge.

10. This form of the forehead, and especially the short hairs
with a forward curve, are manifest on all beautiful heads of Hercules, whether in youth or manhood, and are, with the thickness of neck formerly noticed, also a symbol of his strength.
These hairs seem intended to represent those between the horns
of bulls.   They are, therefore, a characteristic of Hercules, and
distinguish his image from the heads of his beloved Iole, which,
like his own, are covered by a lion's skin.   The hair of this
beautiful woman lies in curls on her forehead, as may be seen,
among other instances, in a head (3), cut in high relief, in the
royal Farnese museum at Naples.   The characteristic in question was one reason, among others, which led me to the true
appellation of a beautiful head, in intaglio, which went by the
name of Iole, but was in fact a Hercules, in the former Stosch
museum.   It is also to be seen in a youthful head crowned with
laurel, cut on a carnelian, by Allion, a Greek artist, which is in
the Grand-ducal gallery at Florence.   A Hercules, therefore, is
also represented in this figure, and not an Apollo, as it is assumed to be.   Another Hercules, cut by Onesas, in the same
gallery, is, like the other, crowned with laurel ; but, in the engravings of it, the forehead has been restored — as the upper
part of the head is wanting in the gem — by persons who had
never noticed the peculiarity in question.   Many coins, especially
of Alexander the Great, bear the impression of a youthful head
covered with a lion's skin ; if connoisseurs in coins had noticed
the foregoing fact, they would have recognized the image of
Hercules, instead of erroneously supposing it to be the head of
Alexander, or some other king.

11. The frontal hair is, likewise, an invariable and infallible
characteristic by which the heads of Alexander the Great can
be distinguished.   But it resembles, in its arrangement, the
hair of Jupiter, — whose son he wished to be considered, — being smoothed upwards, and then falling down again in a curve

on each side of the face, in several divisions. Plutarch, in that passage of the life of Pompey in which it is said that he wore his hair like Alexander, calls this manner of dressing it ἀναστολὴν τῆς κόμης, "a pushing back of the hair": my remarks upon it will be found in the second part of this History.

12. For further confirmation of the utility of the observation made by me as to the short hairs, curving forwards, on the forehead of Hercules, I will remark that it may be applied, in particular, to a youthful head, which, together with a shoulder, is engraved on a gem in the museum of the king of France. This head presents a figure draped with a thin, transparent tissue, which is drawn from the shoulder upon the head, and even over the garland of laurel that encircles the head; at the same time, it veils the lower part of the face, so as to cover the tip of the nose, but still in such a manner that one can plainly distinguish and recognize the features.

13. A special treatise has been written upon this stone, in which it is pretended that the head represents Ptolemy, — king of Egypt, and father of the famed Cleopatra, — who bore the surname of Auletes, or the Flute-player, because he loved to play upon the flute, and that the drapery which veils the lower part of his countenance — for the writer did not perplex himself about the veil over the head and shoulder — is the band termed φορβειά and φόρβιον, which was tied by flute-players over their mouths, and had in it an aperture through which the flute was applied to the lips. There might be some plausibility in this explanatory statement, if we had no definite idea of the band in question; but a triangular altar (4), in the Campidoglio, shows us a Faun, with this band over his mouth, blowing two flutes. As an engraving of this head is to be found in several books, it must of course have been known to the author of the treatise to which I have alluded. We also see a flute-player (5), with his mouth thus bandaged, in a picture from Herculaneum. It is evident from both these instances, that the φορβειά was a narrow band, which passed over the mouth and ears, and was tied on the back part of the head; so that it has nothing to do with the manner in which this figure is veiled.

14. As this head is the only one of its kind, it deserves further investigation, as some conjectures may be made which will come nearer to its true signification. If, with this view, it be compared with the heads of a young Hercules, a perfect resem-

blance between them will be discovered. The forehead has the usual swollen roundness and bigness; the front hair is arranged in the manner previously mentioned; and the cheeks, as low down as the under part of the ear, are beginning to be covered with hair, συγκατιοῦσα ἡ κόμη τῷ ἰούλῳ παρὰ τὸ οὖς, "the hair of his head uniting, near the ear, with the down of his cheek," —

"Cui prima jam nunc vernant lanugine malæ,"

Whose cheeks are now putting forth their vernal down, —

which, according to an ancient commentary, is a precursor of the beard. The ear, moreover, appears to resemble the Pancratiast ear of Hercules.

15. But what meaning can I attach to the drapery which veils this head, and what relation can it have to Hercules? I imagine that by it the artist intended to represent the hero at the time when he was serving Omphale, queen of Lydia. This conjecture is suggested to me by a head of Paris, in the villa Negroni, which is veiled in precisely the same manner, as high up as the edge of the lower lip. This vestment, therefore, appears to have been in common use among the Phrygians and Lydians, — which would naturally be the case with contiguous nations. Besides, these two people were, according to the testimony of Strabo, confounded with each other by the tragic poets, more especially as they had both been governed at one time by Tantalus. Philostratus, moreover, informs us that the customs of the Lydians were, in many respects, the reverse of those of the Grecians; that the former were accustomed to conceal by a thin drapery parts of the body which the latter left uncovered. If these two historical notices be taken into consideration, my supposition ought not to appear unfounded.

16. As neither the Lydians nor the Phrygians existed in the time of Philostratus, it is impossible that he should have founded his remark on personal observation of the Lydian dress. In his day, the customs of those who dwelt in Asia Minor had assumed quite a different aspect. He must, therefore, have derived his information relative to the practice, usual among the Lydians, of wearing mantles, from some more ancient writer, not known to us. Euripides, moreover, speaks of a similar custom among the Phrygians, in that scene of his tragedy of *Hecuba* in which Agamemnon is introduced, who, seeing the murdered body of Polydorus, son of that queen of Troy,

lying before her tent, inquires who the dead Trojan is ; it cannot be a Greek, he says, for he is wrapped in a mantle : —

τίν ἄνδρα τὸν δ᾽ ἐπὶ σκηναῖς ὁρῶ
Θανόντα Τρώων ; οὐ γὰρ Ἀργείων πέπλοι
Δέμας περιπτύσσοντες ἀγγέλλουσί μοι.

He is not speaking here of the vestment in which the dead were
clothed, but of a garb peculiar to the Phrygians, and differing
from the dress of the Greeks. But, if the reader understands
the passage as applicable to the Phrygian dress generally, my
commentary may, in that case, be passed by as unnecessary.

17. I did not make the closing remark of the last paragraph
from any mistrust of the conjecture proposed by me, — that it
was a customary practice among the Lydians to veil the face ;
on the contrary, I think that my explanation of the gem in
question will receive all the confirmation it needs from a painting on a vase of terra cotta, of which an engraving may be
found in the large *Hamilton Collection.* I will mention here,
that this vase was brought from Alexandria, in Egypt, whither
it had been carried, at some earlier period, from the kingdom
of Naples.

18. This picture, undoubtedly, represents Hercules at the
time when he was sold to Omphale, who sits here in company
with three other female figures. The queen is enveloped in a
thin, transparent drapery, thrown over her other dress, which
not only completely covers her left hand, but is even drawn
upwards, over the lower part of the face, upon the nose, precisely in the manner exhibited by the head on the gem. If the
engraver of this head, therefore, had exhibited the whole figure
of Hercules, he would have draped it precisely in this manner ; for even the men, in Lydia, wore a mantle which descended
to the feet, and was called βασσάρα. Generally, it was also
denominated Λύδιος, "Lydian," with the addition of λεπτός,
"thin." We must, notwithstanding Casaubon's conjecture, give
this reading to Athenæus, whose meaning is at the same time
elucidated by the preceding remarks. The right hand of Hercules, who advances toward Omphale, rests upon his club ; and
his left touches her knees, — a form of supplication common
among those who desired to obtain a suit from another. Between these two figures hovers a small male figure, seemingly a
Genius, but it might probably be Mercury, by whom Hercules
was sold to the Lydian queen. If so, it would be the sole

instance among the ancient monuments in which this god has been figured with long wings on his back. Or this winged and perfectly white child may represent the Soul of Iphitus, whom Hercules slew, and may signify that he was sold into slavery in obedience to the oracle of Apollo, that he might expiate the murder. Or it may be Cupid, who calls off Omphale from her conversation, that she may receive, in the youthful hero who presents himself before her, her future lover. The female figure sitting in front of Omphale has her hair cut off short behind, after the fashion of men. This is altogether unusual; and it must, therefore, have some peculiar meaning. I do not know whether to venture a conjecture relative to its signification. But might not this figure, perchance, represent a maiden who had been spayed? — the Lydians having been the first to effect such a change, by artificial means, in the nature of woman. It is said that Andramytes, who was the fourth king of the country before Omphale, invented the operation, in order that he might use such female creatures instead of eunuchs. By what personal mark was a woman of this kind to be indicated, except by her hair? which is short, as young men usually wear it, apparently for the purpose of signifying thereby that her nature as a woman had undergone a change. Young eunuchs, also, wore their hair in this manner. The learned painter of this vase intimated, therefore, by means of such a person, more plainly than he could have done otherwise, the alteration she had suffered, the land in which it was effected, and also the presence of a queen of the Lydians. He may, possibly, have had other reasons, but it is unnecessary for me to inquire further regarding them, as I may then pass over in silence what occurs to me on this occasion relative to the Tribades, and the excessive wantonness of the Lydian women.

19. The reader may, by this time, begin to think the investigation of this remarkable gem a digression. Properly, therefore, I ought to resume the thread of my subject, and notice the beauty of the remaining features of the face. But I cannot refrain from embracing the opportunity to mention two heads of a young hero which perfectly resemble each other. Their configuration is beautiful and ideal. The arrangement of the hair on the forehead is like that of Hercules; and both are encircled by a diadem. The peculiarity in both is a hole above each temple, into which the thumb can be easily introduced, and which

would, therefore, seem to have been made for the purpose of attaching horns. In one head the holes had been filled up by some modern sculptor. From the conformation of the face, and from the hair, we cannot infer that the horns were goats' horns, nor the heads those of young Fauns. The probability is, that small ox-horns were attached here. They were given to the heads of Seleucus I., king of Syria; but these heads do not resemble the likenesses of him. I am consequently of opinion that Hyllus, son of Hercules, is represented by them. His images, like those of Ptolemy Hephæstion, had a horn on the left side of the head; the one on the right side has been gratuitously added by the sculptor. One of these heads is in my possession; the other, in the museum of the Signor Bartolommeo Cavaceppi.

20. The eyes, as a component part of beauty, are still more essential than the forehead. In art, they are to be considered more in regard to their form than their color, because their beauty does not consist in the latter, but in the former, which is not at all affected, whatever the color of the iris may be. With respect to the form of the eyes, generally, it is superfluous to say that one beauty in them is size, just as a great light is more beautiful than a small one. But the size of the eye conforms to the eye-bones, or its socket, and is manifested by the edge and opening of the eyelids, of which the upper describes a rounder curve towards the inner corner of a beautiful eye than the under. All large eyes, however, are not beautiful; projecting eyes never are. The upper eyelid of the lions in Rome, at least of Egyptian lions, opens in such a manner as to describe a complete semicircle. The eyes of heads in profile, on rilievi, and especially on the most beautiful coins, form an angle the opening of which is towards the nose. The corner of the eye towards the nose is deeply sunken, and the contour of it terminates at the highest point of its curve, — that is to say, the pupil itself is in profile. The opening of the eye being truncated in this manner, the head acquires an air of majesty, and an open, elevated look. The pupil of the eye is, also, denoted on coins by means of a raised point on its centre.

I will not repeat here what has already been observed by others, that the word βοῶπις, by which Homer, in particular characterizes beautiful eyes, does not signify *ox-eyed;* but merely remark that the βου, in this as well as in many other words compounded with it, is a prefix, as the grammarians say, signifying enlargement.   Hence the scholiast of Homer translates βοῶπις by μελανόφθαλμος, " black-eyed," and καλὴ τὸ πρόσωπον, "beautiful in face."   The reader can also see what the learned Martorelli says on this point in his *Antiquities of Naples.*

21. The eyes, in ideal heads, are always more deeply seated than they are commonly found to be in nature, and the upper edge of the socket consequently appears to be more prominent. Deeply seated eyes, however, are not a characteristic of beauty, and impart a not very open expression to the countenance. But, as art could not, in this particular, always conform to the teachings of nature, it adhered to the lofty style and the grandeur of conception by which it is characterized.   For, the eyes and eyebrows of large figures being farther removed from the spectator than those of smaller ones, they would be scarcely visible at a distance, if the eyeball had been placed as prominently as in nature, — it being, for the most part, quite smooth in sculpture, and not designated as in painting, — and if, for the same reason, the upper edge of the socket had not been made more prominent.   On this point, therefore, art deviated from nature, and thus brought forth, by means of depth, and of elevation in this portion of the face, greater light and shadow, and imparted more animation and power to the eye, which, otherwise, would have been destitute of expression, and, as it were, lifeless.   This would have been conceded even by Elizabeth, queen of England, who wished her portrait to be painted entirely without shadow.   Art, in this case, rose above nature, and justly, too, and afterwards established from this form of the eyes a rule of almost universal application, even to small figures.   For the eyes of heads on coins of the best days of art lie just as deeply as in those of later date, and the edge of the socket is more prominent ; in proof of which let any one examine the coins of Alexander the Great, and his successors.   In works of metal, some things were signified, which, in the bloom of art, were omitted in those of marble.   Thus, for example, the light, — as artists term it, — or the pupil, was denoted by a raised point on the centre of the eye, on coins bearing the heads of Gelon and Hiero, even prior to the days of Phidias.   But, so far as we know, a pupil was not given to heads in marble until some time during the first century of the Cæsars, and there are only a few which have it.   One of them is the head of Mar-

cellus, grandson of Augustus, in the Campidoglio. For the reason assigned above, and with precisely the same view, eyes appear to have been inserted. This was a common practice among Egyptian sculptors of the earliest ages. In many heads of bronze, the eyes have been hollowed out, and substitutes of a different material introduced. The head of the Pallas of Phidias was of ivory, but the pupil of the eye was a gem. I shall speak particularly of such eyes hereafter.

22. Thus it was well understood and settled what constituted beauty of the eye generally. And yet, without departing from this form, the eye was so differently shaped in the heads of divinities, and ideal heads, that it is of itself a characteristic by which they can be distinguished. In Jupiter, Apollo, and Juno, the opening of the eye is large, and roundly arched; it has, also, less length than usual, that the curve which it makes may be more spherical. Pallas, likewise, has large eyes; but the upper lid falls over them more than in the three divinities just mentioned, for the purpose of giving her a modest, maiden look. But the eyes of Venus (6) are smaller; and the elevation of the lower lid imparts to them that love-exciting and languishing look which the Greeks term ὑγρόν, "liquid." The celestial Venus, or Venus Urania, is distinguished from Juno by an eye of this kind;[1] but as, like Juno, she wears a diadem, she has been confounded with the latter by those who had not noticed her distinctive peculiarity. On this point many modern artists seek to surpass the ancients, and have supposed that by giving to their figures prominent eyeballs, starting from their sockets, they expressed the idea intended to be conveyed by Homer in the term *ox-eyes*, or *large eyes*, as before mentioned. The modern head of the figure, in the villa Medici, erroneously supposed to be Cleopatra (7), has eyes which resemble those of a person who had died by hanging; and a young sculptor, now resident in Rome, has given precisely such eyes to a statue of the Madonna (8) — which he was commissioned to execute — in the church of San Carlo, on the Corso.

23. Nothing, not even the line of the eyelids, escaped the penetration of the ancients in their observation of beauty; for the word ἑλικοβλέφαρος, in Hesiod, seems to apply to a particular form of them. This word has been explained very vaguely and loosely by the host of Greek grammarians since his time, by

[1] Plate XVI, B and C

καλλιβλέφαρος, "with beautiful eyelids." But the scholiast of Hesiod, on the contrary, seems to penetrate into its inner and secret meaning, and thinks that it denotes eyes whose lids describe a line the undulation of which has been compared to the flexure of the young tendrils of the vine, ἕλικες. This comparison, which in its way explains the epithet, may be admitted, if we consider the waving line described by the edge of beautiful eyelids, and clearly seen in the finest ideal heads, as in the Apollo, the heads of Niobe, and especially in the Venus. In colossal heads, as the Juno in the villa Ludovisi, this waving line is drawn yet more distinctly, and more perceptibly expressed. The heads of bronze in the Herculaneum museum have marks on the edges of the lids which indicate that the eyelashes, βλεφαρίδες, were represented by small pins inserted in them.

24. The beauty of the eye itself is enhanced, and, as it were, crowned, by the eyebrow; and the eyebrow is beautiful in proportion to the delicacy of the line formed by the hairs, which is denoted, on the finest heads in sculpture, by the sharp edge of the bone over the eyes. Among the Greeks, such eyebrows were termed *eyebrows of the Graces*. But, if they were much arched, they were compared to a bent bow, or to snails, and in this case were never considered beautiful (9). The former is the ὀφρύων τὸ εὔγραμμον, "graceful line of the eyebrows," which Lucian found so beautiful in the heads of Praxiteles. Petronius, in describing the characteristics of beauty in an eyebrow, uses the following words, — *Supercilia usque ad malarum scripturam currentia, et rursus confinio luminum pene permixta*, "Eyebrows which reach, at one extremity, even to the cheek, and, at the other, almost join the confines of the eye." I believe that, in this passage, we might read *stricturam* instead of *scripturam*, as the latter word conveys no meaning; yet it must be acknowledged that *strictura* cannot be applied here in the sense in which it is used by authors. But, if we extend to it the signification of the verb *stringere*, from which it is derived, Petronius would be understood to say, "even to the boundary of the cheeks;" for *stringere* means precisely the same as *radere*, that is, *to just touch in passing* (10).

25. As the hairs which compose the eyebrows are not an essential part of them, it is not necessary that they should be represented. In portrait-heads, as well as ideal heads, they may

be omitted both by painters and sculptors; and this has been done by Raphael and Annibal Caracci. The eyebrows of the most beautiful heads in marble, at least, are not represented by separate hairs. Eyebrows which meet have already been mentioned. I have stated my opinion to be unfavorable to them, and have good reason to be astonished that Theocritus, the poet of tenderness, could find joined eyebrows beautiful, and that other writers have imitated him in this particular. Among these is Isaac Porphyrogenetes, who gives such eyebrows, σύνο- φρυς, to Ulysses; the supposed Phrygian, Dares, also, to show the beauty of Briseïs, mentions the junction of her eyebrows. Bayle, although he had no knowledge of art, considered this as rather a strange charm in a beautiful woman like Briseïs, and thinks that such eyebrows would not, in our days, be regarded as an attribute of beauty. But he, as well as others, may be assured, that connoisseurs of beauty, even in ancient times, held precisely the same opinion as theirs; among them I will mention Aristænetus, who praises the parted eyebrows of a beautiful woman. The eyebrows of Julia, daughter of Titus, in the villa Medici, and of another female head, in the palace Giustiniani, are joined together. We are not, however, to suppose that their junction, in these instances, was made for the purpose of adding to the beauty of the individuals, but simply to produce a faithful likeness. Suetonius mentions that the eyebrows of Augustus joined; they are not so represented, however, in a single head of him (11). Eyebrows which meet are, as a Greek epigram remarks, an indication of pride and bitterness of spirit.

26. Next to the eyes, the mouth is the most beautiful feature of the face. The beauty of its form, however, is known to all, and requires no special notice. The lips answer the purpose of displaying a more brilliant red than is to be seen elsewhere. The under lip should be fuller than the upper. As a consequence of this formation, there is found beneath it and above the chin a depression, the design of which is to impart variety to this portion of the face, and give a fuller roundness to the chin. In one of the two beautiful statues of Pallas, in the villa Albani, the lower lip projects, but imperceptibly, in order that a greater degree of seriousness may be expressed in her aspect.[1] The

[1] Plate XVIII., B. Front view of the mouth of the Pallas Albani, of the size of the original. — GERM. ED.

lips of figures of the most ancient style are usually closed ; but, in the later periods of art, they are not entirely (12) closed in all figures of divinities, either of the male or female sex ; and this is especially the case with Venus, in order that her countenance may express the languishing softness of desire and love. The same remark holds true of heroic figures. Propertius also refers, in his use of the word *hiare*, to the opening of the mouth of a statue of Apollo, in the temple of this god on Mount Palatine, at Rome : —

" Hic equidem Phœbo visus mihi pulchrior ipso
Marmoreus tacita carmen hiare lyra."

L. 2, *Eleg.* 31, *vers.* 5.

More beauteous than the God his marble form I see ;
Though hushed the lyre, the lips are breathing melody.

In portrait-figures, the reverse is usually the case ; and heads of the Roman emperors, in particular, have the lips invariably closed. The edge of the lips, in some few heads of the older style, is denoted merely by an incised line ; but in others it is elevated (13) quite imperceptibly, and, as it were, pinched up, for the purpose, probably, of indicating more distinctly the line of it in figures which stood at a certain distance from the spectator. Very few of the figures which have been represented laughing, as some Satyrs or Fauns are, show the teeth. Among the images of divinities, only one statue with such a mouth, namely, an Apollo of the older style, in the palace Conti, is known to me.

27. In images whose beauties were of a lofty cast, the Greek artists never allowed a dimple to break the uniformity of the chin's surface. Its beauty, indeed, consists in the rounded fulness of its arched form, to which the lower lip, when short, imparts additional size. In order to give this form to the chin, the ancient artists made the lower jaw larger and deeper than nature usually fashions it, having observed this to be the case in the most beautiful of her conformations. As a dimple — by the Greeks termed νύμφη — is an isolated, and somewhat accidental, adjunct to the chin, it was not regarded by the Greek artists as an attribute of abstract and pure beauty, though it is so considered by modern writers (14). Hence, it is not to be found either in Niobe and her daughters, or in the Albani Pallas, or in Ceres on coins of Metapontus, or in Proserpine on coins of Syracuse, — images of the highest female beauty. Of the finest

male heads, neither the Apollo nor the Meleager (15) of the Belvedere has it, nor the Bacchus in the villa Medici, nor indeed any beautiful ideal figure which has come down to us. The head of an Apollo in bronze, of the size of life, in the museum of the Roman College, and the Venus (16) at Florence, alone have it, as a peculiar charm, not as anything appertaining to the beautiful form of the chin. It was also given to the head of the statue of Bathyllus, which stood in the temple of Juno at Samos, as Apuleius informs us; but, notwithstanding Varro calls this dimple an impress from the finger of Cupid, it does not disprove the correctness of my remarks.

28. A rounded fulness of the chin, therefore, is an attribute of its beauty which was universally acknowledged, and introduced in all figures of superior merit. Consequently, when, in drawings made from them, the lower part of it seems, as it were, to be pinched in, it may be inferred with certainty that the contraction proceeds from the ignorance of the copyist; and when such a chin is found in antique ideal heads, it may justly be suspected that some modern ignorant hand has been attempting to improve upon them. Therefore I doubt whether the beautiful Mercury of bronze, in the Herculaneum museum, had originally such a chin as it now has, especially as we are assured that the head of it was found broken into many pieces. Few heads from modern sculptors are unexceptionable in the chin. In the larger number of them it is too small, too pointed; sometimes, it has the appearance of being pinched in all around. The figures in the works of Pietro da Cortona are always distinguishable by their somewhat small chin. — I forgot to notice another imperfection in the chin of the Medicean Venus (17), namely, its flattened tip, in the middle of which is a dimple. Such flatness of surface is not to be found either in nature or in a single antique head. As, however, our sculptors are continually making copies in marble of this statue, they imitate with the utmost exactness the unusual flatness of its chin, as a beauty, and they cannot be convinced that a broad, flat chin is not beautiful.

29. It was customary with the ancient artists to elaborate no portion of the head more diligently than the ears. The beauty, and especially the execution, of them is the surest sign by which to discriminate the antique from additions and restorations. If, therefore, in a case of doubt as to the antiquity of

engraved gems, it should be observed that the ear is only, as it were, set on, and not worked out with the utmost nicety, the workmanship may unquestionably be pronounced modern (18). In portrait-figures, when the countenance is so much injured as not to be recognized, we can occasionally make a correct conjecture as to the person intended, if it is one of whom we have any knowledge, merely by the form of the ear; thus, we infer a head of Marcus Aurelius from an ear with an unusually large inner opening. In such figures the ancient artists were so particular about the ears, that they even copied their deformities, — as one may see, among other instances, in a beautiful bust belonging to the Marquis Rondinini, and on a head in the villa Altieri.

30. Besides the infinite variety of forms of the ear on heads modelled from life, or on copies of such heads, we observe an ear of quite a singular shape, that is found not only on ideal figures, but also on some which represent particular individuals. The cartilages of it seem to be beaten flat, and swollen; its inner passage is, consequently, made narrower, and the whole outer ear itself is shrunken, and diminished in size.[1] Having, at first, observed this peculiar form of the ear on a few heads of Hercules, I conjectured that a secret meaning was involved in it. The description given of Hector by Philostratus has, I think, furnished me with a key to its explanation.

31. This writer introduces Protesilaus speaking, and makes him describe the stature and characteristics of the Greek and Trojan heroes in the Trojan war. In this narration, he particularly notices the ears of Hector, and says that ὦτα κατεαγὼς ἦν, that is, "his ears were broken and crushed." These injuries were received, not in games of the arena, as Philostratus expressly declares, — because such exercises had not, at that time, been introduced among the Asiatics, — but in contests with bulls. He also explains his understanding of the term, κατεαγὼς ὦτα, "broken ears," by a circumlocution, ἀμφὶ παλαίστραν αὐτῷ πεπονημένα τὰ ὦτα, that is, "ears which have been belabored in the palæstra": such ears he ascribes to Nestor. I do not understand, however, in what sense it could be said of Hector that he got ears of this description in fighting with bulls; and Vigenère, the French translator of Philostratus, was no less perplexed by this statement than myself. I, therefore, believe that,

[1] Plate VIII., B.   A Pancratiast ear.

in the last version of this author, of which an edition was published at Leipsic, the translator has sought to evade all difficulty by means of a general expression, inasmuch as he has
rendered ὦτα κατεαγὼς by *athletico erat habitu.*

32. Philostratus, in this instance, is probably speaking in the
words of Plato, who represents Socrates as making the following inquiry of Callicles : " Tell me, have the Athenians been
made better by Pericles, or, on the contrary, loquacious and
corrupt ? " Callicles answers, — " Who will say this, except
those whose ears are crushed ? " Τῶν τὰ ὦτα κατεαγότων ἀκούεις
ταῦτα : that is, " Who will say this, except people who know
nothing else than how to contend in the arena ? " This was
probably intended as a sarcasm upon the Spartans, who were
less devoted than other Greeks to the arts which Pericles had
introduced into Athens, and fostered there, and who held in
higher esteem athletic exercises, — although Serranus, in his
translation of the passage, has given to it a meaning entirely
different from mine. He renders it thus : *Hæc audis ab iis, qui
fractas obtusasque istis rumoribus aures habent,* — that is, " You
hear these things from persons whose ears are broken and
stunned by such tittle-tattle." My supposition in regard to
the Spartans rests upon another passage of Plato, in the Protagoras, which says, in reference to the characteristics that
distinguished the Spartans from other Greeks, Οἱ μὲν ὦτά τε
κατάγνυνται, " Who, indeed, have their ears crushed." But
even this expression has been wrongly explained by Meursius,
who assumes that the Spartans lacerated their own ears, *aures
sibi concidunt ;* and hence, he understood no better the following words also, ἱμάντας περιειλίττονται ; he supposed the meaning to be, that the Spartans, after having mangled their own
ears, wound leathern thongs around them. But every one will
readily understand that the reference here is to the cestus worn
by boxers, which was bound about the hands. The same explanation of the passage had already been given by a learned
scholar before mine was offered.

33. An athlete with such ears is termed in Lucian ὠτοκάτα-
ξις, " one who has the marks of blows on his ears ; " and Laertius, when speaking of the philospher Lycon, who was a famous
athlete, uses the word ὠτοθλαδίας, which has a similar signification. The latter word is explained by Hesychius and Suidas to
signify τὰ ὦτα τεθλασμένος, " one with crushed ears ; " it cannot

be understood in the sense of *mutilated ears*, applied to it by Daniel Heyne.   Salmasius, who quotes this passage of Laertius, dwells at length on the word ἐμπινής, but passes over without comment the more difficult term ὠτοθλαδίας.

34. In the first place, Hercules has such ears, because he won the prize, as Pancratiast, in the games which he himself instituted at Elis, in honor of Pelops, son of Tantalus, as well as in those which Acastus, son of Pelias, celebrated at Argos. In the next place, Pollux is represented with such ears, because he obtained the victory, as Pancratiast, in the first Pythian games at Delphi.   In the villa Albani is a large rilievo, on which is the figure of a young hero with an ear of this form, to whom I gave, in consequence, the name of Pollux, and, in my *Ancient Monuments,* I have shown the correctness of the appellation.   Such ears may also be observed on the statue of Pollux on the Campidoglio, and on a small figure of the same hero in the Farnesina.   But it is to be remarked that not all the images of Hercules have the ear thus formed.   There are seven statues which represent him as a Pancratiast, and, consequently, with the characteristic of a Pancratiast ; one of them, in bronze, is in the Campidoglio ; of the other six, in marble, one is in the Belvedere, another in the villa Medici, the third in the palace Mattei, the fourth in the villa Borghese, the fifth in the villa Ludovisi, and the sixth in the garden of the villa Borghese. Of heads of Hercules with ears of this shape, I can point to some in the Campidoglio, the palace Barberini, and the villa Albani ; but the most beautiful of them all is a Hermes (19) belonging to Count Fede, which was found in Adrian's villa at Tivoli.   If the Pancratiast ears had been observed on two beautiful bronze busts of a youthful Hercules, of the size of life, in the Herculaneum museum, they alone would have truly denoted the person represented, without any assistance from the conformation, and the fashion of the hair, by which, also, the likeness might have been recognized.   But, neither characteristic having been noticed, the younger bust was pronounced a Marcellus, grandson of Augustus, and the elder, a Ptolemy Philadelphus.   There is a small nude male figure, of bronze, belonging to the family of the Massimi, which, before observing the ears, I had set down as a modern work ; but their Pancratiast form led me, afterwards, to a more correct conclusion. Now, as I am convinced that no one, and especially no artist,

had ever noticed this form of the ear prior to myself, it was of course conclusive evidence to my mind of the antiquity of the head of the figure, and, on more careful examination, I detected in it a resemblance to the heads of Hercules. From the leathern bottle on the left shoulder, this figure would seem to denote Hercules *the Tippler*. I, therefore, believe that the statue of Dioxippus — of whom Pliny makes mention as having been victor in the Pancratium, apparently without exertion or resistance — did not have ears of a form similar to those of a Pancratiast, and that, in this respect, it differed from the statues of other Pancratiasts.

35. The beautiful statue of Autolycus had such ears; and they were given, as a distinctive mark, to many of the finest statues of antiquity, which represented Pancratiasts, and were executed by Myron, Pythagoras, and Leochares. The right ear of the figure in the villa Borghese, erroneously termed a Gladiator (20), likewise has this form, though it escaped observation even at the time when the left ear, being mutilated, was restored. Two ears, thus formed, may be seen on the statue of a young hero in the villa Albani, and on a similar statue which formerly stood in the palace Verospi, but is now in the museum of Henry Jennings, of London. By means of such ears, I think that I have discovered, in the Hermes of a philosopher, in the villa Albani, the philosopher Lycon, successor of Strato, in the Peripatetic sect. In his youth, he had been a famous Pancratiast, and, as far as I can recollect, is the only philosopher of whom this is stated. As, according to Laertius, he had crushed ears, and his shape still showed the development of an athlete, τήν τε πᾶσαν σχέσιν ἀθλητικὴν ἐπιφαίνων, even after he had renounced all gymnastic exercises, the name which I give to this Hermes is thereby rendered very probable. As, moreover, the ears are thus formed on the beautiful youth, of bronze, in the Herculaneum museum, which has the shape of a Hermes, and is inscribed with the name of the artist, Apollonius, son of Archias of Athens, I infer it to be the likeness of a young athlete, and not of the emperor Augustus in his youth, whom, besides, it does not resemble. I observe, in conclusion, that a statue in the Capitoline museum, which is called a Pancratiast, cannot represent a person of this description, because the ears are not shaped in the way which I have described.

36. The ancient sculptors strove to display all their skill not

less in the hair than in the ears.　Hence, the former, as well as the latter, is a sign by which to distinguish the modern from the antique ; for later artists differ so much from the ancients in respect to the hair, partly in its arrangement, and partly in its execution, that the difference must be immediately apparent (21) even to a novice in knowledge of the art.　Of the hair upon the forehead I have already spoken, remarking at the time how it and its peculiar arrangement distinguish a Jupiter, or a Hercules, from other divinities.

37. The workmanship of the hair differed according to the quality of the stone.　Thus, when the stone was of a hard kind, the hair was represented as cut short, and afterwards finely combed, — which I shall again mention in its proper place, — because it is impossible to work out loosely-flowing and curled hair from stone of this sort, since, in addition to its too great hardness, it is also brittle.　In marble, on the contrary, and certainly in male figures executed at a flourishing period of art, the hair was made to curl in ringlets, — except in portrait-figures of persons who had short or straight hair, in which case the artist would necessarily imitate it.　But, though on female heads the hair is smoothed upward, and gathered in a knot on the back of the head, and consequently is without ringlets, still we can see that it follows a serpentine course, and is divided by deep furrows, the object of which is to produce variety, and light and shade.　The hair of all Amazons is executed in this manner, and it might serve as a model to our artists in statues of the Madonna.

38. The hair of all figures which belong to a flourishing period of art (22) is curly, abundant, and executed with the utmost imaginable diligence.　By modern artists, on the contrary, it is scarcely indicated ; this is a fault, especially in female heads.　Hence there is a deficiency of light and shade in this part, for they cannot be produced where the grooves are superficial.　One of the reasons why so little labor has been bestowed upon the hair by modern artists might seem to be that its appearance comes nearer to the reality when it is represented either as smooth, or confined in a mass ; still, on the other hand, art requires even such hair to be disposed in deep curves.　The heads of the Amazons, on which there are no curls, may serve as models in this particular.　There is, moreover, a certain arrangement of the hair, peculiar to the Satyrs

or Fauns, as I shall show hereafter, which has been adopted almost universally by modern artists for male heads, probably because it gives less trouble in the execution. This style appears to have been introduced principally by Algardi.

39. The hair of the Fauns or young Satyrs is stiff, and but little curved at its points. It was termed by the Greeks ἐνθύθριξ, "straight hair," and by Suetonius *capillus leniter inflexus*, "hair slightly bent." By such hair it was, apparently, intended to represent them as having a sort of goat's hair; for the old Satyrs, or the figures of Pan, were made with the feet of a goat. Hence, the epithet φριξοκόμης, "bristly," has been applied to Pan. But if, in the Song of Solomon, the hair of the bride is compared to the fleece of a goat, the remark is to be understood of Oriental goats, whose hair was so long that they were sheared.

40. It is common both to Apollo and Bacchus, and to them alone of all the divinities, to have the hair hanging down upon both shoulders. This fact merits particular attention, because mutilated figures (23) may thereby be recognized as figures of them.

41. Children wore long hair until the age of puberty, as we learn from various sources, and among these Suetonius, in the passage where he speaks of the five thousand Neapolitan children with long hair whom Nero assembled at Naples. Youths who had attained this age were accustomed to wear the hair cut shorter, especially behind, except the inhabitants of Euboea, whom for this reason Homer terms ὄπιθεν κομόωντες, "long-haired behind."

42. I cannot, on this occasion, refrain from saying a few words also in regard to the color of the hair, more especially since a misconception in relation to it has grown out of several passages in the ancient writers. Flaxen, ξανθή hair, has always been considered the most beautiful; and hair of this color has been attributed to the most beautiful of the gods, as Apollo and Bacchus, not less than to the Heroes (24); even Alexander had flaxen hair. I have, elsewhere, corrected the interpretation of a passage in Athenæus so as to make it conform to this idea. The passage in question has hitherto been understood, even by Francis Junius, to mean that Apollo had black hair. But a note of interrogation, placed at the end of it, entirely reverses its meaning; Οὐδ᾽ ὁ ποιητὴς [Σιμωνίδης] ἔφη, λέγων χρυσοκόμαν

Ἀπόλλωνα; " Did not the poet, Simonides, call him the golden-haired Apollo?" Hair of this color is also called μελίχροος, "honey-colored;" and the remark of Lucretius, *Nigra* μελίχροος *est*, " Honey-colored is black," is a confirmation of what I have asserted above; for the poet, when speaking of the false flatteries addressed to women, quotes one in illustration, namely, that a maiden with black hair is called μελίχροος, — thus ascribing to her a beauty which she does not possess. More-over, the interpretation of Simonides hitherto received is a contradiction of the father of poets, who does not even once mention hair of a black color.

CHAPTER VI.

BEAUTY OF THE EXTREMITIES, BREAST, AND ABDOMEN. —
DRAWING OF THE FIGURES OF ANIMALS BY GREEK MASTERS.

1. THE beauty of form of the other parts of the figure —
the extreme parts, hands and feet as well as surfaces — was
determined by the ancient artists, in their works, with equal
regard to congruity.   Plutarch appears to show no more knowledge of art on this point than on any other.   He asserts that
the attention of the ancient masters was exclusively directed to
the face, and that other parts of the figure were not elaborated
with similar assiduity.   It is not more difficult in morals, where
the extreme of virtue borders upon vice, to practise any virtue
within its just limits, than it is in art to execute the extremities,
by the formation of which the artist displays his knowledge of
the beautiful.   But time and man's violence have left few beautiful feet, and still fewer beautiful hands, remaining.   The
hands of the Venus de' Medici (1), which have been the occasion of exposing the ignorance of those who, criticising them as
antique, pronounced them faulty, are modern.   In this respect,
the Venus resembles the Apollo Belvedere, whose arms below
the elbow are also modern.

2. The beauty of a youthful hand consists in a moderate
degree of plumpness, and a scarcely observable depression,
resembling a soft shadow, over the articulations of the fingers,
where, if the hand is plump, there is a dimple.   The fingers
taper gently towards their extremities, like finely shaped columns ; and, in art, the articulations are not expressed.   The
fore part of the terminating joint is not bent over, nor are the
nails very long, though both are common in the works of modern sculptors.   Beautiful hands are termed by the poets hands
of Pallas, and also hands of Polycletus, because this artist was
the first to shape them beautifully.   Of beautiful hands, still
remaining, on youthful male figures (2), there is one on that son

of Niobe who lies prostrate on the earth, and another on a Mercury embracing Herse, in the garden behind the Farnese palace. Of beautiful female hands (3) there are three, — one on the Hermaphrodite in the villa Borghese, and two on the figure of Herse mentioned above : the latter furnishes the very rare, indeed the sole, instance in which both hands have been preserved.   I am now speaking of statues and figures of the size of life, not of rilievi.

3. The most beautiful youthful legs and knees of the male sex are indisputably, in my opinion, those of the Apollo Σαυρο- κτόνος, in the villa Borghese, an Apollo with a swan at his feet, in the villa Medici, a similar one in the palace Farnese, and a Bacchus in the villa Medici.   The beautiful Thetis in the villa Albani, which I shall hereafter describe, has the most beautiful legs (4) of all the female figures in Rome.   The knees of youthful figures are shaped in truthful imitation of the beauty that exists in nature, where they do not show the cartilages with anatomical distinctness, but are rounded with softness and smoothness, and unmarked by muscular movements ; so that the space from the thigh to the leg forms a gentle and flowing elevation, unbroken by depressions or prominences.   Whoever has examined the impressions of footsteps on the sand, especially that of the sea-shore, which is firm, will have remarked that the feet of women are more arched in the sole, and those of men more hollowed at the sides.

4. That this imperfect notice of the shape of a youthful knee may not appear superfluous, let the reader turn to the figures of a youthful age, executed by more modern artists. Few of them, I will not say none, but few of them are to be found which show that the natural beauty of this part has been observed and imitated.   I am now speaking particularly of figures of the male sex ; for, rare as beautiful youthful knees are in nature, they are always still more rare in art, — both in pictures and statues ; insomuch that I cannot adduce any figure by Raphael as a model in this particular, and, much less, by the Caracci and their followers.   Our painters may derive instruction on this point from the beautiful Apollo of Mengs, in the villa Albani.

5. Like the knee, a beautiful foot was more exposed to sight among the ancients than with us.   The less it was compressed, the better was its form ; and from the special remarks upon the

feet by the ancient philosophers, and from the inferences which they presumed might be drawn from them as to the natural inclinations, it appears that their shape was the subject of close observation. Hence, in descriptions of beautiful persons, as Polyxena and Aspasia, even their beautiful feet are mentioned, and history (5) notices the ugly feet of Domitian. The nails are flatter on the feet of antique than of modern statues.

6. Having now considered the beauty of the extremities, I shall next touch upon that of the surfaces, namely, the breast and abdomen. A proudly arched chest was regarded as a universal attribute of beauty in male figures. The father of poets (6) describes Neptune (7) with such a chest, and Agamemnon as resembling him ; and such a one Anacreon desired to see in the image of the youth whom he loved.

7. The breast or bosom of female figures is never exuberant ; and Banier is wrongly informed, when he says, in his description of the figure of Ceres, that she is represented with large breasts ; he must have mistaken a modern Ceres for an antique. The form of the breasts in the figures of divinities is virginal in the extreme, since their beauty, generally, was made to consist in the moderateness of their size. A stone, found in the island of Naxos, was smoothly polished, and placed upon them, for the purpose of repressing an undue development. Virginal breasts are likened by the poets to a cluster of unripe grapes. Valerius Flaccus, in the following passage, alludes to their moderate prominence in Nymphs by the word *obscura* : *Crinis ad obscuræ decurrens cingula mammæ,* — " Hair falling to the zone of the gently swelling breast." On some figures of Venus, less than the size of life, the breasts are compressed, and resemble hills whose summits run to a point ; and this form of them appears to have been regarded as the most beautiful. The Ephesian Diana, which I exclude from the figures of the divinities, is the sole exception to these observations. Her breasts are not only large and full, but are also many in number. In this instance, however, their form is symbolical; beauty was not the object sought. Among ideal figures, the Amazons alone have large and fully developed breasts ; even the nipples are visible, because they represent, not virgins, but women (8).

8. The nipples are not made visible on the breasts either of virgins or goddesses, at least in marble ; in paintings also, in accordance with the form of the breasts in the purity and in-

nocence of life, they should not be prominent. Now, as the nipples are fully visible in the figure of a supposed Venus, of the size of life, in an ancient painting in the palace Barberini, I conclude from this circumstance that it cannot represent a goddess. Some of the greatest modern artists are censurable in this respect. Among them is the celebrated Domenichino, who, in a fresco painted on the ceiling of a room in the Costaguti mansion at Rome, has represented Truth, struggling to escape from Time, with nipples which could not be larger, more prominent, or pointed in a woman who had suckled many children. No painter has depicted the virginal form of the breasts better than Andrea del Sarto; and among other instances is a half figure, crowned with flowers, and also holding some in her hand : it is in the museum of the sculptor Bartolommeo Cavaceppi.

9. I cannot comprehend how the great artist of the Anti‑noüs, wrongly so termed, in the Belvedere, happened to make a small incised circle about the right nipple, which consequently appears as if inlaid, and as large as the part inclosed within the circle. It was probably done for the purpose of denoting the extent of the glandular portion of the nipple. This singularity is to be found in no other Greek figure ; moreover, no one can possibly consider it a beauty.

10. The abdomen is, in male figures, precisely as it would appear in a man after a sweet sleep, or an easy, healthful digestion, — that is, without prominence, and of that kind which physiologists consider as an indication of a long life. The navel is quite deep, especially in female figures, in which it sometimes has the form of a bow, and sometimes that of a small half-circle, which is turned partly upward and partly downward. There are a few figures in which the execution of this part is more beautiful than on the Venus de' Medici, in whom it is unusually deep and large.

11. Even the private parts have their appropriate beauty. The left testicle is always the larger, as it is in nature ; so, likewise, it has been observed that the sight of the left eye is keener than that of the right. In a few figures of Apollo and Bacchus, the genitals seem to be cut out, so as to leave an excavation in their place, and with a care which removes all idea of wanton mutilation. In the case of Bacchus, the removal of these parts may have a secret meaning, inasmuch as

he was occasionally confounded with Atys, and was emasculated like him. Since, on the other hand, in the homage paid
to Bacchus, Apollo also was worshipped, the mutilation of the
same part in figures of him had precisely the same signification.
I leave it to the reader, and to the seeker after beauty, to turn
over coins, and study particularly those parts which the painter
was unable to represent to the satisfaction of Anacreon, in the
picture of his favorite.

12. All the beauties here described, in the figures of the ancients, are embraced in the immortal works of Antonio Raphael
Mengs, first painter to the courts of Spain and Poland, the
greatest artist of his own, and probably of the coming age also.
He arose, as it were, like a phœnix new-born, out of the ashes
of the first Raphael to teach the world what beauty is contained
in art, and to reach the highest point of excellence in it to
which the genius of man has ever risen. Though Germany
might well be proud of the man who enlightened the wise in
our fathers' days, and scattered among all nations the seeds
of universal science,[1] she still lacked the glory of pointing to
one of her citizens as a restorer of art, and of seeing him acknowledged and admired, even in Rome, the home of the arts,
as the German Raphael.

13. To this inquiry into Beauty I add a few remarks which
may be serviceable to young beginners, and to travellers, in
their observation of Greek figures. The first is, — Seek not to
detect deficiencies and imperfections in works of art, until you
have previously learned to recognize and discover beauties. This
admonition is the fruit of experience, of noticing daily that the
beautiful has remained unknown to most observers, — who can
see the shape, but must learn the higher qualities of it from
others, — because they wish to act the critic before they have
begun to be scholars. It is with them as with schoolboys, all
of whom have wit enough to find out their instructor's weak
point. Vanity will not allow them to pass by, satisfied with a
moderate gaze ; their self-complacency wants to be flattered ;
hence, they endeavor to pronounce a judgment. But, as it is
easier to assume a negative than an affirmative position, so
imperfections are much more easily observed and found than
perfections, and it requires less effort and trouble to criticise
others than to improve one's self. It is the common practice,

---

[1] Leibnitz.

on approaching a beautiful statue, to praise its beauty in general terms. This is easy enough. But when the eye has wandered over its parts with an unsteady, rambling look, discovering neither their excellence nor the grounds of it, then it fixes upon faults. Of the Apollo it is observed, that the knee bends inwardly, — though this is a fault rather of the way in which a fracture was mended, than of the artist ; of the presumed Antinoüs of the Belvedere, that the legs bow outwardly ; of the Hercules Farnese, that the head, of which mention has been made, is rather small. Herewith, those who wish to be thought more knowing than others relate, that it was found in a well, a mile distant, and the legs ten miles distant from the body, — a fable which is accredited in more than one work ; hence, then, it happens, that the modern restorations alone are the subject of observation. Of the same character are the remarks made by the blind guides of travellers at Rome, and by the writers of travels in Italy. Some few, on the other hand, err through unseasonable caution. They wish, when viewing the works of the ancients, to set aside all opinions previously conceived in their favor. They appear to have determined to admire nothing, because they believe admiration to be an expression of ignorance ; and yet Plato says, that admiration is the sentiment of a philosophic mind, and the avenue which leads to philosophy. But they ought to approach the works of Greek art favorably prepossessed, rather than otherwise ; for, being fully assured of finding much that is beautiful, they will seek for it, and a portion of it will be made visible to them. Let them renew the search until it is found, for it is there.

14. My second caution is, — Be not governed in your opinion by the judgment of the profession, which generally prefers what is difficult to what is beautiful. This piece of advice is not less useful than the foregoing, because inferior artists, who value, not the knowledge, but only the workmanship, displayed, commonly decide in this way. This error in judgment has had a very unfavorable effect upon art itself ; and hence it is, that, in modern times, the beautiful has been, as it were, banished from it. For by such pedantic, stupid artists — partly because they were incapable of feeling the beautiful, and partly because incapable of representing it — have been introduced the numerous and exaggerated foreshortenings in paintings on plain and vaulted ceilings. This style of painting has become so

peculiar to these places, that, if, in a picture executed on either, all the figures do not appear as if viewed from beneath, it is thought to indicate a want of skill in the artist. In conformity to this corrupted taste, the two oval paintings on the ceiling of the gallery in the villa Albani are preferred to the principal and more central piece, — all three by the same great artist,[1] — as he himself foresaw while engaged upon the work ; and yet, in the foreshortenings, and the arrangement of the drapery after the manner of the modern and the ecclesiastical style, he was willing to cater to the taste of minds of a coarser grade. An amateur will decide precisely in the same way, if he wish to avoid the imputation of singularity, and escape contradiction. The artist who seeks the approbation of the multitude chooses this style, probably because he believes that there is more skill shown in drilling a net in stone [2] than in producing a figure of correct design.

15. In the third place, the observer should discriminate, as the ancient artists apparently did, between what is essential and what is only accessory in the drawing, — partly that he may avoid the expression of an incorrect judgment, in censuring what is not deserving of examination, and partly that his attention may be exclusively directed to the true purpose of the design. The slight regard, paid by the ancient artists to objects which were seemingly not within their province, is shown, for instance, by the painted vases, on which the chair of a seated figure is indicated simply by a bar placed horizontally. But, though the artist did not trouble himself as to the way in which a figure should be represented sitting, still, in the figure itself, he displays all the skill of an accomplished master. In making this remark, I do not wish to excuse what is actually ordinary, or bad, in the works of the ancients. But if, in any one work, the principal figure is admirably beautiful, and the adjunct, or assigned emblem or attribute, is far inferior to it, then I believe we may conclude from this circumstance that the

[1] Antonio Raphael Mengs.

[2] Winckelmann, in this passage, undoubtedly refers to a statue enveloped in a net, in the church of Santa Maria della Pietà, at Naples. The subject is Vice undeceived : a man is represented struggling in a net, and striving to escape from it. The work is a very remarkable one for the patient industry which it proves, as the net is almost entirely detached, touching the figure itself only in a few points. It was executed by Guccirolo. — Tr.

part which is deficient in form and workmanship was regarded as an accessory, or *Parergon,* as it was also termed by artists. For these accessories are not to be viewed in the same light as the episodes of a poem, or the speeches in history, in which the poet and historian have displayed their utmost skill.

16. It is, therefore, requisite to judge mildly, in criticising the swan at the feet of the above-mentioned beautiful Apollo in the villa Medici, since it resembles a goose more than a swan. I will not, however, from this instance, establish a rule in regard to all accessories, because in so doing I should at the same time contradict the express statements of ancient writers, and the evidence of facts. For the loops of the smallest cords are indicated on the apron of many figures clothed in armor. Indeed, there are feet, on which the stitching between the upper and under soles of the sandal is executed so as to resemble the finest pearls. We know, moreover, in respect to statues which once existed, that the least details about the Jupiter of Phidias were finished with the utmost nicety, also how much industry Protogenes lavished upon the partridge in his picture of Ialysus, — to say nothing of numerous other works.

17. In the fourth place, if they who have had no opportunity of viewing antique works should see, in drawings and engravings of them, parts of the figures manifestly ill-shaped, let them not find fault with the ancient artists ; they may be assured that such deformities are to be attributed either to the engraver, or to the sculptor who repaired them. Occasionally, both are in fault. In making this remark, I have in mind the engravings of the statues in the Giustiniani gallery, all of which were repaired by the most unskilful workmen, and those parts which were really antique copied by artists who had no relish for antiquity. Taught by experience like this, I am governed accordingly in my judgment of the bad legs of a beautiful statue of Bacchus leaning upon a young Satyr, which stands in the library of San Marco, at Venice. Although I have not yet seen it, I am convinced that the faulty portion of it is a modern addition.

18. In this section on the essential of Greek art, — all that ralates to the drawing of the human figure being concluded, — I have a few remarks on the representation of animals to add to those which I have already made in the second chapter· of this book. It was not less an object with the ancient Greek artists

than with the philosophers, to investigate and understand the nature of beasts. Several of the former sought to distinguish themselves by their figures of animals : Calamis, for instance, by his horses ; Nicias, (9) by his dogs. The *Cow* of Myron is, indeed, more famed than any of his other works, and has been celebrated in song by many poets, whose inscriptions still remain ; a dog, by this same artist, was also famous, as well as a calf by Menæchmus. We find that the ancient artists executed animals after life ; and when Pasiteles made a figure of a lion, he had the living animal before his eyes.

19. Figures of lions and horses of uncommon beauty have been preserved ; some are detached, and some in rilievo ; others are on coins and engraved gems. The sitting lion, of white marble, larger than life, which once stood on the Piræus, at Athens, and is now in front of the gate of the arsenal at Venice, is justly reckoned among the superior works of art. The standing lion in the palace Barberini, likewise larger than life, and which was taken from a tomb, exhibits this king of beasts in all his formidable majesty. How beautiful are the drawing and impression of the lions on coins of the city of Velia! It is asserted, however, even by those who have seen and examined more than one specimen of the living lion, that there is a certain ideal character in the ancient figures of this animal, in which they differ from the living reality.

20. In the representation of horses, the ancient artists are not, perhaps, surpassed by the moderns, as Du Bos maintains, on the assumption that the Greek and Italian horses are not so handsome as the English. It is not to be denied, that a better stock has been produced by crossing the mares of England and Naples with the Spanish stallion, and that the breed of the animal in these countries has been very much improved by this means. This is also true of other countries. In some, however, a contrary result has happened. The German horses, which Cæsar found very bad, are now very good ; and those of France, which were prized in his time, are at present the worst in all Europe. The ancients were unacquainted with the beautiful breed of Danish horses ; the English, also, were unknown to them. But they had those of Cappadocia and Epirus, the noblest of all races, the Persian, Achæan, Thessalian, Sicilian, Etruscan, and Celtic or Spanish. Hippias in Plato says, " The finest breeds of horses belong to us." The writer above mentioned also

evinces a very superficial judgment, when he seeks to maintain the foregoing assertion by adducing certain defects in the horse of Marcus Aurelius. Now this statue has naturally suffered, having been thrown down and buried in rubbish. As regards the horses on Monte Cavallo, I must plainly contradict him; the portions which are antique are not faulty.

21. But, even if Grecian art had left us no other specimens of horses than those just mentioned, we might presume — since a thousand statues on and with horses were made anciently where one is made in modern days — that the ancient artists knew the points of a fine horse as well as the ancient writers and poets did, and that Calamis had as much discernment of the good qualities and beauties of the animal as Horace and Virgil, who describe them. It seems to me, that the two horses on Monte Cavallo at Rome, the four of bronze over the porch of St. Mark's church at Venice, may be considered beautiful of the kind ; and there cannot exist in nature a head more finely shaped, or more spirited, than that of the horse of Marcus Aurelius. The four horses of bronze, attached to the car which stood on the theatre at Herculaneum, were beautiful, but of a light breed, like the Barbary horses. One entire horse has been composed from the fragments of the four, and is to be seen in the court-yard of the royal museum at Portici. Two other bronze horses, of a small size, also in this museum, may be mentioned among its greatest rarities. The first one, with its rider, was found in Herculaneum, May, 1761 ; all four of its legs, however, were wanting, as were also the legs and right arm of the rider. It stands on its original base, which is inlaid with silver. The horse is two Neapolitan palms in length ($20\frac{3}{4}$ in. Eng.) ; he is represented on a gallop, and is supported by a ship's rudder. The eyes, a rosette on the frontal, and a head of Medusa on the breastband, are of silver. The reins themselves are of copper. The figure on the horse, which resembles Alexander the Great, also has eyes of silver, and its cloak is fastened together, over the right shoulder, by a silver hook. The left hand holds the sheath (10) of a sword ; the sword, therefore, must have been in the right hand (11), which is wanting. The conformation resembles that of Alexander in every respect, and a diadem encircles the head. It is one Roman palm and ten inches ($16\frac{1}{4}$ in. Eng.) high, from the pedestal. The second horse was, likewise, mutilated, and without

a rider. Both these horses are of the most beautiful shape, and executed in the best manner. Since then, a horse of similar size, together with an equestrian Amazon, has been discovered in Herculaneum. The breast of the horse, which is in the act of springing, rested upon a Hermes. The horses on some Syracusan and other coins are beautifully drawn; and the artist who placed the first three letters, MIΘ, of his name under a horse's head on a carnelian of the Stosch museum was confident of his own knowledge, and the approbation of connoisseurs.

22. I will take this occasion to repeat a remark which I have made elsewhere, — that the ancient artists were not more agreed as to the action of horses, that is to say, as to the manner and succession in which the legs are lifted, than certain modern writers are, who have touched upon this point. Some maintain that the two legs of the same side are lifted at the same time. This is the gait of the four antique horses at Venice, of the horses of Castor and Pollux, on the Campidoglio, and of those of Nonius Balbus and his son, at Portici. Others are positive that their movement is diagonal, or crosswise, — that is to say, that they lift the left hind-foot after the right fore-foot; and this assertion they ground on observation, and the laws of mechanics. In this way are disposed the feet of the horse of Marcus Aurelius, of the four horses attached to the chariot of this emperor in a rilievo, and of those which are on the arch of Titus.

23. Besides these, there are in Rome several other animals, executed by Greek artists in marble and on hard stone. In the villa Negroni is a beautiful tiger (12), in basalt, on which is mounted one of the loveliest children, in marble. A large and beautiful sitting dog (13), of marble, was carried a few years ago to England. It was probably executed by Leucon, who was celebrated for his dogs. The head of the well-known goat (14) in the palace Giustiniani, which is the most important part of the animal, is modern (15).

24. I am well aware that, in this treatise on the drawing of the nude figure by Greek artists, the subject is not exhausted. But I believe that I have discovered the right end of the clew, which others can seize, and safely follow. No place can compare with Rome in the abundance of its facilities for verifying and applying the observations which I have offered. But it is impossible for any one to form a correct opinion in regard to

them, or to obtain all the benefit which they are capable of yielding, in a hasty visit. For the impressions first received may not seem to conform to the author's ideas; yet, by oft-repeated observation, they will approximate more and more nearly to them, and confirm the experience of many years, and the mature reflections, embodied in this treatise.

NOTES.

NOTES.

The authors of the notes are designated by the following signatures: W., Winckelmann; Germ. Ed., the German Editor, Meyer; L., Lessing; A., Amoretti, author of an Italian translation; F., Fea, also an Italian translator; D., Desmarest; S., Siebelis; E., Eschenburg.

PREFACE TO HISTORY OF ART.

1. AFTERWARDS explained by the author as Electra and Orestes. — GERM. ED.

2. Baldinucci, *Vita di Bernini*, p. 72. Bernini, *Vita del Cav. Bernini*, cap. 2, p. 13. Bernini may, perhaps, have esteemed too highly a fragment of a group known by the name of Pasquino, at the corner of the Corsini palace, in Rome. But it is unquestionably an admirable work, worthy of a Greek master. There are several ancient repetitions of this work extant. According to Visconti (*Mus. Pio-Clem.*, Tom. VI. pp. 21–31), this torso, as well as other similar groups, represents Menelaus holding in his arms the dead body of Patroclus. — GERM. ED.

3. The wound in the right thigh, and the consternation expressed on the face and in the whole figure, render it highly probable that this statue represents Adonis, wounded by a boar, as Visconti (*Mus. Pio-Clem.*, Plate 31) also maintains. — F.

PREFACE TO NOTES ON THE HISTORY OF ART.

1. WINCKELMANN has made a mistake here, or rather a clerical error. It is scarcely possible that he did not know that the Marcus (not Quintus) Curtius in the Borghese villa is a modern figure, — by Bernini, it is said; only the plunging horse on which he sits is antique, and of admirable workmanship. (*Sculture della Villa Borghese*, Tom. I. Stanza I. No. 18.) — GERM. ED.

2. This work represents not the death of Agamemnon, but the vengeance inflicted by Orestes on Ægistheus and Clytemnestra, on account of the murder of Agamemnon. — GERM. ED.

BOOK I.

CHAPTER I.

1. Gerh. Voss. *Instit. Poët.*, lib. 1, p. 31.

In Mesopotamia there were images of the gods from the time of Abraham. (Joshua xxiv. 14.) Jacob commanded his family to put away all images of the gods. (Gen. xxxv. 2.) Rachel stole the idols from Laban, her father. (Gen. xxxi. 19.) — F.

2. Not all the obelisks in Rome were erected in Egypt by Sesostris. Pliny (lib. 36, cap. 9, sect. 14, n. 5), at least, mentions only a single obelisk set up by Sesostris, which was afterwards erected in the Campus Martius, whether by Augustus, as Fea maintains, or not, we are unable to determine. Pliny certainly does not expressly assert it. — F. and Germ. Ed.

3. Psalm cxxxv. 16 speaks only of a head; but in Psalm cxv. 4–7, hands and feet of figures of gods are mentioned. — F.

4. Scylac. Peripl., p. 50, seq. Suid., v. ἕρμα. The name Hermes, Mercury, to whom such stones, it is pretended, were first erected, would, even according to its derivation in Plato (*Cratyl.*, p. 408, B), have no application to those. — W.

Tzetzes (*Chiliad.* 13, *Hist.* 429, v. 593) says that every statue was termed Hermes. — F.

Ἀνδριάς Πανδίονος, in Aristophanes (*Pac.*, v. 1183), was a Hermes of this kind, and one of twelve at Athens on which were suspended the rolls of soldiers; it cannot, therefore, signify a column, as the translators have rendered it. — W.

The Hermes by which Mercury was originally represented, probably owes its shape to some mystic allusion, as also Macrobius (*Saturnal.*, lib. 1, c. 19), Suidas (v. ἕρμα), and Codinus (lib. 100, cap. 29) maintain. Or its form may depend on the fable which relates that the hands and feet of the god were cut off, whilst he was sleeping, as Servius (*Ad Virgil. Æn.*, lib. 8, v. 138) cites, and as he is found represented on a marble wrought in mosaic. According to Pausanias (lib. 4, cap. 33), the Athenians were the first to give to the Hermes a quadrate form. Cicero (*Ad Attic.*, lib. 1, *epist.* 8) mentions some Hermæ of which the trunk or shaft was of Pentelic marble, and the heads of bronze. A Hermes terminating in a lion's paw may be seen among the *Pictures of Herculaneum* (Tom. IV. p. 5). — A. and F.

In the *Notes on the History of Art*, Winckelmann makes the following remarks upon the Palladium, as one of the oldest figures known to us : " It was, as Suidas and others relate, of wood, and, according to Apollodorus (*Bibl.*, lib. 3, p. 20), four feet and a half high, if, as Hesychius states, a πῆχυς is to be reckoned as a measure of a foot and a half. If the said Palladium should have been, as it seems, the figure upon whose knees Theano, wife of Antenor, and priestess of the same Pallas, placed a robe (Homer, Ἰλ. ζ. v. 303), then, if we take the verbal meaning of the passage, it must have been represented, not in a standing, but in a sitting position. But the more ancient Greeks, and their artists of the best periods, have either distinguished this latter Pallas from the Palladium, or they have understood the phrase ἐπὶ γούνασιν not verbally, as *a placing on the knees,* but to mean that Theano placed her peplon at the feet of the goddess, — as it certainly can be explained. The Pallas on a fragment of one of the most beautiful of the ancient rilievi, in the museum of the author, in which Ajax is striving to engage the love of Cassandra, is represented standing, like the Palladium, on engraved gems, in the hand of Diomedes. On another beautiful work in the arches under the palace of the Borghese villa, exhibiting not the love, but rather the violence of Ajax towards Cassandra, we see this Pallas, similar to the Palladium on engraved gems, in form of a Hermes or Terminus, and, like that figure and all others prior to the time of Dædalus, standing with closed feet, ποσὶ συμβέβηκος, as low as which a garment is signified. She holds her right hand before her breast, upon her ægis, and a spear in her left, differing in this respect from the Palladium, in whose right hand authors place a spear, and in the left a spindle (Apoll., lib. 100 ; Tzetzes *in Lycoph.,* v. 363) ; so, too, another very ancient statue of this goddess at Erythræ, in Achaia, likewise holds a spindle, and bears on its head a ball. (Pausan., lib. 7, p. 534.) " — GERM. ED.

5. Clemens Alexandrinus (*Cohortat. ad Gent.,* no. 2, p. 13), whom Eusebius quotes, makes no mention whatever of this triangle. That it was a figure of mysterious import among the Egyptians, Plutarch (*De Is. et Os.,* p. 373) testifies, and Caylus also (*Recueil d'Antiquit.,* Tom. II., *Antiq. Egypt.,* p. 11) remarks. Of the Hermæ, or rather of the simple, somewhat regular or four-sided stones which Sesostris caused to be placed as boundary stones in the countries conquered by him during his campaign in Asia, Diodorus Siculus (lib. 1, § 55) relates, that male sexual parts were given to some of them, in order to indicate the warlike and brave of the nations subdued by him ; and on the contrary, female parts to others, to denote the cowardly and contemptible. Herodotus (lib. 2, cap. 102) testifies to the latter, and says (lib. 2, cap. 106) that Hermæ with female sexual parts were found in Syria even in his time. — F.

6. Saturn and Serapis were not divinities of Greek origin. Tacitus (*Hist.,* lib. 4, cap. 81), Plutarch (*De Is. et Os.,* p. 361), Clemens Alexandrinus (*Cohort. ad Gent.,* no. 4, p. 42), Macrobius (lib. 100), Origen (*Contra Cels.,* lib. 5, no. 28, p. 607), and others, assert unanimously that the Egyptians were adverse to the divinities introduced by the Ptolemies, and did not in any way blend their own deities and sacred usages with those of the Greeks. — F.

7. I here term Egyptian, not those works executed by their ancient artists, but those which were wrought in later times, perhaps in the third or fourth century of the Christian era, and mostly in greenish basalt, and those which are marked with symbolic signs, and divinities, of the Egyptians. — W.

8. Inscriptions are also found on the figure itself. A small statue of Isis, of wood, in Caylus (*Rec. d'Antiq.,* Tom. V., *Antiq. Egypt.,* Pl. II., no. 1, 2), has writing over the whole robe, from the middle of the body to the feet. In the museum of the Borgia family, in Velletri, several very ancient Egyptian images of deities are found in hard stones, porcelain, and sycamore, which show hieroglyphs graven into or painted on the

figure. Mention is made by Guasco (*De l'Usage des Stat.*, ch. 10, p. 296, ch. 12, p. 323) of similar statues. There is writing on the body of the very ancient Sphinx, of bronze. (Cayl., Tom. I. Pl. XIII. p. 44. Fea, Tom. I. p. 60.) — F.

9. Needham even published an explanation of these signs, which had been palmed off on him by a Chinese in Rome, who had no more knowledge of his own language than other young persons of that country who are educated at Naples, in a college founded for them; and not one of them knows the writing which is seen on Chinese utensils, fabrics, &c., because, as they say, it is the language of the learned. For as these are children whom their parents have exposed, and whom the missionaries have sought out, rescued from death, brought up, and sent out to this country as soon as they were sufficiently old, they of course acquire only a moderate knowledge of their own language. — W.

The Chinaman of whom Needham made inquiries was the predecessor of Winckelmann in the Vatican library, and knew many Chinese words; but in the present case he was manifestly a deceiver. Having, probably, been informed of the hot dispute which had arisen among the learned in regard to the age and originality of the Chinese and Egyptian people, he wrote — in order to favor his own nation, and to show that the Chinese language was one and the same with the ancient Egyptian — on some Chinese manuscripts in the Vatican library the signs and characters which, as he knew, are found on the Turin head. — F.

10. Lib. 14, p. 948. Tyrwhitt wishes to read Σ τόπα ἔργα or Σκοπάδεια ἔργα, and Favorinus explains σκολιά by ἀνίσα, δύσκολα, δυσχερή, *unequal, disagreeable, harsh.* — S.

11. Casaubon did not translate Strabo; he occupied himself solely with a critical examination of the text, without giving any heed to the faults of translation. — F.

CHAPTER II.

1. THE most ancient artists wrought also in pitch. Hercules, having given burial to Icarus, the son of Dædalus, the artist, from gratitude, made a statue in pitch of the hero. (Apollod., lib. 2, cap. 6, n. 4.) Yet Pausanias (lib. 9, cap. 11) says of this same statue, that it was made of wood. Junius also forgets pitch (lib. 3, cap. 9) when he enumerates the several materials of ancient statues. — L.

2. Pausan., lib. 1, cap. 3. Ceramicus was the name of a street in Athens, in which this porch and others were situated. The particular porch so called took its name, not from the works in clay with which it was adorned, but from Ceramicus, son of Bacchus and Ariadne. Pliny (lib. 35, cap. 12, sect. 45) derives the name from the workshop of Chalkosthenes, a worker in clay, which was located there. Yet another place of the same name, on the outside of Athens (Cic., *De Leg.*, lib. 2, cap. 36), was devoted as a burial-spot for those who had fallen in battle. (Meurs., *Ceramicus Geminus*, Oper., Tom. I. cap. 1, p. 466.) — F.

It should read, "On the roof of the royal porch in the Ceramicus." — S.

3. Vermilion was used (Plin., lib. 33, cap. 7, sect. 36), because it was a
lively and very favorite color. — F.

4. Della Valle, *Viagg.*, Parte III. Lett. 1, § 7, p. 37 ; § 13, p. 72.

Among the Ethiopians, not only the deities were painted with vermilion, but also the chief men of the nation painted themselves with it.
(Plin., lib. 33, cap. 7, sect. 36.) The Egyptians, likewise, occasionally
painted the images of their divinities with such a color, as we see by a
painting in the *Museo Herculaneo* (Tom. IV. tav. 52), and find confirmed
in the *Museo Borgiano*. In Rome, the practice of painting the statues of
the divinities continued even to the time of Arnobius. (*Contra Gent.*, lib.
6, p. 196.) — F.

5. In one of these frieze ornaments, which represents a woman holding a *cista mystica*, "a mystic box," and which belonged to the Abbé Visconti, we see three holes ; the fourth is wanting, because the fragment is
somewhat mutilated. The number of the holes, as well as their form,
shows clearly that they were intended for the nails by which the bas-
reliefs were fastened to the wall. Besides, these heavy models, wrought
from clay, could not have been supported by a cord in the workshop of
the artist. — F.

6. Pausan., lib. 6, cap. 18. Praxidamas, of Ægina, who conquered in
boxing, in the fifty-ninth Olympiad, and Rhexibius, an Opuntian, who,
in the sixty-first, obtained the victory among the Pancratiasts, caused
statues to be erected to themselves in Olympia, as the prize combatants.
They were made of wood, — that of Praxidamas being of cypress, and
that of Rhexibius of fig-wood. — GERM. ED.

7. For this reason, Clement of Alexandria includes Diagoras among
the wisest men of antiquity, because he showed by such an act the sound-
ness of his judgment in regard to the images and deities of antiquity ;
and he is very much astonished that any one should number him among
atheists. According to this writer, the image must have been small, as
Diagoras took it in his hands, with the words that he would do with it as
Euristheus did with one of the same kind. — F.

Pausanias, especially in his second book, speaks of many other statues
and images of wood which were still in existence in his day, and among
them of a very ancient figure of Apollo Lycius, which was made by
Attalus, the Athenian, and which, with a temple, was dedicated by
Danaus to the god at Argos, at the same time. (Cap. 19.) He is, moreover, of the opinion, that all images of the earliest periods, and particularly the Egyptian, were of wood. In Rome as well as throughout Italy,
artists continued to make statues of the gods in wood, even after marble
and bronze had come into use, — until after the conquest of Asia. (Plin.,
lib. 34, cap. 7, sect. 16.) — GERM. ED.

8. Herod., lib. 2, cap. 129. In the time of Pausanias there stood at
Corinth two wooden images of Bacchus, entirely gilded with the exception of the face, which was painted red with vermilion. (Pausan., lib.
2, cap. 2.) — F.

9. The most usual practice was to make the face, hands, and feet of
ivory, like the statue of Pallas in Ægira, the other parts being of wood,
partly gilded and partly painted. (Pausan., lib. 7, cap. 26.) A naked

Venus, of which Pygmalion became enamored, was entirely of ivory (Clem. Alex., *Cohort. ad Gent.*, n. 4, p. 51), as was in Rome the statue of Minerva in the Forum of Augustus, and that of Jupiter in the temple of Metellus. (Plin., lib. 36, cap. 5, sect. 4, n. 12.) The Olympian Jupiter was of ivory and gold. (Pausan., lib. 5, cap. 11.) — F.

10. Some one in Rome has a wolf's tooth, on which the twelve deities are wrought. — W.

The author is not correct in his belief that wolf's teeth do not decompose, because he had seen one of the kind which had been preserved until his time. But this is not sufficient proof, since pieces of ivory also have been preserved, which, according to Winckelmann and others, decomposes, like the still harder teeth of other animals. (Buffon, *Hist. Natur.*, Tom. VII., *Des Loups*, p. 46.)

It was also customary to cover books with ivory tablets, and especially those called Diptycha, which the consuls and other magistrates were wont, at the festivities and public games occasioned by their induction into office, to give to their friends. (Gothofred., *Ad. Cod. Theod.*, lib. 15, tit. 9, l. 1.) — F.

11. Statues of wood and of bronze were also clothed. (Pausan., lib. 2, cap. 11.) Dionysius the Younger caused a statue of Jupiter, which he had despoiled of its golden garment, to be dressed, in mockery, in a woollen garment. (Clem. Alex., *Cohort. ad Gent.*, n. 4, p. 46.) From Tertullïan (*De Idolatr.*, cap. 3, n. 3) it seems to have been the custom to provide the images of the deities with embroidered garments. — F.

12. Lib. 8, cap. 14; lib. 9, cap. ult.; lib. 10, cap. 38.

Pausanias says expressly, that there were brazen statues before the age of Rhæcus and Theodorus (Tom. III. cap. 17, l. 6); but they were not of one piece, but in several pieces, fastened together by nails. — S.

13. He engraved a lyre on the gem of Polycrates. (Clem. Alex., *Pædagog.*, lib. 3, cap. 11, p. 289.) — F.

14. The death of Pisistratus is placed, without dissent, in the sixty-third Olympiad, five hundred and twenty-eight years before Christ. — GERM. ED.

15. Columns, also, were made from glass. (Clem. Alex., *Recognit.*, lib. 7, cap. 12, 13, and 26.) Goguet (*De l'Origine des Lois*, liv. 2, ch. 2, art. 3) maintains that the columns in the theatre of Scaurus were of glass, according to Pliny (lib. 36, cap. 15, sect. 24, n. 7). The reader desirous of information concerning the works in glass of the ancients is referred to Buonarroti (*Osservazioni sopra Alcuni Frammenti di Vasi Antichi di Vetro, Ornati di Figure, Trovati nei Cimeterei di Roma*). — F.

16. Lib. 35, cap. 6, sect. 30. Pliny states in many passages, that all kinds of gems were so skilfully imitated, as to render it difficult to distinguish the artificial from the natural; as, for example, the opal (lib. 32, cap. 6, sect. 22), the carbuncle (lib. 37, cap. 7, sect. 26), the jasper (cap. 8, sect. 37), the sapphire, the hyacinth, and so of all colors (lib. 36, cap. 26, sect. 67). On this point the reader is referred to Galeotti (*Museum, Præfat.*, § 20, p. 22) and Buonarroti (*Osservaz. Istoric., sopra Alcuni Medagl., Prefaz.*, p. 16). — F.

17. It is several years since this vase was in the Barberini palace, it having been sent to England, where it is known under the name of the Portland vase. It was found in one of the largest marble sepulchral

urns, still preserved in the Capitoline museum, which, for a long time, was supposed to be the tomb of the Emperor Alexander Severus and his mother, Mammæa. Copies, as well of the vase as of the sepulchral urn, may be found in the fourth part of the *Museo Capitolino* (tav. 1, 2, 3, 4, p. 1); also in Piranesi's *Antichità Romana* (Tom. II. tav. 33 – 35); of the vase alone, in La Chausse (*Mus. Rom.*, Tom. I. sect. 1, tab. 60 – 62, p. 42). — F. and GERM. ED.

18. This is the case with the famous, admirably wrought head of Tiberius in the Gem-cabinet of the Florentine gallery. (*Mus. Flor.*, Tom. I. tav. 3.) This head is as large as a hen's egg; and hence it was believed to be cut out of an unusually large turquoise. But it clearly appears, on closer and more careful examination, that the supposed turquoise is not a natural product, but a glass paste.

Statues were also prepared from amber, *electrum*, — a name which was afterwards given to a certain compound of gold and silver. In regard to statues of glass, the reader is referred to Pliny; of iron, to Pausanias and Pliny; of bone, to Arnobius; of lead, to Publius Victor; of wax, to Appian, Ovid, Statius; and, finally, of gypsum, to Pliny, Pausanias, and Tertullian. — F., from Junius (*De Pict. Vet.*).

CHAPTER III.

1. THE heads only of these figures are given, as the remarks of Winckelmann apply specially to them, the remainder being principally modern. — GERM. ED.

2. Burmann, *Præf. ad Inscript. Gruter.*, p. 3. — GERM. ED.

BOOK II.

CHAPTER I.

1. THIS observation should have been used by those who have of late written much on the similarity between the Chinese and the ancient Egyptians. — W.

2. No idea can be formed of the shape of Egyptian heads from engravings, as of a mummy in Beger (*Thes. Brand.*, Tom. III. p, 402), and another, described by Gordon (*Essay towards explaining the Hieroglyphical Figures on the Coffin of an Ancient Mummy*, London, 1737, fol.). — W. The figure in Beger is not that of a mummy. — L.

3. Herodot. lib. 2, cap. 30. Diodorus (lib. 1, § 67) sets the number at more than two hundred thousand men. He also says (lib. 3, § 3) that the Egyptians, as a colony of the Ethiopians, adopted from the latter the custom of taking great care of the dead body. — F.

4. Herodot., lib. 3, cap. 24. A mummy of this kind was presented by the Cardinal Alexander Albani to the Institute at Bologna; another is in London; and each has its ancient case of preserved sycamore, which, like the bodies, is painted. The third painted mummy is at Dresden, among the royal antiquities. Now, as the faces of all these mummies have the same color, it cannot be maintained, as Gordon wishes, that the London mummy was a person from Nubia. — W.

5. Juvenal, *Sat.* XV. v. 45. Quintil., lib. 1, cap. 2. Juvenal is speaking, not of Alexandria, but of Canopus, a city lying in the vicinity of Alexandria, of which the licentiousness was extreme. (Juvenal, *Sat.* VI. v. 84. Strab., lib. 17, p. 1153, Princ. Stat. *Sylv.*, lib. 3, cap. 2, v. 111. Senec. *Epist.*, 51.) — F.

6. Chrysostom (*Orat.* II. p. 162) says that only the art of poetry was forbidden, on account of its seductive influence. This statement must, however, be understood with some limitation, since he also says (*Homil.* VIII. *in Matth.*, no. 4) that "Egypt had been for a long time the land of poets." — F.

7. Compare Martini, *Storia della Musica*, Tom. I. cap. 11.

Plato (*De Legib.*, lib. 2, p. 656) says that, from the earliest ages, music had not only been practised in Egypt, but even been defined and regulated by immutable public laws; he had found musical compositions here of so great beauty, that they must necessarily have been created by a god, or by a god-inspired man.

It may be maintained that the Egyptians used musical instruments and sang hymns at all their festivals, even the smallest, as happened, according to Philostratus (*Vita Apollon.*, lib. 5, cap. 42, *in fine*), when the priests accompanied to Upper Egypt the lion, in which, as Apollonius said, was the soul of King Amasis. — F.

8. The monastic mode of life probably originated, not in Egypt, but in Palestine. At least there were monks here earlier than in Egypt, according to the unanimous testimony of ancient authors. — F.

9. Fleury (*Hist. Eccles.*, Tom. VII. lib. 70, cap. 9) does not speak, as Winckelmann thinks, of Lower Egypt alone, but rather of all Egypt; and he puts the number of eremites at seventy-six thousand. Many of them, probably, were not Egyptians. Persons from all parts resorted to this land, where the religious sentiment was held in respect, and where they found more suitable places, partly for leading a recluse life, and partly for escaping the persecutions of the heathen. — F.

10. Among the Greeks in Egypt the Greek Tau had the form of a cross, as it is seen in a very valuable ancient manuscript of the Syrian New Testament, on parchment, in the library of the Augustines in Rome. This manuscript, in folio, was executed in 616, and has marginal notes in Greek. Among others I notice here the word I+ΔIϤЄ instead of HTAIRE. — W.

11. The Egyptians and most of the important cities of Greece and Asia, for the purpose of obtaining the favor of Adrian, and, through it benefits and privileges, voluntarily erected temples to Antinoüs, dedicated to him sacred groves, oracles, and priests, stamped coins in his honor, and represented him, in images, under the form and with the attributes of their divinities. (Buonarroti, *Osservaz. Istor. sopra Alcuni Medagli*, cap. 2, p. 25. Bottari, *Mus. Capit.*, Tom. III. tav. 56.) — F.

12. There is no ground for the assertion of a Greek writer of the Middle Ages (Codin., *Orig. Constant.*, p. 48), that human figures were wrought only in a part of Egypt, and that, on this account, the inhabitants were termed *Men-makers,* ἀνθρωπόμορφοι. — W.

CHAPTER II.

1. AMONG the ancient Egyptian works yet extant, the two Lions on the ascent to the Campidoglio are indisputably the most satisfactory in an artistic point of view. The shape of the beasts is, on the one hand, well conceived, and, on the other, well represented also in compact and very powerful proportions. These qualities, in connection with the quiet position, and extreme simplicity of the outlines, give to the whole a truly grand character. The Lion on the left has been broken into several pieces, and again put together; the other has suffered less. The two Egyptian Lions at the Fontana Felice, on the square in front of the Baths of Diocletian, have just as much repose of attitude and simplicity of outline, but less of grandeur in the whole. Of the great Sphinx in the Borghese villa, it is to be remarked that the head is modern. Two smaller, better-preserved Sphinxes, — the one of green, the other of blackish basalt, — in the park of the villa above mentioned, belong to the best and most beautiful monuments of ancient Egyptian art. — GERM. ED.

2. The ears are not too high on the heads of the figures on the Obelisk of the Sun, in the Campus Martius, nor on a small figure of an Egyptian priest, of yellow breccia, in the *Museo Pio-Clementino.* In the latter, however, they seem to be set a little too far backward. — F.

3. Winckelmann was undoubtedly wrong when he believed that the feet of the figure of Laocoön were of unequal length. The right leg of the larger boy, from the knee to the foot, is censured as being somewhat longer than the other. It is usual to excuse this, as well as the too great length of the left foot of the Apollo Belvedere, by saying that the artist may have intentionally added so much to these somewhat retreating parts as they would possibly lose to the eye of the spectator by being withdrawn. But we are very much afraid that an arrangement of this kind is a still greater fault than those which it is intended to excuse. For a plastic work in which such a system of enlargement of the more distant parts, and also a consequent proportionate diminution of nearer parts, was introduced, would necessarily, from the derangement of all proportions, present profiles offensive both to the sight and the taste. However, the antique masterpieces in question need no such elaborate exculpation, because the inequality in the length of the legs of the son of Laocoön, as well as in the feet of Apollo, is far more trifling, especially in the latter, than it is usually stated to be. Moreover, in regard to the unequal length of the feet of a few Egyptian statues, the excuse, founded on reasons of perspective, is still less applicable — because art in them is simpler and ruder — than to Greek statues, and

it is therefore best to hold the thing for precisely what it is, an error. — GERM. ED.

4. Raffei (*Osservazion. sopra Alcun. Mon. Antic.*, tav. 4, fig. 1, p. 49) holds this kneeling figure (Plate VI.) to be a priest or priestess, showing to the initiated three gold mysterious images in a little box, termed by Clemens of Alexandria (*Strom.*, lib. 5, not. 7) κωμασία and by Synesius (*Calvitii Encom.*, p. 73) κωμαστήριον.

Fea, also, supposes these and similar statues to be priests and initiated women, who carried about in processions the statues of the gods worshipped by them, and who were, on this account, named παστόφοροι, *shrine-bearers*, or θαλαμηφοροι, *bed-bearers*. (Apulej., *Metam.*, lib. 11, pp. 369–371; Id., *De Abstinen.*, lib. 4, p. 363.) It was usual for such processions to stand still from time to time (Philostr., *De Vita Soph.*, lib. 2, cap. 20; Meurs., *Eleusin.*, Tom. II. cap. 27, p. 534), when the priests, kneeling, probably presented to the people the images of the deities, either to be worshipped or kissed. In this way the Emperor Commodus, who was so enthusiastic in the worship of Isis, was accustomed to carry around the image of Anubis. (Spartian. in *Anton. Carac.*, cap. 9. Apulej., loc. cit., p. 377.)

The engraving of the figure mentioned in the text may be found in Fea. (Tom. I. tav. 6.) — GERM. ED.

5. This statue is neither an Anubis nor an Osiris, but a female figure, probably representing Isis. (See engraving in Fea's translation, Tom. I. tav. 8.) The sex would be more easily recognized, if those who had the charge of restoring the hands, arms, and legs had given to them more pleasing forms. She has, like the figure on the Isiac Tablet (Jablonsky, *Conject. in Tab. Bemb.*, § 7; *Miscell. Berolin*, Tom. VII. p. 330), a cat kind of head, resembling the lion tribe. — F.

6. Two heads of Isis with horns are found on engraved gems in the Stosch Cabinet (Nos. 40, 41), but they are of a later date, and of Roman workmanship. — W.

7. In the Florentine gallery, there is a round pedestal, of grayish granite, wrought smooth only on one side, with a sacrificial procession on it, one of the figures in which actually holds a *sistrum*. This monument, seemingly very ancient, was probably carried from Rome to Florence, but Winckelmann could not have known it. — GERM. ED.

8. Salmasius (*Exercit. in Solinum*, p. 998) infers from a passage in the poet Gratius, that the linen in Egypt could hardly be sufficient to clothe the priests. Pliny, however, enumerates four kinds of Egyptian linen; and the poet seems to have intended merely to denote the great number of priests. — W.

9. Men and women wore a loosely hanging dress, without a girdle, as even their statues show, except on occasions of mourning, at which time the custom among them was altogether opposite to that of the Greeks. (Herodot. lib. 2, cap. 85.) In order to be able to gird themselves in such cases, they sewed, according to Herodotus (lib. 2, cap. 36), a loop or band under the garment, deviating from the practice of other nations. Girded garments were also used at religious celebrations and processions by the numerous priests and initiated women engaged in them, as may be seen in the *Isiac Procession* in the Mattei palace. (Lens, *Du Costume*, liv. 1, chap. 2.) — F.

10. Egyptian male figures also have very frequently a neck-band hanging down upon the breast; others have a sort of stola; and others still are wholly draped — F.

The stola was a loose dress which reached from the neck to the ankles; over this was worn the pallium, the blanket or cloak of the Romans. — Tr.

11. According to Visconti (*Mus. Pio-Clem.*), the hip-cloth or apron, as well as the usual hood, of male Egyptian figures, is not a cloth arranged in folds, but a striped stuff. In proof of this, he quotes a passage from Plutarch (*De Is. et Os.*), which says: " The priestly and sacred garments of the Egyptians are striped alternately with black and white, in order to signify that, in man's conceptions of the deities, there are many things clear and certain, but many obscure and doubtful. " — Germ. Ed.

12. In Egypt the royal dignity was hereditary. If there was no successor in the royal family, then one was selected from the priests or warriors. In the latter case, the elected must join himself to the class of priests, in order to be instructed in Egyptian wisdom, but not for the purpose of exercising the priestly functions. (Platon. *Politic.*, p. 150. Plutarch., *De Is. et Os.*, Princ., p. 354.) — F.

13. This figure, which has gone into the Pio-Clement museum, is not a female, but a male figure, as the shoulders, breast, and hands show It is probably a Pastophor, who holds in a small box the image of a seated Cercopithecus, a long-tailed ape. The feet are not visible, because there are none; part of the head is a restoration.

14. Now in the Pio-Clement museum. This sparrowhawk is of gray basalt. — F.

15. This figure, wrought from imperfect basalt, or basaltic granite, which on being struck emits a sound, as do all figures executed from a similar stone, passed afterwards into the Pio-Clement museum, and found in Visconti a learned interpreter. According to him, it represents an Egyptian priest of Horus. The bands which go from the cap down beneath the chin — but which are not given in the engravings from the monument — were intended, not to fasten it, but to represent a portion of the false beard tied on, though the beard is no longer clearly to be seen, because the statue has been damaged and restored in this very place. Other grounds corroborative of his opinion, together with the explanation of this remarkable monument, may be read in the *Pio-Clement Museum* (Tom. II. pp. 31–39), in which there is also a copy of it (tav. 16). In Caylus (Tom. II. pl. 7, no. 4) there are two similar figures, confirming Visconti's opinion, one of which has a cap, like that of Aldus Manutius; the other (Tom. IV. pl. 1, no. 5) has a simple cap, very slightly raised, resembling that usually worn by the priesthood in Italy. — F. and Germ. Ed.

16. Jacob Gronovius (*Præf. ad Thes. Antiq. Græc.*, Tom. VI. p. 9) has, in this place, given scope to his imagination, and represented to himself figures seeming to have their heads covered by the skins of small Maltese dogs, the tails of which stand upwards over the forehead; and he believes that he sees here the true derivation of the word κυνῆ, the *helmet*, as being in the most ancient times made of the skin of a dog's head. On other Egyptian heads we see a lizard instead of a serpent. (Beger, *Thes. Brand.*, Tom. III. p. 301.) The above-mentioned conceit of this

learned man appears still more groundless, when we examine two male
youthful Hermæ (Fea, Tom. I. tav. 11, 12) in the Albani villa, which are
covered with the skins of dogs' heads, as Hercules is with the lion's hide;
two paws of the skin are tied around the neck.   They probably represent
Lares or Penates, the household gods of the Romans, which, as Plutarch
relates (*Quest. Rom*, p. 176), were imaged with the head thus covered.
That most ancient kind and shape of helmet are seen still more plainly
on a beautiful Pallas, of life-size (Fea, Tom. I. tav. 13), in the same villa,
which wears the skin of a dog's head instead of the usual helmet, in such
a manner that the upper jaw together with the teeth lies below the forehead of the goddess. — W.

We are not willing to believe that the skin on the heads of this Pallas
and the two Hermæ is that of a dog.   It resembles, in all respects, the
skin of a lion, as seen on innumerable heads of Hercules, in every kind
of monument.   And we are authorized to believe that the two Hermæ
actually represent this hero in a beardless state, as there is great similarity, even in the features, to those of Hercules on other monuments.
— F.

17.   In connection with Egyptian dress, a doubt has occurred to me in
regard to the antiquity of an ode of Anacreon, in which the Parthians are
mentioned, and the tiara or cap as their distinctive mark (Brunck., *Ana-
lect.*, Tom. I. p. 112; Anacr. *Carm.*, n. 55): —

Καὶ Πάρθιους τίς ἄνδρας
'Εγνώρισεν τιάραις;

And some one recognized the Parthian men by their tiaras.   How did the
Greeks become acquainted with the name of Parthians in Anacreon's
time ? — W.

18.   Pococke's *Descript. of the East*, Vol. I pl. 61.   In Caylus (*Recueil
d'Antiq.*, Tom. IV., *Antiq. Egypt.*, pl. 4, no. 4) is a Horus with ear-rings.

Bracelets are seen both on male and female figures.   They are placed
about the wrist of a male statue which was transferred from the Rolandi
museum to the Pio-Clement museum, and mentioned at page 184 (see
Plate VII.); also on the Isis in the Capitoline museum, already cited,
and on the figure published by Pococke.   The Pastophora of green basalt, in the Pio-Clement museum, has arm-bands in form of a serpent.
Other figures in Caylus and Montfaucon have them about the upper part
of the arm, even indeed about the ankles.   Herodotus (lib. 4, cap 168)
also says that the women of the Adyrmachidæ wore iron rings on the
legs.   Pharaoh gave to Joseph a golden neck-band.

The Egyptians wore rings also on the fingers, as is shown by Ælian (*De
Nat. Animal.*, lib. 10, cap. 15), Plutarch (*De Is. et Os.*), and Aulius Gellius
lib. 10, cap. 10), and by several mummies. — F.

CHAPTER III.

1. WHEN the author wrote this passage, he had not observed that the two statues of Isis, of basalt, in the Capitoline museum, of which he had just before spoken, actually have hieroglyphs, engraved as well on the base as on the column against which they stand. He afterwards informed himself better on this point also, and in the *Preliminary Treatise to the Monuments*, § 22, he mentioned the hieroglyphs on the statues named, and from this circumstance appears to have changed his opinion in regard to the time when such a mode of writing went out of use. In the paragraph referred to, he disputes not only the Father Kircher, who (*Œdip. Ægypt.*, Tom. III. p. 515) maintains that the practice and knowledge of hieroglyphs were lost from the time of the conquest by Cambyses, but also others, not named, who conjecture that this happened at the commencement of Greek rule in Egypt. It is probable, however, that the knowledge and use of hieroglyphic writing may have still continued at that time, gradually diminishing as the religion and mythology of the Greeks extended more and more widely in Egypt, and at length entirely ceased. This opinion continues, not only to be admissible in regard to the discoveries which have since been made, but also to receive from them additional confirmation. — F.

2. The obelisk from the Circus of Caius, which stands in front of St. Peter's church, and was erected by the son of Sesostris, who performed no deeds that made him celebrated, appears, for this reason, to be without hieroglyphs, for Herodotus and Diodorus state that the erection of such monuments was a privilege of those kings who had immortalized their names by action. — W.

3. In the first edition, of 1764, page 54, may be seen the following passage : "Of the two former of these statues, the under-garment is visible only by the sleeves, which are denoted by means of a raised edge or prominence ; the breasts seem to be entirely bare, so transparent and fine must the texture be imagined." In order not to throw over this passage any more obscurity, which could be cleared only by a view of the statues in question, the editors have thought themselves obliged to retain unchanged the reading of the text in the Vienna edition. — GERM. ED.

4. Maffei, *Raccolta di Stat.*, fol. 148. Now in the Pio-Clement museum. — D.

5. Visconti, who has given a copy of one of these statues in the *Pio-Clement Museum* (Tom. II. tav. 18), and an explanation of it (pp. 41–43), maintains, on the other hand, that these statues did not have, in the least, the features of Antinoüs. They were, originally, an architechtonic ornament on the temple of Canopus, at Adrian's villa (Raffei, *Osserv. sopra Alcun. Ant. Mon.*, tav. 6, p. 60), probably as an imitation of those colossal figures, twelve cubits high, at the entrance of the temple of Apis, in Egypt, — Bearers, Telamons, or Caryatides, so called ; a supposition which is also rendered very probable by a sort of base on their heads that supplied the place of a capital. For ourselves, we are unable, in this case, to decide either for or against Winckelmann, because the height at which these two figures have been placed, near a door of

the Pio-Clement museum, makes it very difficult to examine the features of the face. This much, indeed, is certain, that the character of the forms of all parts of the body resembles that of the figure of Antinoüs. The resemblance, however, might be viewed less as a portrait-resemblance than as a peculiarity of the predominating style of art in the time of Adrian. — GERM. ED.

6. Warburton's *Essay on Hieroglyphics*, Vol. I. p. 294. The same may be said of Pauw (*Recherch. Philosoph. sur les Egypt. et les Chin.*, Tom. I., lib. 1, p. 45), who, following Jablonsky's opinion (*Specim. Nov. Interpr. Tab. Bemb.*, no. 1, § 5; *Miscell. Berolin.*, Tom. VI., pp. 141, 142), holds this tablet to be a calendar, made in Italy after the Egyptian mode, in the second or third century. Caylus (*Rec. d'Antiq.*, Tom. V. pl. 14, p. 44) looks upon it as an Egyptian work, though of an antiquity not earlier than the Christian era. — F.

7. The term Canopus is applied to vases made of fine clay, which served to filtrate the water of the Nile, and render it clear and fit for drinking, and having on the cover the head of a person or animal. This is the form under which Egyptian mythology seems to have represented Canopus, the god of the water of the Nile. The name is derived from the city of Canopus, near which was found the clay whereof these vessels were made. It is said by the Greeks, that Menelaus, on his return from Troy, stopped at one of the mouths of the Nile to refit, and that whilst there his pilot, named Canopus, was bitten by a viper, and died of the wound. The city was erected over his tomb, and derived its name from him. The deity thus symbolized by the Egyptians was probably the good Genius of the Nile, the Serapis of the temple of Canopus. — TR.

8. This is the most appropriate place to remark, that, in the Pio-Clement museum, there is a large Canopus of valuable white alabaster, the belly of which is covered, however, not with figures wrought in bas-relief, but with spiral grooves. A small one of terra-cotta, with a belly quite smooth, together with the head or cover of another, also of terra-cotta, is in the collection of Campanian, Etruscan, and other vases in the Florentine Gallery. — GERM. ED.

9. The word Abraxas or Abrasax is applied by antiquarians to a certain kind of engraved gems on which the word Abraxas is sometimes found. The term is intended to signify Mithras or the Sun, who is, in the language of the Gnostics, the lord of the 365 days: the Greek letters in the word Abrasax are supposed to signify three hundred and sixty-five. These gems were much worn by the heathen, and also by many of the early converts to Christianity, as amulets or protectors against disease. The reason of the practice is apparent, if we reflect that the Sun and Apollo were the same, and that Apollo was the god of healing.

These gems are of different sizes and figures; sometimes they are in the shape of finger-rings.

The emblems borne by them are very numerous. On some may be seen the names of saints, of angels, and even of Jehovah; on others, Mithras or the Sun, Isis, Osiris, Serapis, the cock, the dog, the lion, the ape, — in fact, every kind of object which the Egyptians placed among their deities; on others, monstrous compositions of animals, and obscene images, Phalli and Ithyphalli.

The engraving on these gems is rarely good. The reverse, on which is the word Abraxas, is said to be sometimes of a lower and more modern taste than the obverse. The characters are usually Greek, but sometimes Hebrew or Coptic. The date of them is chiefly of the third century. — Tr.

10. Many specimens of Abraxas may be seen in Montfaucon. (*Antiq. Expl.*, Tom. II., part 2, pl. 144, *seq.*) — F.

11. The statue of Memnon also is quite naked, and without a hip-cloth, like the figures here mentioned. (Fea, Tom. I, tav. 4.) In Caylus (*Recueil*, &c.) several small figures of this kind may be found. — F.

12. This figure (Fea, Tom. I., tav. 14) appears to me to be that of a priest of a procession in honor of Isis, who, according to Apuleius (*Metam.*, lib. 2, p. 372), was dressed in a white, scant garment, descending from the breast to the feet. From the position we might believe that it is the one which bore a light. — F.

CHAPTER IV.

1. INSTEAD of κατὰ τὴν ὀροφήν, read κατὰ τὴν ὀσφύν, (Aristot., *De Histor. Animal.*, lib. 1, p. 14,) ἐχόμενα τούτων, γαστὴρ καὶ ὀσφὺς, καὶ αἰδοῖον, καὶ ἰσχίον (Herodot., lib. 2, cap. 40), and reflect that κατά is never used to signify motion towards, but relation and sequence. Rhodomann's and Wesseling's conjecture of κορυφήν is altogether inadmissible. The ancient reading ὀροφήν comes nearer to the probable correct one. — W.

Winckelmann has fallen into an error here, probably in consequence of quoting from memory. The passage to which he refers has not the slightest application to sculpture. It merely states the sequence of the different parts of the body from the head downwards. The passage stands thus: Μετὰ δὲ τὴν κεφαλήν ἐστιν ὁ αὐχὴν, εἶτα στῆθος καὶ νῶτον. . . . . Καὶ ἐχόμενα τούτων γαστὴρ, καὶ ὀσφὺς, καὶ αἰδοῖον, καὶ ἰσχίον. "After the head comes the neck, then the chest and back, &c. Following these are the belly, and hips, and pubis, and ischium." — Tr.

2. The fact, that the Antinoüs in the Capitoline museum was made in two portions, must be ascribed, not to imitation of the Egyptian style, but rather to the nature of Parian marble, which, according to Pliny (lib. 36, cap. 8, sect. 13) and Isidor (*Etym.*, lib. 16, cap. 5), was not found in very large blocks, as Visconti judges from the Juno Lanuvina, thirteen Roman palms (9 ft. 6 in.) high, which was transferred from the Paganica palace to the Pio-Clement museum; this statue was originally composed of several pieces, jointed together, of the finest Parian marble. — F.

The remarks made by Visconti, in his explanation of the upper half of a beautiful Bacchus executed in this way, may be applied more appropriately to the Capitoline Antinoüs, consisting of two parts. "For the sake of more convenient carriage, statues were prepared in several pieces, usually in two, those statues especially, as I believe, which were executed at a distance from the place of their destination, for the use or adornment of the palaces and villas of private persons, and in order that they might even be easily transferred from one place to another at the fancy of their possessors. Three female statues in the Capitoline museum, and one which represents the Emperor Adrian in armor, in the Ruspoli palace, are prepared in this manner; and the lower half of all of them, as well as of the Bacchus mentioned above, is lost." — GERM. ED.

3. Diod. Sic., lib. 1, § 47. But Pococke, in his description of this statue (Vol. I., book 2, chap. 4, p. 289), says that it is composed of five pieces, and the engraving in Fea also shows this. — GERM. ED.

4. Winckelmann's conjecture is also acknowledged by Fea as satisfac·tory, from the evidence of a fragment, still remaining beneath the chin of the statue, of the antique ground-surface, which seems to have been concave. Besides, the surrounding part, of modern workmanship, consists, not of marble, but of stucco. — GERM. ED.

5. It is superfluous to remark, that a great scholar, Scaliger (*In Scaligerian.*), and a more modern traveller, Motraye (*Voyage*, Tom. II. p. 225), have allowed themselves to dream that granite is a product of art. In Spain there is an abundance of all kinds of granite, and it is the commonest rock there. It is also found in Germany and other lands. — W.

6. Montfaucon considers this statue of Isis to be of black basalt; Fea, of basaltic granite. — GERM. ED.

7. The pavement of the most ancient Roman streets, prior to their improvement by Trajan, as the Appian Way, in the direction of the Pontine Marshes, is of limestone. The Romans made use of the stone which was nearest at hand. — F.

8. It is not an Anubis, but an ape, and probably of the kind described by Aristotle. (*De Histor. Animal.*, lib 2, cap. 8.) — F.

9. It has since been repaired. Mr. Byres possesses a similar head three inches high, well preserved, and far more beautiful. This, however, as well as that in the Albani villa, also lacks the Modius. — A. and F.

10. This statue was found, nearly forty years ago, in digging the foundations of the Roman Seminary of Jesuits in the Campus Martius, the locality in which the temple of Isis anciently stood; and in the same section (Donati, *Rom. Vet. ac Rec.*, lib. 1, cap. 22, p. 80), though on land belonging to the Dominicans, was found the above-mentioned Osiris with a hawk's head, now in the Barberini palace. The alabaster of that statue is purer and whiter than Oriental alabaster generally, as Pliny (lib. 36, cap. 8, sect. 12) asserts of Egyptian alabaster. The author of a treatise on valuable stones (Giovanni da R. Lorenzo, *Dissertaz. sopra le Pietre Preziose degli Antichi*, Part I. cap. 2, § 23; *Saggi di Dissertaz. dell Acad. di Cortona*, Tom. I. p. 29) has not got this statement, because he believes it impossible to find any Egyptian statue in alabaster. Moreover, his opinion — that, even if the Egyptians did make statues of alabaster, they must have been very slender, and of the shape of mummies — is restricted by this statue. For the base of it is four and a half Roman palms (3 ft. 3 in.) in length, and the height of the stool on which the figure sits, including the base, to the hips of the figure, is as much. Any one who knows that alabaster is a petrifaction formed from water,

and has heard of the great vases in the Albani villa, ten palms (7 ft. 4 in.) in diameter, can imagine still larger pieces. Alabaster is also formed in the ancient aqueducts of Rome. When repairs were making on one of them, leading to St. Peter's church, which had been built by a Pope some centuries before, a deposit of tartar, a true alabaster, was found on the inside, and the Cardinal Girolamo Colonna had table-slabs sawed from it. The formation of alabaster can also be seen in the vaults of the Baths of Titus. — W.

Visconti says, in the *Pio-Clement Museum* (Tom. II. p. 39): " The glorious fragment of the seated statue, of alabaster, in the Albani villa, should have been restored with the symbols of Horus, whose color, according to the traditions of the priests, was white." — F.

11. Lib. 36, cap. 22, sect. 43. — Pliny names this very stone (lib. 36, cap. 8, sect. 13) sienite, from the city of Syene, which lies on the confines of Egypt and Ethiopia. He adds (sect. 14), that obelisks were made from it. It is therefore probable, that the stone called Pyropœkilos is a granite, and not a porphyry. From the small specks or white points with which the red color of the granite is intermixed, it is termed Leptosephos. — F.

12. Visconti (*Mus. Pio-Clem.*, Tom. VI. p. 73) disputes Winckelmann's statement in regard to porphyritic statues of the age of the Ptolemies; he maintains the impossibility of referring to that date, with probability, any one of the works of art now extant; indeed, it might even seem as if the ancients did not begin to make use of this exceedingly hard kind of stone prior to the reign of the Emperor Claudius. From the passages quoted by him from ancient authors, this statement, however, is not made altogether clear; and if a decision should be formed from obvious appearances in existing works of art, then Winckelmann, who is manifestly a better connoisseur than Visconti, is right. For all the characters of the style and taste of different periods, exhibited by the ancient monuments of plastic art, must be unworthy of dependence, and the history of art, in so far as it is based on them, would have little value left, if the so-called Juno in the Borghese villa, and the torso of a draped female statue on the ascent to the Capitol, should prove not to have been executed at an earlier date than the time of the Emperor Claudius. — Germ. Ed.

13. In the Florentine cabinet of gems is preserved a mask, or, to speak more plainly, a face, seemingly of ancient Egyptian workmanship. It is nearly of life-size, and is made of a very hard gem, almost like chrysoprase, though of a somewhat feebler lustre, and of a dull color, bordering on leek-green. The eyes are inserted, and are made of enamel, imitating the white and pupils of the real eye. — Germ. Ed.

The celebrated Peiresc, in one of his unpublished letters to Menetrier of 1632, in the library of the Cardinal Albani, mentions two works shaped like mummies, one of which was of touchstone, the other of a white stone somewhat softer than marble. They were excavated behind, so that they seem to have been the covers of coffins in which embalmed bodies were contained. Both pieces were covered with hieroglyphs. They were brought from Egypt to Marseilles, and the trader to whom they belonged asked fifteen hundred pistoles (nearly $3,000) for them. — W.

14. The mother of emerald is, according to Lessing (*Briefe Antiquar. Inhalts*, Br. 25), nothing else than the Prasius or Gemma Prasina of the ancients. Winckelmann's assertion, that it is the matrix of emerald, is refuted by experience, since emeralds are never found in it. It is difficult, however, to determine what Winckelmann understands by plasma of emerald. — A connoisseur has closely examined the table-slabs mentioned above, and has discovered that they consist of two translucent plates of gypseous mica or fine diaphanous alabaster, placed together, — a green mass or coating having been put between them. The edges are so well preserved and framed, that it is not easy to discover the deception. — E.

15. It is not probable that it is white-lead, because this paint becomes blackish by animal or mineral vapors, — as we see by some modern paintings. We may, therefore, more readily believe that the ground-color on the mummies is chalk, mixed with glue or gum. — F. and GERM. ED.

CHAPTER V.

1. PROBABLY the Phœnicians never had any statues or bas-reliefs in marble ; if they had had either, the Romans would not have failed, after the subjugation of them, to carry to Rome works of art of this kind, — as they did from Etruria, Greece, and Egypt. Even the silence of historians in recounting the plunder collected in Carthage, and in other Egyptian cities, favors this assumption not less than the fact, that, although the number of eminent works of art disinterred in Rome is so large, not a single fragment of a statue or bas-relief has been found, relating to the Phœnician nation. The Romans, it is true, frequently made use of the Numidian or Lybian marble, called at the present day African breccia, yet only in the formation of columns, pavements, and partition-walls (Juvenal, *Sat.* VII. v. 182), because it was unsuitable for statues on account of being irregularly spotted, and of different colors. M. Lepidus was the first to carry such Numidian marble to Rome : he ornamented the atrium of his house with it. (Plin., lib. 36, cap. 6, sect. 8.) The Emperor Adrian caused a hundred pillars of Lybian marble to be carried to Rome, and twenty to Smyrna, for the purpose of decorating the Gymnasia erected by him in those cities. (Pausan., lib. 1, cap. 18 ; *Marmor. Oxon.*, 21.) — F.

2. Bochart, *Phal. et Can.*, lib. 4, cap. 35 ; Goguet, lib. 4, cap. 2, art. 1, p. 236. — Sidon was celebrated for its manufacture of linen, tapestry, and costly lawns, for its skill in working metals, in carving wood, and the discovery of glass ; Tyre, by the dyeing of cloths, and especially by its discovery of purple-color, and through its works in ivory. — F.

3. Passeri (*Pict. Etrusc.*, Tom. I. p. 21) mentions that vases with Phœnician characters on them, but without pictures, are found in Sicily. — F.

4. The Academy of Cortona possesses several Carthaginian coins of bronze, and two of silver. — F.

5. The Carthaginian coins stamped in Sicily are certainly very beautiful, and hardly inferior to the best Greek coins. But it would be hazardous to regard them as specimens of art produced by the Carthaginians themselves, and to look upon them as a standard of the taste among this people. For, in all probability, the dies of these coins were made in Sicily, and by Greeks. If this were not the case, then some peculiarity in taste, workmanship, &c., could at least be pointed out. But, as Winckelmann himself observes, they are distinguishable from beautiful Greek coins merely by the Punic writing. Furthermore, admirable monuments of another kind, of Carthaginian origin, or at least accounts of such monuments, must also still be in existence; for it is, if not impossible, yet in the highest degree improbable, that there should have been among the Carthaginians die-cutters of so extraordinary skill, and, on the other hand, neither sculptors, nor founders, nor painters of reputation. The Boethus mentioned by Pausanias cannot be brought into the argument here, because he had lived in Greece, had worked in the taste of the Greeks, and had acquired from them his skill. So, also, an Iceland landscape-painter, and a designer of Calmuck descent (Feodor in Karlsrühe), have recently become famous among us; yet art does not therefore flourish in Iceland or among the Calmucks. — GERM. ED.

6. There are none of the latter kind in Golzius (*Magna Græcia*); these were found in the Grand-Ducal gallery at Florence and the royal Farnese museum at Naples. — W.

7. Salmas., *Ad Tertull. de Pallio*, p. 56. — Salmasius rather shows that the Carthaginians were accustomed to wear mantles, and that they had different kinds, double and single, round and four-cornered. He could not, also, be of a different opinion without contradicting Tertullian, on whose book *De Pallio* he intended to comment. — A.

8. The Mosaic Law, it is true, forbade the making of images of the gods for worship, but did not prohibit images of angels, men, and beasts for ornament, or in commemoration. Even Moses himself prepared Cherubim for the ark of the covenant; and Solomon made others, of gigantic size, for the temple, and also twelve oxen of bronze as a support of the brazen sea, so called. (1 Kings vii. 23.) In later times, the Jews extended the Mosaic Law to every kind of figures. (Origen, *Contra Celsum*, lib. 4, cap. 37.) Flavius Josephus relates that the Jews requested Vitellius not to allow the Roman standards to pass through their country, because they imitated the figures of eagles and other animals. (*Antiq. Jud.*, lib. 18, cap. 4, n. 3.) — F.

9. Bianchini, *Histor. Univ.*, cap. 31, p. 537. — In the rich Russian imperial cabinet of engraved gems there are some very admirable Persian pieces, as we know from casts of them. — GERM. ED.

10. The Persian women usually wore two garments, as we may infer from Diodorus (lib. 17, § 35). Among the monuments of Persepolis communicated by Bruyn (*Voyage en Perse*, Tom. II. p. 169) is found a female figure, dressed in a tunic with sleeves, which holds with one hand the hem of a garment. Probably this is the purple tunic called Sarapis by Pollux (lib. 7, cap. 13, segm. 61) and Hesychius. The latter quotes under the word Sarapis a few words of Ktesias, from which he would infer that this garment was common both to men and women. The latter girdled themselves with sashes, which were made with fringes.

(*Schol in Æschyl. Pers.*, v. 153.) Men and women wore expensive shoes, necklaces of jewels, ear-rings, bracelets, and rings on the fingers and joints. (Brisson. loc. cit., lib. 2, § 196.) — F.

11. Brisson. (lib. 1, § 46) speaks in detail of the different kinds of caps and coverings of the head of the Persians, and remarks that the kings wore caps running to a point, and the other Persians caps bent forwards. (Lens, loc. cit., p. 192, pl. 29.) — F.

12. Herodot., lib. 1, cap. 131. — Probably, one of the principal causes why the formative arts were unable to attain any special degree of excellence among the Persians was also the limited use of them, as they were employed only in the imitation of warlike and bloody subjects. *Apud Persas*, says Ammianus Marcellinus (lib. 24, cap. 6), *non pingitur vel fingitur aliud præter varias cædes et bella*, "Among the Persians, nothing is painted or imaged but various kinds of death, and wars." Compare Brissonius, lib. 3, § 92. — L.

13. Plutarch, *In Pompeio*, p. 633. — The worship of the god Mithras, a symbol of the sun and fire, originated in Persia, and here he remained the principal divinity until the time of Zoroaster. The horse was sacrificed to him, as the animal which corresponded most nearly to so swift-footed a deity. (Herodot., lib. 1, cap. 216. Ovid, *Fast.*, lib. 1, v. 383. Xenophon, *Cyroped.*, lib. 8, p. 215.) This deity was afterwards worshipped also in Rome, and in other cities of the Roman empire, and especially in Milan (Gruter, *Inscript.*, p. 34, no. 9), as is likewise proved by the bas-reliefs mentioned above. — F.

14. Plin., lib. 34, cap. 8, sect. 19, § 9. — The artists whom Cambyses brought from Egypt to Persia built, according to Diodorus (lib. 1, p. 46), the celebratèd palaces of Persepolis and Susa, or embellished them, as Wesseling (loc. cit., not. 80) and Saint-Croix (*Journal des Savans*, Juin, 1765, p. 1277) explain this passage of Diodorus. — F.

15. That the Egyptians and Persians had commercial intercourse with each other may be inferred partly from the fact that the latter held rule over the former for the space of one hundred and thirty-five years (Diodor. Sic., lib. 1, § 44) ; and partly from many monuments, in which the Egyptian and Persian styles of art appear blended. (*Cayl. Rec. d'Antiq.*, Tom. I. pl. 18, pp. 55, 56 ; Tom. III. pl. 12.) — F.

16. Palæphatus (*De Invent. Purpuræ*) relates that the Phœnician kings and other notables of this nation carried small idols on their persons, in order that greater respect might be shown to themselves. — F.

17. According to Adler (*Mus. Cufic. Borgian.*, p. 105), the Druses do not descend from the Franks, but are an Asiatic race, deriving its origin from a Persian of the name of Drusus, who lived about 1017. Their religion is a mixture of Mohammedanism, Christianity, and arbitrary additions. Adler mentions the figure of an ox, covered with characters, which was one of their idols, and is now in the Borgian museum at Velletri. — F.

BOOK III.

CHAPTER I.

1. In the *Ancient Monuments*, No. 79, the author speaks of five such representations of the hero Echetlus on Etruscan burial-urns, one of which is executed in alabaster of Volterra, and one in marble. In the numerous collection of Etruscan monuments in the Florentine gallery, there are found, besides, no less than eighteen burial-urns of terra-cotta, painted, and all ornamented with this scene. (Montfaucon, *Antiq. Expl.*, Suppl., Tom. V. pl. 57, not. 2. Dempster, *Etrur. Regal.*, Tom. I. tab. 54.) — F. and GERM. ED.

2. Plat. *Polit.*, p. 315. — Plato says, that there was a law among the Etruscans which commanded human sacrifices ; but that, in his time, it had ceased to be obeyed, and was acknowledged as wicked. — F.

3. In reply to all this may be adduced the great love of the Etruscans for music, insomuch that they were the inventors of several musical instruments. In all their cities there was a theatre, in which were exhibited not only gladiatorial games and tragedies, but also comedies and pantomimic dances. The climate of Tuscany, at the present day, is not of a kind which predisposes to melancholy. — F.

4. This statement, it is true, is found to be confirmed by many Etruscan burial-urns ; yet, it must also be remarked, on many others joyous pictures are presented, as games, dances, weddings, festivals, and similar subjects, as any one can easily convince himself by reference to Gori and others. — F.

5. Fabrett., *Inscrip.*, cap. 6, p. 243, not. 5. — This very scene is found represented in a sort of work composed of many-colored stones, called *Commesso* (Ciampini, *Vet. Monum.*, Tom I. tab. 24j, in the Albani villa. To it alludes, also, a Greek inscription, not yet published, which is on the surface of one half of a column, that has been sawed in two, in the Capponi mansion at Rome, and from which I will quote only the line which alludes to this representation: ΗΡΠΑCΑΝ ΩC ΤΕΡΠΝΗΝ ΝΑΙΑΔΕC ΟΥ ΘΑΝΑΤΟC, *The Nymphs, not Death, carried away the beautiful girl.* — W.

6. Montfaucon (*Antiq. Expl.*, Tom. V. pl. 71, p. 123) has not been more successful than others in discovering the true representation of this urn. — W.

7. Dionys. Halic., *Antiq. Rom.*, lib. 7, cap. 72. — On a large rilievo, sawed from a burial-urn, in the Albani villa (copied in Zoega's *Bas-reliefs*, No. 27), are represented a woman seated, and a maiden standing, in a larder, together with gutted animals, hanging up, and other edibles, — a picture similar to the one of which there is an engraving in the *Giustiniani Gallery ;* above are the following lines from Virgil (*Æn.*, lib. 1, v. 611) : —

> " Dum montibus umbræ
> Lustrabunt, convexa polus dum sidera pascet,
> Semper honos, nomenque tuum, laudesque manebunt."

There was formerly in Rome a sepulchral urn on which was even represented an indecent scene, *Spinthrian,* so called; and the following words of the inscription still remained: ΟΥ ΜΕΛΕΙ ΜΟΙ, *It does not concern me.* Something still worse, together with the name of the deceased, may be seen on a work of this kind belonging to the sculptor, Cavaceppi. — W.

CHAPTER II.

1. APOLLODORUS, lib. 1, cap. 7, § 9. — If, therefore, the phrase πτεροφόρων σχημάτων, in a passage of Euripides which has been preserved by Longinus (*De Sublim.*, p. 66), is translated *winged chariots,* the translation is not to be censured, as a critic thinks, and who supposes that he explains it more correctly by *winged horses* (Rutgers., *Var. Lect.*, lib. 1, cap. 10); yet he is in error, for the wings are attributed, not to the horses, but to the chariot. Meanwhile, the word πτεροφόρος, *winged,* is found as an epithet of the chariot of the son of Theseus, used by the same poet (*Iphig. Aul.*, v. 251) to denote its swiftness. — W.

Since Winckelmann wrote this, so many new discoveries of ancient monuments have been made, that representations of winged cars on works of Greek art are scarcely to be considered any longer as objects of rarity. The reader is referred to the *New Collection of Hamilton Vases,* and to Visconti (*Pitture d'un Antico Vaso Fittile Appart. al Sig. Principe Poniatowsky*). — GERM. ED.

2. In the *Ancient Monuments,* the author has explained this figure in the same manner as he has done here. Visconti (*Mus. Pio-Clem.*, Tom. VI. pp. 6 and 85) has shown that the figure with the tongs in its hand originally represented Vulcan, and that only the upper part, which was lost, has become, by unskilful restoration, of a female shape. In the fourth volume of Visconti (*Mus. Pio-Clem.*, tav. agg.) an engraving of all three sides of this work, together with an account of the restorations, may be found. — GERM. ED.

3. The question, which figure on the Borghese three-sided altar the author particularly intended here, is not without difficulties. In the upper row, near Neptune, stands a goddess, who holds something in her hand, which at the time when Winckelmann wrote, and before the monument had been cleaned, was probably indistinct, and may have looked like flowers. But it is, as can now be discerned without difficulty, ears of wheat, and the figure of Ceres. In the lower row, the first of the three Hours has in her hand a flower with a long stem, unless it may, perchance, be a twig with young fruit. But it is altogether improbable that the author should not have correctly known these three figures, especially as they are wrought on that side of the monument which, even in his day, could be conveniently seen. — GERM. ED.

4. This statement of the author is remarkable, for it presents the point from which we are to judge all his opinions on Etruscan and ancient Greek art; it is also to be viewed as the limit to which he advanced in his knowledge of these monuments. Many may have more

knowledge now in regard to them, but they must also have the modesty
to remember that Winckelmann's capital has been at interest for a long
time ; and since then some additional monuments of the ancient style
have been discovered, and others have been studied with more attention.
He has, indeed, rendered to antiquarian knowledge one of the most valuable of all services, by removing one of the greatest obstructions ; for
he checked the previous extravagant prejudices in favor of Etruscan
art, and claimed for the Greeks the many important monuments which
an antiquated error had adjudged to the Etruscans. In consequence of
this view, any further remarks which we may have to make in regard to
monuments still included by the author among works of Etruscan art
must be considered, not as a contradiction of his opinion, but simply as
an advance on the path opened by him. — GERM. ED.

5. Gori, *Mus. Etrusc.*, Tom. II. tab. 155. — The Chimæra of bronze,
in the gallery at Florence, diminished, and with omission of modern restorations, may be seen in Plate XI. (after Dempster, *Etrur. Regal.*, Tom.
I. tav. 22). The expression of this monster is wild and ferocious. The
bones and muscles are rendered with much knowledge, and very power-
fully. About the outlines there is, generally, a certain degree of hardness, corresponding well with the character of the whole. The tail
terminates in a serpent, which is biting the horn of the goat. A portion
of the horn, and the serpent, are modern restorations. On the right fore-
foot are a few Etruscan letters, which Buonarroti (*Ad Dempst.*, p. 93)
and Gori (*Mus. Etrusc.*, Tom. II. p. 293) read as *tinmcuil ;* but Passeri
(*Lettr. Roncagl.*, Tom. XXIII. ; *Racc. d'Opusc.*, Lettr. 10) as *tinmicuil.*
Scholars have given different opinions in regard to the meaning of this
writing. It would be very difficult, taking into consideration our
deficient knowledge of the Etruscan language, to determine who has
given the true signification. — GERM. ED. and A.

6. There are cogent reasons for regarding the Genius, of bronze, in the
Barberini palace, as one of the most ancient works of Greek art, rather
than an Etruscan monument. The following characters all accord with
Greek works of the old style : the shoulders are very broad in proportion to the whole figure ; the chest, though flat, is strongly prominent,
and the nipples are not placed far enough to the sides ; the hair fits
about the forehead like a band of single packthreads lying close
together ; the thighs and other limbs give evidence of knowledge on
the part of the artist, and of an endeavor after a beautiful shape. The
high antiquity of this figure seems to be manifest also from the features
of the face, which are not handsome ; yet they do not therefore denote a
portrait, but rather art still in an ungracious state. — GERM. ED.

7. Dempster, *Etrur. Regal.*, lib. 1, tab. 40. — The Haruspex, as he is
called, is of full size and standing, has one arm and hand raised, and is
conceived as if in act of addressing an assembled multitude. His hair
is cropped, he wears shoes, or, if you will, half-boots, fastened with
straps in the usual way, as high up as the lower part of the calf of the
leg, an under-garment with short sleeves, and over it the mantle, by
which the left arm, that hangs down straight, is covered even to the
hand ; the fourth or ring finger is ornamented with a seal. In the whole
of the figure we recognize an image prepared with the utmost fidelity
after the likeness of a particular individual, and treated so much in

detail, that even the seams of the under-garment are rendered. We therefore acknowledge ourselves to be wholly of the author's opinion, that this statue belongs to the later period of Etruscan art. Its style and taste give absolutely no probable ground for throwing its origin farther back than to an age shortly preceding the time of the first Roman emperors, as we believe we have ascertained by observation. — GERM. ED.

8. The beard of Etruscan figures is not a sure sign of their high antiquity, since, as the author himself afterwards acknowledges, Jupiter, Vulcan, and Æsculapius, in the most ancient Etruscan works, are represented without beard. — A.

9. This Minerva is one of the charming figures that were produced by the cultivated taste of Greek art in the later period when earnestness and grandeur also had disappeared, and the pleasing had acquired exclusive control. Hence, she is an uncommonly lovely shape ; her helmet is very becoming to her; and the robe is thrown with studied elegance about the body and the left arm, which is resting on the side. An engraving of it may be seen in the *Florentine Museum* (Tom. III. tab. 7). — GERM. ED.

10. Olivieri, *Marm. Pisaur.*, p. 4. Gori, *Mus. Etrusc.*, tab. 87. — The Genius, so called, of bronze, in the Florentine gallery, of which an engraving may be found in the *Florentine Museum* (Tom. III. tav. 45, 46), might be regarded as an Iconic statue, erected probably to a young Greek as an honorary testimonial of a victory obtained in the Games. A simple attitude, good proportions, a beautiful shape on the whole, and noble features, give to it especial value. The locks of hair, lying flat one on another, are somewhat stiff and wiry, and the ribs also are rendered a little thin, — characters from which we may infer that this statue was executed prior to the introduction in art of that style whose special aim it was to produce the beautiful and pleasing. — GERM. ED.

11. The Romans, under their kings, were already in possession of this promontory, for Tarquinius Superbus sent a colony thither (Liv., lib. 1, cap. 56) ; and in the earliest alliance between Rome and Carthage, which was arranged under the first Consuls, Lucius Junius Brutus and Marcus Horatius, Circeum is named among the four cities on the seashore, held by the Romans, which they did not wish to have harrassed by the Carthaginians. The same condition is repeated in the very same words in the next following treaty between the two parties. (Polyb., lib. 3, p. 180.) Cluverius, Cellarius, and others have not touched upon this. The first league was concluded twenty-eight years prior to the expedition of Xerxes against the Greeks; and the statue in question must, if it were possible for it to be Greek, have been made before this time, in conformity with the knowledge of Greek art. But the Volsci, who occupied the promontory of Circeum (Liv., lib. 2, cap. 39), had no intercourse or commerce, especially at that time, with the Greeks, though they had with the Etruscans, their neighbors ; so that, if we take into consideration only the time and the locality, this Apollo should be regarded as an Etruscan work. — W.

12. This statue was found in a small temple on the shore of a lake, called Lago di Soressa. This lake, which belonged to the house of the Prince Gaetani, formerly discharged itself into the sea through a canal ;

but the channel having become obstructed, the water for a long time stood very high in the lake. In order to make it convenient for fishing, it was necessary to let the water run off. The ancient canal was cleared out. In it were found a few small skiffs of the ancients, which were fastened with nails of metal; and, when the water in the lake itself was fallen, the temple came in sight; in it the Apollo was found. Even now is visible the marble niche, with very finely executed ornaments, in which the statue formerly stood. — W.

13. *Galler. Giustin.*, Tom. I. tav. 17. — The Giustiniani statue, which is known under the name of the Vestal, has in all its parts something angular, very severe and precise, and consequently little that is pleasing. It may even be objected that it is stiff. The folds of the robe are in perpendicular lines; and, thus, the old Greek style shows itself throughout. Yet it deserves to be remarked of this monument, that it has been finished with especial care, smoothly and accurately. — GERM. ED.

14. The described bas-relief in the Albani villa, the *Rearing of Bacchus by Leucothea*, is unquestionably very ancient, and, in its relation to the history of art, one of the most remarkable monuments. But it has no similarity with any Etruscan work of undoubted genuineness; it is executed from a Greek marble of coarse grain; and it corresponds generally so well with the monuments now acknowledged as ancient Greek, that we have no scruple in holding it to be the oldest known work of the kind. The nose and lips of Leucothea are restorations, and also some of the right hand. Both hands of the child are new. — GERM. ED.

15. Eustathius (*Comment. in Iliad.*, lib. 19, p. 1249) remarks, that it was customary among the Pelasgians to represent Mercury with a beard. He is seen imaged in this manner on divers monuments, even on Roman. (Foggini, *Mus. Capitol.*, Tom. IV. p. 299.) Pausanias (lib. 7, cap. 22) relates that a Mercury with a beard was to be seen in the middle of the market-place at Pharæ, in Achaia. — F.

16. Scaliger (*Poët.*, lib. 1, cap. 14) explained it in this way. Pollux, however, does not in those passages ascribe the beard to Mercury, but to the tragic masks. The epithet σφηνοπώγων, *having a wedge-shaped beard*, was used in reference to Mercury in Artemidor (II. 42). — F. and GERM. ED.

17. The round altar in the Capitoline museum, with figures of Mercury, Apollo, and Diana, is Greek, and not Etruscan. And it is by no means ancient Greek, but a later imitation of the ancient Greek style, as we have become convinced, by frequent opportunities of studying it. In the features of Apollo we perceive the fully complete ideal of this god. The mouth is not drawn upwards; the elongated eyes are not depressed near the nose; the forms of the body are not meagre, — marks which uniformly characterize works really of a primeval origin. The body and limbs are, on the contrary, of a youthful plumpness, and not without size; and the transitions of one part into another are softly handled. The ear is somewhat lower than it ought to be according to rule; whereas, in monuments of indisputably great antiquity, the ear is usually placed too high. From the workmanship of the hair also, we are authorized to anticipate the later origin of this work, for it is not so wiry as it would have been according to the manner of the most antique style. The handling too of the marble indicates far greater freedom and dexterity.

We cannot, consequently, assent to the author's opinion in regard to this monument any further than to admit that it is in the ancient style, but executed by a later artist, as we have seen that, in the times of the Ptolemies and of Adrian, works were finished in the ancient Egyptian style. It might possibly be the case, that the three figures in question were actually copied from a primeval work, with improvement in charac- ter and form. This latter conjecture derives additional probability from the circumstance that there once existed in the Albani villa an ancient monument on which were represented the figures of Minerva, Apollo, Diana, and Mercury, the latter three being almost exactly like those on the Capitoline altar. Mercury is very deficient in the youthful grace, the nimbleness, the lightness, the delicacy in shape and features, in short, in the characteristics which the beautiful style of art has elsewhere accorded to images of this deity. But Winckelmann recollects that, in remote antiquity, this god must also have been represented with a beard. Conse- quently, it is not to be wondered at, if, in a work imitative of the prime- val style, the beard should have been adopted. We observe, however, not less in Mercury than in Apollo of that ideal conformation which is a departure from the genuine antique style. We must not, also, overlook the Pancratiast ear, partly because of its introduction by the artist with appropriate significance, and partly because it has never before been noticed. Diana cannot be seen so conveniently as the other figures, on account of the place in which the monument now stands in the Capitoline museum. But she, too, is shaped ideally, having a grand, almost Juno- nian character; and the execution appears, generally, to be highly elabo- rated. — GERM. ED.

18. *Description of Engraved Gems*, Class 2, Div. 16, No. 1720. Such a bow was probably called *patulus*, " open " : —

Imposito patulos calamo sinuaverat arcus

" Having fitted the arrow, he had bent the open bows."
(Ovid. *Metam.*, lib 8, v. 30.)

But the other was called *sinuosus*, "curved " . —

Lunavitque genu sinuosum fortiter arcum.

" And with his knee he forcibly bent the curved bow into a crescent shape."
(Ovid. *Amor.*, lib. 1   *Eleg.*, I v. 23.) — W.

19. *Mus. Capitol.*, Tom. IV. tab. 22. In the *Capitoline Museum* of the Marquis Lucatelli (p. 23), it is erroneously stated that this work was found at Nettuno on the sea-shore. The Cardinal Alexander Albani has contradicted the statement in an autograph note to this work. It formerly stood in a villa, outside of the Porta del Popolo, belonging to the Medici family; and the Grand-Duke Cosmos III. made a present of it to the Cardinal, by whom it was put into the Campidoglio, together with his previously made collection of antiquities. — W.

If we, also, feel inclined to restore this monument to ancient Greek art we merely express more plainly the author's conjecture in regard to it since he manifests very distinctly his doubts of its Etruscan origin. But he unquestionably errs in looking upon it as of later workmanship than the square and the round altars — both in the Capitoline museum — of which mention was made shortly before; for the round well-curb in question, ornamented with figures of the twelve superior deities, may be one of the most ancient Greek works. We will present the reasons in confirmation of our opinion, and, for the sake of greater clearness, will illustrate them by an accurate copy of the head and a portion of the figure of Juno (Plate XV.), one of the best preserved figures on the monument. In the first place, much labor and care have been expended on the working of the marble; and it is evident that the artist has devoted his utmost powers to it, although with better success in some points than in others. He had not yet learnt how to handle easily his material, and the effort is visible. But this rude manipulation is in exact correspondence with the equally uncultivated taste, design of the forms, &c. We may consequently presume that the work is actually an original one, regarded at least as a whole, — not an imitation, perhaps, of a more ancient work, — and the production of a good master, and therefore capable of giving us some information as to the state of art at the time when it originated. In the second place, it is very clear, from the conformation, features, and proportions of the figures, that this monument belongs to an earlier age, and to a less cultivated style of art, than the above-mentioned square or round altar, and, on the other hand, is later than the bas-relief of Leucothea in the Albani villa, and may have been executed about the same time with the three-sided altar in the Borghese villa. It is well known, that, on all antique Greek monuments which formerly passed for Etruscan, the figures are in stiff positions, that the free hands are clasped together, that the fingers are sometimes stuck straight out, frequently somewhat crooked, the garments ample, the folds for the most part straight and lying flat one upon another &c. Enough has also been said of the rather large mouth and its upturned corners, of the oblong and not deeply set eyes, the smallish chin, and of the hairs lying near each other like wires or stout threads. But the fact has been more rarely remarked, and never properly appreciated, that, with all the slimness and visibly superfluous length of the figures of this ancient style, still the heads are too large. It was a necessary condition of the progress of art to a higher degree of cultivation, that the doctrine of proportions, as the basis of beauty, only gradually attained exactness. We may therefore infer the higher or lower antiquity of figures on primeval monuments from the greater or less symmetry and good proportion of the parts to each other. For the figures of better proportions will naturally be nearer to the age of more refined taste in art, than those in which the ruder proportions are still exhibited. But, in this as in all other cases, we must beware of one-sidedness, and not despise any one of the other signs which may help us to a better insight into the different ages, tastes, and styles of the ancient monuments. If there are distinctive marks, then it must be conceded that each land, each age, has its peculiar way of impressing itself on the products of art, and consequently there will be a rise and decline in art. Let each monument, therefore, be carefully scrutinized, and a judgment not be formed until all the circumstances have been weighed ; but never let the voice of doubt proclaim that it is difficult, even impossible, to determine by the workmanship the age of the early monuments.

It is evident that the back part of all the heads of the Capitoline well-mouth is too small. The ears are set far back, but are finished, almost throughout, in the most diligent manner, as may be seen, for instance, on the Jupiter, Vulcan, Minerva, and especially Neptune. The last was the favorite subject of the artist. With the exception of the widely opened mouth, and something which seems to be teeth, his mien is good, the forehead and eyebrow-bones tolerably well formed, as are also the other portions of the body; however, neither he, nor Jupiter, nor Mars, nor Minerva, nor several others, although slim in shape, has more than six heads and a half in height, — if the head is assumed as a measure. Vulcan, indeed, has a little more length than this; but in him the ribs are deep, almost to an excess. Apollo, who is still taller, has very long thighs; and hence his figure contains, for a portion of it, seven lengths perhaps; the mouth, somewhat widely opened, is drawn upwards at the corners, and shows the teeth a little. The artist probably made an attempt to represent the god as singing to the accompaniment of his lyre, and failed. Mercury has features nearly resembling the barbaric, and although, like the other figures, he is turned in profile, still the whole eye is visible. His legs look shrivelled; on the other hand, the goat, which he draws after him, is happily done. Mars and Hercules are both young and beardless, as are Vulcan and Mercury. The first is tolerably well shaped, as a whole; the second is represented moving on tiptoe, as if dancing; his mouth is drawn very much upwards, and his eye is almost like that of Mercury. His muscles and sinews are not more strongly rendered; but the artist conceived the laudable idea of letting the hair stick out short, and in small, crisp curls, from beneath the lion's hide. The forehead is high and vigorous. — Among the female figures, Juno appears the most admirable, and is also in the best preservation. The engraving is a satisfactory presentation of her. Cybele, Venus, Diana, and Minerva give no occasion for special remarks. Their proportions are precisely the same as those already pointed out in reference to Minerva. — The whole work is broken into many pieces, and has suffered much on its lower as well as upper edge. The right foot of Juno may be a modern restoration. All the figures have been more or less injured. — GERM. ED.

20. Pausan., lib. 1, cap. 39. — Pamphos is a poet, according to whom Ceres, after the abduction of her daughter Proserpine, sat, in the shape of an old woman, by a well in the vicinity of Megara and Eleusis. There is no mention in Pausanias of a representation of this subject in stone, near a well. — F.

21. This gem has been described in two treatises by Father Carlo Antonelli, professor at Pisa; that is, he relates anew the entire history of these and other heroes of the time, giving all the passages in ancient authors except those which I shall quote from Statius. In regard to art he had nothing to say. — W.

22. This figure holds in its hand a scraper, with which it seems to be scraping itself. The action is rendered still more probable by comparison with the four figures on an Etruscan cup, also holding scrapers, in Caylus (Rec. d'Antiq., liv. 2, Antiq. Etrusc., pl. 37.) Two of them are in a somewhat constrained posture, and resemble the figure on the gem in question Visconti (Mus. Pio-Clem., Tom I. tav. 13, in fine, p. 23, not a) believes, not without reason, that Tydeus is represented here in the act of purifying himself from his involuntary homicide of his brother Menalippus, as Hyginus relates. (Fab., 69.) — F.

23. It would almost seem as if Statius had seen this gem ; or else all figures of Tydeus must have been drawn in just such a manner, that is, with large and visible bones and knotty muscles ; for the language of the poet appears to describe and explain the gem, just as the gem, on the other hand, may illustrate the poet · —

> " Quamquam ipse videri
> Exiguus, gravia ossa tamen, nodisque lacerti
> Difficiles ; nunquam hunc animum natura minori
> Corpore, nec tantas ausa est includere vires."
>
> *Theb.*, lib. 8, v 643. — W.

24. Ἰλ. ψ. v. 140. Pausan., lib. 1, cap. 37. — We will here state briefly whatever remarks we have to make upon the three engraved gems classed by the author among Etruscan works. Winckelmann's own assertion in regard to the first gem, — representing the *Council of the Five Greek Heroes against Thebes*, — that the writing on it is more like the ancient Greek than that of other Etruscan works, gives rise to the supposition that it may actually be a primeval Greek work, and that probably both the figures of Tydeus and Peleus, of which mention is made, are also of the same origin. Visconti (*Mus. Pio-Clem.*, Tom. I. p. 95) even supposes that he finds in the former the copy of a celebrated work by Polycletus (*destringentem se*, "scraping himself"; Plin., lib. 34, cap. 8, sect. 19) But, in opposition to this assumption, it should at all events be stated, that the gem must be older than the work of art of which it is supposed to be a copy. We hold it, however, to be difficult, indeed quite impossible, to point to figures of similar art and kind in other works of unquestionable Etruscan origin; whilst, on the other hand, it could be easily done in regard to ancient Greek monuments. We must also add here, as a remark of general application, that engraved gems are truly valuable monuments, that we are indebted to them for the preservation of a great number of admirable conceptions, and that the good and best among them have, besides, excellent characteristics in regard to the skill of execution ; but in investigations into the state of art, as to the date, style, and taste, it would not be well to assign to them great weight in proof. From the smallness of their size, the characteristics never stand forth with sufficient distinctness. Better deductions on these points will be obtained from coins, but the larger bronzes and works in marble are always to be preferred even to these. — GERM. ED.

CHAPTER III.

1. THE Consuls cited by Dio Cassius are Lucius Cæsar, L. Marcius, and C. F. Figulus, whose consulship happened in the year 690 of the foundation of Rome. The historian mentions that the she-wolf was in the Capitol; so too Cicero, in his third *Oration against Catiline*; and both assert that she was struck and tumbled over by lightning. Such a thunderbolt would necessarily have produced some other effect than a simple rent or injury to the thigh. Cicero (*De Divinat.*, lib. 1, cap. 12,

In Catiln. Orat., 3, cap. 8), in the words, *Hic silvestris erat Romani nominis altrix*, " Here *was* the forest-nurse of the Roman name," leads us to antici- pate that she was no longer in existence in his day. Of the child which represented Romulus he says, in the *Oration* cited, *fuisse meministis*, " you remembered that it *was*." Nardini (*Roma Antica*, lib. 5, cap. 4, p. 200) and Ficaroni (*Le Vestig.*, lib. 1, cap. 10, p. 37) have not given heed to these words, since they believed that this she-wolf was in the Capitol even at the time when they wrote.

The other she-wolf, the one mentioned by Dionysius of Halicarnassus, was made, in the year of Rome 457 (Liv., lib 10, cap. 16, not. 23), by direction of the Ædile Curules Cneus and Quintus Ogulinus, from fines which had been levied upon certain usurers, and, as a memorial of the two founders of the city who had been suckled by a she-wolf, was set up in that temple. This was probably the Capitoline she wolf, as it is called. Fulvius Ursinus (Nardini, *loc. cit.*) is also of the same opinion. She too was, perchance, afterwards struck by lightning, if the injury, or, more correctly, the injuries, — which are found on both thighs, — are not ascribable to another cause. — F.

We dare not, indeed, presume to decide upon the disputed point, which of the two she-wolves mentioned by authors may be the one now present in the Capitol; but observation shows us a stiff, angular style of draw- ing in this monument. The hair about the neck is, as it is usual in pri- meval works, but slightly raised, and arranged in rows; the manner throughout is rude, and somewhat awkward, yet not without spirit and stern expression. A work of art of such a character, even though of Etruscan workmanship, can hardly have originated in the year 457 of the building of Rome, coinciding nearly with the one hundred and twentieth Olympiad. The injuries on the hind legs of the animal are plainly to be seen, and certainly render it probable that it is the very same one which was once struck by lightning. — GERM. ED.

CHAPTER IV.

1. BAS-RELIEFS, or rather fragments of bas-reliefs, in terra-cotta, and painted with different colors, were found in the year 1774 at Velletri; and they were considered to be Volscian works. The drawing of the figures is stiff; their shape is slender; and the faces have barbarously rude features. These monuments represent chariot-races and other sub- jects, and seem in reality very ancient. The manner or style resembles the most nearly the black profile-kind of figures on the oldest painted vessels of terra-cotta. Fea, who has had one of these fragments en- graved (Tom. III. p. 5), likewise recognizes their similarity to the paintings on the most ancient Greek vases, and conjectures that they might possibly be copies from better originals, — a point which we are not willing to decide. I have also to notice, that a small work, under the title, *Bassi Rilievi Volsci in Terra Cotta* (1785, fol), has been pub- lished, with colored engravings, for the purpose of explaining the monu- ments, looked upon as Volscian works, which are at present in the Borgia museum at Velletri. — GERM. ED.

2. Not the whole camp, but a space set apart, in the middle of the camp, was, not surrounded, but covered, like a tent, with linen cloths, over the dimensions stated. One legion, consisting of sixteen thousand men, was termed *linteata*, not because they were dressed in linen, but because each individual of it was required to take a solemn oath of fidelity in this place covered with linen cloths. — F.

3. I will remark here, that five Greek inscriptions were afterwards discovered on a beautiful vase in the Grand-Ducal cabinet at Florence, — an engraving of which was published by Dempster (*Etrur. Regal.*, tab. 62, 63), and also by Passeri (*Pict. Etrusc.*, Tom. I tab. 58, 59), — after it had been cleansed by washing.

Of these inscriptions, or rather superscriptions, of some figures painted around the upper part of the vase, Visconti (*Mus. Pio-Clem.*, Tom. II. p. 62, not. b) has given a learned explanation, and has also introduced into a supplementary plate a copy of the vase itself and of its pictures. We must however remark, that, at the time when there was still a strong belief in the Etruscan origin of the painted vases, they seem to have been studied only in a hasty manner. But since they have come into increased esteem as works of art, — and great numbers of them have been recently discovered, and more interest generally has been awakened in regard to such monuments, — so many of them with Greek inscriptions have also become known, that they are hardly to be classed any longer among antiquarian rarities. Indeed, it would hardly be possible to find a considerable collection of vases which could not show one or more with a Greek inscription. — GERM. ED.

4. Fea, who does not willingly let an opportunity pass of defending against Winckelmann the Etruscans and those who have written in their favor, here again quotes Guarnacci (*Orig. Ital.*, Tom. II. lib. 7, cap. 1, p. 305), who says : "A part of these vases were collected by Cardinal Gualtieri himself, but the larger portion were a gift to him from Signore Bargagli, at that time Bishop of Chiusi, the place in which they were found." We are unable, indeed, to determine how much credit may or may not be given to the statement of Guarnacci in regard to the Gualtieri vases, — which afterwards went into the Vatican Library, — to the prejudice of what Winckelmann asserts concerning them. We must, however, admit that the ocular evidence is very much in Winckelmann's favor. For in the Vatican collection just mentioned there are found, with the exception of the vase to be seen in Passeri (*Pict. Etrusc.*, Tom. III. not. 297), on which is a hovering, black, winged Genius, only a very few painted vases which could really pass for Etruscan, or which visibly differ from those which are brought from Naples and are of Greek workmanship. — GERM. ED.

5. As the author has made mention of all large collections which were in existence at his time, or were known to him, it seems proper that we should present a brief notice of the collections, known to us which were either formed in his time, but had escaped his observation, or which have been brought together since. We will, however, make the preliminary remark, that the Hamilton Collection mentioned by Winckelmann, and published by D'Hancarville, was transferred by its owner to the British Museum, for the sum of eight thousand pounds.

Mr. Hamilton afterwards made at Naples a new and still more con-

siderable collection of painted vases, of which drawings were executed
under W. Tischbein's supervision, and explanations furnished by the
Chevalier Italinsky. The work was published in four folio volumes.
This collection also was destined for England; but a portion of it was
lost by shipwreck; the remainder was sold in London, for forty-five hundred guineas, to Mr. Hope, who is said to be the possessor of more than
fifteen hundred such vases.

In Naples there were formerly two collections, which probably still
exist. One of them is the royal collection, quite considerable both for
the number and size of the vases. It was, at one time, arranged in a
special room in the Gallery at Capo di Monte. The other belongs to the
Vivengio family, at Nola, and may amount to about three hundred good
pieces, all of which were found about the city named.

The Museum of the Institute at Bologna possesses a number of painted
vases, several of which are good.

According to Millin's account in the *Musée des Arts*, there are in
France fifty very admirable vases, and an equal number in the manufac-
tory of porcelain at Sévres. The same antiquarian gives, in the work
cited, a more circumstantial account of a collection belonging to M. de
Parois, which contains more than five hundred pieces; he has also furnished engravings and explanations of several remarkable pieces in it.
(*Monumens Antiq. Ined.*) Frequent mention is made of a collection,
probably of considerable size, which was formed at Malmaison by the
Empress Josephine; and in Millin's *Peintures de Vases Antiques* are copies
of several beautiful vases which it contained.

Germany cannot boast of any great wealth in painted ancient vases.
The sole large collection is that of Count Lamberg, in Vienna, which
he formed when he was Austrian Ambassador at Naples, in 1780. In
the Museum of Antiques at Dresden a few of such painted vases are to
be found, and among them three or four with remarkable representations. A few, also, are preserved in the ducal library at Weimar,
which were brought from Italy by the late Duchess Amelia. Among
them, however, there is only one deserving of notice, on which is a picture of the rape of Cassandra. — GERM. ED.

6. D'Hancarville, on the contrary, believes that the small vases were
not playthings merely, but that they were sacred utensils in the Lararia
or house-chapels of the ancients, as the larger vases were in the public
temples. — F.

7. In a hall of the Studii at Naples is found the vase of Vivengio,
as it is called, which represents the misfortunes of the family of Priam.
It is of extraordinary beauty of form, ornament, and painting. It
was found enclosed in another earthen vessel of coarser quality. —
GERM. ED.

8. *Nem.* 10, *Epod.* β, v. 68, Ἐν ἀγγέων ἕρκεσιν παμποικίλοις, *In cases,
painted of various colors, for containing vases*, to which the Scholiast adds,
in an explanatory manner, ἐξωγράφηντο γὰρ αἱ ὑδρίαι, *for the water-pitchers
were painted with figures.* — W.

These Greek words are very much distorted in the Vienna edition
and in the French translation of 1802. The passage itself has been
misunderstood even by the Scholiast. The poet is speaking of a vessel
of baked clay, filled with oil, in an artistically-wrought brazen case. — S.

9. D'Hancarville maintains that the large, beautiful, and painted vases were votive offerings, hung up in the temples, and there serving as ornaments. The objection to this is, that all the vases, without any exception, have been taken from tombs; and it is difficult to conceive how they could come there from the temples. The conjecture proposed by more modern inquirers is, that they were given to youths as memorials, when they put on the manly robe and were initiated into the mysteries of Bacchus, and were afterwards deposited in their tombs. This supposition is certainly a more acceptable one. — GERM. ED.

10. Many trials have been made, and many mixtures proposed, to imitate the blackish-brown color with which the ancient vases are painted. The arts of fabrication, however, are precisely the point in which we are superior to the ancients. But their whole life was penetrated by art and taste; and in the most trifling monuments, beauty and grace unite in the most pleasing manner with appropriateness. In short, an animating breath has been breathed by art into everything which originates from refined antiquity. Herein is the deficiency of our time; let us seek to supply it. — GERM. ED.

11. To vases painted with several colors, the delicate, variegated colors were not applied until the vase had been once baked. This is the reason why they have not usually united firmly with the clay, for they fall off easily in scales, or can be scratched off. — A.

12. A rogue named Pietro Fondi succeeded in counterfeiting these vessels. He resided generally at Venice and Corfu; many pieces of his workmanship remain in Italy, but most of them have gone to foreign countries. This is the same man of whom Apostolo Zeno speaks in one of his letters. (*Lettere*, Vol. III. p. 199.) The deception is, however, easily discovered, even by those who have no great knowledge of drawing; the clay used in them is coarse, and the vases are consequently heavy. On the other hand, the vases of the ancients are made of an uncommonly pure clay, and their smoothness seems as if it were blown upon them; in the others, the contrary is the case. — W.

In the *Notes to the History of Art*, the following memorandum occurs: —

"I have seen some few of the modern counterfeits of this kind among the genuine vases of Count Simonetti in Rome, which were likewise collected in Nola. The vases are either ancient in themselves, the deception being confined solely to the figures on them, which are produced by rubbing off the antique black polish, in which case they have a yellowish color, the color of the baked clay itself; or they are entirely new and painted with oil-colors; the latter kind is also distinguishable by its weight in comparison with the lightness of the antique. If a person has no chance to make the comparison, then the drawing of the figures affords in each case an accurate means of distinction. On one of the vases mentioned is introduced a Chinese figure with a halberd in its hand; and on another, a narrow cloth is thrown about the belly of a male figure, after the manner of more modern pictures. — W.

The Vasari family at Arezzo, and other manufacturers in Italy and England, had counterfeited such vases. In the Grand Ducal collection of painted vases, in Florence, some imitations by the former may be found. (Lanzi, *Giornale de' Letterati*, Tom. XLVII. Art. 1, p. 166.) — F.

13. Plaut. *Pœn.*, Act 5, Sc. 5, v. 34. Quintil., lib. 1, cap. 5. — It was a shaggy garment, worn by the ancient Etruscans, Sardinians, and other nations. (Dempster, *De Etruria Regali*, Tom. I. lib. 3, cap. 54.) — F.

14. The marble of Luna, also called the Ligustic (Serv. *ad Æn.*, lib. 8, v. 720), surpassed the most beautiful kinds of white Greek marble in whiteness at least, if not in hardness. (Plin., lib. 36, cap. 5, sect. 4.) Nevertheless, no Etruscan work of the more ancient style has been found, made of this marble; hence it might be inferred with probability, that it was unknown to the ancient Etruscans, whatever Fea may object to the inference, and however little his explanation may agree with Pliny's use of language (loc. cit.). Mention is made by Pliny (lib. 36, cap. 6, sect. 7) and by Strabo (lib. 5, p. 349) of this same marble.

Among the many buildings in Rome constructed of this marble, the temple of Apollo, erected by Augustus on the Palatine Hill, was specially pre-eminent. (Serv. *ad Æn.*, lib. 8, v. 720.) — GERM. ED.

BOOK IV.

CHAPTER I.

1. THE priest of a youthful Jupiter at Ægæ, the priest of the Ismenian Apollo, and he who led the procession in honor of Mercury, at Tanagra, with a lamb on his shoulder, were all young men who had gained the prize of beauty. The city of Egesta, in Sicily, erected to a certain Philip, — who was a citizen, not of that place, but of Crotona, — merely on account of his exceeding beauty, a tomb, as to a deified hero, on which sacrifices were offered to him. — W.

The enthusiasm with which the youth and beauty of the bloom of life were extolled by the Greeks might be shown from many passages of the ancient writers, especially Plato. Instead of all of them, we will quote only a single passage from Xenophon (*Sympos.*, cap. 4, § 11), which he puts into the mouth of Critobulus: — Ὄμνυμι πάντας θεούς, μὴ ἑλέσθαι ἂν τὴν βασιλέως ἀρχὴν ἀντὶ τοῦ καλὸς εἶναι. "I swear, by all the gods, that I would not choose the power of the [Persian] king in preference to beauty." — GERM. ED.

2. Called καλλιστεῖα. — W.

3. The inhabitants of the Lipari islands erected, at Delphos, as many statues to Apollo as they had taken vessels from the Etruscans. (Pausan., lib. 10, cap. 16.) — W.

4. Pausanias (lib. 6, cap. 8) relates this of Eubotas of Cyrene, to whom the oracle of Jupiter Ammon had predicted victory — F.

5. Only occasional mention is made of slingers. (Thucyd., lib. 4, cap. 32; Euripides, *Phœnissæ*, v. 2149.) — W.

6. Gedoyn, in this opinion, thinks he has distinguished himself above the common crowd of writers. (*Histoire de Phidias, Acad. des Inscrip.*, Tom. IX., *Mém.*, p. 199.) A superficial English writer (Nixon, *Essay on*

Sleeping Cupids), notwithstanding he had visited Rome, follows him in it. — W.

7. Namely, the Lesche, " a place in Sparta, as in most Greek cities, appropriated to social meetings for the purpose of conversation." (Pausan., lib. 10, cap. 25.) — The painting at Delphos represented the taking of Troy, as I find in an ancient manuscript scholium upon the Gorgias of Plato, which has preserved the inscription on it, as follows : —

Γράψε Πολύγνωτος, Θάσιος γένος, Ἀγλαοφῶντος
Υἱός, περθομένην Ἰλίου ἀκρόπολιν.

" Polygnotus, a Thasian by birth, son of Aglaophon, painted the destruction of the citadel of Troy." — W.

8. Winckelmann can have read the words of Juvenal, *lances Parthenio factas*, only in the catalogue of Junius. For, if he had looked into Juvenal, he would not have allowed himself to be misled by the ambiguity of the word *lanx ;* but would have immediately perceived, from the connection, that the poet did not mean the basins or scales of a balance, but plates and bowls. Juvenal commends Catullus, because, in a dangerous storm at sea, he had imitated the beaver, by throwing into the sea his most valuable articles, that he and the ship might not sink together. He says that, among these silver dishes for the table, there were also plates with embossed work, executed by Parthenius. Parthenius, says the ancient scholiast, *cælatoris nomen*, is the name of a carver in relief. — L.

9. Polybius, lib. 4. Lessing censures Winckelmann, as if there were nothing in this passage to confirm his assertions. But the censure is unjust ; for the testimony of the historian verifies Winckelmann's quotation. — Thespiæ, Olympia, Cos, and Cnidos, also, together with many cities and islands, were especially famed for their statues. — GERM. ED.

10. He was called " the Shadow-painter," σκιαγράφος (Hesychius, σκιογράφος). The reason of the appellation is therefore obvious. Hesychius, who has taken σκιογράφος for σκηνογράφος, that is, " the Tent-painter," is to be emended. (Hesych., *ex edit. Alberti*, Tom. II. p. 1209.) — W.

It should be remarked that the term σκηνογράφος, here rendered " Tent-painter," (Germ. *Zelt-Maler,*) signifies more properly " Scene-painter." By the epithet " Shadow-painter," σκιογράφος, applied to Apollodorus, is to be understood a painter in chiaroscuro, or light and shade. — TR.

11. Μηδὲν ἐν προσευχαῖς ὑπὲρ αὐτοῦ [Καίσαρος], μὴ ἄγαλμα, μὴ ξόανον, μὴ γραφὴν ἱδρυσάμενοι, " Placing nothing in honor of him [the emperor] in the oratories, — neither polished statue, nor rude image, nor picture." (Philo, *de Virt. et Legat. ad Caium.*) — GERM. ED.

12. An entertainment to the gods, in which their images were laid upon couches, and meats served to them in public. — TR.

CHAPTER II.

1. W<small>HEN</small> many statues were collected together, they were distinguished by numbers, probably in reference to the place which they occupied in the row. This at least may be inferred from the Greek letter *H,* engraved on the socle of the statue of a Faun, in the palace Altieri. It was, therefore, the seventh in the range. As the same letter was cut on a bust of which a Greek inscription makes mention, it is to be inferred that this bust was the seventh of those formerly set up in the temple of Serapis. For the same reason, the letter *N,* engraved on the shaft that serves as a support to the Amazon of Sosicles, in the Capitoline museum, denotes that it was the thirteenth in some former collection. — F.

2. To many of our readers the remarks of Winckelmann upon Michael Angelo and Bernini may seem harsh, perhaps unjust. He was not, in fact, particularly partial to either, as it appears from other passages; we must, however, take into consideration the stand from which he contemplated the style of these masters. He does not judge these celebrated artists, in the least degree, according to the standard of modern art, — much less does he wish to decide what rank they are to take in the list of modern artists, — but he compares what they have done with the highest idea of beautiful form derived from the masterpieces of antiquity; and in this respect, he is right beyond dispute. Wholly in the same sense, and with precisely such a special reference to beauty of form, is also to be understood a well-known *bon-mot* of Nicholas Poussin, who is said to have remarked of Raphael, — "Compared with the moderns, he is an angel; but with the ancients, an ass." — G<small>ERM.</small> E<small>D.</small>

3. There were, at one time, two well-executed heads, of basalt, in the villa Albani. The more beautiful one, of which Winckelmann speaks, was formerly named Cleopatra, and afterwards Berenice. It possesses noble and very regular features, and is, in every respect, an exquisite work of art. The nose is a modern restoration. — The second head is not equal to the first, either in beauty of features or in skilful execution. At first, it was called Berenice, but afterwards Lucilla. The nose and chin are repaired. — G<small>ERM.</small> E<small>D.</small>

4. Let no one be induced by the passage in the text to think of portrait-likeness, — of which Winckelmann certainly did not intend to speak (see section 33 of this chapter), — since he would, in such case, entirely mistake the genius of ancient art. When the ancient authors, in speaking of Phryne, Lais, and other celebrated women whose favors were venal, mention that great artists modelled their masterpieces after them, they did not, by any means, intend to be understood that portraits of them were actually made, that is to say, that the individual parts of their shape and features were copied, but — even though the passages should express ever so clearly another meaning — that these beautiful persons supplied the great artists, in the conception of their ideal conformations, as of Venus, for example, with an outward occasion, and probably, in the execution of their figures, served them as models. If the abso-

lute ideal invented by each artist, and standing in a perfect state before his mental vision, had not always predominated over every thing external, then would the works of art neither have deserved, nor attained, the high celebrity which has fallen to their lot. Even though Phryne may have been faultlessly beautiful, and have shown herself ever so complaisant to Praxiteles, still the Venus of Cnidos was no portrait of her, because a likeness requires an imitation of the features of the individual, whereas ideal images exclude it. If, from the analogy of all ancient works of art still extant, we may, as we must, believe that the celebrated Venus of Cnidos, by Praxiteles, is an ideal image of the goddess, a general type of the highest feminine grace and beauty of form, we shall also be able to maintain, on indisputable grounds, that this image may, in some respect, have resembled every very beautiful woman; the most beautiful woman, indeed, who has ever lived, or will live, may have the greatest resemblance to that image; and, in so far as Phryne may have been extraordinarily beautiful, the ancients might believe, and say with truth, that the masterpiece of Praxiteles resembled her. But the intelligent, and connoisseurs, at least, did not understand by this expression a common portrait-likeness, as we clearly perceive from the circumstance, that Arellius, who lived shortly before Augustus (Plin, lib. 35, cap. 10, § 37), incurred the reproach of scandalous and blasphemous conduct, because the goddesses painted by him always resembled the courtesans in whom he happened, at the time, to be interested. — Germ. Ed.

5. Translators render the word σύνοφρυς by *junctis superciliis*, "joined eyebrows," as the connection in the text requires; but it might be translated "proud," according to the explanation of Hesychius. It is said, however (La Roque, *Mœurs et Cout. des Arabes*, p. 217), that the Arabians think eyebrows which meet beautiful. — W.

6. Not merely two, but four, such recumbent Hermaphrodites are in existence, or at least known. One, at Paris, which has been for a long time in France; a second, in the Florentine gallery, is the one mentioned by the author; a third, and the most celebrated, is that in the villa Borghese, near Rome, likewise noticed by the author; a fourth, and, as it seems to us, the best in execution, is in the palace Borghese, in Rome. Whether, as Visconti supposes, the celebrated Hermaphrodite of Polycletus, in bronze, mentioned by Pliny (lib. 34, cap. 8, § 19), may have been the original from which the four figures just named were copied in ancient times, we do not pretend to decide. It is possible, but still not capable of proof. On the contrary, we do not venture even to assert that either of the marbles in question may be an original work, although the two Borghese figures possess indisputably very many admirable qualities. If we consider them in respect of invention, and the predominating idea, there is scarcely one among all the antiques which could be named as possessing more excellences. The equivocal, undecided nature of the forms, wavering between male and female, between boy and maiden, is rendered with wonderful delicacy, and weighed, as it were, in the nicest balance.

It was the intention of the artist to represent this Hermaphrodite as sleeping, it is true, yet sleeping unquietly, and excited by voluptuous dreams. He is turned almost entirely over, and the undulating line of the body, occasioned by its position, lends to him an extraordinary charm, and denotes a style in art that had not only advanced to the extreme of refinement in search of the pleasing, but had, indeed, already strayed beyond it into the realms of voluptuousness. In so far as we may presume to draw an inference from these characteristics, as to the age when the work in question was executed, it could not well be earlier than after the time of Alexander the Great, when Greek rule, manners, and art prevailed in Asia.

Among the four repetitions, still extant, of this recumbent Hermaphrodite, the one first mentioned, which is said to have been retouched by a modern artist, has the least value as a work of art. It was disinterred at Velletri, and has been known a longer time than the others.

The forms of the Florentine Hermaphrodite are elegant, the contour soft and flowing, the flesh tender. Some few slight inaccuracies, however, are visible; and the handling, especially of the hair, also allows room for conjecture that it is a copy, executed in the time of the Roman emperors. He lies on the spread skin of a lion or tiger, the end of which is also wrapped about the left arm. This latter particular distinguishes the Florentine in some degree from the three other repetitions. — The nose is new; probably, also, both legs, the whole of the right thigh and half of the left, the socle, and the skin spread underneath. Accurate observers will probably find that the characteristics of the male sex are, in this figure, somewhat more modest, short, and quiet, than in the two Borghese statues; this is not, however, an original ancient variation, but merely an effect of the delicate scrupulousness of the artist by whom the restorations were made.

The celebrated figure in the villa Borghese deserves to be ranked before the Florentine, partly on account of its better preservation, and partly because the forms are, generally, even more flowing and elegant. Notwithstanding these admirable qualities in the execution, still there is observable about the mouth, eyes, and in other important points, a certain want of spirit, of living expression, which cannot be lacking in any truly original work, or at least not in one so perfect in conception as this. Although the Florentine Hermaphrodite is wrought from Greek marble, and this from Italian, still we should be inclined to regard the latter as the more ancient, judging from the indications of the handling. — The tip of the nose, four fingers of the left hand, the left foot as high as the small of the leg, a trifling portion of the drapery, and the mattress, — which passes for a masterpiece of its kind, — are new, and from the hand of the celebrated Lorenzo Bernini.

The fourth Hermaphrodite, in the gallery of the palace Borghese at Rome, appeared to us, after repeated examination, always more tender and fleshlike in execution, and the forms more lovely, and to melt more softly into one another, than is the case with the figure at the villa.

Besides these monuments, in which the idea of the Hermaphrodite is conceived in the finest poetical sense, and realized in a style of art that cannot be surpassed, there are several others, differing in position and action, yet representing the same subject. Of these, Winckelmann mentions a small upright figure in the villa Albani. We will notice only one other, exceedingly beautiful in its execution, which is kept locked up in a closet, in the villa Borghese, because the posture is somewhat bold. It is nearly of the size of life, stands bent a little backwards, and is covered with female drapery, the front part of which is lifted up by both hands. Nothing can be seen lovelier, smoother, rounder, and especially softer, than these features, these limbs. The face, it is true, has not a high character, — this would not be consistent with the rest, — but it is very pleasing, round, and lovely, full of passion and delight. The skill of the artist has enabled him to introduce about the cheeks and mouth a something which is not exactly vulgar, but yet has a touch of common humanity, — a trace of sensuality, — and even by this very means to enhance the fascination of his work. — The end of the nose, the greater portion of the head and hair, the right leg, the left foot, and the characteristics of the male sex, are modern.

This figure was originally intended for a niche, since the reverse side is very carelessly handled, or rather is only sketched. It is said to have been found not far from Mount Portio, on the place where one of the villas of Lucius Verus was probably situated; we do not intend, however, to intimate, by this remark, that we believe it to have been executed during the reign of this emperor. On the contrary, it has all the characteristics of a purely Grecian work of the later, effeminate style, and, moreover, the marble is Greek. — GERM. ED.

7. In the heads of Jupiter, the eyes are large and well opened, but not round; so that, in this respect, they resemble less closely the conformation of the lion than one might probably suppose from Winckelmann's words. (See Plates I. and II., two of the finest heads of Jupiter, in which the eyes, forehead, and frontal hair are represented.) — GERM. ED.

BOOK V.

CHAPTER I.

1. IT would be a fault in female figures with bared breasts, if the nipples, as an essential part of them, were not visible, that is to say, were not indicated at all. They are, however, always signified, and even made visible through the dress, in all antique figures, even those representing virgins. Yet, as in beautiful women, so also in beautiful youthful statues, they are neither large nor prominent, but, as it were, still immature for fulfilling the offices of maternity. — GERM. ED.

2. It is now in the Pio-Clement museum. Visconti believes either that the child in the arms of the goddess represents Mars, or that the monument, taken as a whole, is a symbol of Juno Lucina. — F.

3. Ancient art has transmitted to us Fauns of different characters, or, in other words, it has thought proper to present the ideal of them in different modes, and under forms more or less noble. The remark of Winckelmann is well grounded, that several statues and heads of young Fauns are of uncommon beauty, and apparently conceived and represented as though of divine origin, and relatives of Bacchus; for example,

the many similar young Fauns, noticed by him, standing at rest against the trunk of a tree, which pass for copies of the (so called) περιβόητος, " The Celebrated," of Praxiteles.

The beautiful young Faun, also, which, together with three antique repetitions of it, stands in the museum at Dresden, is equally pleasing, yet still more noble and divine, in its conception. (A profile of the head alone may be seen in Plate III., fig. A.) A fifth figure, resembling the Dresden statues, is in the villa Ludovisi, at Rome. The head in particular is extremely lovely, and well preserved. The young Faun blowing a flute — of which there are, likewise, numerous copies — is charmingly graceful, although the shape generally is somewhat less noble. There are two such figures in the Capitoline museum, and several in the villa Borghese, one of which is of surpassing excellence. Unsatisfactory engravings of this most beautiful figure may be found in Perrier (*Statue*, No 48), and in the *Sculture del Palazzo della Villa Borghese*. In the latter of these works the conjecture is offered, whether the celebrated Faun, painted by Protogenes, and bearing the epithet ἀναπαυόμενος, " The Reposing," might not have been the original of this monument in marble. Indeed, the many repetitions of it, and the skill and wisdom which prevail in the disposition of its parts, as well as the elegance and tenderness of the forms, place it beyond all doubt that it must have had for its original a work highly celebrated in antiquity. But we should not conjecture that original to have been a painting, unless the probability of this were based upon very peculiar circumstances.

The celebrated Silenus carrying the young Bacchus in his arms, in the villa Borghese, is also to be enumerated among the estimable, noble figures of the Bacchus family. — Note 9 will give further information in regard to this beautiful monument.

The Fauns which Winckelmann appears to designate properly by the epithet *Simi*, that is, flat-nosed, are conceived after a different and lower ideal. They have a broader and flatter face, eyes not deeply set, and, for the most part, a somewhat sunken nose with a thick tip; the mouth is proportionately wide, and the face usually distorted with laughter. Warts, like those which goats have, are often put under the jaw, near the neck. In other respects, their conformation is always vigorous and agile, though occasionally slender; and pervaded by strongly marked muscles and sinews, as required by their occupation of roaming through woods and fields. The first place among figures of this kind and character properly belongs to the celebrated sleeping Faun of the Barberini collection. The sleep in which he lies sunk after fatigue, and the relaxation of all the muscles of the limbs, are expressed in a manner which cannot be improved; it is, indeed, inimitable. We can almost hear the deep respiration, see how the wine swells the veins, how the excited pulses beat.

The second place belongs to the Faun playing the Scabellum,[1] in the Tribune at Florence. Not only do the faultless harmony throughout, and the highly naive simplicity in the gesture, and in the keeping of all the parts, challenge our admiration, satisfy the requirements of the understanding, and perfectly accomplish the object in view, but this

[1] A kind of musical instrument which was played by the pressure of the foot ; it always gave the same tone. — Tr.

figure, like the Barberini sleeping Faun, just mentioned, delights also the feelings themselves, as a bright, glorious image of nature unrestrained. It is, moreover, one of the most learned figures, or, to speak more correctly, one of those in which we see a masterly display of anatomical skill, profound knowledge of the action of the muscles, and of the manner in which the will affects them previously to the moment of action. The foot, which is about to press the Scabellum, with the sole attached, is raised; the tendons which move the toes are in a state of the most forcible contraction; but he is impatient to hear the sound; hence the calf of the leg already begins to swell, and the great back cord of the leg is becoming tense for a downward blow. — The head is modern, yet very good, full of expression, and in harmony with the whole; also both arms, a considerable piece of the left heel, and all the toes of the right foot. These restorations are all from the hand of one artist, said to be Michael Angelo.

An excellent figure, almost as large as life, in the Capitoline museum, also belongs from its character to this same lower class of the Faun-ideal. It is carrying fruits in a skin by which it is girt. (A profile-likeness of the head may be seen in Plate III., fig. B.) The naïve expression of joyousness, which gives life, as it were, to this admirable work of art, delights the spectator. It is, besides, one of the best-preserved figures; for even the right hand, which is raised and holding forth an apple, is antique, with the exception of the fingers. On the head, only the tip of the nose is somewhat injured. A couple of toes on each foot, and other trifling parts are modern restorations.

In this second class, or inferior Faun-ideal, are to be included the bald, flat-nosed Sileni, with large, and occasionally hairy, belly and thighs, and also somewhat short proportions. Good standing figures of this kind are to be found in the Pio-Clement museum, at the entrance of the palace Lanti, in the gallery Giustiniani, and in the museum at Dresden.[1]

The sinking Silenus, supported by a Faun, on the great Borghese vase, and another, which might be named " The Reeling," upheld by two Fauns, on the beautiful bas-relief in the Pio-Clement museum, belong here, although they seem to be more noble in form, and to constitute a class intermediate between those just mentioned and the beautiful Borghese Silenus holding the young Bacchus in his arms, to which reference has already been made.

Finally, there remains to be considered still a third class, and this the lowest of such ideal conformations, — namely, the long-horned and goat-footed, to which, in the language of art of the present day, the name of Satyr is usually and exclusively applied, although, anciently, the Greeks comprehended under this term all the kinds above named, without exception.

If we see the Fauns, so called, of the second class almost always represented in a state of mind excited by wine even to waggishness, excessive gayety, jumping, and dancing, so the ancient artist made use of the Goat-footed as the true Merry-Andrew. For this reason, we find on engraved gems, as well as in a Herculaneum painting, one of these mon-

[1] An engraving from a statue in the Pio-Clement museum may be seen in Plate V. — TR.

grels engaged in a butting contest with a real male goat. In the villa Borghese there is another, who is sitting down, and occupied with comic gravity in extracting a thorn from the foot of a robust Faun, who behaves himself in a manner quite unseemly. In the *Pio-Clement Museum* (Vol. I., Plate 50) may be found a group of a still lower character, though superior in execution, in which a Satyr, with lustful impatience, is striving to strip the dress from a struggling Nymph. When ancient art deviates still farther, into the representation of dubious or shameless subjects, it does, indeed, occasionally make use of the lower kind of Fauns, but more frequently of the Goat-figures. — GERM. ED.

4. This Satyr or Faun of Praxiteles was termed ὁ περιβόητος, The Praised. According to Pausanias (lib. 1, cap. 20) and Athenæus (*Deipnosoph.*, lib. 13, cap. 6), it was of bronze, aud was standing even in their time, that is, about A. D. 174, in the Tripod street, at Athens. Among the figures which pass for probable copies of this masterpiece, so celebrated in antiquity, the one which was carried from the Capitoline museum to Paris is, in respect to execution, the most valued. But, however beautiful it may be, still there are observable about it, as in most ancient copies, certain indications of haste and negligent handling. The drill has been much used, and, on more careful examination, errors are discoverable; for example, the retracted right foot is much shorter than it ought to be. — The nose, the back part of the head, and both fore-arms and hands are modern. — GERM. ED.

5. Winckelmann has given a wrong interpretation to the passage in Pausanias (lib. 2, cap. 13) from which he probably derived this statement. Pratinas and Aristias were not artists in marble and bronze, as Heyne first remarked, but two dramatic poets, who, like Æschylus, wrote satirical dramas also, σάτυροι, the chorus of which was composed of Satyrs. — GERM. ED.

6. *Lacinæ a cervice binæ dependentes* (Plin., lib. 8, cap. 50, sect. 76), " Two flaps pendent from the neck." They are visible on a beautiful young Faun sleeping on a rock, among the Herculaneum bronzes (*Antich. d' Ercolano*, Vol. VI., Plate 40), and in another plate (No. 42), which represents an elder Faun, or a Silenus, stretched out upon a skin. These pendants are still more clearly visible on a beautiful Faun of red marble, in the *Pio-Clement Museum* (Vol. I., Plate 47). — F.

7. It was found near the celebrated tomb of Cæcilia Metella, and belonged to the Institute at Bologna, where it was seen by Breval and Keissler, who make mention of it. — W.

The bust, not the head alone, of the Faun mentioned here, which belongs to the second class designated in Note 3, could hardly be equalled in regard to the industry bestowed upon the execution of it. All the parts are finished with the greatest accuracy; but, as the whole has been very smoothly polished, the reflected light from the surface produces a certain appearance of hardness, which is not favorable to the really admirable monument. It is, besides, in perfect preservation; only the right side of the face is a little stained with something green, probably from lying, whilst in the ground, in contact with bronze. For this reason the French term it *le Faune à la tache.* — GERM. ED.

8. Watelet, *Reflex. sur la Peinture*, p. 69. — GERM. ED.

9. The Borghese Silenus is, beyond question, the noblest of all the im-

ages of the instructor of Bacchus which have come down to us. It is one of those glorious, purely human representations which perfectly content the eye, the understanding, and the feelings. The invention, arrangement, purity of the outlines, and consummate elegance of the forms, equally demand praise and excite astonishment. From the workmanship generally, and from the hair in particular, we may infer that this work belongs to the most flourishing period of art. It may also be reckoned among those which have been admirably well preserved. — According to our observation, the left hand, and the fingers of the right hand, of Silenus, and several parts of the figure of the child, are modern. — It was found amid the ruins of the gardens of Sallust, at the same time with the large Borghese vase. — GERM. ED.

10. In regard to the statue from which this engraving is copied, Visconti (*Chiaramonti Mus.*, Vol. II., p. 29) remarks as follows: — " The ancient monuments still remaining which relate to Dionysius or Bacchus, and his numerous followers, usually divided into the various families of Satyrs, Fauns, Sileni, Pans, Mænades, &c., are so frequent, that they are to be found everywhere in museums, and as the ornaments of dwelling-houses, of gardens, and of villas. But images which represent the primitive Silenus, the instructor of Bacchus, are rare. Although the poets and writers of satires travesty him as old, very fat, and pot-bellied, resembling a wine-skin, deformed, as Lucian caricatures him, and as he is often represented on bas-reliefs, in the Bacchic scenes upon sarcophagi so common in museums, still the original character of Silenus is much more noble, since he is understood to have bred and educated Bacchus or Dionysius, in whom is personified the uncivilized state of the world, and its passsage from a rude to a more cultivated condition. He was the head, the leader, of that troop of old Satyrs who were called Sileni after him, and who accompanied Bacchus in his Indian campaign, which was undertaken for the purpose of civilizing the barbarians. The Orphic Hymns invoke him under the name of the bravest and best of the Sileni; the titles which they give him denote veneration; they pronounce him to be honored alike by gods and men. . . . . In the more ancient Theogony, Silenus was regarded as the depositary of science, which, in his capacity of instructor, he communicated to Bacchus, who made use of it to civilize mankind, still in a rude and savage state.

" This figure, which falsifies all the erroneous notions entertained of Silenus, shows him in his original character, as the foster-father and instructor of Bacchus. Now this latter, taken in a moral sense, is nothing more than a symbol of the refinement of the world from a state of barbarism, and the former is a symbol of the knowledge which had nurtured, guided, and assisted him.

" Like his foster-child, he is naked; his aspect is noble and affectionate, as suitable to the educator of a god, whom he holds in his arms and presses to his bosom. The child is caressing him in turn, and gracefully extends his hands to the other's cheeks. His head is bald; the goat-ears, — denoting an origin in common with the Satyrs and Panisci, and partaking of the bestial and the human, — and the Panther's skin, upon the left arm, are attributes which show that Silenus possesses two natures, a mortal and a divine, a material and an intellectual. His nose is flat, his face broad, and the expression composed of hilarity, benevolence, and

sagacity. The wreath of ivy-leaves and ivy-berries around the head of
each tells of the perpetual youth of Bacchus, and the strength and
sweetness of the bonds with which barbarism binds the minds of men.
— Tr.

11. Of this statue (*Pio-Clem. Mus.*, Vol. I., Plate 46) Visconti remarks
as follows : — " A distinction is commonly received among antiquarians
which assists them greatly in classifying the so much varied images of
the rustic deities who are the followers and companions of Bacchus.
Having observed them sometimes with the lower limbs goat-like, at other
times only with capriform ears, and again with tail and horns, now in
advanced life, and now in youth, they gave the name of Satyrs to those
which, in the expression of the countenance, in the hair, and the goat-
like haunches and legs, resembled the antique representations of the
god Pan. The term Faun they applied to those which are seen with
ears and tail alone, and sometimes with the rudiments of horns, but of
which the legs and thighs are wholly human ; if, however, they were not
of youthful or manly age, but in advanced or mature life, then they were
no longer termed Fauns, but Sileni. Some, with greater exactness,
have wished, indeed, to distinguish by different names the different
kinds of Fauns, — confining this appellation to those which, with a
human form, have the ears, horns, and tail of a goat, and calling by the
name of Tityri those rare figures of Bacchanals which have nothing of
the goat shape.

" The exactness of such authors certainly deserves some praise, since it
attempts to make different ideas correspond to different names, — which
does much to promote clearness ; but they seem to go too far, in seeking
to derive such a division — which can have no other object than the con-
venience of artists and antiquarian nomenclature — from the ideas of the
ancients, and in censuring, for want of precision, those classic writers
who have not observed it. In refutation of such an opinion, it is sufficient to reflect, that images are found, of Greek workmanship and of
remote antiquity, of all the diversified kinds of Bacchanals, although we
are certain that the Greeks never knew Fauns except by the name of
Satyrs or Sileni, which was applied indifferently to all the followers of
Bacchus. Still, however, even the Greeks sometimes distinguished the
individual characters of various deities of a similar kind, and perhaps
they knew no distinction more usual than that of Pan and Silenus. The
former was commonly figured in semi-capriform resemblance ; to the
latter were given a bald forehead, a flat nose, a long beard, a hairy breast,
and a short and corpulent person. In Pan they recognized one of the
most ancient divinities of Arcadia and of shepherds ; in Silenus, the
instructor, the companion, the general of Bacchus. All classic writers
agree in the characteristics noticed above, and no description is more
lively than that given of the two by Lucian, who refers to them, at the
head of the conquering army of India, in these words : — ' Under the
god, there were two generals ; one of them was a short, very fat, pot-
bellied, tremulous old man, with flat nose, and large, upright ears ; the
other, a monster man, from the middle downwards resembling a goat,
with hairy legs, horns, long beard, choleric,' &c. By these two portraits of Pan and Silenus, we can recognize them in the monuments ;
but in the sculptured images of the latter we find the very same variety

which we perceive in the authors who speak of him. Whilst some of them present him to us as a drinking, ridiculous old man, others describe him as a wise man, so far removed from hypocrisy, that he allows himself to be confounded with the class of voluptuaries, — who knows, however, the causes and ends of things, and whose breast is filled with a pure philosophy. This is the idea in regard to Silenus given in the sixth Eclogue of Virgil; and such must have been the idea of the Greek artist of the beautiful statue of the Pincian villa, in which this demigod is represented holding the infant Bacchus in his arms, and with features and limbs so noble in form, as to denote him to be a wise person, one to whom the education of a god might be intrusted. The sculptor of the marble before us has taken another view of Silenus, and represented him as the allegorical personage of intoxication. In the features of the face, and the shape of the limbs, he has adhered to the comic description by Lucian, with the exception of the ears, which in the image are not capriform. Though what the figure holds in its hand is a modern restoration, still there is no doubt as to the action of squeezing a bunch of grapes into a cup. — The perfection with which the skilful artist has expressed his conceit cannot be sufficiently comprehended by one who has not the marble itself before him. The head, which is crowned with the leaves and berries of the ivy, is of an admirable character, and the naturalness and fleshiness of the fat, hairy trunk is the utmost to which sculpture can attain." — Tr.

12. As Winckelmann does not particularly designate the head of Pan in the Capitoline museum, of which he makes mention here, it is doubtful whether he means a Hermes in the miscellaneous room, which formerly bore the name of Jupiter Ammon, or the Satyr-Mask, that is, merely the face without any back part, which probably still stands in the Capitoline museum, in the room of the great Vase. The latter is uncommonly beautiful, and executed with exquisite expression of character; it is, however, very much injured. The head of the (so called) Jupiter Ammon in the miscellaneous room is, indeed, also good, yet the execution of it is far from being so admirable. It has a noble character, approximating even to the majestic; together with the horns of a ram, and pointed ears. Winckelmann was probably induced to regard this monument as an image of Pan particularly by the hair, because it is curled over the forehead quite differently from that on the heads of Jupiter. — The nose is a restoration.

A statue of Pan of the size of life, in a sitting posture, and of pretty good workmanship, may be found in the villa Borghese. But the most admirable head of Pan is in the mansion Rondinini; it may even dispute superiority with the Capitoline Mask, just mentioned. — The nose and mouth, and also some locks of the beard and hair, are new.

Furthermore, there is a Pan's head, but little observed, in the garden of the villa Medici; it stands on a Hermes, in front of the pavilion in which formerly stood the Cleopatra, or properly Ariadne, now in Florence. The ideal character, that is, the mixture of human with goatish features, is clearly and admirably expressed. — Germ. Ed.

13. The knee, and also the legs towards the ankle, of the Apollino, so called, formerly in the villa Medici, but now in the Tribune at Florence,

are usually considered less beautiful than the rest of the figure. There may, perhaps, be some truth in the criticism, if it be viewed in detail, and not according to its general signification and effect as a whole. For our own part, however, we think very favorably of it, and, after repeated attentive examination, have never been able to detect those strikingly neglected portions by which the harmony of the whole is disturbed. Even if the legs near the ankle-joint do appear too much developed and too little youthful, it proceeds from the circumstance, that the figure was broken precisely in this place, and probably has been retouched, as the uneven outline leads one to infer.

In judging of this work, we must reflect that it is in the highest degree probable that it was executed in the time of Alexander's successors, and therefore in the later periods of Greek art, when artists began to aim at a general pleasing effect, rather than to produce the exact shape and perfect finish of each particular part. Hence, the idea of the head of this figure is certainly very beautiful, indeed lofty, in general; but still we are not always willing in this case, as we are, for example, in that of the Niobe and her two loveliest daughters, to follow closely the drawing of the forms into its details. It was neither the artist's intention to render every particular accurately, nor did so severe and punctilious treatment comport with the flowing softness of this later style. If such points are taken into consideration, each fresh view of the Apollino will reveal new beauties to every person competent to judge of art. The flow and soft undulation of the outlines is wonderful; the principal or middle line of the figure cannot possibly have more sweep, more that is elegant, noble, and fascinating. The leaning attitude, the position of one hand upon the head, as well as the supporting of the other, denote repose; but the spirit of the godlike youth is in action; lofty feelings are swelling his tender breast, and animating his beautiful countenance; he seems to be listening to the song of the Muses. — The hands, nose, and that part of the hair which is gathered in a net on the crown of the head, are modern. — The execution is masterly, although extremely delicate; on the feet we see the indications of a boldly handled chisel. Originally this figure was polished smoothly, and it still retains some lustre. — GERM. ED.

14. The idea of this Genius, especially of the head, really seems to have come from heaven. Nevertheless, even this head, although the most successful portion of the figure, shows very evident marks of being an antique copy. With all the beauty and pure proportion of the parts, still we discover, in the arrangement of the hair, a few sections of it which are quite stiff; and the use of the drill is visible about the mouth. Yet the gracefulness of the turn, the elegant sweep of the middle line, the nobleness and dignity of the whole shape, and the soft and flowing character of the forms, point to an original produced in the most flourishing period of Greek art. That this figure, however, is not itself an original, but a copy, is evident partly from the remarks already made in regard to the head, and partly from the fact that the other members also evince no really accurate knowledge flowing from the artist's own mind, but — if we may permit ourselves a harsh expression — they are executed with a superficial mechanical skill wholly inadequate to the lofty subject for which it was required.

A slight sketch of this monument is to be found in the second volume of the *Sculture del Palazzo della Villa Borghese*, Stanza IX., No. 11. In the explanation, (p. 94 of the same volume,) it is, moreover, asserted that the appellation of Genius is probably not correct, and that the work might very well be an imitation of the celebrated Thespian Cupid of Praxiteles, which, there is good reason to suppose, carried neither bow nor arrow.

It is our belief that there are modern additions to this figure, — namely, the left leg as far as the foot, both fore-arms, the tip of the nose, the larger portion of the wings, and also the upper part of the drapery, which is thrown over the trunk of a tree, against which the figure leans. The lower antique fragment of this drapery falls in very admirable folds. — GERM. ED.

15. This is the figure of which Flaminio Vacca (Montfauc., *Diario Ital.*, p. 193) speaks; he believes it to be an Apollo, but with wings. Montfaucon has had it engraved from a frightful drawing. (Montfauc., *Antiq. Expl.*, Tom. I., Plate 115, No. 6.) — W.

16. The Apollo in the rooms of the Conservatori is a beautifully executed half-figure without arms, which appears to represent the god in boyhood, and not larger than life. The hair is confined very elegantly on the crown of the head, and the eyeballs are denoted by a cavity. — GERM. ED.

17. Winckelmann's Works, Vol. III., p. 195, § 14. — GERM. ED.

18. This Group has been carried to Naples. — GERM. ED.

19. The Mercury with a well-preserved antique purse in the hand was set up in the palace of the villa Borghese after Winckelmann's time. It is a large, well-executed statue, and in a remarkable state of preservation; it does not, however, belong to the best class of images representing Mercury. To say nothing of the (so called) Belvedere Antinoüs, which Visconti has shown to be probably a Mercury, it is excelled by the seated Mercury, in bronze, from Herculaneum, and also by an erect statue, in marble, of the size of life, in the Florentine gallery. In the latter, the right leg is crossed over the left, one hand is placed on the side, and the other rests on the trunk of a tree. Although it has been broken into many fragments, still only the hands and fore-arms, and a piece of the right foot, appear to be modern. The features are pleasing and delicate, and the outlines of the whole figure very flowing.

The beautiful little statue in the *Pio-Clement Museum* (Vol. I., Plate 5) also merits mention in this place. It represents Mercury as a child, with the finger placed upon the mouth cunningly, as though he had just committed some little bit of roguery, and was begging the spectator to keep silence. There are several antique copies of this charming monument, one of which is in the villa Borghese, and still another is mentioned by Winckelmann.

But a head of Mercury, covered with the Petasus, or little hat, far excels in point of artistic merit all the monuments just enumerated. It is said to be no longer in Rome, but to have been sent to England. Casts and numerous copies have made it known in almost all cultivated countries. (See an outline in Plate VI.) — GERM. ED.

20. The celebrated seated statue of Mars in the villa Ludovisi is executed in a soft and pleasing manner in Greek marble. The position announces careless repose; the forms of the limbs are beautiful, yet

their beauty does not in the least detract from the expression of heroic strength. The head has a glorious, noble, appropriate character. On the left shoulder marks are visible, as if something had been broken off, — an appearance which suggests the inference, that originally another figure stood close to it. — The nose, and the right hand and foot, are modern restorations. Of the Cupid which sits at the feet of the god, the head, and also the arms and right foot, are new. — GERM. ED.

21. The candelabra here mentioned passed afterwards from the Barberini palace into the Pio-Clement museum. Drawings of them have frequently been made, but the best and most correct is to be found in the *Pio-Clement Museum*, Vol. IV., Plates 1–8. — GERM. ED.

22. Several modern antiquarians believe that they have discovered an image of the bearded Mars in the admirably executed colossal figure in the Capitoline museum, known under the name of Pyrrhus. Winckelmann, in the tenth book, eleventh chapter, conjectures that it may represent Agamemnon; and, in the same place, he also denies that a beard has been given to Mars, in any one instance, in works of ancient art.

In the villa Borghese stands a figure similar to the Capitoline, but smaller, the head of which, being lost, was restored by a copy from the latter. On the other hand, the antique legs of the former, with their armor, have been preserved, which in the Capitoline figure were wanting, and have been badly restored. On coins of the Bruttii and Mamertini are to be seen bearded heads, which also pass for images of Mars. — GERM. ED.

23. Visconti (*Pio-Clement Museum*, Vol. I., p. 62) considers the statue in the villa Pamfili, which is known by the name of Clodius, to be a young Hercules of this description in female garb. We, however, believe that this 'beautiful and rare monument represents the young Theseus or Achilles. But our object at present is not disputation, but to mention a few works of distinguished merit, which are veritable images of the youthful Hercules. We commence, as we ought, with a marble statue in the Florentine gallery, in which the hero, still as a child, is strangling the serpents that were about to wrap him in their folds. This work is somewhat larger than life, and, according to our feeling, there is no one which displays the wonderful art of the ancients in the conformation of ideal, or, to speak more correctly, of idealized shapes, more strikingly, gloriously, and grandly than this.

In this child, who, resting upon his knees, seems to be merely sporting with the serpents, we already see the germ of the future hero, the powerful, indefatigable, invincible hero. The whole figure is so excellent, that every thing in it deserves praise and high esteem, and no one part goes beyond or falls behind the others in congruity or fineness of shape. Still, however, the Herculean forehead, chest, and ribs, the powerful hips, and also the left knee, seem to be positively exquisite, indeed, wonderfully successful. — The right leg and half of the thigh, the tip of the nose, and the right ear, are modern restorations.

Another serpent-throttling little Hercules, differing, however, in attitude from the Florentine Hercules just described, and undoubtedly of later workmanship, exists among the antiquities of the villa Borghese. — Another figure, in this same collection, which is pronounced a young Hercules, we should be inclined to regard as a restored Cupid, with the spoils of Hercules. — On the celebrated beryl, engraved in intaglio by Cneius (ΓΝΑΙΟC), in the Strozzi collection of gems, the hero is represented at the age of adolescence. — A few years ago, there was found in the villa Aldobrandini, near Rome, the head of a young Hercules, beautifully wrought in marble, of the size of life, and crowned with grape-leaves. The eyes and mouth have an expression of joyousness; the cheeks are of moderate fulness; and the ears approximate in shape to those which are considered characteristic of the Pancratiasts; and yet — which seems to us remarkable — they have not wholly the character of such an ear, but merely the commencement of it, or a tendency to it. — The artist by whom the nose was awkwardly restored may also have worked off something from the damaged chin, and from the under lip; hence these parts, although properly not new, contrast ill with the others. — GERM. ED.

24. Among the monuments of ancient art, there have been preserved not only many images of Bacchus, but also some few of high perfection. In our judgment, the upright figure of him, in the garden-building at the entrance of the villa Ludovisi, near Rome, is one of the most beautiful. The noble forms of the body flow into one another with incomparable softness and grace, like gentle waves of bland oil, and the eye of the beholder glides over them, back and forth, with insatiable delight. — The head, which may not, indeed, be the original head belonging to the statue, has a frightful modern nose, and in other respects is by no means excellent. The left knee is modern, and so also appear to be both arms. — Visconti (*Mus. Pio-Clement*, Vol. IV., p. 99) believes that the little winged heads, which, as buckles or latchets, adorn the shoe-straps on the feet of this statue, denote Acratus.

Of equal beauty with this monument is the glorious torso of another statue of the god, which may be found engraved and explained in the *Mus. Pio-Clement.*, Vol. II., Plate 28, with the accompanying remark, that it was valued very highly by Mengs.

The gallery of antiques at Paris contains a statue corresponding to the torso just mentioned, which, it is said, is admirably executed, and also well preserved.

Omitting other beautiful images of Bacchus which adorn different museums, we will mention further only a torso of a seated figure, larger than life, and of exceeding beauty and art, which was formerly an admired object among the Farnese antiquities, but will now be found in Naples. — GERM. ED.

25. Among the most exquisite detached heads of Bacchus, we do not hesitate to assign the first place to that wonderful work of art, known by the name of the Capitoline Ariadne. Winckelmann was the first to relinquish this appellation, thinking that he recognized in it a Leucothea, from the band on the forehead. His reasons for this supposition were properly disputed by Visconti. The monument then passed among antiquarians, almost universally, for the most beautiful of the heads of Bacchus, and as such it was removed to Paris. The original name, however, appears to have again become gradually the favorite. Modern French works which treat of antiquities refer to it anew as Ariadne. We acknowledge ourselves, however, particularly inclined to the opinion that it is a head of Bacchus; for, as our readers will have learned from

the text, the equivocal character of the conformation, wavering between male and female, is in part conformable to the ideal character of Bacchus, and in part belongs to the modern restorations, — namely, a considerable piece of the nose, the under lip, and the upper part of the breast, — which were made under the conviction that the head was female. In regard, however, to this truly wonderful monument, we may still be permitted to remark, that there are few others in which the extreme subtilty with which the idea is conceived is carried out so consummately in execution. Although the forms are uncommonly delicate, they are not, on this account, any the less large; and the execution, with extraordinary softness, is still very decided. In a word, if we were to choose among all the collected works of Greek sculpture, we should be unable to select one more exquisite in itself than this, and more worthy of the most brilliant period of art, and, moreover, of the most celebrated masters of this period. (Plate IX., an outline of the head of this statue.) [1]

In the miscellaneous room of the Capitoline museum another head of Bacchus is to be found, which is little inferior in excellence of execution to the one just mentioned, the Ariadne, as it is called; like the latter, it has a fillet round the forehead. — The nose is modern; cheek and neck injured; eyes excavated, perhaps for the purpose of being filled with some other substance.

A second head of Bacchus, in the same place, has a lofty character. The tip of the nose, the chin, and the neck are restorations. — A third, and smaller one, in the same place, also with a fillet round the forehead, has always been acknowledged as a Bacchus, and very much prized on account of its pleasing features, although the execution does not indicate the best age of art; for the hair is deeply hollowed by the drill, the ears are placed much too low, the left eye is turned a little obliquely upwards, and is also a little smaller than the other. As the eyes, however, are in other respects of pleasing shape, and may be regarded as characteristic, in reference to the Bacchus-ideal, an engraving of them is given in Plate X., fig. B, B.

In conclusion, we will mention a fourth head of Bacchus in the same collection. It stands in a gallery in front of the chambers, on a high column, and for this reason is rarely observed. It is larger than life, and crowned with ivy. The locks of hair, falling down somewhat over the forehead, — which is in itself of a very noble character, — point out to our recognition the son of Jupiter. Love and joyousness look forth from the oblong and narrow eyes; the mouth seems to open for pleasure, for enjoyment; the plump cheeks denote a cheerful state of comfort, and are delicately rounded.

The execution of this monument shows an industry quite remarkable, and the handling is in a style wholly peculiar to itself; for the hair, the eyelids, &c., are deeply hollowed underneath, for the purpose of obtaining stronger shadows, and, thereby, greater distinctness when the head is viewed at a distance. — The restorations consist of a few locks of hair, and the larger portion of the nose; the lips also have suffered much. — GERM. ED.

26. The Hermes of a bearded or Indian Bacchus, mentioned in the

---

[1] See frontispiece. — TR.

text as belonging to the sculptor Cavaceppi, is no longer in Rome. But there is no lack of beautiful heads of the kind, in different museums. Of the entire figures of this Bacchus, the most beautiful, without doubt, is the one which is called by the name of Sardanapalus. (*Mus. Pio-Clement*, Vol. I., Plate 41.) A half-figure, not remarkable for much merit, is still to be found in the Vatican museum. We will, moreover, mention in this place the meritorious head of a bearded Bacchus on coins of Thasus; and as the Bacchus-ideal is very clearly expressed in it, we have thought proper to introduce an enlarged outline of it. (Plate X., fig. A.)

The shape, as well as the workmanship, of this head displays a style which is noble, grand indeed, and at the same time severe, — leading us to infer that it is a copy from a glorious temple-statue of the high style; and the same characteristics justify us in ascribing to the coin, without hesitation, a higher antiquity than appears to belong to the Sardana-palus, as it is called, and to the many bearded heads similar to it, that were formerly known by the name of Plato, but which are now acknowledged, all of them, to be images of the Indian Bacchus.— GERM. ED.

27. The difference in the images of Hercules, pertinently noticed by Winckelmann, demands especial attention, for it furnishes a key whereby we may obtain a clear insight into the seeming mystery of the conformation of this hero, especially in the celebrated Farnese statue, and also in some heads engraved on gems.

We are obliged, indeed, to assume two, essentially different, ideal conformations of Hercules. The one which represents him in the career of his exploits and his labors does not aim to ennoble him, but merely to express the extreme measure of the capacity of physical strength and action which can be exhibited in the human shape. As such a design was not to be accomplished in any other way than by an exaggeration of the usual lineaments and forms, art created the powerful bull-neck, the strong, broad shoulders, the firmly interlocking attachments of the massy muscles: neither did it neglect the full projecting sinews and veins;— the former being requisite to denote strength generally; the latter, to indicate exertions either actual or past. This is the class of images or ideals of Hercules, considered in his human condition, of which the Farnese statue may be regarded as the universal representative.

The other ideal conformation, of higher conception, aims to present Hercules in a perfect, deified state. He has achieved the deeds which prepared for him the way to Olympus; he is raised above all earthly needs; he enjoys a blissful repose, and is even a beneficent deity.

We now clearly comprehend what a great difference of shape the admirable art of the Greeks could and must give to an image designed on this principle, in contradistinction to the other; how much more noble, pleasing, mild, and beautiful it must have been. These considerations lead, also, to the conclusion, that the torso which stood in the Belvedere of the Vatican is to be regarded as the principal monument of the nobler ideal of Hercules. Here we anticipate the objection, that many statues, as well as rilievi, represent the hero under the nobler image, notwithstanding he is engaged in the performance of his exploits. We might, perhaps, evade this objection by replying, that even the ancients have not always understood the spirit of ancient art and of its greatest masters, for from this very cause originated the degeneracy of taste and the decline of art. But the circumstance can be explained satisfactorily in yet another way. It is susceptible of proof, that the nobler ideal of Hercules was invented and perfected at an earlier date than that according to which the hero is represented in the Farnese statue and some other monuments. The latter, indeed, was not generally adopted before the age of Lysippus, and, although completed, appears never to have attained a legitimate authority, since the images of this second class vary, in respect to the features of the face, far more than those of the first. The fundamental idea, however, remains always the same. Now if in many works of a later age we see the nobler, or, if I may so express myself, the divine, shape of Hercules predominant, — even in images representing him in the performance of his labors, — such monuments are either to be viewed as imitations of more ancient works, or, as we have reason to believe, owe their origin to a misunderstanding of the conception.

The most beautiful of the heads of Hercules of the nobler kind still extant, larger than life, and representing the hero at the age of manhood, we know only from casts, which are frequently seen in Rome, as well as in collections elsewhere. The marble is said to have gone to England. The fragment of another, still larger, head of Hercules, admirably executed, stands in the smaller garden-palace of the villa Ludovisi, at Rome. The mouth, beard, ears, and back part of the head have been preserved; the forehead, nose, and eyes, on the other hand, are modern restorations.

It cannot escape attentive observers, that many images of Hercules, even of the nobler kind, have the swollen Pancratiast ears, — which, properly, does not appear to be consistent with the deified condition of the hero. But such ears are given to him, beyond doubt, merely with an allegorical signification, as the tutelary god of the arena.

In order to give the reader some idea of what has been said of the ideal conformation of Hercules, we shall present, in Plate VII., Letter A, an engraving of the forehead, together with the arrangement of the hair, of that glorious head mentioned above as having been carried to England; under letter B, in the same plate, the profile of another noble Hercules, after a beautiful Greek coin; and in Plate VIII., Letter A, the head of the Hercules Farnese. — GERM. ED.

28. In this passage, in which Winckelmann ascribes to the images of Jupiter a uniform look of serenity, as a characteristic expression, he appears to have thought principally of two heads only, to be mentioned hereafter, and others similar to them, which were probably copied from the great masterpiece of Phidias, at Olympia, if not immediately and exactly, still with sufficient fidelity to make us acquainted, generally at least, with the idea, the spirit, and the features of it.[1] It is, however, more than probable that there may have been deviations, — not deviations from the shape, which, having been once accepted, had become, as it were, a legal standard, — but variations in expression; and Visconti's remark, provided it is not extended beyond the limits of the conditions

[1] Plate II. — TR.

specified, appears to be very correct, — that the epithets applied to Jupiter, as μειλίχιος, " the Gracious," *ultor,* " the Avenger," *tonans,* " the Thunderer," ὅρκιος, " the Guardian of Oaths," and equally also a passage in Pausanias (lib. 6, cap. 24), justify the inference that a difference of expression conforming to these epithets existed in the several images of the god to which they were applied.

Among the statues of Jupiter still in existence, the large seated figure, formerly in the mansion of the Verospi, but now in the museum of the Vatican, is perhaps one of the most excellent. Among the busts and single heads, the colossal one which was found in the excavations at Otricoli is the most valued. Visconti asserts that it is the largest of all the heads of Jupiter now in existence. But he is certainly in error; for there is to be found in the Florentine gallery a similar head, just as large, and also in as good, perhaps in even a still better, state of preservation; a kind, lofty, glorious being; noble, serene, and grand beyond all imagination, especially when viewed in profile. The gentle inclination of the head to the right side gives him an uncommon still grace, and becoming mildness. The hair and beard, which are very elegantly arranged, encircle the god-like face with clustering curls. — The nose is new; also some small portions of the hair and breast.

Another head of Jupiter, considerably larger, but much injured, formerly stood outside, and near, the palace of the villa Medici. It was removed thence to Florence, and now adorns the garden Boboli. (Plate I. shows the forehead, eyes, and arrangement of the hair.) In respect to high moral expression, and lofty majesty, it has, perhaps, preëminence even over those mentioned above.

The Capitoline museum also possesses an admirable, though smaller, head of Jupiter, which formerly stood in the mansion della Valle, and was very much esteemed. — The nose is new, and the hair slightly damaged; moreover, the head does not appear to be well placed upon the bust; it does not, in fact, seem to belong to it. — GERM. ED.

29. This Pluto afterwards passed from the villa Mattei into the Pio-Clement museum.[1] Visconti, who has engraved and explained it under the name of Serapis, says that it is made of iron-gray basalt. He approves, however, the name given to it by Winckelmann, because several images of Serapis were found which had the attribute of Pluto, namely, the dog Cerberus. But these images belong only to the Sinope-Alexandrian idolatry, with which the purely Greek Pluto had nothing in common, — as one may see on many bas-reliefs representing the Rape of Proserpine, in none of which Pluto has this head-dress.

Visconti remarks further, that all the statues of Pluto still extant are of moderate workmanship, and not decidedly different from Serapis. The sole head of Pluto without a Modius and the physiognomy attributed to Serapis is in the possession of the prince Chigi. It is a work of wonderful merit. The severe countenance and tangled hair at once proclaim the sovereign of the lower world. — GERM. ED.

30. This great head of white marble, and wearing a Modius, is of admirable workmanship, and in good preservation. It corresponds, however, but little to what Winckelmann says of the stern aspect of the

---

[1] Plate XI. This head is engraved after that in the *Pio-Clement Museum,* Vol. VI., Plate 14. — TR.

images of Pluto, since it has rather a mild look. The same is the case with the colossal bust of Serapis, with rays about the head, in the Pio-Clement museum.[1] (See, Plate XIII., another, smaller marble bust of Jupiter Serapis.) We must, therefore, if Winckelmann's opinion in regard to the severe countenance of Pluto is correct, — and it seems to be founded upon the nature of the case itself, — make a distinction between images of Pluto and those of Serapis, — assigning to the former those with a stern look, and those with a mild expression to the latter. But if no distinct separation can be made even in this way, and the faces of Pluto and Serapis flow one into the other, and these in their turn pass over into the character of Jupiter, then we must consider that all such perplexing monuments come from a later Greek age, — in which much that was foreign had been introduced into the Greek mode of thinking, and even art itself no longer adhered firmly to the original images whose character was regarded as canonical, — or that they are, altogether, works executed in the days of the Romans, when many kinds of strange idolatries were intermingled, a confusion which must have made itself felt in some degree by art and its productions. — GERM. ED.

31. Besides Pluto or Serapis, other deities wore the Modius on their heads, — as Isis, Fortuna, and a Priapus in De la Chausse (*Mus. Roman.*). Winckelmann found a Fortuna with this head-dress in the Stosch museum; he also conjectures that even Ceres may have this attribute.

In the museum Odescalco there is a soldier holding in his hand a small Victoria with the same badge. In shape the Modius resembles a basket of rushes or reeds. A beautiful head of white marble in the cloister of Sant' Ambrogio at Naples — which, according to the assigned character, must be a Pluto — is deserving of note, because an olive-branch, together with ears of grain, can be seen in the bushel or Modius which it wears. — F.

32. The statue of Æsculapius, and especially the head of it, in the villa Albani, is the most beautiful known image of this deity; it even surpasses a colossal figure which stands in the garden of the villa Borghese, in a temple built expressly for it, although the latter is highly remarkable, partly on account of the goodness of the execution, and partly on account of its rare size. The attitude is that most usual in statues of this deity; the right hand holds a staff entwined by a serpent; the left hand, together with the arm, is folded in the mantle, and rests upon the side. The head, considered by itself, has a kind, benevolent, wise character; but is softer and less grand and vigorous than Jupiter's, which it almost exactly resembles in the disposition of the hair, — thus affording a confirmation of Winckelmann's remark. — The right arm, together with the staff and snake, and also the toes of the right foot, are modern restorations.

According to Visconti, the charming group of Æsculapius and Hygeia, in the Pio-Clement museum, is the sole round work in marble which represents these divinities united. Though the heads of both are ancient, still they did not originally belong to the figures.

A remarkable statue, bearing the name of Æsculapius, formerly stood in the Pitti palace, at Florence, and is probably there still. The head

[1] Plate XII. This head is engraved after that in the *Pio-Clement Museum*, Vol. VI., Plate 15. — TR.

resembles those of the (so called) Plato, or Indian Bacchus, and is probably the portrait of a celebrated physician of antiquity, in whose whole
figure the artist intended to give an approximate likeness to the character of Æsculapius. The execution of the nude part of the breast,
shoulders, &c., is soft, beautiful, and natural. The folds of the robe are
admirably arranged, simple, and elegant. — It is much to be regretted
that this noble work of art has been broken into many pieces, and been
twice restored. The earlier restorations consist of the nose, a piece of
the right cheek, the left hand, the right arm, and both feet; the later, of
a piece of the forehead above the right eye, the fore-finger of the modern
left hand, and the tips of the fingers of the right, which is placed upon
the hip. — GERM. ED.

33. This statue of Neptune, of which the style is good and the execution commendable, was carried from the villa Medici to Florence. (Plate
XIV., Letter A.) Another statue, conjectured, though without full certainty, to be a Neptune, and restored as such, may be found in the *Pio-
Clement Museum* (Vol. I., Plate 33).

The images of this deity seem to be, on the whole, very rare; since, in
addition to the two large statues just mentioned, and a well-executed
small one among the antiquities at Dresden, we know of only a few
other figures on rilievi, but not a single remarkable head or bust. —
GERM. ED.

34. Visconti (*Mus. Pio-Clement.*, Plate 5, Vol. VI.) remarks in the
following terms upon the head from which this engraving is copied: —
"The eyebrows and scaly cheeks, the beard and hair falling in waves,
like water, the dolphins fancifully entangled in the beard, and, finally,
the waves which encircle the chest and shoulders of this colossal Hermes, are all characters which lead us to conjecture that a marine god is
here represented. At the first glance, it might be supposed to be Ocea-
nus, the first-born of the Titans; but, on closer observation, we recognize a sea-deity of the second rank, as, for instance, a Triton. . . . . The
Bacchic wreath of vine-leaves and ivy is worn by Nereids and Tritons,
who are frequently seen celebrating the orgies and festivals of Bacchus,
and decorated with his emblems and habiliments. It is uncertain why
the ancient artists denoted so close a connection between Bacchus and
the deities of the sea; whether because they regarded him as the symbol
of the watery element; or whether because his religious rites, having
been brought into Greece from transmarine colonies, may be said to have
come, as it were, from the sea, and to have been carried thither by the
Nereids; or whether, in fine, this community of emblems and symbols,
which the marine deities have with him, may have been derived from
Leucothea, the aunt and nurse of Bacchus, and also a sea-goddess, and
from Palæmon, her son, the god of harbours and seamen, and his cousin
and foster-brother. . . . . The horns, like those of a calf, projecting
from his temples, instead of nippers or claws, which are observed on
other antiques, evidently refer both to the roaring of the stormy sea, and
to earthquakes, which, in ancient times, were supposed, with some reason,
to have had their cause in subterranean waters, — a terrible phenomenon,
which it was customary to ascribe to Neptune principally, and indirectly
to the secondary deities of the sea. As the Bacchic Hermæ were used
as ornaments for the walks in the beautiful gardens of ancient Rome, so

these Triton figures served a similar purpose in the maritime places in which her citizens loved to dwell." — TR.

The two colossal Tritons' heads, in the villa Albani, mentioned in the text, altough equally well executed, are far inferior in artistic merit, and in nobleness and dignity of character, to the Hermes described above, which was found, after Winckelmann's time, at Pozzuoli, and placed in the Vatican museum.

In the Pio-Clement museum there are also two other monuments, very valuable in point of execution, belonging to this class. The first consists of a Triton, or properly a Sea-centaur, who is carrying off a Nymph, — together with a pair of frolicsome Amorini. The figures of this group, which originally embellished a fountain, are not quite of the size of life; it was found in a *pozzolana*-pit near Rome, outside of the Porta Latina. The second is the half-figure of a Triton, somewhat larger, and of still better execution; it was discovered at Sant' Angelo near Tivoli. Engravings of these two monuments may be seen in the *Pio-Clement Museum*, Vol. I., Plates 34 and 35.

The bust in the Capitoline museum, of which Winckelmann makes mention in the text, a few lines above, is a double Hermes, very well executed, and in good preservation, that may be found in the miscellaneous room; the fins about the eyes are rendered more plainly on this than on any other monument. In the same room there is also a bust which was formerly held to be a Faun; it is without horns, has pointed ears, and, in respect to the features of the face, resembles the half-figure in the Pio-Clement museum mentioned above. This, likewise, represents a Triton. The head is well preserved, and admirably executed. The breast appears to be modern. — GERM. ED.

35. The picture by Poussin here mentioned, or at·least one wholly similar, is in the Florentine gallery. The objections made by Winckelmann are well grounded, for Theseus has a pretty strong beard, and the background of the picture is ornamented with extensive ruins, amidst which, among other things incongruous with the subject represented, occurs an arch having Corinthian pilasters. However, this landscape in the background is precisely the most valuable portion of the painting, for the figures are neither well conceived nor well arranged, nor are they carefully drawn. — GERM. ED.

CHAPTER II.

1. ALSO Diana, as Visconti shows (*Mus. Pio-Clement*, Vol. I., Plate 10, Note *b*). — F.

2. Heyne seeks to prove, from many odes-to be found in the Greek Anthology, that the Medicean Venus is to be considered as standing before Paris, and Böttiger, in his valuable notices, justifies Heyne's conjecture. — GERM. ED.

3. The Venus of the Capitoline museum must be numbered among the most beautiful figures of this kind. She is somewhat larger than the Venus de' Medici, and more developed in regard to the character of her shape. In artistic merit she is but little inferior to the other; and

her attitude, as Winckelmann observes, is altogether the same. Instead of a dolphin, a tall unguent-vase stands by her side, upon which is placed a cloth ornamented with fringe. — The nose, the thumb and fore-finger of the left hand, and the thumb and middle finger of the right hand, are restorations. The restoration of the nose was not happily made; indeed, the beautiful face was disfigured by it: whether this is the case now, we do not know. The lips, especially the upper one, are somewhat damaged. An engraving of this statue may be found in the *Monum. Antiques du Musée Napoléon*, Tom. I., Plate 56. — GERM. ED.

4. The Venus of Menophantus was discovered on the slope of Monte Celio, in Rome, and subsequently came into possession of Prince Chigi. The attitude of this statue is nearly the same as that of the Venus de' Medici; but with her left hand she holds before herself the end of a drapery, trimmed with fringe, which falls down on the scroll — or, as Visconti (*Mus. Pio-Clement*, Vol. I., pp. 19, 92) supposes it, the jewel-box — bearing the inscription, and serves as a support to the figure.

The head possesses much that is lovely, and, as repects the ideal expressed in it, and also in the arrangement of the hair, it resembles the heads of the Medicean, Capitoline, Dresden, and other exquisite statues of Venus. The forms, generally, are elegant and slender; and the faultless proportions justify the supposition that the original copied by Menophantus was an admirable work.

Though the handling of the flesh, as well as of the hair, indicates a practised and skilful artist, still it is far from having attained that bewitching, tender softness which we perceive in the Capitoline Venus, and other works of the best periods of art. As far as we can judge from the mechanical indications, it does not seem to belong even to the earlier times of the Roman empire. — The nose and both arms are modern; some repairs have also been made in the drapery; and there are some slight injuries on the lips. (See the engraving, *Mus. Pio-Clement*, Vol. IV., Plate 68.) — GERM. ED.

5. This is stated in the following inscription on a cube, at her feet, on which falls the drapery that she holds before her abdomen : —

ΑΠΟΤΗC

εΝΤΡωΑΔΙ

ΑΦΡΟΔΙΤΗC

ΜΗΝΟΦΑΝΤΟC

εΠΟΙεΙ

"Menophantus made [me] after the Venus in Troas." [1]

We know, however, nothing more respecting this artist than of the original from which he copied. Troas lay in the Trojan territory, other-wise called also Alexandria and Antigonia; and we find a victor men-tioned (*conf.* Scaliger, *Poet.*, lib. 1, cap. 24) who had obtained the first prize in the great games of Greece. In regard to the form of the letters, the reader can see my remarks (*Monum. Antiq. Inedit.*, p. 221) on the statue, recently discovered, bearing the name of Sardanapalus. — W.

6. Several antiquarians are disposed to doubt the existence of such antique higher ideals of Venus, or images of the Venus Urania. But

---

[1] Incorrectly rendered in the text by *Troy*. — TR.

Pausanias (lib. 1, cap. 19) mentions a Hermes that was to be found at Athens, in the character of Venus Urania; also (lib. 3, cap. 23) an image in wood representing the goddess as armed; and (lib. 6, cap. 25) a statue by Phidias, of ivory and gold, in which the Venus Urania was represented as standing with one foot on a tortoise. It is not to be supposed that an artist like Phidias would have given to his image no definite character suitable to the idea to be expressed. Such a supposition is rendered even the less probable when we know that in the vicinity of the Venus Urania of Phidias stood a Venus Vulgivaga of bronze, seated on a goat,—a work by Scopas. Unless there had been striking differences in the two statues, Pausanias would not have contrasted them with one another in the way he has done. Hence we believe with Winckelmann, that such statues of Venus Urania did really exist and do exist now; and that they are distinguished from other images of Venus partly by loftier majesty and earnestness, and partly by the diadem, which is higher in the middle, and slopes gradually to each extremity.

Winckelmann has contented himself, in another place, with adducing as an example of this Venus a bust, or rather a head,—for the rest is modern,—in the villa Borghese; it possesses, however, but little merit of execution.

The most beautiful known heads of the heavenly Venus are,—

(1.) One of admirable Greek marble in the museum at Mantua. It is adorned with a diadem, like a Juno; but the features are the features of Venus, with the exception that a far higher, more earnest meaning than usual pervades them.—This remarkable monument has suffered somewhat in the eyes, and also in other places.

(2.) In the Florentine gallery there is a well-known estimable statue which bears the name of Venus Urania (Gori, *Mus. Flor.*, Vol. III., Plate 30); it bends slightly forward, and holds the gathered drapery before its middle. Both arms, together with the right foot, are new, and the drapery has been retouched. The head, which is a masterpiece of beauty and noble grace, surpasses the body, and apparently does not belong to it, although the statue rightly owes its name to the head.— It is a pity that it is so much injured. The nose, the under lip, the chin, the greater portion of the neck, and the two locks of hair knotted on the crown of the head, are modern restorations; but the diadem is a genuine antique. The features generally exhibit about the same character as those in the monument just mentioned, at Mantua.

(3.) A head, furnished with a diadem, and of which the forms, not less beautiful than appropriate, proclaim it to be a head of Venus, was formerly in the museum at Cassel.

(4.) The gallery of antiquities at Dresden also possesses a beautiful fragment of such a head, which, by being set upon a figure not originally belonging to it, has been restored as a Ceres.

In Plate XVI., Letters B and C, we present two eyes, one drawn after the Dresden fragment, and the other after the head formerly to be found at Cassel. By these engravings we hope to show how great a mistake is usually made in regard to most of the images of this kind, in naming them Juno, on account of the diadem. — GERM. ED.

7. Well known to the lovers of antiquity by the name of the Ludo-

visi Juno. It is incomparably grand and lofty, and yet lovely and beautiful beyond measure. The tip of the nose is the only restoration; in other respects, — the marks of a few bruises on the right cheek excepted, — this glorious work is not perceptibly injured. The left eye seems to be somewhat flatter than the right; the difference, however, is probably not original; time and accident may have occasioned some abrasion at this point. (See Plate XVI., Letter A, the face of this Juno in profile.)

Besides this colossal head of Juno, there are two other admirable heads of the same goddess in the villa Ludovisi. One of them, somewhat larger than life, stands near the former in the library of the villa. The features are lovely, yet without detracting any thing from the majesty and loftiness of the character; a drapery or veil floats from the head, behind the high diadem. This beautiful monument is not perceptibly injured, with the exception of the tip of the nose, which is modern, and a few injuries to the neck where it unites with the chest. — The other, which is twice as large as life, and, consequently, must be classed among the colossal heads of Juno, may be found in the smaller garden-palace of the same villa, on the staircase leading to the upper apartments. The features are large and noble; but the handling of the flesh, and the deep grooves between the locks of hair, appear to point to the times of the Roman empire.

We will add that the imperial musuem at Paris possesses a head of Juno resembling the smaller Ludovisi head, which is likewise larger than life, and has a veil behind the diadem. (*Monum. Ant. du Musée Napoléon*, Tom. I., Plate 5.) A colossal head of Juno of superior execution, but without a diadem, may, it is said, be found at Sarsko-Selo, near St. Petersburgh. — GERM. ED.

8. Roma was occasionally represented with a short tucked-up robe, almost like an Amazon; she may be seen draped in this manner on different rilievi; but at times she has long drapery, and is armed, and so far resembles Pallas. Of this kind are, in particular, some few seated figures, among which the one of porphyry, over the fountain by the palace of the senator on the Capitol, has the most artistic merit. Her charming face is slightly averted; the drapery clings to the body in folds which are numerous, it is true, but yet arranged with uncommon prettiness.

In the court of the palace of the Conservatori is another Roma, of marble, somewhat larger, likewise seated, but far inferior to the former. The folds of the drapery are meagre and deep, and form no masses. The head and shoulders as low as the breasts are modern; also the hands and the advanced left foot. The antique picture in the palace Barberini represents Roma in long clothes, and seated; a tolerably successful colored engraving of it may be found in the *Almanac of Rome*, of the year 1810, published by Sickler and Reinhart.

We must not omit the almost colossal marble head of Roma in the villa Borghese. In regard to the skill displayed in the execution, it is unquestionably to be esteemed more highly than any other of the known monuments relating to this subject. On the helmet Romulus and Remus are wrought in relief. — The breast and one half of the nose are modern; and the slightly injured lips have been mended with stucco.

Finally, we would remark that the helmet of Roma usually has not a projecting front, which the greater number, and the most beautiful, of the images of Pallas have, but it lies close to the forehead, as the Roman soldiers were accustomed to wear it. — GERM. ED.

9. Winckelmann means here the perfectly preserved statue of Pallas, which, as far as we know, still stands in the villa Albani, and is certainly one of the admirable monuments of the high style. (See a profile outline of the face in Plate XVIII., letter A.) The forms are not delicate, for that would be contrary to the idea of power; neither are they soft, for softness would detract from the severe earnestness, the loftiness, of her countenance; they are not even to be termed elegant, for that would not comport with the elevation and grandeur which were the principal objects of the artist; but they are divinely pure, beautiful, and lofty. The folds of the drapery are masterpieces of drawing, and of the finest selection, although they are not kept in masses so broad and undisturbed as to enable them to produce, by shade and light, a strong and particularly a pleasing effect. This monument, however, may have been executed before light and shade had been accurately observed, and the rules of their application to the plastic arts discovered.

It will be seen from these remarks that we are nearly of the same opinion as Winckelmann in regard to the high merit of this noble monument. We do not, however, by any means, intend on this account to disparage in the least other celebrated images of Minerva. The former Giustiniani statue — now in the possession of the Senator Lucien Bonaparte, if we do not mistake — is no less valuable; and although it seems to come from the same age of the severe style, still, for the taste of the present day, it possesses more of those characteristics that invite and attract. Of late, greater, indeed nearly the greatest, reputation has fallen to the share of the almost colossal Pallas of Velletri (see an outline of the face in Plate XVII.), although in pure merit as a work of art it is probably inferior to the two just named; at least, it does not excel them. An outline of this monument may be found in Millin (*Monum. Ant. Ined.*, Vol. II., Plate 23), and a beautifully executed engraving in the *Musée François*, by Robillard Peronville (livr. 26). Similar to it, or else admirably copied, like it, from the same exquisite prototype, is the bust which formerly stood in the villa Albani, of proportions about as large as those of the statue last named, and which is to be less highly valued only in so far as it is not in so good a state of preservation; for a considerable portion of the nose is new, and restorations are observable in the under lip, also, as well as on the lower eyelid. — GERM. ED.

10. In the gallery of the palace Colonna is a glorious Diana in long drapery, the wonderful head of which is probably the most beautiful of all the heads of this goddess now remaining. The features are delicate and of exceeding beauty; her bearing divinely lofty, and, undisturbed by nearer objects, she looks, with an earnest, eager gaze, straight forward into the far distance. A slight expression of pride and coyness relieves, or rather elevates, the indifference of her character. The drapery of this noble, slender figure lies in elegant folds. The execution is generally good, and the monument so well preserved throughout, that even the hands are for the most part antique. On the head, merely the nose needed to be restored.

Among the most beautiful images of Diana we must enumerate also the torso of a slender figure, having long drapery, in the villa Borghese, which is known by the name of La Zingarella, " The Gypsy Girl."

The statue of Diana in short drapery, which has been in France since the time of Henry the Fourth, is also celebrated, and without doubt justly, although we say so not from our own judgment, having never seen it. It represents her in the action of running, with a hind by her side. Engravings of this valued monument may be found in the *Musée François*, Livr. 15, and *Monum. Ant. du Musée Napoléon*, Tom. I., Plate 51. — GERM. ED.

11. There is nothing more common than to see in museums figures restored as Ceres, and nothing, on the contrary, is more rare than really genuine statues of this goddess. Even Winckelmann himself was unable to refer to a single one.

The sole figure in marble, of the size of life, which can be regarded with certainty as an image of Ceres, stands in the villa Borghese. The head is of lofty beauty, and wears the pointed diadem, about which lies a wreath of wheat-ears. The mantle is admirably executed, with the single exception that the folds are too numerous. — The nose is a restoration; the upper lip is somewhat injured; the greater part of the wreath of wheat-ears may possibly also be a modern work. So, too, we judge the chaplet of flowers in the left hand, and the bunch of wheat-ears in the raised right hand, to be new.

Another, larger figure, in the same place, likewise beautifully executed, is one of the spurious images mentioned above, which has been converted into a Ceres merely by the attributes given to it by the modern restorer. — GERM. ED.

12. The third volume of the *Monumenti Antichi Inediti* never appeared. — GERM. ED.

13. Sophocles terms the Furies ἀεὶ παρθένους, "always virgins," in *Ajax*, verse 837 The tragic writer, Æschylus, was the first, as Pausanias (lib. 1, cap. 28) relates, who represented them with snakes in their hair. But the statues of these divinities in the temple consecrated to them, which was situated on the Areopagus at Athens, did not have a fearful character, any more than the images of the other subterranean deities standing in the same temple. — GERM. ED.

14. Visconti (*Mus. Pio-Clement.;* Vol. XI., p. 64) thinks that the arm of the Perseus, in the palace Lanti at Rome, mentioned by Winckelmann, and also the Medusa's head, are of modern workmanship. He likewise expresses many doubts in regard to the name of this statue, since the ægis over the shoulder belongs not to Perseus, but rather to a statue of Jupiter, or of a deified Augustus. The decision of this latter point we will leave to others more learned than ourselves. But on account of the Medusa's head, which Winckelmann pronounces the most beautiful in marble, we should be pleased to hear the reasons why Visconti holds it to be a modern work. We have frequently examined with attention, and never without astonishment, this admirable, and, in our opinion, antique monument. It is an ideal in which there is a glorious blending of the pleasing with the terrible, of soft forms with fierceness of character. The good effect of the whole is disturbed, or at least impaired, by the badly restored nose, and the awkward way in which the injured lips

have been botched. The chin is very small, but very prominent; the mouth is large; the corners of the mouth deep. The line of the forehead and the beginning of the nose, as far as the antique part extends, waves and bends in a gentle and pleasing manner; the eyes are closed; the cheeks, pretty in form, not very round, yet showing with soft outlines the muscles and bones.

It is very probable that Winckelmann did not know the celebrated head — properly face or mask — of Medusa, which stood in the palace Rondinini, larger than life, and wrought of white marble, in high relief. This admirable work is executed with rare industry, but conceived in a much severer sense, and with less loveliness, than the head just mentioned in the palace Lanti, or the beautiful small Medusa-head wrought in high relief on the cuirass of a bust of the Emperor Adrian in the Capitoline museum. The forms, however, are large, and even beautiful, although they incline, as the artist intended, to the fierce and terrible. For this purpose, the teeth, also, are exhibited in the open, poison-exhaling mouth. A certain hardness and sharpness visible in the features, as an expression of rigidity, is another masterly and intentional stroke. — One wing of the nose and the extreme tip of it, together with some trifling restorations of the snakes, are the sole modern parts. — GERM. ED.

15. It will appear inconceivable to many how Winckelmann could doubt, for a time, the genuineness of a monument of ancient art so justly admired as is the head of Medusa engraved by Solon. But who will come forward and say that he has judged erroneously on such subjects?

It is to be remarked, that Fea, in reference to this work of Solon (*Storia delle Arti*, Tom. I., p. 324, note C), falls into the very remarkable error of speaking of it as a cameo; whereas every tyro in knowledge of ancient art — every one, indeed, who has seen only one impression of the Medusa's head by Solon — must know that it is an intaglio, or deeply cut stone, and not a cameo, or cut in relief. Fea also asserts that the gem is still whole, and that Winckelmann's account of its fracture into two pieces must apply to some other cameo. — GERM. ED.

The reader will find in Plate XIV., Letter B, an engraving of this very beautiful head, which is not, probably, excelled by any one, unless it may be the intaglio mentioned in the text as having been executed by Sosicles. The original gem by Solon is in the Florentine museum; and an engraving of it may be found in the second volume, plate seventh, of the *Museum Florentinum*, from which the present engraving is copied. — TR.

16. The most important of the still extant statues of Amazons appear to be copied principally from two originals of ancient celebrity, which nearly resembled each other in shape and features, but differed in action. This circumstance Winckelmann has overlooked, and hence erroneously supposes that all Amazon-statues are made with a wound in the breast, or, more properly, under it. The Amazon-statue which formerly stood in the villa Mattei, and was afterwards transferred to the Pio-Clement museum, undoubtedly possesses the most merit as a work of art. An engraving of this monument may be found in the *Mus. Pio-Clement.*, Vol. XI., Plate 28, in the *Musée François*, Liv. 57, and in the *Statues* published by Piranesi.

This figure may without hesitation be classed among works of the severe style of Greek art at the time when it was gradually becoming milder, and was beginning to incline to the more tender, to the beautiful, and the pleasing. We see in it — and the idea is carried into execution with a felicity that cannot be surpassed — a noble, vigorous female form, perfectly developed in every limb by constant exercise, standing in a state of repose, with the right hand bent across the head, and with the left hand, which hangs by its side, holding a bow. — The modern restorations are the right leg, as low as the ankle, including a portion of the knee; likewise both arms, the nose, chin, and under lip; the neck is doubtful.

One of the Amazon-statues in the Capitoline museum — of which the text makes mention in the following paragraph — is perfectly similar to that just described, especially since it has been lately restored, and one of those well-preserved heads, formerly kept in the miscellaneous room, been placed upon it, as Winckelmann wished. This figure also has an extraordinary degree of merit, and if it must yield the superiority in lofty, pure beauty to the above-mentioned statue in the Pio-Clement museum, it appears able, nevertheless, to dispute with it the palm in pleasing grace. — One half of the nose, the raised right hand, and also the left, the left foot, and the toes of the right, are modern; the leg, from the lower edge of the knee to the ankle, is either badly joined, or else is a modern restoration.

Another Amazon in the Capitoline museum is remarkable, partly because the name, CωCIKΛH, is engraved on the trunk of a tree which serves as a support, and partly because it differs from the figures before mentioned, not only in posture and in the folds of the drapery, but even in expression. She has a wound below the right breast; the right arm is held up over the head, whilst the left is employed in lifting the robe from the wound. Hence, the face exhibits an expression of pain and suffering; whilst, on the other hand, the two figures first mentioned are without a wound, and appear merely serious and unconcerned. The work of Sosicles — if it be assumed that the name engraved denotes the artist by whom the work was executed — is, however, not altogether so slender in its proportions as the others; it may also have lost somewhat of its original sharpness and the learning of its finish, rubbed off by the hands of modern artists. The head has never been broken from the trunk, and, with the exception of the tip of the nose and a small portion of the under lip, it has also no restorations. On the other hand, the whole of the raised right arm, and the left fore-arm, together with that piece of the robe which the hand raises from the wound, are modern work, as are also two toes of the left foot. It is probable that the legs are the original antique legs, but that they have been retouched about the ankles, where they were broken off from the feet; on this account, the latter appear somewhat heavy, and the former too slender.

Pliny (lib. 34, cap. 8, § 19) speaks of five Amazons by celebrated masters, which were kept in the temple of Diana at Ephesus. The one most esteemed was by Polycletus; the second by Phidias; the third by Ctesilaus; the fourth by Cydon; and the fifth by Phradmon. The Amazon of Ctesilaus showed her wound; it is, therefore, scarcely to be doubted, that, in the above-mentioned Capitoline statue bearing the name of Sosicles, and in other similar works, we possess more or less accurate copies of it. Though the action of the Amazon of Polycletus is not known positively, still it is possible that the figures holding a bow may be copies from it; for the most esteemed work would, probably, be copied the most frequently, and with the greatest exactness. Indeed, if it were not that Pliny includes all the above-mentioned five Amazons in the temple of Diana at Ephesus among the bronze images, that glorious statue of the villa Mattei might pass for the original executed by Polycletus himself. The Amazon of Phidias stood leaning on a lance, as Lucian relates (*Imagin.*, lib. 11, cap. 4); but as yet we have no known copy of it. Of the works of Cydon and Phradmon we possess no circumstantial account, and therefore cannot recognize the copies, of which there are perhaps some still extant. We find ourselves in a similar embarrassment in regard to a sixth celebrated Amazon-figure, executed in bronze by Strongylion, which obtained the epithet Εὔκνημος, on account of the beauty of its legs. (Plin., lib. 34, cap. 19, § 21.)

It deserves, however, a passing remark, that we occasionally also see Amazons on horseback, in different attitudes, — as, for example, the Herculaneum figure in bronze (*Mus. Ercol.*, Vol. VI., Plates 63, 64), and the marble figure in the garden of the villa Borghese, dashing against a warrior, who, supported on one knee, is defending himself with sword and shield against her assault; beneath the horse sits, crouched together, another warrior, who serves as a support to the Amazon. There were formerly in the palace Farnese two single figures of mounted Amazons. Of the numerous Amazon-figures which have been preserved on rilievi, engraved gems, and in paintings on vases, our present purpose does not require us to speak. — GERM. ED.

17. The Diana Venatrix (so called) stands in the round hall of the palace Pamfili. It is dressed in a short robe, almost after the manner of the Amazons; so that there appears to be some ground for Winckelmann's conjecture. It is worth inquiry by future investigators, whether the partly antique dog by the side of the figure belonged orignally to it, or whether it is an ancient fragment arbitrarily adjoined to it in modern times. In the former case, this figure is distinguished in a remarkable manner from all other Amazons. — The workmanship of this monument is good. A portion of the head, and likewise the arms and legs, are new. — GERM. ED.

18. Petit, *De Amazon*, cap. 33, p. 259. — GERM. ED.

19. It will be difficult to adjust the dispute between the lovers of art and the connoisseurs in horses, respecting the beauty or ugliness of the antique images of horses. For he whose taste has been cultivated in the noblest and most beautiful forms of works of art will judge differently from one who is accustomed to prefer that which is rare, or useful, or perhaps merely customary. An English horse without a docked tail would not please the latter, whilst, on the other hand, the former considers docking of the tail to be an outrage against nature. The same difference of opinion may be said to exist in regard also to beauty of shape in men. But enough! The horse of Marcus Aurelius on the Capitol is more admirable than any one that has been executed by modern artists; yet it is not of so fine, elegant, and active an appearance as the horses of the two Balbi in the Bourbon museum at Naples, and

these in their turn must yield to the four horses which adorn the portal of the church of St. Mark, at Venice. — GERM. ED.

20. Winckelmann is right in saying that the ancient lions are ideal in shape. They are so, in so far as art, when forming her creations, poetically elevated them above the bare reality of nature. But they who suppose that it substituted in the place of lions another and an imaginary race of animals are very much in error, and their censure on this account is misapplied. It has done to lions neither more nor less than to other beasts, and to beasts generally not more than to man. It can be asserted, with just as much appearance of truth, that the ancient statues are unlike actual men, as that the ancient images of lions are unlike real lions. The Colossus of Phidias, on Monte Cavallo, in Rome, looks, in truth, no more like a pitiful, oppressed, starved citizen, than the great lion couchant before the Arsenal at Venice, or the standing lion, wrought in relief on the staircase of the palace Barberini, at Rome, is to a miserable, worried lion of a menagerie. — GERM. ED.

CHAPTER III.

1. THIS Dancer was afterwards transferred to the Pio-Clement museum. Visconti (Vol. III., Plate 30, pp. 39, 40) has given an engraving and explanation of it. He first says, that the chaplet with which the beautiful head of this figure is adorned is formed, not of flowers, but of ivy-blossoms. He then goes on to remark, — "Though this statue does not exhibit in its forms the nobleness and slenderness observable in other yet more admirable works of sculpture, still it is to be classed among the masterpieces of antiquity, on account of the truth, grace, and softness with which the shape and features of a beautiful woman are copied, who, in the Campanian pleasure-gardens, — where the statue was discovered, — had, probably, once fascinated by her allurements a voluptuous crowd." — GERM. ED.

2. Pausan., lib. 6, cap. 25. Translators have not rightly understood this form of speech, Τὸν ἕτερον τῶν ποδῶν ἐπιπλέκων τῷ ἑτέρῳ. They have rendered it by *pedem pede premere*, "to set one foot on the other"; whereas it should have been rendered by *decussatis pedibus*, which in Italian signifies *gambe incrocicchiate*, "with the legs crossed." — W.

3. If this doubt of Winckelmann were to obtain credit, how many other coins would be rejected as not genuine! Providence, standing and resting against a column, is seen in this attitude on a coin of Alexander Severus (Musellii *Numismat. Antiq.*, Part 11, Tab. 75, No. 7); another female figure (No. 8) in a similar position; Perpetual Security, on a coin of the Emperor Gallienus (Tab. 223, No. 6), and on a coin of the Emperor Tacitus (Tab. 234, No. 4); Public Joy, on the reverse of two coins of Julia Mammæa (Tab. 182, Nos. 2, 3); the Peace of Augustus on a coin of Æmilianus (Banduri, *Numism. Imperat. Roman.*, Tom. I., p 92). — F.

This attitude is, however, usually given only to figures in which it is intended to express stability and repose.   Hence, all of them, as far as we know, lean against the stump of a column. — GERM. ED.

4. Winckelmann deserves infinite credit for having discovered and unfolded, more clearly than any other antiquarian, the high merit of these masterpieces.   But when he says that this state of unspeakable anguish, of horror-struck sensibility, leaves the features unchanged, and thus allowed the embodiment in these figures of the highest and purest beauty, it seems as if he wished to defend the artist of Niobe and her daughters merely by an ingenious explanation, or to praise him conditionally, and tacitly concede the justice of the matter-of-fact objection usually made by incompetent judges, that the work is deficient in force of expression.   But we maintain that it needs for its defence no such display of elaborate reasons.   We must simply acknowledge what is obvious, that the artist's conception of his figures is raised far above the level of common nature, and that, in the execution of his idea, he has everywhere continued true to that justness and purity of taste which avoids whatever is not beautiful.   In a word, in order to judge correctly of this wonder of ancient art, we must soar into the regions of poesy, and not erroneously suppose that the progress of the action in a highly tragic work of art should be the same as where death happens in the ordinary way.   Considered in this manner, Niobe and her daughters need no justification, or any supposition of inexpressiveness resembling the stupefaction of anguish, but they are unconditionally correct and excellent in conception and execution. — GERM. ED.

5. The expression of pain is much stronger in the Laocoön than in the Niobe.   But it must be considered that this work was intended to solve the problem of expressing a real bodily pain, and therefore admitted, indeed .required, the manifestation of painful sensations to be more strongly indicated.   Moreover, this work is the production of art at a later period, when it was more finished in itself, and required more finish in its productions, — when its style was refined, noble, and beautiful, but not so elevated as that of the Niobe.   No one can prize the Laocoön more highly than we do ; it is a miracle, the sum and abstract of all art ; but a godlike spirit streams from the Niobe, and impels heavenward the feelings of the spectator. — GERM. ED.

6. Marcus Agrippa on this work has no beard ; the architect and soldier have beards. — F.

7. Among the ancient Romans, the symbol on coins and other monuments of the conquest of a province was a woman in a sitting posture, supporting her head on her hand, and her elbow on the knee, which was drawn up.   In this manner the conquest of Judea is symbolically represented on numerous coins of Vespasian and Titus ; so, likewise, is the conquest of Germany, Sarmatia, Armenia ; and that of Dacia may be seen on a beautiful bas-relief under the statue of Roma Triumphans in the palace of the Conservatori, on the Capitol.   Still, I do not venture to doubt the genuineness of the coin adduced by Winckelmann, because old coins of an impression hitherto unknown are daily found. — F.

8. It is evident from the connection, that Winckelmann has committed a clerical error here, in writing " celebrated head of Prudence," instead of " celebrated head of Justice " ; for the former is represented as aged,

and, although well executed, is not much esteemed; but the latter is a celebrated work. She is young, beautiful, and of a voluptuous cast of countenance; she is, moreover, a little more nude than is proper. From Christian decency, therefore, and because a Spaniard once became enamoured of her, she has been invested with a bronze garment, so constructed, however, that it can be unscrewed; and a gratuity from the lovers of nudities will procure its removal. — GERM. ED.

9. The Santa Susanna of François Quesnoy, called Fiammingo, stands in the church of the Madonna di Loretto in Rome. It is a marble statue, about, or perhaps a little above, the natural size. A crown and sceptre lie at her feet; in her right hand she holds a palm-twig, and with her left it was probably intended that she should point at the crown and sceptre at her feet; but she actually points over and beyond them. The execution of this work is very elaborate; the style of the forms inclines to the tender, beautiful, and noble; the drawing is well understood, the proportions faultless, the features charming, and the turn of the figure very pleasing. The drapery, as a whole, is prettily disposed, but the masses are wanting in purity and repose. — GERM. ED.

10. The statue of Santa Bibiana stands in the church of the same name in Rome. It is accounted the masterpiece of the celebrated Bernini. It is a figure in white marble, of about the size of life, and is executed with extreme industry, polished, and hollowed out beneath. The handling of the flesh is uncommonly soft and tender. This work, considered in regard to conception, is fundamentally poetical and good. The artist wished to represent the saint as looking towards heaven with rapture and delight in the enjoyment of blessedness. But the idea is not carried out with the requisite degree of elevation. We see in the holy Bibiana nothing more than a youthful figure in an attractive attitude, with a pretty face and delicate hands, but whose features and whole air express a terrestrial, sensual well-being and pleasure, rather than the pious enraptured joy of a blessed saint. The drapery is prettily arranged, but its folds, according to this master's usual manner, are extraordinarily deep. — GERM. ED.

11. This celebrated picture with half-figures, by Leonardo da Vinci, was formerly in the Borghese Aldobrandini gallery at Rome, but it is said to have been removed to England a few years since. The purity of form, and the expression, in the youthful Christ are altogether exquisite; the heads of the Pharisees are full of character, and seemingly alive; the coloring, also, appears to be more lively and florid in this picture than in other works of the same artist. — GERM. ED.

12. The Madonna del Sacco, as it is called, is a fresco painting in the cross-passage of the convent of the Santa Annunziata, in a lunette over the door which leads into the church. It represents the Holy Family reposing whilst on their flight into Egypt. — GERM. ED.

13. The Pietà of Annibal Caracci represents Mary with the dead body of Christ in her lap, and two small weeping angels. The grouping, drawing, and expression are glorious, grand, and vigorously pure; the strong and somewhat darker coloring of which this artist made use in his earlier life harmonizes well with the tragic subject of the picture. — GERM. ED.

CHAPTER IV.

1. The author appears to contradict here what he has said in the previous paragraph. — Germ. Ed.

2. It seems as though we ought to infer just the reverse, for the connection of the text throughout shows that the neck is believed to swell after indulgence in the pleasures of love. Twice the measure of the neck must, therefore, lengthen the string. It is, consequently, a sign of inviolate chastity, if, when the middle of the measure is held in the mouth, the two ends scarcely meet upon the head; a greater length indicates the reverse. — Germ. Ed.

3. Winckelmann probably refers, in this passage, to a head of Bacchus, the ears of which are placed too low, in the miscellaneous room of the Capitoline museum. He calls it Leucothea, because he considered himself authorized to apply this name to all Bacchic heads with a band on the forehead, if the features were in a measure undecided. His reasons, however, have been found insufficient. We must also recollect that this head is not strictly one of the doubtful kind; for this reason it has, as far as we know, always been considered as a Bacchus, and is still considered such. — Germ. Ed.

4. The author was unquestionably wrong in his belief that the feet of the Laocoön are of unequal length. It is objected to the right leg of the larger boy, that it is longer from the knee to the foot than the other. The same excuse is usually made, in this instance, as for the undue length of the left foot of the Apollo Belvedere, namely. that the artist intentionally added so much to these more remote parts, because their increased distance would necessarily detract from their size as seen by the observer. But we much fear that this justification is a greater fault than those it is intended to excuse. Such a system of enlargement of the more distant, and consequently corresponding diminution of the nigher limbs, if introduced into a plastic work of art, would necessarily unsettle all proportions, and produce profiles offensive both to the eye and taste. Fortunately, the masterpieces in question need no such elaborate justification. The inequality in the length of the legs of the son of Laocoön, as well as in the feet of the Apollo, is, especially in the latter, much more trifling than it is said to be. These grounds of defence, based on perspective effect, are less applicable to the unequal length of the feet of some Egyptian statues, in which the art is simpler and ruder, than to Greek statues. It is therefore best to consider these deviations simply as errors. — Germ. Ed.

5. Instead of "and thence (the depression above the chin) to the tip of the chin," we must read "from the depression to the point of the chin are two parts"; that is to say, as much space is given to the chin, from its depression to its point, as there is from this same depression to the lower extremity of the nose, or one sixth of the whole length of the face. "The breadth of the nose to the edges of the nostrils contains one such portion"; this passage must be understood to mean, that the nose must be as broad as the length of an eye, or equal in its breadth to the length of the chin. It appears to us, moreover, to be incorrectly stated, that the "length of the mouth is equal to the length of the eyes"; whereas

it is half as long again, as Winckelmann himself also thought, since he adds, "and to the height of the chin measured to the opening of the mouth," which is actually a length and a half of that of the eyes. — GERM. ED.

6. This remark of the author is more applicable to plastic works than to painting. We know, from many passages of the ancient writers, that the painters both of the earlier and later periods frequently represented in their works large, intricate compositions, as, for instance, Micon, in his *Battle of the Amazons with the Athenians*, Euphranor, in his *Battle of Mantinea*, &c. But it cannot be denied, that, in the most valued works of the ancient painters, the utmost simplicity in composition and the severest economy in figures were observed. — GERM. ED.

7. If it be conceded that all the ancient artists derived their subjects from Homer, the admission must at least not be understood in a strictly literal sense. We must not believe that they, like so many of the moderns, translated the words of the poet into images. If this had been the case, the inquiry might be made, why so many antique monuments are difficult of explanation; and we might, with some show of truth, draw therefrom an inference unfavorable to the excellence of ancient art. But the case is actually otherwise. The formative artist did not sacrifice his freedom of thought to the poet. He did not even copy him. He only worked up in his own way the material which the poet elaborated in his way; but both drew from the same primitive spring, tradition. It cannot, however, be denied, that the material of such plastic embodiments, especially at a later period, was taken from Homer. But the artist did not anxiously cling to the words of the poet; they were to him rather a stimulus to invent and compose in his own way. For the ancients had a better knowledge of what pertained to poetry, and what to the plastic arts, than the moderns appear to have. — GERM. ED.

CHAPTER V.

1. THE Greek profile, as it is called, in which the forehead and nose form nearly a straight line, is even now, according to the statements of travellers, to be found in nature, and especially in the southern parts of Europe. — GERM. ED.

2. I cannot think that Winckelmann meant to state in this passage that the Giustiniani Pallas, and the Vestal (so called), in this palace, are works of the same old style. The Vestal is much more ancient, and denotes a taste still uncultivated. The Pallas, on the other hand, is one of the most glorious images of this goddess, and may be regarded as a genuine work of the high style of Greek art. — GERM. ED.

3. By these characteristics we distinguish a beautiful figure of Iole with the attributes of Hercules, which was in the possession of Count Firmian, of Milan. It is of marble; its height is two feet two inches and a half. In some places modern restorations are observable. — GERM. ED.

4. This triangular work is in the palace of the Conservatori, at Rome. The workmanship is admirable. On one side is a Faun, with a band over his mouth, blowing two flutes. On the second side is also a Faun. On the third is a Bacchante The ornaments under this bas-relief, consisting of volutes and chimæras, and serving as feet, seem to be an imitation of the more ancient Greek style. — Germ. Ed.

5. *Pitture d' Ercolano*, Tom. IV., Tav. 42. The mouth-band of flute-players is also seen on a youthful figure in long drapery, on a painted vase in William Hamilton's first collection, published by D'Hancarville (Vol. I., Plate 124). — Germ. Ed.

6. The eyes of the Venus, compared with the other parts of her face, are not really small; they are merely a little less opened, for the purpose of imparting a look of sweetness. — Germ. Ed.

7. The Cleopatra (so called) has been carried from the villa Medici to Florence. Besides, Visconti (*Mus. Pio-Clement*, Tom. II., p. 90) has shown that similar recumbent statues represent Ariadne. — Germ Ed.

8. Winckelmann means the Judith of the sculptor Le Brun. — F.

9. In Tuscany, persons with such eyebrows are called *stupori*, "dullards" — Germ. Ed.

10. It is impossible that Lucian can have considered the sharpness of the edge of the bone over the eyes a beauty in the works of Praxiteles, because this artist, as Winckelmann himself observes in another place (Book IX., chap. 11), renounced this manner of forming it. The passage in Lucian might, therefore, be understood of the beautiful sweep or arch which Praxiteles gave to the edge of the bone over which the eyebrow is placed, — a meaning, also, which seems most applicable to the words τὸ εὔγραμμον. — Germ. Ed.

11. Joined eyebrows, such as Suetonius represents Augustus to have had, are actually to be seen in an admirably executed head of Augustus, of white marble, in the *Pio-Clement Museum* (Tom. VI., Plate 40). This is also the sole known likeness of him in advanced life. — Germ Ed

12. The parted lips, in images of the gods and heroes executed at a period when art was distinguished for the loftiness and beauty of its style, are, in our opinion, owing to the same cause to which Winckelmann, quite correctly, attributes the deeply seated eyes. By opening the lips it was proposed to obtain stronger shades, greater effect, and increased animation. The desired result has certainly been produced in a fitting manner — Germ. Ed.

13. The somewhat projecting border of the lips is not, like deeply seated eyes, an ideal endowment, furnished by art; it may be regarded as truly an imitation of nature, — especially in figures which belong to the severe and high style, in which the forms of each part are rendered with the utmost possible exactness. Accurate observers will undoubtedly have often noticed this shape of the edges of the lips as natural in young, well-formed persons. — Germ. Ed.

14. Franco, *Dial. della Bellezza* (Part I., p. 27). Also Paolo Antonio Rolli, in the following lines (*Rime*, p. 13) : —

" Molle pozzetta gli divide il mento,
Che la beltà compisce, e il riso, e il gioco
Volan' gl' intorno, e cento grazie e cento." — W.

" His chin, where every beauty now 's expressed,
A dimple soft divides, by Love impressed.
About it smiles and sportive jests are found,
And troops of graces flutter in its round."

15. The Antinoüs (so called); this statue Visconti (*Mus. Pio-Clement.*, Vol. I., Plate 7) takes to be a Mercury. — F.

16. In the *Trattato Prel.*, Cap. IV., p. 56. Winckelmann adds, — " Since the above-named Venus has a dimple, since one was also to be seen on the statue of Bathyllus at Samos (Apul., *Florid.*, Cap. XV., Tom. 2), I have conjectured that the Venus might perhaps be a portrait-statue of a beautiful woman who had a dimple in her chin. Artists were therefore obliged, in regard to this part, to deviate from the true and ever-present idea of the beautiful." — F. (Compare Note 4, Book IV., ch. 2.)

17. If the author had had the Venus before him when writing this remark, it could hardly have escaped his observation, that the right side of the chin had been injured, and repaired with stucco. Probably the entire chin has been retouched, and its fulness somewhat diminished, especially at its under part. — GERM. ED.

18. The remark on the beauty of the ears is fully borne out by heads of great excellence, and particularly by busts, which should be examined near at hand, — as, for instance, by the bust of young Commodus in the Capitoline museum, and other busts, of which the remaining parts also are not carelessly executed. The ears of many other heads, and especially of statues, are often neglected. — F.

19. This Hermes has since passed into the Pio-Clement museum. — GERM. ED.

20. It is the right ear which has been restored. — GERM. ED.

21. Winckelmann is correct in his remark as to the striking difference in the handling of the hair between ancient and modern works of plastic art. Careful investigators of antiquity will also be more inclined to attach great importance to the very different modes of treatment of this part, as we can affirm from experience, confirmed in many ways, that, in criticising differences of style, and in determining the age to which any monument of art belongs, the workmanship of the hair is a character of the utmost significance. The hair can never be represented by the plastic artist as natural in appearance, but only in a conventional manner; its arrangement, therefore, expresses the prevailing taste, the ideas and views of each particular period. Later imitators probably paid even less attention to such accessories; so that their peculiarities, or rather the peculiarities in style of their age, are manifested most strikingly in the hair. — GERM. ED.

22. The execution of the hair during the old style of Greek art was somewhat stiff, and deficient in variety. Even those monuments which approximate to the high style, that is, to the time of Phidias, still retain some traces of this harsh, wiry manner, though they show a constantly increasing beauty and elevation, and that noble simplicity which always accompanies, and constitutes a part of, the great and the noble. After this epoch in art, the hair has more motion and softness; it appears to have been arranged now very elegantly in ringlets, especially in the im-

ages of Venus, Apollo, and Bacchus, like dry yellow or brown hair, which has a natural curl. This good style continued, with various slight modifications, from the time of Alexander until the Romans made themselves masters of the whole civilized world. But, immediately after the first Cæsars, an artificial curl of the hair was introduced, and executed with an exceeding industry. In Adrian's time it seems as though it was intended to represent the hair dripping with oil. Under Marcus Aurelius and Lucius Verus, the manner was one of almost endless nicety and labor, — each single hair of the beard and head being rendered in numberless little curls. Thus it went on until shortly after the time of Septimius Severus and Caracalla, when elaborateness of execution expired with art itself. Everything is now more negligently finished, and becomes gradually coarser, and more deficient in merit, until finally, in the likenesses and other works executed during Constantine's reign, as well as shortly before and after it, we perceive, instead of a characteristic representation of the hair and beard, nothing more than holes irregularly bored, which, when viewed as a whole, resemble a wasp's nest.— GERM. ED.

23. By means of this observation upon the hair, Visconti also was led to recognize a Bacchus in the torso of a statue in the Pio-Clement museum. — GERM. ED.

24. As, for instance, Theseus (Seneca, *Hippolyt.*, vers. 649); Œdipus (Euripides, *Phœnissœ*). Jason also was described in precisely the same manner (Philostrat., *Icon.* 7 ; *Opera*, Tom. II.). — GERM. ED.

CHAPTER VI.

1. THE right arm of the Venus de' Medici, from the shoulder, and the left from the elbow, are modern. — GERM. ED.

The hands are by Bernini, and are a disgrace to the statue. — TR.

2. Beautiful antique hands are indeed rare, yet not so rare as one might suppose from this passage. The list of well-preserved hands on ancient statues might be considerably enlarged, if any advantage were to be derived from it. Thus, for instance, both hands and several fingers of the Capitoline Venus are really antique. The right hand, an exquisite little hand, of a well-executed statue, in marble, about half the size of life, of Leda, in the Capitoline museum, is perfectly preserved. The same may be said of a Muse in the Pio-Clement museum; and antique hands in good preservation might be specified from every considerable collection of antiques. — GERM. ED.

3. The hands and feet of a young Cæsar holding a Parazonium, in the Pio-Clement museum, are ancient, as are also those of the seated child with a goose. In the same museum, among the fragments, may be found the right arm, well preserved, and the hand, of a Pallas; so, likewise, the feet of the most celebrated statues are antique. Two female hands of natural size and exceeding beauty, of Parian marble, were found some years ago. They are now in the possession of Prince Borghese. In the right hand is a butterfly; in the left, a flute.

Near the place where these hands were disinterred, a small torch was discovered, on which the butterfly had probably rested, — to signify the warmth which love imparts to the soul. — F.

4. The right leg of the elder son of Laocoön justly holds a place among the most beautiful legs of youthful figures; for the shape of it is admirable, incomparably pure and elegant. Of aged male figures, the legs of Laocoön himself, and also those of the Borghese Silenus holding the infant Bacchus in his arms, deserve the first rank. General opinion pronounces the legs of the last-mentioned statue to be, unquestionably, the most beautiful of all that remain. — GERM. ED.

5. Very many beautiful feet have come down to us; so that whoever attempts to designate the most beautiful may perchance omit others fully as beautiful. Casts of the feet of the Medicean Venus usually serve artists as models of delicate female feet. Among the feet of male figures, those of the Apollo Belvedere, the Capitoline Antinoüs, the Borghese Silenus, the Laocoön, and the Farnese Hercules, are particularly esteemed. — GERM. ED.

As Winckelmann has not thought proper to enter more fully into the details of beauty in a foot, I will endeavor to supply the omission. A beautiful foot, both of the male and female figure in youth, is rounded in its form; and in the female the toes are delicate, and have dimples over their first joints, which should be very gently marked. Though the foot of the male figure has greater squareness, it should not show more distinctly its anatomical structure. The second toe is the longest of all, and separated by a distinct interval from the great toe, from which it is turned by a slight inclination outward. The heel should not project, for this is a distinguishing mark of brutes. The sole should be arched, and the instep consequently raised; the reverse is observed in animals. The foot of a European is half the length of the leg, measured to the top of the knee-pan; its breadth, in a straight line across the upper joint of the little toe, is one third of its length. The anterior part of the foot is intended by Nature to be much broader than the heel; but shoemakers and fashion have decided that this construction is erroneous. It astonishes me that any mother, who looks with fondness upon her infant's foot in all its natural beauty, with its anterior breadth, and the toes smooth, separate, distinct, can ever submit it to the painful and deforming compression which the tyranny of custom requires, and from which, as yet, escape is almost impossible. — TR.

6. See the graphic description of Agamemnon in Homer (*Iliad*, lib. 2, vers. 479). — GERM. ED.

7. The breast was consecrated to Neptune. In the images of him on antique gems, he is represented as far down as the lower extremity of the chest (*Descript. des Pierres gravées du Cab. de Stosch*), which is not so usual with respect to the other gods. — W.

8. The author, in this passage, seems to intimate exactly the reverse of what is stated in the first chapter, second paragraph, of this book. To us the truth appears to lie between the two statements. In the Amazons the ancients wished to represent heroines, vigorous women, able to endure the toils of war, and who neither courted nor shunned the joys of love. Such a character requires perfectly developed forms, without regard to aught else. Accordingly, the best images of Amazons do not

appear as scarcely budding maidens, with breasts which are just beginning to swell, but exhibit the fully matured capacities of youth. On this
account, their breasts are neither exuberant, as in women who have
borne many children, nor flat, and, as it were, unripe, as in figures of
Pallas, Diana, and others, designed as images of a maidenly character
that shuns the endearments of love. — GERM. ED.

9. (Pliny, lib. 35, cap. 11, § 40.) The dogs of Lysippus are praised by
Pliny (lib. 34, cap. 8, § 19) ; also one painted by Protogenes (lib. 35, cap.
10, § 36) ; but Pliny prized above them all a bronze dog, represented
licking his wound, which formerly stood in the temple of Juno on the
Capitoline hill. It was destroyed when the Capitol was burnt, during
the popular commotions occasioned by the partisans of Vitellius. This
dog was esteemed so highly, that guards were appointed by a public
decree to watch it, and their lives were answerable for its safety. (Pliny,
lib. 34, cap. 7, § 17.) — GERM. ED.

10. The left hand holds the rein. The sword-sheath is suspended
beneath the left arm by a belt passing over the right shoulder. —
GERM. ED.

11. Which is the case now. — F.

12. It is of blackish marble (*bigio morato*), and partly restored. Two
of granite, of not quite full size, are in the Pio-Clement museum. — F.

13. Dallaway (Vol. II. p 134) says, that the sitting dog which is mentioned as having been carried to England was sold, a few years previously, by Mr. Jennings to Mr. Duncombe, of Yorkshire, for £1,000
sterling. Two similar ones are in the Pio-Clement museum ; one in the
palace Chigi ; and two in the gallery at Florence. All of them are well
executed. The one which went to England may, however, have been
the best. It was repaired by Cavaceppi, who introduced an engraving
of it into his *Raccolta d' Antiche Statue*, but who, unaptly enough, holds it
up as a work of Phidias. An admirable group of two greyhounds, —
called by the ancients Spartan hounds (Aristænet., *Epist.*, lib. 1, epist.
18), — playing with each other, is to be found in the Pio-Clement museum. A repetition of it is in the museum of Lord Townley, of London.
Both these groups, together with several other figures of dogs, were
found on a hill, now called Dog-hill, in the vicinity of the ancient city of
Lanuvium. — GERM. ED.

14. Not only the head, but all the extremities of the celebrated Giustiniani goat, are by a modern hand. In size, it is larger than life ; and
the antique work is admirable, and of a truly grand character.

A sitting wild-boar, in marble, above the natural size, is in the Florentine gallery. It is one of the principal pieces among the figures of animals now remaining. It could not have been unknown to Winckelmann,
however he may have accidentally omitted to notice it. A powerful and
noble style is manifest in all the forms of this admirable beast. The
expression is in a high degree natural and lively. The handling is bold,
careful, and worthy of a great master ; and the stiff, harsh character of
the bristles cannot be improved. In Gori's *Museum Florentinum* (Vol. III.,
Plate 69) there is a tolerable engraving of it. In the villa Borghese is an
antique repetition of it, somewhat less in size, of gray marble ; it is well
executed. — GERM. ED.

15. In the rich collection of animals in the Pio-Clement museum there

is a very beautiful goat, Amalthæa, to the beard of which the hand of a child still remains attached. Also a fallow-buck of natural size and color, of Oriental alabaster; a sow, of white marble, with twelve pigs under her; an eagle and a stork, of superior execution; the head of a rhinoceros, less than the natural size; a crocodile, of touchstone, about four palms long. There is, besides, in the *Capitoline Museum* (Vol. III., p. 162) a crocodile of natural size, of Parian marble. It is, however, to be remarked, that antique figures of animals are, upon the whole, rare. Consequently, a large number of counterfeits of all kinds have been prepared and sold by rogues, in modern times, as genuine works. — F.